D1545859

Great
Nineteenth-Century
French Short Stories

Great
Nineteenth-Century
French Short Stories

EDITED BY

ANGEL FLORES

DOVER PUBLICATIONS, INC.
New York

Published in Canada by General Publishing Company, Ltd., 30 Lesmill Road, Don Mills, Toronto, Ontario.
Published in the United Kingdom by Constable and Company, Ltd., 10 Orange Street, London WC2H 7EG.

This Dover edition, first published in 1990, is an unabridged republication of the work first published in 1960 by Doubleday & Company, Inc., Garden City, New York, under the title *Nineteenth Century French Tales*.

Manufactured in the United States of America
Dover Publications, Inc., 31 East 2nd Street, Mineola, N.Y. 11501

Library of Congress Cataloging-in-Publication Data

Great nineteenth-century French short stories / edited by Angel Flores.
     p.   cm.
    Reprint. Originally published under title: Nineteenth century French tales. Garden City, N.Y. : Doubleday, 1960.
    ISBN 0-486-26324-X
    1. Short stories, French—Translations into English. 2. Short stories, English—Translations from French. 3. French fiction—19th century—Translations into English. I. Flores, Angel, 1900–
PQ1278.G74   1990
843′.0108′009034—dc20

                                                         90-3008
                                                                CIP

Preface

Most of today's anthologies of French stories in English translation tend to give an inadequate impression of French literature of the nineteenth century—the impression that it can be mirrored in a group of more or less realistic tales by certain well-known experts in the art of reporting "cases" or of tailoring piquant anecdotes in "precise" colors. So stereotyped have these collections become they might be the work of a single compiler who never wearies of repeating his favorite numbers: inevitably a Balzac story, a Stendhal, a Mérimée, a Flaubert, a Maupassant, a Zola . . . The present volume attempts to avoid this well-trodden path. It shows non-realistic trends rarely associated with the circumscribing and inadequately termed French *clarté*. Contrastingly enough, it reveals an imaginative flow that, paralleling realism and naturalism, spreads toward the fantastic and the macabre, toward expressionism and surrealism. Furthermore, these pages endeavor to reflect nineteenth-century popular taste including some best-sellers (Eugène Sue, Paul de Kock, Frédéric Soulié) who today are relegated to mere footnotes if they are indeed mentioned at all. In addition, care has been taken to represent writers who, although unnoticed in their day, blazed new trails: Aloysius Bertrand, who invented the poem in prose; Laforgue, who anticipated the sophistication of the 1920's; Borel and Lautréamont, who uncovered a world relished a century later by the surrealists. The Maupassant here rep-

resented with "Who Knows?" almost suggests a Kafkan
world and hardly the slick author of the forever anthologi-
cal "Boule de suif" and "The Necklace." Benjamin Constant's little "classic" *Adolphe* stands, unique, to represent
the analytical current that, deepening through Stendhal,
led to the mighty maelstrom of Marcel Proust.

These considerations and the fact that the stories themselves make absorbing reading justify, it is hoped, the publication of this new anthology of French short stories.

A. F.

Contents

Adolphe

BY BENJAMIN CONSTANT

TRANSLATED BY MURIEL KITTEL

BENJAMIN CONSTANT
1767–1830

Born at Lausanne of French Protestant parents, Constant studied at the universities of Oxford, Erlangen, and Edinburgh and showed an early interest in philosophy and politics. He became a leading orator and pamphleteer, playing significant roles under Napoleon and Louis XVIII, now suffering exile, now holding important positions. In 1794 he met Madame de Staël, who fascinated him but tired him with her imperious domination, which lasted for seventeen years, despite the disclosure of his secret marriage to Charlotte von Hardenberg in 1808. "Adolphe" (1816) is essentially the account of this liaison—its vicissitudes and final rupture. It is to this brief novel rather than his ambitious *Cours de politique constitutionnelle* (3 volumes) or his ponderous *History of Religion* (12 volumes) that Constant owes his immortality, for *Adolphe*, in the poignant intensity of its drama, subtle analysis of motivations, and sober style, is a landmark in the development of French fiction.

ABOUT CONSTANT: Harold Nicolson, *Benjamin Constant*, N.Y., Doubleday, 1949. OTHERS: Geoffrey Scott, *The Portrait of Zélide*, N.Y., Scribner's, 1927; John Middleton Murry, *The Conquest of Death*, London, P. Nevill, 1951; David Cecil, *Poets and Story-Tellers*, London, Constable, 1949; Martin Turnell, *The Novel in France*, N.Y., Vintage, 1958.

I

At the age of twenty-two I had just completed my studies at the University of Göttingen. My father, minister to the Elector of ————, intended me to travel through the most noteworthy countries of Europe; he then wished me to join him, enter the department he directed, and there be trained to take his place someday. I had won, by fairly persistent labor in the midst of a dissipated life, successes that had distinguished me from my fellow-students, and that had roused in my father hopes that were probably much exaggerated.

These hopes had made him very indulgent toward the many excesses I had committed. He never let me suffer the consequences of my errors. He had always granted and sometimes anticipated my demands in this respect.

Unfortunately his conduct was more noble and generous than affectionate. I was thoroughly aware of all his claims to my gratitude and respect, but no confidence ever existed between us. There was an ironical factor in his character that sorted ill with my disposition. At that time I wished only to abandon myself to those primitive and passionate feelings that lift the soul out of the common sphere and inspire it with disgust for everything around it. I found in my father, not a censor, but yet a cold and sarcastic observer, who would first smile with pity, and then quickly end the conversation with impatience. During my first eighteen years, I cannot remember ever having an interview with him of more than an hour. His letters were

affectionate, full of reasonable and sensitive advice, but we
were hardly in each other's presence before there appeared
in him a sense of constraint, which I found inexplicable,
and which affected me painfully. I did not then understand
the nature of shyness: that internal suffering that pursues
us even to the most advanced age, that forces our deepest
feelings back into our hearts, that freezes our words, that
makes unnatural on our lips all that we try to say, and that
will only allow us to express ourselves in vague phrases, or
in somewhat bitter irony—as if we wished to punish our
feelings for the pain we experience in our inability to express them. I did not realize that my father was shy even
with his son, and that often, after long expecting from me
some evidence of affection (which his apparent coldness
seemed to forbid), he would leave me with tears in his
eyes and complain to others that I did not love him.

My feeling of constraint with him had a great influence
on my character. Just as shy as he, but more restless because I was younger, I grew accustomed to keep all my
feelings to myself, to make only solitary plans, to count only
on myself for their execution, and to regard the advice, interest, help, and even the mere presence of other people as
an annoyance and an obstacle. I formed the habit of never
speaking of what I was doing, of tolerating conversation
only as a troublesome necessity, enlivening it by constant
levity to make it less boring to myself, and to help conceal
my true thoughts. This resulted in a certain absence of
spontaneity with which my friends today still reproach me,
and in a difficulty in maintaining serious conversation that
I still find hard to overcome. At the same time this situation
gave rise to a burning desire for independence, a great impatience with the ties surrounding me, and an invincible
terror of contracting new ones. I was at ease only when
alone; and this aspect of my personality has still so great
an effect that, even now, when I have to decide between
two issues, and on most trivial occasions, I am disturbed
by a human face, and my natural impulse is to escape in
order to deliberate in peace. I had not, however, the depth
of egoism that such a character would seem to imply;

while I was interested only in myself, I found myself only faintly interesting. I had deep within myself a need for tenderness of which I was unaware, but that, being completely unsatisfied, would detach me in turn from every object that attracted my curiosity. This indifference to everything was further strengthened by the idea of death; an idea that had affected me while quite young, and that I have never thought men could easily manage to forget. At seventeen I had witnessed the death of an old woman whose strange and remarkable mind had begun to develop my own. This woman, like so many others, had at the beginning of her career thrown herself into society, of which she was ignorant, with the feeling of great spiritual strength, and truly powerful faculties. Then—also like many others —by refusing to submit to artificial but necessary conventions, she had seen her hopes betrayed, and her youth pass without pleasure: old age had reached her at last but had not subdued her. She lived in a château near one of our estates, unhappy and withdrawn, her mind her sole resource, and analyzing everything with her mind. In inexhaustible conversations over nearly a year, we had considered life in all its aspects, with death always as the end of all; having talked of death with her so much, I saw death strike her before my eyes.

This event filled me with a feeling of uncertainty about our destiny, and with a vague dreaminess that has never left me. My favorite reading was poetry that emphasized the brevity of human life. I considered no end worth the trouble of any exertion. It is rather curious that this feeling has grown weaker with my increase in years. Could it be that there is something doubtful in hope, so that when it disappears from a man's career, this career takes on a stricter and more positive character? Could it be that life seems to gain reality as all illusions vanish, just as a mountaintop is more clearly seen on the horizon when the clouds are dispelled?

After leaving Göttingen, I went to the small town of D——. This town was the residence of a prince, who, like the majority of German princes, mildly governed a small

territory, gave protection to the enlightened men who settled there, allowed complete freedom to all opinions, but
who, limited by ancient custom to the society of his courtiers, gathered around himself only men who were largely
insignificant or mediocre. I was welcomed at this court
with the curiosity that any stranger will arouse who comes
to break the round of monotony and etiquette. For several
months I saw nothing to capture my attention. I was grateful for the politeness shown me; but either my shyness prevented me from taking advantage of it, or the weariness of
an aimless activity led me to prefer solitude to the colorless
pleasures I was invited to share. I hated nobody, but few
people inspired my interest. However, men are wounded
by indifference, which they attribute to ill-will or affectation; they are unwilling to believe that their company can
be naturally boring. Sometimes I tried to control my boredom by retreating into deep silence; this silence was taken
for contempt. At other times, weary of my own taciturnity,
I indulged in several witticisms, and my wit, once set in
motion, carried me to excess. In one day I would reveal
everything ridiculous I had observed in a month. The recip-
ients of my sudden and involuntary expansiveness were not
at all grateful—and they were right, for it was the need for
speech that seized me, not confidence. During the conversations with the woman who had first developed my mind,
I had acquired an invincible aversion for all commonplace
maxims and dogmatic formulas. Whenever I heard mediocrity talking complacently about well-established and quite
incontrovertible principles, matters of morality, convention,
or religion—topics it willingly puts in the same category—I
felt myself compelled to contradict, not because I would
adopt the contrary opinions, but because I was impatient
with such fixed and unimaginative beliefs. In addition,
some instinct warned me to distrust these general axioms
that were so utterly unexceptionable and so innocent of
subtlety. Fools make a compact and indivisible unit of their
morality so that it may interfere as little as possible with
their actions and leave them free in all details.

By this conduct I soon gained a great reputation for

levity, banter, and malice. My bitter words were taken as
proof of a spiteful nature, my witticisms as attacks on all
that was respectable. Those whom I had made the mistake
of ridiculing found it convenient to identify themselves with
the principles I was accused of calling in doubt. Since I
had unintentionally made some people laugh at the expense
of others, all of them united against me. It was as if, in
exposing their weaknesses, I had betrayed a confidence, and
as they had shown me their true natures they had thereby
obtained from me in return a promise of silence: but I had
absolutely no knowledge of having accepted such a burdensome agreement. They had found pleasure in giving themselves free rein; I had found it in observing and describing
them; and that which they called treachery seemed to me
a quite innocent and legitimate reward.

I have no intention of justifying myself here; I long ago
gave up this easy and frivolous habit of an inexperienced
mind; I merely wish to say—and for the sake of others than
myself (now retired from the world)—that it takes time to
become accustomed to the human race as it has been
formed by our self-interest, affectation, vanity, and fear. The
astonishment felt in early youth at the sight of such an artificial and elaborate society indicates natural feeling rather
than a wicked disposition. Society has, moreover, nothing
to fear from such a nature; it weighs so heavily on us, its
dull influence is so powerful, that it loses no time in shaping
us in the universal mold. We are no longer surprised at
anything but our former surprise; and we find ourselves
well enough off in our new form, just as we finally breathe
freely in a crowded theater, where at first we had breathed
only with difficulty.

If any escape this general fate, they keep their secret dis-
agreement to themselves. They recognize the seed of vice
in most pleasantry; they no longer jest about it because
contempt has taken the place of ridicule, and contempt is
silent.

In the small society around me there then developed a
vague uneasiness about my character. They could point to
no criminal act, they could not even deny several occasions

that might have indicated generosity or devotion, but they said that I was immoral and unreliable—two epithets happily invented to insinuate facts that are unknown, and to stimulate invention where knowledge is lacking.

II

Absent-minded, inattentive, and bored, I was quite unaware of the impression I was making; I was dividing my time between studies that I frequently interrupted, projects that I did not carry out, and pleasures that barely interested me, when a circumstance, superficially trivial, effected an important revolution in my disposition.

A young man with whom I was quite intimate had been seeking for some months to gain the favor of one of the least insipid women in our society; I was his disinterested confidant in this enterprise. After lengthy efforts he succeeded in gaining her love, and since he had never concealed his reverses and sufferings, he felt obliged to tell me of his success. Nothing could equal his transports and excessive joy. The sight of such happiness made me regret that I had not yet tried it myself; up to that time I had had no affair with a woman that could have flattered my self-esteem; a new future seemed to open before me; deep in my heart I felt a new desire. There was doubtless a great deal of vanity in this desire, but it was not all vanity—perhaps even less than I thought myself. Men's feelings are confused and mixed, formed from a multitude of varied impressions that escape observation, and speech, always too clumsy and too general, may well serve to disguise but never to define them.

In my father's house I had adopted a fairly immoral attitude toward women. My father, while strictly observing the outward conventions, would often make frivolous remarks about liaisons. He regarded them as excusable if not permissible amusements, and considered only marriage to be a serious matter. His guiding principle was that a young man should take care to avoid what was called a folly: that is, to form a permanent engagement with someone who was not completely his equal in fortune, birth, and external advantages, but otherwise, provided there was no question of marriage, he considered that all women could be taken and later left without inconvenience. I have seen him smile with a certain approbation at that parody of a well-known saying: "It does them so little harm, and gives us so much pleasure."

Nobody realizes what a profound effect such sayings have on the very young, or how deeply astonished children can be at an age while their opinions are still doubtful and wavering, when they hear the direct rules they have been given contradicted by jests that everyone applauds. These rules then seem to be nothing more than trite formulas that their parents have agreed to repeat to salve their consciences, while the jests hold the real secrets of life.

Troubled by a vague emotion, I said to myself: "I want to be loved," and looked about me. I saw nobody who might inspire my love, nobody who seemed capable of accepting it; I questioned my heart and my tastes—I felt no motion of preference. I was in this state of internal agitation when I made the acquaintance of the Count of P——, a man of forty, whose family was connected with mine. He suggested that I should go to see him. Unfortunate visit! He had living with him his mistress, a Polish woman, celebrated for her beauty although she was no longer very young. In spite of her disadvantageous position this woman had frequently displayed a superior character. Her family, fairly distinguished in Poland, had been ruined during that country's troubles. Her father had been proscribed; her mother had sought refuge in France, taking her daughter with her; the mother's death had left the daughter in complete isolation. The Count of P—— had fallen in love with her. I have never heard how this affair began; when I first saw Ellenore it was already of long standing and almost consecrated. Was it the misfortune of her situation or the inexperience of her youth that forced her into a way of

life that was equally distasteful to her upbringing and habits, and also to her pride, which was one of the remarkable
elements in her character? All that I know, all that everyone knew, is that when the Count of P—— had lost almost
all his fortune, and was threatened with the loss of his liberty, Ellenore had given him such proofs of her devotion,
had so contemptuously refused the most brilliant offers,
and had shared his dangers and his poverty so zealously
and even joyfully, that the most scrupulous severity could
not refuse to do justice to the purity of her motives and
the disinterestedness of her conduct. It was owing to her
activity, courage, and good sense, to sacrifices of all kinds
that she bore without complaint, that her lover had been
able to recover a part of his fortune. They had come to
D—— to attend to a court action that might completely restore the count to his former wealth, and they planned to
stay for about two years.

Ellenore had only an ordinary mind, but her ideas were
just, and her expression of them always simple and sometimes striking through the nobility and elevation of her feelings. She had many prejudices; but they were all directly
opposed to her interest. She attached the highest value to
regularity of conduct, precisely because her own was considered irregular. She was very religious, because religion
rigorously condemned her way of life. In conversation she
severely repulsed everything that other women would have
considered innocent pleasantry, because she was always
afraid that her position authorized people to use vulgarities
with her. She would have liked to receive only men of the
highest rank and most irreproachable conduct, because the
women to whom she shuddered to be compared usually
attract a mixed society: as they are resigned to the loss of
respect, they look only for amusement in their social relationships. In short, Ellenore was at war with her destiny.
She protested, so to speak, in every word and deed against
the class in which she found herself placed; and as she
felt that reality was stronger than she, and that her efforts
did not change the situation, she was very unhappy. She
brought up the two children she had borne to the Count

of P—— with excessive strictness. Her attachment to them was more passionate than tender, and it was possible to suspect that an element of revolt was mingled with it, and that this made them somehow tiresome. When anyone made a well-meant remark about her children's growth, their promising talents, or their future careers, she would pale at the thought that she must one day tell them of their birth. But the slightest danger, an hour's absence, would bring her back to them with an anxiety in which could be detected a touch of remorse and a desire to give them by her caresses the happiness that caresses had not given her. This conflict between her feelings and her position in society had given her a moody disposition. Often she was dreamy and silent, sometimes she spoke impetuously. Since she was tormented by one particular idea, she could never remain completely calm, even in the most general conversation. But this very fact gave to her manner something passionate and unexpected, which made her more interesting than she normally would have been. The strangeness of her situation took the place of novelty in her ideas. Like a fine storm, she was observed with interest and curiosity.

Coming to my notice at a moment when my heart craved love, and my vanity success, Ellenore seemed a conquest worthy of me. She herself found pleasure in the company of a man different from those she had met before. Her circle was composed of a few friends or relatives of her lover and their wives, who had been compelled by the count's influence to receive his mistress. The husbands were devoid equally of feeling and ideas; the wives differed from the mediocrity of their husbands only in being more nervous and restless, because they lacked the calmness that comes from regular occupation with business. A lighter wit, a more varied conversation, a peculiar blend of melancholy and gaiety, of despondency and enthusiasm, astonished and attracted Ellenore. She spoke several languages, not very correctly, but always vivaciously and sometimes gracefully. Her ideas seemed to reach the light through obstacles, and to emerge from the struggle more agreeable, more naïve, and more original; for a foreign idiom rejuvenates thought and frees it from forms of expression that seem either commonplace or affected. We read the English poets together; we went for walks together; I would often visit her in the morning and again in the evening; I discussed a thousand things with her.

I had intended to make a study of her mind and character from the standpoint of a cool and impartial observer; but every word she uttered seemed clothed with inexplicable grace. The aim of pleasing her gave me a new interest in life and enlivened my existence in an unusual way. I attributed this almost magical effect to her charm; I would have enjoyed it more fully but for my attachment to my self-esteem. This self-esteem was a third party between Ellenore and myself. I felt obliged to press on as quickly as possible to the goal I had set myself. Consequently I did not give myself up unreservedly to my feelings. I longed to speak because I thought I had only to speak to succeed. I did not believe that I loved Ellenore, but by now I could not have relinquished the idea of pleasing her. She was constantly in my thoughts; I made innumerable plans; I invented innumerable ways to win her, with that ignorant conceit that is always confident of success because it has never made any attempt.

Nevertheless, an invincible shyness held me back: all my speeches died on my lips, or ended quite differently from my intentions. I struggled inwardly, I was indignant with myself.

I finally sought an argument that would extricate me from this struggle with honor in my own eyes. I told myself that nothing should be hurried, that Ellenore was too unprepared for the declaration I was meditating, and that it would be better to wait longer. In order to live at peace with ourselves we almost always disguise our incapacities and weaknesses as calculations and systems; this satisfies that part of us which is, so to speak, the spectator of the rest.

The situation continued to be drawn out. Each day I fixed tomorrow as the certain date for a positive declaration, and each tomorrow passed as yesterday. My shyness left me as soon as I went away from Ellenore. I then renewed my clever plans and deep designs, but no sooner was I back in her presence than I again felt nervous and troubled. Anyone who read my heart in her absence would have taken me for a cold and insensitive seducer; anyone who saw me in her presence would have seen me as a novice in love, tongue-tied and passionate. Both judgments would be equally mistaken; there is no complete unity in man, and hardly anyone is altogether sincere or altogether false.

Convinced by these repeated experiences that I should never be bold enough to speak to Ellenore, I decided to write to her. The Count of P—— was away. The long struggles I had had with my own character, the impatience I felt at my inability to overcome it, my uncertainty about the success of my attempt infused my letter with an agitation that was very like love. Fired by my own style, as I finished writing I experienced a touch of the passion that I had sought to express as forcefully as possible.

Ellenore saw in my letter that which was natural to see there: the transient rapture of a man ten years younger than herself, whose heart was opening to feelings hitherto unknown to it, and who deserved more pity than anger. She replied kindly, gave me affectionate advice, offered me her sincere friendship, but told me that she could not see me until the count returned.

This reply shattered me. My imagination, inflamed by the obstacle, took control of my whole being. The love that an hour before I had congratulated myself on pretending I suddenly felt as a violent reality. I rushed to Ellenore's house; I was told she was out. I wrote to her; I implored her to grant me a final interview; in heart-rending terms I described my despair and the fatal projects her cruel decision inspired. For the greater part of the day I waited in vain for a reply. I could only calm my unspeakable torment by telling myself that tomorrow I would brave every obstacle to reach Ellenore and speak to her. A few words came from her in the evening: they were gentle, I thought

I detected in them a touch of regret and sorrow, but she persisted in her resolution, which she told me was unshakable. I called on her again in the morning. She had left for an unknown destination in the country. Her servants had not even any means of forwarding her letters.

For a long time I stood motionless at her door, unable to believe in any further chance of finding her. I was astonished by my suffering. My memory recalled the time when I had told myself that I was only interested in a success, that this was merely an attempt I could easily abandon. I had no conception of the violent, uncontrollable anguish that was now tearing my heart. Several days passed in this manner. I was incapable equally of amusement or study. I wandered ceaselessly in front of Ellenore's door. I walked about the town as if I hoped to meet her around every street corner. One morning during one of these aimless wanderings, which helped to replace agitation by fatigue, I saw the Count of P——'s carriage: he was returning from his journey. He recognized me and got out. After a few commonplaces I spoke to him of Ellenore's sudden departure, taking care to conceal my emotion. "Yes," he said. "One of her friends a few miles from here has been in some trouble that Ellenore thought she could help and sympathize with. She left without consulting me. She is a person who is at the mercy of her feelings, and her ever-active spirit can almost find repose in devotion to others. But I need her here too much; I am going to write to her: she will certainly come home in a few days."

This assurance quieted me; I felt my suffering lessen. I was able to breathe freely for the first time since Ellenore's departure. Her return was less prompt than the count had hoped; but I had resumed my usual way of life, and the anguish I had felt began to disappear, when, a month later, the Count of P—— let me know that Ellenore was to arrive that evening. Since he felt it important for her to maintain the place in society that her character deserved and her situation seemed to preclude, he had invited to supper several women from among his relatives and friends who were willing to visit Ellenore.

My memories revived, confused at first, later with greater vividness. My self-esteem was bound up with them. I was embarrassed and humiliated to meet a woman who had treated me like a child. I seemed to see her, smiling, as I approached, at the calming effect of a short absence on the intoxication of a youthful head, and I detected in that smile a certain contempt for me. My feelings were gradually reawakened. That very day I had risen without a thought for Ellenore; an hour after hearing of her arrival her image floated before my eyes, dominated my heart, and I was sick with fear that I might not see her.

I stayed at home all day, I kept myself hidden, as it were, I trembled lest the least move should prevent our meeting. Nothing indeed was more simple or more certain, but I wished it so ardently that it appeared impossible. Impatience devoured me: I looked at my watch every second. I had to open the window to breathe; my blood was burning in my veins.

At last I heard the hour strike when I was to go to the count's. My impatience immediately changed to timidity; I dressed slowly, I no longer felt in a hurry to get there; I was so terrified lest my expectation should be deceived, and the presentiment of the pain that I risked was so intense, that I would have willingly agreed to postpone everything.

It was fairly late when I entered the count's house. I saw Ellenore sitting at the end of the room; I dared not go toward her, for it seemed as if everyone's eyes were on me. I hid myself in a corner of the drawing room behind a group of men who were talking. From there I observed Ellenore; she seemed slightly changed, she was paler than usual. The count found me in my hiding place; he came to me, took me by the hand, and led me to Ellenore. "I present to you," he said, laughing, "one of the men most astonished by your unexpected departure." Ellenore was talking to a woman next to her. When she saw me her words died on her lips; she was completely tongue-tied. I was almost so myself.

People could hear us; I asked Ellenore some trivial ques-

tions. We both resumed an appearance of calm. Supper was
announced; I offered Ellenore my arm, which she could
not refuse. "If you do not promise to receive me tomorrow
at eleven o'clock," I said as I led her away, "I shall leave
immediately, I shall abandon my country, my family, and
my father, I shall break all ties, renounce all obligations,
and go no matter where to end as soon as possible a life
that it pleases you to poison."

"Adolphe!" she replied, and hesitated.

I made a movement to leave. I do not know what my
features expressed, but I have never felt such a violent
spasm.

Ellenore looked at me. Fear mingled with affection in
her face. "I will see you tomorrow," she said, "but I implore you——" Many people were following us and she could
not finish her sentence. I pressed her hand with my arm and
we went to the table.

I should have liked to sit next to Ellenore, but the master of the house had decided otherwise; I was placed almost
opposite to her. At the beginning of dinner she was dreamy.
When someone addressed her she replied gently, but
quickly lapsed into abstraction. One of her friends, struck
by her silence, asked her if she were sick. "I have not been
well lately," she replied, "and even now I am still very
shaky." I wanted to make a good impression on Ellenore;
by showing myself to be amiable and witty, I wished to
make her favorably disposed toward me, and to prepare
her for the interview she had granted me. So I tried numerous ways to hold her attention. I led the conversation to
subjects I knew interested her; our neighbors joined in; I
was inspired by her presence. I succeeded in getting her
to listen to me, soon I saw her smile; the joy I felt was so
great, my looks expressed such gratitude, that she could
not help being moved. Her sadness and inattentiveness disappeared; she no longer resisted the secret charm that
filled her soul at the sight of the happiness I owed to her;
and when we left the table our hearts were in accord as
if we had never been separated. "You see," I said, giving
her my hand to return to the drawing room, "my life is

in your power. What have I done that you should find pleasure in making it a torment?"

III

I passed a sleepless night. I no longer had any thought of calculation or strategy: I really felt that I was genuinely in love. I was no longer motivated by the hope of conquest: the need to see the woman I loved, to rejoice in her presence, dominated me exclusively. Eleven o'clock struck. I went to see Ellenore; she was waiting for me. She wanted to speak; I asked her to listen. I sat down beside her, for I could hardly stand, and proceeded to speak as follows— though not without frequent interruptions:

"I have not come to protest against the sentence you have pronounced; I have not come to withdraw a declaration that may have offended you: I could not even if I would. The love you refuse is indestructible. The effort I am making now to speak to you calmly is proof of the force of the emotion that offends you. But I did not ask you to listen in order to hear more about my passion; on the contrary, I came to ask you to forget it, to receive me as before, to dismiss the memory of a moment's madness, not to punish me for the secret you know I should have kept locked in my heart. You are familiar with my situation, with my character that is said to be strange and uncivilized, with my heart that is alien to all worldly interests, that is solitary in the midst of society, and yet suffers from the isolation to which it is condemned. Your friendship sustained me; without this friendship I cannot live. I have become accustomed to seeing you; you have let this pleasant custom grow and take form: what have I done to lose this sole consolation of a sad and melancholy existence? I am horribly unhappy; I no longer have the courage to bear such long-drawn-out unhappiness. I hope for nothing, I ask for nothing, I want only to see you, but I must see you if I am to live."

Ellenore remained silent. "What are you afraid of?" I went on. "What am I asking? Only that which you grant to any indifferent acquaintance. Is it society you fear? This society, absorbed in its solemn frivolities, cannot understand a heart like mine. How can I help being prudent? Does not my life depend on it? Ellenore, grant my prayer: you will even find some pleasure in it; you should feel a certain charm in being loved like this, in seeing me near you, thinking only of you, living only for you, owing to you every sensation of happiness I can still feel, rescued by your presence from suffering and despair."

I continued in this vein for a long time, answering all objections, rephrasing in numerous ways all the arguments in my favor. I was so submissive, so resigned, I was asking so little, and I would have been so unhappy if she had refused.

Ellenore was touched. She imposed a number of conditions; she consented to see me only infrequently, when many others would be present, and provided that I never spoke to her of love. I promised everything she asked. We were both pleased: I with having regained the advantage I had almost lost, Ellenore with being generous, understanding, and prudent, all at once.

The very next day I took advantage of the permission I had won; I continued to do so on the following days. Ellenore no longer thought of the need for keeping my visits infrequent; she soon found nothing more natural than seeing me every day. Ten years of fidelity had given Count P—— complete confidence. He allowed Ellenore the utmost freedom. He had had to struggle against the opinion that wished to exclude his mistress from the society in which he had to live: consequently he was pleased to see Ellenore's circle grow; a full house proved his personal triumph over opinion.

Whenever I arrived I noticed an expression of pleasure in Ellenore's eyes. And her eyes turned naturally to me whenever she was amused by the conversation. If anything interesting were being described she would always call me over to listen. But she was never alone. Whole evenings would pass when I was unable to say anything to her privately beyond a few trivial and interrupted words. It was not long before I grew irritable at such constraint. I became gloomy, silent, moody, and bitter in my speech. I could hardly control myself when others were talking privately to Ellenore; I would rudely interrupt them. I did not care whether I offended anyone, and I was not always checked by fear of compromising her. She complained to me of this change. "What do you expect?" I said impatiently. "You doubtless think you have done a great deal for me; I must tell you that you are mistaken. I fail to understand your new way of life. Before, you lived in a retired manner; you fled from tiring company; you avoided these eternal conversations that drag on precisely because they should never have been begun. Today your door is open to the entire world. In asking you to receive me, one would think I had obtained the same favor for the whole universe. I must say that, after having seen you live so prudently before, I little expected to find you so frivolous now."

I detected in Ellenore's face a feeling of displeasure and sadness. "Dear Ellenore," I said, suddenly softening, "don't I really deserve to be distinguished from the hundreds of bores who besiege you? Has friendship no secrets? Is it not distrustful and shy in the midst of noise and the mob?"

Ellenore was afraid to be unyielding lest she provoke a return of that imprudent conduct that made her alarmed for both of us. The idea of breaking with me no longer entered her mind: she consented to receive me alone occasionally.

The strict rules she had imposed on me were then quickly relaxed. She let me describe my love, gradually she became used to this language, soon she confessed that she loved me.

I spent several hours at her feet, saying that I was the happiest of men, lavishing on her countless assurances of love, devotion, and undying regard. She told me how much she had suffered in trying to avoid me, how often she had hoped I would find her in spite of her efforts, how the least noise she heard seemed to announce my arrival, what confusion, joy, and fear she had experienced at seeing me again, how, through mistrust of herself, and in order to reconcile the dictates of her heart with those of prudence, she had given herself up to the distractions of society and cultivated the crowd that before she had avoided. I made her repeat the smallest details, and this story of a few weeks seemed to us the story of a lifetime. Love makes up for length of time in memories by a kind of magic. All other attachments need the past; love creates a past to surround us by its enchantment. It gives us, so to speak, the sense of having lived for years with someone who, until lately, was practically a stranger. Love is only a luminous point, and yet it seems to take possession of time. A little while ago it did not exist, in a little while it will exist no more, but as long as it does exist it sheds its light equally on the time before and the time to come.

But this calm did not last long. Ellenore was the more on guard against her weakness because she was haunted by the memory of her errors; and my imagination, my desires, and a theory of self-conceit that I was unaware of myself all revolted against such a love. Always shy, often irritable, I complained, I raged, I covered Ellenore with reproaches. More than once she was ready to break off a relationship that brought only worry and confusion into her life. More than once I pacified her by my prayers, denials, and tears.

"Ellenore," I wrote to her one day, "you don't realize all that I suffer. Near you or away from you I am equally unhappy. During the hours that we are apart I wander aimlessly, bent under the burden of an existence I cannot endure. Society irritates me, solitude crushes me. These nondescript people who watch me, who know nothing of my affairs, who look at me with curiosity without interest, astonishment without sympathy, these people who dare to speak to me of subjects other than you, wound me mortally. I flee from them, and then when I am alone I search in vain for a breath of air to relieve my stifled chest. I throw myself on the ground that ought to open and swallow me forever; I place my head on the cold stones that ought to cool the burning fever that consumes me. I drag myself to that hill overlooking your house; I remain there, my eyes fixed on the retreat I shall never share with you. And if I had met you earlier you could have been mine! I could have clasped in my arms the only being that nature has made for my heart, for my heart that has suffered so much because it was looking for you and only found you when it was too late! When these hours of madness are over at last, and the moment when I may see you has come, I set off trembling for your house. I am afraid that everyone I meet will guess the feelings within me; I stop, I slow my steps, I put off the moment of happiness—the happiness that everything threatens, that I think I am always about to lose; imperfect and tormented happiness that every minute is conspired against by fearful events, jealous eyes, tyrannical whims, and your own will! When I reach your threshold and half open your door, a new terror strikes me: I enter like a guilty man asking pardon of everything I see, as if all were hostile, as if all envied me the hour of happiness I am about to enjoy once more. The slightest noise frightens me, the slightest movement nearby terrifies me, the very sound of my own footsteps makes me draw back. When I have almost reached you I still fear that some obstacle may suddenly come between us. I see you at last: I see you and breathe again; I look upon you and come to rest like the fugitive who touches the soil of the sanctuary that is to save him from death. But even then, when my whole being yearns toward you, when I have a desperate need to relax after so much agony, to place my head on your knees, to let my tears flow freely, even then I must restrain myself by force, even close to you I must live a life of effort: not a moment of effusion, not a moment of surrender. Your eyes watch me; you are embarrassed, almost annoyed by my distress. Some kind of constraint has replaced that delightful time when at least you admitted your love for me. The time flies, other interests demand your attention; you never forget them, you never postpone the moment when I must leave. Strangers come, I may see you no longer; I feel I must run away to escape the suspicions surrounding

me. I leave you more upset, more torn, more insane than
before. I leave you and relapse into that terrible isolation
where I struggle with myself without finding a single soul
on whom I can lean and rest for a moment."

Ellenore had never been loved like this before. The
Count of P—— had a very real affection for her. He had a
great deal of gratitude for her devotion and a great deal of
respect for her character, but his manner always carried
with it a trace of superiority over a woman who had given
herself to him openly and without marriage. It was generally held that he could have made a more honorable alli-
ance; he never said so to her—perhaps he never said so to
himself, but what remains unsaid may still be true, and
whatever is true will be guessed.

Up to this time Ellenore had no conception of the passionate feeling, of the life lost in her own that my very
rages, injustices, and reproaches only proved irrefutably.
Her resistance had heightened all my sensations and ideas;
I turned from those outbursts that frightened her into submission to tenderness and idolatrous regard. I looked upon
her as a heavenly being. My love was almost a cult and
appealed to her all the more because of her fear of being
as deeply humiliated by others as she was reverenced by
me. In the end she gave herself to me completely.

Woe to the man who, in the first moments of a love
affair, does not believe it to be eternal! Woe to him who in
the arms of the mistress he has just won still keeps a fatal
prescience and foresees that he will be able to detach himself. A woman whose heart has carried her away has at
that moment something touching and sacred. It is not
pleasure, or nature, or the senses that corrupt, but our calculations that are conditioned by society, and the reflections
that spring from experience. I loved and respected Ellenore
immeasurably more after she had yielded. I walked
proudly among men; I looked at them with a conqueror's
eyes. The air I breathed was a pleasure in itself. I rushed
to nature to thank her for the immense and unhoped-for
blessing she had deigned to grant me.

IV

Love's magic spell! Who can describe it? That persuasion
that we have found the being destined for us by nature;
that sudden light that shines over life and seems to explain
its mystery; that strange value attached to the most minor
circumstances; those swift hours whose details escape us
because of their very sweetness, and leave in our souls only
a long memory of happiness; that wild gaiety that often
mingles for no reason with our habitual tenderness; that
great pleasure in presence, that hope; in absence that detachment from all vulgar cares, that superiority to all our
surroundings; that certainty that from now on the world
cannot reach us where we are; that mutual understanding
that guesses every thought and responds to every feeling—
love's magic spell, even he who has felt it cannot describe it!

The Count of P— had to go away for six weeks on urgent business. I spent that time with Ellenore almost without interruption. Her attachment seemed to have increased
with the sacrifice she had made me. She never let me leave
her without trying to keep me. When I went out she asked
me when I would come back. Two hours apart were unbearable to her. She would fix the precise moment of my
return. I agreed joyfully, I was grateful, I was happy in
the feeling she showed for me. But still the demands of
ordinary life cannot be bent arbitrarily to our desires. It
was sometimes inconvenient for me to have all my steps
marked out in advance, to have all my minutes counted in
this way. I was compelled to hurry all my projects, and
to break most of my ties. I did not know what to say to
my acquaintances when they proposed some engagement
that in a normal way I should have had no reason to refuse.
While I was with Ellenore I did not regret in the least
losing those social pleasures that had never greatly interested me. But I should have liked her to let me give them

up more freely, I should have felt it sweeter to come back
to her of my own accord, without telling myself that it was
time to go and that she was anxiously waiting for me; and
without the thought of her distress mixing with the happiness I would have on my return. Ellenore was certainly an
ardent pleasure in my life, but she was no longer a goal:
she had become a tie. Besides, I was afraid of compromising her. My continual presence must surprise her servants
and her children, who could observe me. I trembled at the
idea of upsetting her life. I felt that we could not be united
forever, and that I had a sacred duty to respect her secu-
rity; I therefore advised her to be prudent, while still assur-
ing her of my love. But the more advice I gave her of this
sort, the less she was willing to listen to me. At the same
time I was horribly afraid of hurting her. As soon as I saw
an expression of pain on her face, her will became mine;
I was only at ease when she was pleased with me. Whenever I managed to leave her by insisting on the need to
absent myself for a short time, the image of the suffering
I was causing her followed me everywhere. A fever of remorse would seize me, increasing every minute until I could
bear it no longer. I would fly to her, looking forward to the
pleasure of comforting and pacifying her. But as I approached her house, a feeling of resentment against this
curious tyranny would mingle with my other feelings.
Ellenore herself was passionate. I believe that she felt for
me an emotion she had never felt for anyone. In her earlier
affairs her heart had been crushed by a painful sense of
dependency; with me she was perfectly at ease, because
we met in perfect equality: she felt that she had recovered
her self-respect in a love that was devoid of all calculation
or self-interest; she knew that I was sure that she loved me
for myself alone. But her complete freedom with me meant
that she hid none of her emotions from me; and whenever
I came back to her room, impatient at coming earlier than
I would have liked, I would find her sad or annoyed. I had
suffered for two hours away from her at the thought of
what she was suffering away from me; now I had to suffer
two hours with her before I could pacify her.

Nevertheless, I was not unhappy. I told myself that it was sweet to be loved, even with these demands; I felt that I was doing her some good; her happiness was necessary to me and I knew that I was necessary to her happiness.

Besides, I had a confused idea that by the very nature of things this affair could not last; sad though this was in many ways, it nonetheless served to calm me in my bouts of fatigue or impatience. Ellenore's ties with the count, the disparity of our ages, the difference in our situations, my departure—which many circumstances had already delayed, but the date was near—all these considerations induced me still to give and receive as much happiness as possible: I was so sure of the years that I would not quarrel with the days.

The Count of P—— returned. He was not slow to suspect my relationship with Ellenore; each day he received me more coldly and more morosely. I spoke urgently to Ellenore of the risk she was running, I begged her to let me interrupt my visits for a few days, I urged the interests of her reputation, her fortune, and her children. She listened for a long time in silence; she was as pale as death. "In one way or another," she said, "you will soon be leaving; let us not hasten the moment; do not worry about me. Let us gain days, let us gain hours: days and hours are all I need. Adolphe, some presentiment tells me that I shall die in your arms."

So we went on as before, myself constantly worried, Ellenore constantly sad, the count silent and anxious. Finally the letter I was waiting for came: my father ordered me to return to him. I took the letter to Ellenore. "Already!" she said when she had read it. "I did not think it could be so soon." Then, bursting into tears, she took my hand and said, "Adolphe, you see that I cannot live without you; I do not know what will happen to my future, but I implore you not to leave me yet: find some excuse to stay. Ask your father to let you prolong your visit for another six months. Is six months so long?" I wanted to oppose her plan, but she cried so bitterly, she was trembling so violently, her features bore the print of such heart-rending suffering that

I could not go on. I threw myself at her feet, I clasped her in my arms, I assured her of my love, and I left to write to my father. And actually as I wrote I was inspired by the knowledge of Ellenore's distress: I alleged countless reasons for delay, I underlined the usefulness of continuing at D—— some courses that I had been unable to take at Göttingen, and when I sent my letter to the mail I fervently hoped that I would win the consent I asked.

I went back to Ellenore in the evening. She was sitting on a couch; the count was near the fireplace, fairly far from her; the two children were at the end of the room, not playing and wearing the expression of astonishment that children have when they are aware of some trouble but do not suspect its cause. I told Ellenore by a gesture that I had done as she wished. A gleam of joy shone in her eyes but quickly disappeared. We said nothing. The silence became embarrassing to all three of us. Finally the count said, "I am told, sir, that you are preparing to leave." I answered that this was unknown to me. "I think," he went on, "that at your age one should not delay in taking up a career, but," he added, looking at Ellenore, "perhaps everyone here does not agree with me."

I did not have long to wait for my father's reply. As I opened his letter I trembled at the pain a refusal would give Ellenore. I even thought that I would feel this pain with equal bitterness. But as I read his consent, all the inconveniences involved in a longer stay suddenly sprang to my mind. "Another six months of trouble and constraint," I said to myself, "six months of offending a man who has been my friend, six months of exposing a woman who loves me; I am running the risk of depriving her of the only position where she can live peacefully and with respect; I am deceiving my father—why?—to evade temporarily a distress that is sooner or later inevitable. Do we not feel this distress daily, minutely, drop by drop? I am only doing Ellenore harm; my feeling, as it is now, can never satisfy her. I am sacrificing myself for her without achieving her happiness; and as for myself, I am living here futilely, lacking independence, lacking a moment's freedom, unable to breathe in peace even for an hour. Still occupied by these thoughts, I went to Ellenore. I found her alone. "I am staying another six months," I told her.

"You tell me the news very coldly."

"Because I confess that I greatly fear the consequences of this delay for both of us."

"It does not seem as if they could be very troublesome for you at least."

"You know very well, Ellenore, that I never think chiefly of myself."

"Neither do you think very much of other people's happiness."

The conversation had taken a stormy turn. Ellenore was hurt by my regrets at a time when she thought I should be sharing her joy. I was hurt by her victory over my earlier resolutions. The scene became violent. We broke into mutual reproaches. Ellenore accused me of having deceived her, of having had only a passing fancy for her, of alienating the count's affection from her, of throwing her back into that equivocal position in public opinion from which she had spent her life trying to escape. I was annoyed to see that she turned against me things I had done only in obedience to her, and through fear of hurting her. I complained of the extreme constraint I suffered, of my youth wasted in inactivity, of the tyranny she exercised over all my movements. As I spoke I saw her face suddenly covered with tears. I stopped, I retreated, I denied, I explained. We kissed, but a first blow had been struck, a first barrier passed. We had both spoken irreparable words: we could ignore them but we could not forget them. Some things can be left unsaid to ourselves for a long time, but once they are said we repeat them constantly.

We lived for four months in this unnatural relationship that was sometimes delightful but never completely free; we still found pleasure in it but the magic was gone. Nevertheless, Ellenore's attachment to me did not weaken. Even after the bitterest quarrels she was just as anxious to see me and would fix the time of our meetings as if our union were the most peaceful and tender possible. I have often thought that my own conduct helped to keep Ellenore in this mood. If I had loved her as she loved me, she would have been calmer; she would have thought of her own accord about the risk she was taking. But she hated all idea of prudence because all the prudence came from me; she did not think through her sacrifices, because she was too busy getting me to accept them; and she had no time to grow cool toward me, because all her time and energy were directed toward holding me. The new date fixed for my departure drew near, and as I thought about it I experienced a mixture of pleasure and regret: like a man who must purchase certain health by a painful operation.

One morning Ellenore wrote to me to come to her at once. "The count forbids me to see you," she said. "I have no intention of obeying this tyrannous command. I have followed this man into exile, I have saved his fortune, I have served all his interests. He can do without me now, but I cannot do without you." It can easily be guessed what entreaties I used to dissuade her from a plan that was inconceivable to me; I spoke to her of public opinion. She replied that this opinion had never been just to her. "For ten years I have done my duty better than any wife, and public opinion has nonetheless kept me from the position I deserved." I reminded her of her children. "My children are the Count of P——'s. He has recognized them, and he will take care of them. They will be only too happy to forget a mother who had nothing but shame to give them." I redoubled my prayers. "Listen," she said, "if I break with the count, will you refuse to see me? Will you?" she repeated, seizing my arm with a force that made me shudder.

"Certainly not," I replied, "and the more unfortunate you are, the more devoted I will be to you. But consider——"

"I have considered everything," she interrupted. "He is coming back—leave me now, and do not come here again."

I passed the rest of the day in inexpressible torment. Two days went by without news of Ellenore. I was miserable at not knowing what was happening to her; I was even miserable at not seeing her, and I was surprised at the pain this deprivation caused. Nevertheless, I wanted her to give up the plan that made me so fearful for her, and I was beginning to hope that she had done so, when a woman brought me a note in which Ellenore begged me to visit her on such a street, in such a house, on the third floor. I rushed there, still hoping that, since she could not receive me at the count's, she wished to see me for the last time elsewhere. I found her making preparations for a permanent residence. She came to me, both happy and shy, and trying to read my feelings in my eyes. "All is over," she told me. "I am completely free. I have fifteen hundred francs a year from my own fortune. That is enough for me. You will be here for another six weeks. When you leave, perhaps I can settle near you, or perhaps you will come back to see me." And as if she feared a reply she plunged into a mass of detail about her plans. She tried every argument to persuade me that she would be happy, that she had sacrificed nothing for me, that the decision she had made was right for her, independently of me. It was obvious that she was making a great effort, and that she only believed half of what she was saying. She was deafening herself with her own words for fear of hearing mine; she was eagerly prolonging her speeches to put off the moment when my objections would plunge her back into despair. I could not find it in my heart to make any; I accepted her sacrifice, I thanked her for it, I told her it made me happy; I went further: I assured her that I had always wanted an irrevocable decision to impose on me the duty of never leaving her. I attributed my former wavering to a feeling of delicacy that forbade me to consent to anything that would jeopardize her situation. In short, I had no thought but to keep her from all pain, all fear, all regret, and all uncertainty as to my feeling for her. All the time I was speaking to her I had no other aim, and my promises were sincere.

V

The separation of Ellenore and the Count of P—— had the effect on public opinion that one would have expected. In one instant Ellenore lost all the benefit of her ten years of devotion and fidelity; she was put with all the women in her class who unscrupulously indulge in one affair after another. Because of the desertion of her children she was regarded as an unnatural mother, and women of irreproachable reputation smugly repeated that the loss of the most essential feminine virtue soon infects all the rest. At the same time they pitied her—so as not to forgo the pleasure of blaming me. My conduct was called that of a seducer, an ingrate who violated the laws of hospitality, who for the sake of a passing whim had sacrificed the peace of two people, of whom he should have respected the one and taken care not to offend the other. Several of my father's friends made serious representations to me; others, less frank with me, made me feel their disapproval by oblique suggestions. The young men, on the other hand, were delighted by the skill with which I had supplanted the count, and by numerous pleasantries, which I vainly tried to repress, congratulated me on my conquest and promised to follow in my footsteps. I cannot describe what I had to suffer from both this harsh censure and this shameful praise. I am convinced that if I had been in love with Ellenore I should have won opinion over to us. For such is the power of true feeling that, when it speaks, it silences false interpretations and artificial conventions. But I was only a weak, grateful, and dominated man. I was not sustained by any feeling that sprang from the heart. So I expressed myself with embarrassment, I tried to put an end to the conversation, and if it went on, I terminated it by a few rough words to show the others that I was ready to quarrel with them. Indeed, I would have much rather fought with them than replied.

Ellenore soon saw that opinion was turning against her. Two relatives of the count whom his influence had compelled to receive her made a sensational rupture; under the guise of stern moral principles they were delighted to give free rein to the malice they had so long controlled. The men continued to visit Ellenore, but a certain familiarity crept into their tone, which showed that she no longer had the support of a powerful protector or the justification of an almost sacred union. Some visited her, they said, because they had always known her; others because she was still beautiful, and her recent lightness of conduct gave them hopes they did not try to disguise from her. Everyone justified his relationship with her, which meant that everyone thought his relationship needed justification. And so the unfortunate Ellenore saw herself fallen forever into that state from which she had tried all her life to emerge. Everything combined to crush her spirit and wound her pride. She regarded the desertion by some people as proof of their scorn, and the attentions of others as the indication of an insulting expectancy. She was miserable in solitude, she was embarrassed in society. Ah! certainly I should have comforted her; I should have pressed her to my heart and said, "Let us live only for each other, let us forget these people who misunderstand us, let us be happy just with our own regard, with our own love." I tried to do this, but how can a resolve based on duty rekindle a dying passion?

Ellenore and I concealed our thoughts from each other. She dared not confide in me the sorrows of a sacrifice that she knew I had not asked. I had accepted this sacrifice: I dared not complain of a misfortune I had seen but had not had the strength to prevent. So both of us were silent on the one subject that was constantly in our minds. We lavished caresses on each other, we spoke of love; but we spoke of love because we were afraid to speak of anything else.

As soon as a secret comes between two hearts in love, as soon as one of them decides to conceal a single thought from the other, the charm is broken and the happiness destroyed. We can make amends for anger, injustice, even for lack of attention, but dissimulation introduces a foreign element into love that makes it seem unnatural and tarnished in its own eyes.

By a curious inconsistency, while indignantly rebutting the slightest insinuation against Ellenore, I myself in general conversation added to the wrong done to her. I had submitted to her wishes, but I had taken a violent dislike to women's domination. I continually declaimed against their weakness, their demands, the tyranny of their grief. I proclaimed the most hardhearted principles, and the same man who could not resist a tear, who yielded to silent sorrow, who was pursued in absence by the image of the suffering he had caused, showed himself in every word to be scornful and pitiless. All my explicit praises in Ellenore's favor could not destroy the impression made by such conversation. People hated me; they pitied Ellenore but they did not respect her. They were annoyed with her for not inspiring her lover with more consideration for her sex, and more respect for ties of the heart.

Since Ellenore's break with the Count of P—— a man who visited her regularly had revealed an ardent passion for her, and by his indiscreet persecution had forced her to refuse to see him. This man indulged in such outrageous jests at her expense that I could not tolerate him. We fought; I wounded him seriously, I was wounded myself. I cannot describe the mixture of confusion and terror, gratitude and love on Ellenore's face when she saw me after this event. In spite of my entreaties she took up her residence with me; she did not leave me for a single moment until I was convalescent. She read to me during the day, she sat up with me for most of the night, she watched my slightest movement and anticipated my every wish; her ingenious kindness increased her abilities and doubled her strength. She assured me constantly that she would not have survived me; I was imbued with affection and torn with remorse. I wished that I could have found something in myself to reward such a constant and tender attachment; I called to my aid memories, imagination, even reason and feelings of duty: all futile efforts! The difficulty of the situation, the certainty that the future would separate us, and perhaps a kind of rebellion against a bond I was unable to break consumed me inwardly. I reproached myself for the ingratitude I forced myself to hide from her. I was miserable when she seemed to doubt a love that was so necessary to her; I was equally miserable when she seemed to believe in it. I felt that she was nobler than I, I despised myself as unworthy of her. It is a terrible misfortune to be unloved when one is in love, but it is a greater one to be loved passionately when one no longer loves. I would have given the life I had just risked for Ellenore many times over if she could have been happy without me.

The six months that my father had granted me were now over; I had to think of leaving. Ellenore made no attempt to oppose my departure, she did not even try to delay it, but she made me promise that I would come back to her after two months, or else allow her to join me. This I solemnly promised. What would I not have agreed to at a moment when I saw her struggling with herself to control her grief? She could have extracted from me a promise not to leave her; deep in my heart I knew that her tears would not have been disobeyed. I was grateful that she did not exercise her power; I felt that I loved her better for it. Besides, I myself could not part without deep regret from one who was so completely devoted to me. There is something very profound in affairs that go on for a long time. Without our realizing it they become such an intimate part of our lives. At a distance we may calmly resolve to break them, and we think we are waiting impatiently to do so, but when the moment comes, it fills us with terror, and such is the strangeness of our wretched hearts that it is excruciatingly painful to leave those whom we have lived near without pleasure.

During my absence I wrote regularly to Ellenore. I was torn between the fear that my letters would hurt her and the desire to depict only what I really felt. I could have wished her to guess my feelings, but to guess them without suffering. I congratulated myself when I was able to

substitute the words "affection," "friendship," "devotion"
for "love," but then I would suddenly picture poor Ellenore,
alone and sad, with only my letters for comfort; at the end
of two cold and formal pages I would quickly add several
ardent or tender phrases designed to deceive her afresh. So
that without ever saying enough to satisfy her, I always
said enough to mislead her. Curious falsehood! Its very success worked against me, prolonged my torment, and was
intolerable.

I anxiously counted the days and hours as they slid by;
I prayed for the passage of time to slow down; I trembled
as the day approached when I should have to fulfill my
promise. I could not conceive of any way of leaving; I could
discover none whereby Ellenore could come and live in the
same town as myself. Perhaps—to tell the truth—I did not
want it. I compared my peaceful and independent life with
the life of hurry, confusion, and torment to which her passion condemned me. I found it so pleasant to be free, to
go and come, leave and return without anyone caring. I
was resting, as it were, in the indifference of others after
the strain of her love.

All the same, I dared not let Ellenore suspect that I
should have liked to abandon our plans. She had understood from my letters that it would be difficult for me to
leave my father; she wrote that consequently she was beginning her preparations to leave. For a long time I did
nothing to oppose her resolve. I gave her no definite answer; I mentioned vaguely that I should always be delighted to know that she was happy—and then added: to
make her happy; pitiful equivocations, strained expressions
that I groaned to see so obscure and trembled to make any
clearer. I finally decided to speak frankly to her; I told myself that I owed it to her; I aroused my conscience against
my weakness; I fortified myself with the thought of her
peace against the image of her suffering. I strode about
my room reciting aloud what I proposed to say to her. But
I had hardly written a few lines when my mood changed;
I no longer saw in my words the meaning they were to
convey, but only the effect they could not help produce;

in spite of myself a supernatural power controlled and directed my hand, and I limited myself to advising a few months' delay. I had not said what was in my mind. My letter carried no trace of sincerity. The arguments I gave were feeble because they were not true.

Ellenore's reply was violent; she was indignant at my wish not to see her. What did she ask of me? Only to live somewhere near me, unknown. How could I fear her presence in a secret retreat in the middle of a big city where no one knew her? She had sacrificed everything for me—fortune, children, reputation; she asked no other return for her sacrifice than to wait for me like a humble slave, to spend a few minutes a day with me, and enjoy the moments I could spare her. She had resigned herself to two months' absence, not because she thought absence necessary, but because I seemed to want it; and when—after painfully adding day to day—she had finally come to the date I myself had fixed, I proposed that she begin the long torment over again! She could have been mistaken: perhaps she had given her life to a hard, unfeeling man. I was master of my actions, but I was not her master to force her to suffer, abandoned as she was by the man for whom she had made a total sacrifice.

Ellenore soon followed this letter; she let me know of her arrival. I went to her, firmly resolved to show a great deal of joy; I was impatient to reassure her heart, and to give her some happiness and calm—at least for a moment. But she had been hurt; she looked at me mistrustfully and soon detected my efforts; she stung my pride by her reproaches; she insulted my character. She showed me to be so despicable in my weakness that she turned my anger against her more than against myself. A mad fury possessed us: all consideration was abandoned, all delicacy forgotten. It was as if we were hurled against each other by Furies. Everything that the most implacable hatred had invented about us we applied to each other; and these two unhappy beings, who knew only each other in the world, who alone could do each other justice, who alone could understand

and comfort each other, seemed to be irreconcilable enemies furiously bent on destroying each other.

We parted after a scene lasting three hours; and for the
first time in our lives we parted without explanations, without amends. I had hardly left Ellenore before a profound
grief replaced my anger. I was in a kind of stupor, completely stunned by what had happened. I repeated my
words to myself in astonishment: my behavior was inconceivable to me; I wondered what there was within me that
could have maddened me.

It was very late; I dared not return to Ellenore. I promised myself that I would see her first thing in the morning,
and went back to my father's house. It was full of people,
and it was easy in such a crowd to keep myself withdrawn
and my distress hidden. When we were alone my father
said, "I am told that the Count of P——'s former mistress
is in town. I have always allowed you the greatest freedom,
and have never wanted to know anything about your love
affairs, but it is not suitable for you to have a declared
mistress, and I warn you that I have taken steps to ensure
that she leave here." He left me as he finished speaking. I
followed him to his room; he motioned me to withdraw.
"Father," I said, "as God is my witness, I wish her to be
happy, and for that I would consent never to see her again;
but take care what you do. While you think you are separating us, you may well bind her to me forever."

Immediately afterward there came to my room a valet
who had been with me on my travels and knew of my rela-
tions with Ellenore. I charged him to find out immediately,
if he could, what the measures were that my father had
mentioned. He came back after two hours. My father's secretary had confided to him under vow of secrecy that the
next day Ellenore was to be served with orders of expul-
sion. "Ellenore driven out," I cried, "driven out in disgrace!
When she came here only for my sake—when I have broken
her heart, and seen her weep without pity? Where shall she
lay her head, unhappy soul, wandering alone in a world
where I have ruined her reputation? To whom could she
tell her grief?" My mind was soon made up. I won over

my servant and showered him with gold and promises. I ordered a post-chaise for six in the morning at the city gates. I made countless plans for my eternal reunion with Ellenore: I loved her more than ever, my whole heart had come back to her, I was proud to protect her, I was eager to hold her in my arms, love had completely repossessed my soul. The fever I felt in my head, heart, and senses threw my life into utter confusion. If at that moment Ellenore had wished to part from me, I would have died at her feet in order to keep her.

Day came; I rushed to Ellenore. She was in bed, having wept all night; her eyes were still moist, her hair disheveled; with surprise she saw me enter. "Come," I said. "Let us go." She tried to reply. "Let us go," I went on. "Have you any other protector or friend on earth but me? Are not my arms your only refuge?" She resisted. "I have serious and personal reasons," I added. "Follow me, for heaven's sake." I carried her off. On the way I covered her with caresses, I pressed her to my heart. I replied to her questions only with kisses. I finally told her that when I realized my father wished to separate us I had felt that I could not be happy without her, that I wished to dedicate my life to her and to ratify our union with every kind of bond. At first her gratitude was extreme, but she soon detected contradictions in my story. By dint of entreaties she extracted the truth from me. Her joy vanished, her face clouded with a dark shadow. "Adolphe," she said, "you are mistaken about yourself: you are generous, you are devoting yourself to me because I am persecuted. You think you feel love, when all you feel is pity." Why did she say these fatal words? Why did she reveal a secret I wished to ignore? I forced myself to reassure her; perhaps I succeeded; but the truth had entered my soul and the emotion was destroyed. I was determined to carry out my sacrifice, but I was no longer happy in it, and already I harbored a thought I was again reduced to conceal.

VI

On our arrival at the frontier I wrote to my father. My letter was respectful, but it had an undertone of bitterness. I resented the fact that he had tightened my bonds while meaning to break them. I told him that I would not leave Ellenore until she was comfortably settled and no longer needed me. I begged him not to force me to remain permanently bound to her by persecuting her. I waited for his reply before deciding on our establishment. "You are twenty-four years old," he replied. "I will not exercise an authority that is almost at an end, and that I have never used; I will even conceal your strange actions as far as I can; I will spread the rumor that you have left by my orders and on my business. I will contribute liberally to your expenses. You yourself will soon realize that the life you are leading is not suitable for you: your birth, talents, and fortune give you a better place in the world than that of companion to a woman with neither country nor home. Your letter proves to me that you are already feeling dissatisfied with yourself. Remember that there is nothing to be gained by prolonging a situation of which you are ashamed. You are wasting the best years of your youth, and this loss is irreparable."

My father's letter dealt me repeated and bitter blows: he told me only what I had told myself many times; many times I had been ashamed of dribbling away my life in obscurity and inaction. Reproaches and threats would have been more welcome to me: I should have had some pride in resisting him, and I should have felt the necessity of gathering my resources to defend Ellenore from the dangers that threatened her. But now there were no dangers. I was perfectly free, and this freedom only increased the impatience with which I bore the yoke that appeared to be of my own choosing.

We settled in Caden, a little town in Bohemia. I told myself again that, since I had undertaken the responsibility for Ellenore's fate, I must not make her suffer. I managed to control my feelings; I repressed even the slightest signs of discontent, and used all the resources of my mind to create an artificial gaiety that would veil my profound sadness. This effort had an unexpected effect on me. We are such flexible creatures that we end by experiencing the feelings we pretend. I partially forgot the troubles I hid. My perpetual jests dispelled my own gloom, and the assurances of affection I gave Ellenore spread a gentle feeling in my heart that was very like love.

There were times when I was prey to troublesome memories. When alone I would give way to attacks of uneasiness; I would make countless extraordinary plans for a sudden break out of the sphere in which I didn't belong. But I suppressed these feelings as bad dreams. Ellenore seemed content. How could I disturb her happiness? Nearly five months passed in this way.

One day I saw that Ellenore was distressed and that she was trying to hide from me a thought that preoccupied her. After long entreaties on my part she made me promise that I would not oppose the decision she had made, and confessed that the Count of P—— had written to her: his lawsuit had been successful, he gratefully remembered the help she had given him and their ten years' liaison. He offered her half his fortune, not to rejoin him (which was no longer possible) but on condition that she left the ungrateful and treacherous man who had parted them. "I have replied," she told me, "and you guess correctly that I have refused." I guessed only too well. I was touched, but in despair at the new sacrifice Ellenore was making for me. In any case I dared make no objection. My attempts in this direction had always been so fruitless! I withdrew to consider what line I should follow. It was clear that our bonds should be broken. They were grievous to me, they were becoming harmful to her, I was the only obstacle to her finding herself a comfortable place in society and the consideration that sooner or later follows wealth. I was the

only barrier between her and her children; I had no further
excuse that I could see. To yield to her in these circumstances was no longer generosity but culpable weakness.
I had promised my father to regain my freedom as soon
as Ellenore no longer needed me. Finally it was time to
take up a career, to begin an active life, to win some claim
to men's regard, and make good use of my abilities. I went
back to Ellenore, believing myself unshakable in my plan
of forcing her not to reject the Count of P——'s offer, and
to tell her, if necessary, that I no longer loved her. "Dear
friend," I said, "we sometimes struggle against our destiny,
but we always end by yielding to it. The laws of society
are stronger than man's will; the most imperious ideas are
broken by the force of circumstance. We vainly persist in
consulting only our hearts, sooner or later we are bound to
listen to reason. I cannot keep you any longer in a position
equally unworthy of us both: I can do it neither for you
nor for myself." While I spoke without looking at Ellenore,
I felt my ideas becoming vaguer and my resolution weak-
ening. Wishing to recover my strength, I went on hurriedly.
"I shall always be your friend; I shall always have the deepest affection for you. The two years we have been together
will never be effaced from my memory—they will always
remain the most wonderful period of my life. But love—
that transport of the senses, that involuntary intoxication,
that obliviousness to all duty—Ellenore, I no longer feel it."
For a long time I waited for a reply without raising my
eyes to her. When I finally looked at her, she was motionless; she was looking at everything as though she could
recognize nothing. I took her hand, it was cold. She pushed
me away. "What do you want of me?" she said. "Am I
not alone, alone in the world, without a soul to understand
me? What else have you to say to me? Haven't you said it
all? Isn't it all over, over forever? Let me alone, leave me
—isn't that what you want?" She tried to move away but
faltered. I tried to hold her back; she fell unconscious at
my feet. I lifted her up, kissed her, and brought her back
to life. "Ellenore," I cried, "come back to yourself, come
back to me; I love you, I love you most tenderly. I was

deceiving you—so that you could make your choice more freely." The credulity of the heart is inexplicable. These simple words, contradicted by so many before them, restored life and confidence to Ellenore. She made me repeat them several times; she seemed to breathe hungrily. She believed me: she was intoxicated by her own love, which she took for ours, she confirmed her reply to the Count of P——, and I was more committed than ever.

Three months later there was a new possibility for change in Ellenore's situation. By one of those changes of fortune common to faction-torn countries Ellenore's father was recalled to Poland and his property restored. Although he scarcely knew his daughter, who had been taken to France by her mother at the age of three, he wished to establish her close to him. The rumor of her adventures had reached him only vaguely in Russia, where he had been throughout his exile. Ellenore was his only child. He was afraid to be alone; he wanted to be looked after; he sought only to discover his daughter's whereabouts, and, as soon as he had found out, warmly invited her to join him. She could feel no real affection for a father she could not remember having seen. Nevertheless, she felt it her duty to obey: in this way she would ensure a large fortune for her children and resume the rank in society of which her misfortunes and conduct had deprived her, but she told me positively that she would not go to Poland unless I went with her. "I am no longer at an age," she said, "when the soul is open to new impressions. My father is a stranger to me. If I stay here, others will quickly gather around him; he will be just as happy with them. My children will have the Count of P——'s fortune. I know very well that I shall be generally blamed —I shall be considered an ungrateful daughter and a callous mother—but I have suffered too much; I am no longer young enough for the world's opinion to weigh too heavily on me. If there seems any bitterness in this, Adolphe, you have only yourself to blame. If I had any illusions about you, I would probably consent to an absence, when its bitterness would be lessened by the prospect of a sweet and lasting reunion. But you would like nothing better than

to think of me as six hundred miles away, peacefully content in the bosom of my family, and surrounded by wealth.
You would write about it to me in such sensible letters—
I can imagine them in advance: they would break my heart,
and I do not want to expose myself to them. I have not
the consolation of telling myself that by sacrificing my
whole life to you I have succeeded in inspiring you with
the love I deserve, but at least you have accepted the sacrifice. I have already suffered enough from the hardness of
your manner and the coldness of our relationship; I submit
to the torments you inflict on me—I will not face any additional ones."

There was something harsh and violent in Ellenore's tone
and voice, which indicated firm determination rather than
deep or moving emotion. For some time she would become
irritated beforehand when she asked me for something—as
if I had already refused it. She commanded my actions
but knew that my judgment disapproved of them. She
would have liked to penetrate the intimate sanctuary of
my thought to break down the silent opposition that made
her angry with me. I spoke to her of my situation, of my
promise to my father, of my own desires; I entreated, I
became angry. Ellenore was immovable. I hoped to awaken
her generosity, as if love were not the most selfish of feelings, and therefore the least generous when wounded. I
made a curious effort to soften her toward the misery I
felt in staying with her; I only managed to exasperate her.
I promised to visit her in Poland, but my promises were
lacking in warmth and generosity and she saw in them only
impatience to leave her.

The first year of our stay in Caden came to an end without any change in our situation. When Ellenore found me
gloomy or depressed, she would first be troubled, then hurt,
and finally her reproaches would wring from me a confession of the weariness I wanted to conceal. For my part,
when Ellenore seemed happy, I would be irritated to see
her enjoying a situation that cost me my happiness, and I
tormented her in this brief pleasure by insinuations that
showed what I really felt. And so we would attack one

another in turn by oblique statements, only to retreat immediately into general protestations and vague justifications in order to relapse into silence. For we each knew so exactly what the other would say that we would be silent to avoid hearing it. Sometimes one of us would be ready to yield, but we missed the right moment to come together. Our suspicious and wounded hearts could not meet again.

I often wondered why I remained in such a painful situation: my answer was that if I went away from Ellenore she would follow me, and I should have provoked a fresh sacrifice. I finally told myself that I must give her this last satisfaction, and that she could ask nothing further from me once I had resettled her in the midst of her family. I was going to propose that I follow her to Poland, when she received word of her father's sudden death. He had made her his only heir, but his will was contradicted by later letters that distant relatives were threatening to have validated. In spite of the little contact between her and her father Ellenore was painfully affected by his death; she reproached herself for having abandoned him. Soon she blamed me for her failure. "You have made me fail in a sacred duty," she said. "Now it is only a matter of my fortune: I shall sacrifice it to you still more easily. I shall certainly not go alone to a country where I shall only meet enemies."

"I had no desire to make you fail in your duty," I replied. "I confess that I should have liked you to be willing to consider that it was also painful to me to fail in mine. I was unable to obtain this justice from you. I yield to you, Ellenore; your interest takes precedence over all other considerations. We shall leave together whenever you wish."

We actually set out. The distractions of the journey, the novelty of the sights, the efforts we made at self-control occasionally brought us some fragments of intimacy. We had been used to each other for so long, and had experienced so many different circumstances together, that we found that every word and almost every gesture evoked memories that took us suddenly back to the past and filled us with involuntary tenderness, as lightning breaks the dark-

ness without dispelling it. It was as if we were living in a
kind of memory of the heart that was powerful enough
to make the idea of parting sorrowful, but too weak for
us to find happiness in being united. I gave myself up to
these emotions as a rest from my usual constraint. I should
have liked to give Ellenore some evidence of affection that
would have contented her; I sometimes spoke to her of
love, but these emotions and words were like pale leaves,
drained of color, that by some trace of dying vegetation
grow languidly on the branches of an uprooted tree.

VII

As soon as she arrived, Ellenore was able to take possession of the disputed property on condition that she would
dispose of it only when the lawsuit was decided. She settled herself on one of her father's estates. My father, who
never discussed anything directly in his letters to me, contented himself with filling them with insinuations against
my journey. "You informed me that you would not leave,"
he said. "You explained to me at length all your reasons
for not leaving: consequently, I was convinced that you
would leave. I can only pity you when, with your independent mind, you always do what you do not want to do.
Moreover, I cannot form an opinion about a situation that
I only know imperfectly. Up to now you have seemed to
me to be Ellenore's protector, and in this role there has
been something noble in your actions that elevated your
character, whatever the object of your attentions may be.
Today your relationship is no longer the same; you are no
longer protecting her, she is protecting you; you live with
her as a stranger whom she is introducing to her family. I
make no judgment on a situation of your own choosing,
but since it may have inconveniences, I should like to mitigate them as far as I can. I am writing to Baron T——, our
minister to the country you are in, to recommend you to

him. I do not know whether it will suit you to make use of this recommendation; at least regard it only as proof of my interest, and in no way as an attack on the independence you have always successfully managed to defend against your father."

I stifled the reflections this style of writing aroused in me. The estate I was living on with Ellenore was not far from Warsaw; I went into the city to see Baron T——. He received me in a friendly way, asked me why I was in Poland, and questioned me as to my plans. I did not quite know how to reply. After a few minutes of embarrassing conversation he said, "I am going to speak to you frankly. I know what motives brought you to this country—your father has told me; I may even say that I understand them: there is no man living who has not found himself, at some point in his life, torn between the desire to break off an inconvenient affair and the fear of hurting the woman he has loved. The inexperience of youth greatly exaggerates the difficulties of such a situation; it likes to believe in the truth of all those demonstrations of sorrow that replace the weapons of strength and reason in a weak and excitable sex. The heart suffers but self-esteem is gratified, and such a man who really believes he is sacrificing himself to the despair he has caused is actually only sacrificing himself to the illusions created by his own vanity. The world is full of passionate women; every one of them has protested that she will die if she is deserted; every one of them is still alive and has found consolation." I tried to interrupt. "Forgive me, young friend," he said, "if I express myself rather harshly, but the good I have heard of you, your promising talents, and the career you ought to be following, all oblige me to speak openly to you. I can read your mind in spite of and better than you can; you are no longer in love with the woman who dominates you and drags you after her; if you still loved her you would not have come to me. You knew your father had written to me; you could easily foresee what I had to say to you. It has not annoyed you to hear me state those arguments that you repeat to yourself constantly but always in vain. Ellenore's reputation is far from being intact."

"Please let us put an end to this useless conversation," I replied. "Unfortunate circumstances were responsible for Ellenore's early years: she can be unfavorably judged by misleading appearances, but I have known her for three years, and no living creature has a loftier soul, a nobler character, a purer or more generous heart."

"As you please," he replied, "but these are details that opinion does not take into account. The facts are positive and public—do you think you can abolish them by preventing me from recalling them? Listen," he went on, "in this world one must know what one wants. You do not intend to marry Ellenore?"

"Probably not," I said. "She herself has never wished it."

"Then what do you intend to do? She is ten years older than you. You are twenty-six; if you take care of her for another ten years, she will be old and you will have reached middle age without having begun or achieved anything that satisfies you. You will be possessed by boredom, she by ill-humor; every day she will seem less pleasing to you, every day you will be more necessary to her; and the outcome of an illustrious birth, a brilliant fortune, and a distinguished mind will be to vegetate in a corner of Poland, forgotten by your friends, lost to fame, and tormented by a woman who will never be pleased with you whatever you do. I will add only one word more and then we will not return to a topic that embarrasses you. All roads are open to you: literature, the army, the civil service; you could aspire to the most distinguished marriage; you are capable of every success, but remember, between you and any kind of success lies an insurmountable obstacle, and that obstacle is Ellenore."

"I thought I owed it to you, sir, to hear you in silence," I replied, "but I also owe it to myself to declare that you have not shaken me. I repeat, nobody but myself can judge Ellenore; nobody else sufficiently appreciates the truth of her sentiments and the depth of her feeling. As long as she needs me I will stay with her. No success could compensate me for leaving her unhappy, and should I have to limit my career to giving her support by sustaining her in her troubles, and protecting her with affection against the injustice of an ignorant world, I would still consider I had not spent my life in vain."

I left after these words, but who can explain the extinction of the emotion that dictated them, even before I had finished speaking? By returning on foot I hoped to postpone seeing Ellenore, whom I had just been defending. I crossed the city hurriedly—I was impatient to be alone.

When I was well into the country I slowed my pace, and was beset by a host of thoughts. Those fatal words echoed around me: "Between you and any kind of success lies an insurmountable obstacle, and that obstacle is Ellenore." I cast a long, sad look at the time that was now gone beyond return; I recalled the hopes of my youth, the confidence with which I had thought to command the future, the praises I had won for my first attempts, the dawn of reputation I had seen glow and disappear. I repeated to myself the names of several of my fellow-students whom I had treated with the utmost disdain and who, simply by determined effort and routine lives, had left me far behind on the road to fortune, consideration, and fame. I was oppressed by my lack of action. As misers see in the treasure they hoard all the things it could buy, so I saw in Ellenore the deprivation of all the successes to which I might have aspired. It was not a single career that I regretted: since I had tried none, I regretted them all. Since I had never used my abilities, I imagined them to be limitless, and cursed them; I wished nature had made me weak and mediocre, if only to save me from the remorse of having voluntarily debased myself. Any praise or approval of my mind or knowledge seemed an intolerable reproach: it was like hearing admiration for the vigorous arms of an athlete loaded with chains in the depths of a prison. When I wished to regain my courage and tell myself that it was still not too late to act, the image of Ellenore rose before me like a ghost and thrust me back into nothingness; I was seized by fits of rage against her, yet by a curious blend of feeling this rage did not lessen in the least the terror I felt at inflicting it on her.

My soul, wearied by these bitter feelings, suddenly sought refuge in contrary ones. A few words, spoken at random by Baron T—— about the possibility of a pleasant and tranquil marriage, made me create an ideal companion. I thought of the peace, consideration, and even independence that such a life offered; for the bonds I had been trailing for so long made me infinitely more dependent than any authentic marriage could have done. I imagined my father's joy: I felt an impatient desire to resume in my country and in company with my equals the place that was my due. I imagined myself leading an austere and irreproachable life in answer to the judgments made against me by cold and frivolous malice, and to all the reproaches heaped on me by Ellenore.

"She constantly accuses me," I said to myself, "of being hard, ungrateful, and pitiless; if only heaven had granted me a woman whom convention allowed me to acknowledge, whom my father would not be ashamed to accept as a daughter, I would have been infinitely happier in making her happy. My feelings, which are misunderstood because they are suffering and hurt, are imperiously commanded to give proof of themselves; my heart refuses to do so in face of anger or threats. But how delightful it would be to indulge them with the beloved companion of a regular and respected life! What have I not done for Ellenore? For her sake I have left my country and my family, for her sake I have wounded the heart of an aged father who still suffers far away; for her sake I am living in this place where my youth wanes in solitude, without fame, without honor, and without pleasure. Do not these sacrifices, prompted by neither duty nor love, prove what love and duty *could* inspire me to do? If I am so afraid of the suffering of a woman who controls me only by her suffering, how much more tenderly would I keep all trouble and pain from a woman who commanded my devotion without reservation or remorse! What a different person would I seem then! How quickly would I lose that bitterness of which I am now

accused because its cause is unknown! How grateful would
I be to heaven, how well-disposed toward men!"

As I went on in this strain, my eyes were moist with
tears; countless memories poured into my mind like a flood
—memories that my relationship with Ellenore had made
hateful to me. Everything that recalled my childhood, the
places where my early years were spent, the companions
of my early games, the old relatives who had first showered
me with marks of interest—all wounded and hurt me. I was
reduced to repressing the most attractive images and natural desires as if they were guilty thoughts. But the companion my imagination had suddenly created for me went
naturally with all these images and sanctioned all these desires; she shared all my duties, all my pleasures, and all
my tastes; she reunited my present life with that period
of my youth when hope had opened such a vast future
before me, a period from which Ellenore had separated
me as by an abyss. My memory retraced the smallest details and the tiniest objects: I saw again the old castle where
I had lived with my father, the woods surrounding it, the
river touching its walls, the mountains bounding its horizon;
all this seemed so clearly present and so full of life that it
filled me with almost unbearable trembling. And among
these scenes my imagination set a young and innocent creature who made them lovelier and animated them with hope.
Plunged in this reverie, I wandered on, still with no fixed
plan, without saying that I must break with Ellenore, and
having only a dim and confused notion of reality. I was
like a man, crushed by trouble, who has been consoled by
a dream and feels that the dream is almost over.

Suddenly I found myself at Ellenore's castle, which I
had been unconsciously approaching; I stopped and took
another road, pleased to postpone the moment of hearing
her voice again.

The day was dying, the sky was serene and the countryside deserted; men had finished their work and left nature
to herself. My thoughts gradually took on a more somber
and impressive tinge. The night shadows, thickening every
minute, the vast silence around me that was interrupted

only by infrequent and distant sounds, induced in me a calmer and more solemn feeling that replaced my fantasy. My gaze wandered over the graying horizon: its limits were no longer visible; this somehow gave me a sensation of immensity. I had not experienced anything like this for a long time; constantly absorbed in purely personal reflections, with my eyes always on my own situation, I was a complete stranger to any general ideas. I had thought only of Ellenore and myself: Ellenore, who inspired me only with pity mingled with weariness, and myself, who no longer inspired esteem. I had shrunk, as it were, into a new kind of egoism, an egoism that lacked courage and was discontented and humiliated. I was grateful to be able to give birth to thoughts of a different nature, and to rediscover the power of self-forgetfulness and so to surrender to disinterested meditation; my soul seemed to be emerging from a long and shameful degradation.

Almost the whole night passed in this way. I walked at random; I passed through fields, woods, and villages where all was still. Occasionally, in some distant dwelling, I would see a pale light piercing the darkness. "There perhaps," I said, "some wretched soul is restless with sorrow, or struggles with death—death, which does not seem to have convinced man of its inexplicable mystery, even by its daily recurrence; that certain end that neither consoles nor pacifies us, toward which we feel habitual carelessness and only passing terror! And I too," I went on, "yield to this pointless inconsistency. I rebel against life as if life were endless; I spread misery about me in order to recover a few wretched years that time will soon snatch from me. Ah! Let me give up these futile efforts, let me enjoy the passage of time, and the days hurrying one after the other; let me remain a quiet and indifferent spectator of an existence already half spent, let me seize it and tear it apart: we cannot prolong its time—is it worth arguing about?"

The thought of death has always had great power over me. In the midst of my strongest emotions it has always sufficed to calm me immediately; it now had its usual effect on my spirit. My attitude toward Ellenore grew less bitter;

all my irritation disappeared; only a gentle, almost tranquil feeling remained after this night of delirium; the physical weariness I felt probably contributed to this tranquillity.

It was almost daybreak. I could already distinguish various objects. I realized that I was quite a long way from Ellenore's house. I pictured her anxiety and was hurrying to reach her as fast as my weariness allowed, when I met a man on horseback whom she had sent to look for me. He told me that she had been distracted by fear for twelve hours; she had gone to Warsaw and searched the suburbs, and then gone home in inexpressible torment. The villagers had spread out in all directions over the countryside in order to find me. This account filled me at first with rather painful irritation. It annoyed me to be subjected by Ellenore to this tiresome supervision. In vain I told myself that it was because of her love for me; was not this love also the cause of all my unhappiness? Nevertheless I managed to subdue this feeling for which I reproached myself. I knew that she was worried and distressed. I mounted the horse and quickly covered the distance separating us. She received me with transports of joy. I was moved by her emotion. Our conversation was brief, because she soon thought I needed rest; so I left her this time, at least, without saying anything to wound her heart.

VIII

I awoke the next day still pursued by the thoughts that had disturbed me the night before. My agitation increased on the following days. Ellenore tried in vain to probe the cause; I replied to her impetuous questions with forced monosyllables; I hardened myself against her insistence because I knew only too well that frankness on my part would be followed by suffering on hers, and that her suffering would require further dissimulation from me.

Worried and surprised, she had recourse to one of her

friends to discover the secret she accused me of concealing;
eager to deceive herself, she looked for a fact where there
was only a feeling. This friend spoke to me about my
strange moods, the trouble I took to discourage all thought
of a lasting tie, and my inexplicable need for rupture and
isolation. I listened to her for a long time in silence. Up to
this point I had told no one that I no longer loved Ellenore;
my lips refused to utter such a thought, which I regarded
as treachery. But I wanted to justify myself, so I told my
story with care, praising Ellenore highly, agreeing that my
behavior was inconsistent but attributing it to the difficulty
of our situation—all without letting a word slip that would
prove definitely that the difficulty lay in my lack of love.
The friend was moved by my account; she saw generosity
in what I called weakness, misfortune in what I said was
harshness. The same explanations that infuriated Ellenore's
passionate nature seemed to convince the impartial mind
of her friend. We are just when we are disinterested. Whoever you may be, never entrust your heart's interests to another: the heart alone can plead its own cause, the heart
alone can probe its own wounds. Every intermediary becomes a judge; he analyzes, compromises, concedes the
idea of indifference, admitting it as possible and recognizing it as inevitable; he thereby excuses it and indifference
is surprised to find itself legitimate in its own estimation.
Ellenore's reproaches had persuaded me that I was guilty:
I learned from her supposed defender that I was only unfortunate. I was led into making a complete confession of
my feelings. I agreed that I felt devotion, sympathy, and
pity for Ellenore, but I added that love had no part in my
self-imposed duties. This truth, until then locked in my
heart, and only occasionally revealed to Ellenore at the
height of distress and anger, seemed to take on more reality
and power by the simple fact that I had confided it to
someone else. It is a serious and irrevocable step to reveal
suddenly to a third person the hidden recesses of an intimate relationship; when light enters this sanctuary it de-
fines and completes the destruction that darkness had been
hiding in its shadows; in the same way bodies sealed in

tombs will preserve their original form until the outside air enters and reduces them to dust.

Ellenore's friend left me. I do not know what account she gave of our conversation, but as I approached the salon, I heard Ellenore speaking in an excited tone. She stopped when she saw me. But she soon began to make various general remarks, which were really particular attacks. "Nothing is more extraordinary," she said, "than the zeal of certain friends. Some people will eagerly take charge of your interests, only to betray your cause more thoroughly; they call it devotion; I would prefer hatred." I quickly understood that Ellenore's friend had taken my side against her, and had annoyed her by not seeming to judge me to be sufficiently guilty. I was aware of being almost in league with another person: this was yet another barrier between our hearts.

A few days later Ellenore went further. She was incapable of any self-control; as soon as she thought that she had cause for complaint, she immediately demanded an explanation, without tact or calculation: she preferred the risk of a break to the strain of pretense. The two friends parted, never to be reconciled.

"Why do you bring strangers into our intimate discussions?" I said to Ellenore. "Do we need a third person in order to understand each other? And if we do not understand each other, what third person could remedy the situation?"

"You are right," she said, "but it is your fault. Until now I did not need to ask anyone's help to reach your heart."

Suddenly Ellenore announced that she planned to change her way of life. I gathered from her conversation that she attributed the discontent that was consuming me to the solitude in which we lived. She would exhaust all the wrong explanations before accepting the true one. We usually spent monotonous evenings alone together, dividing them between silence and ill-humor; the spring of long conversations had run dry.

Ellenore decided to attract to her house various noble families living in her neighborhood or in Warsaw. I could

easily foresee the difficulties and dangers of her attempts;
the relatives who were disputing her inheritance had revealed her past mistakes and spread countless slanderous
rumors about her. I shuddered at the humiliations she
would have to face, and tried to dissuade her from this
enterprise. My arguments were useless; my fears wounded
her pride, although I expressed them carefully. She supposed that our connection embarrassed me because of her
equivocal life; this only made her more anxious to recon-
quer an honorable position in society. Her efforts were
partly successful. The fortune she possessed, her beauty
only slightly dimmed by time, the very rumor of her adventures—all aroused curiosity. She soon found herself surrounded by a large circle, but she was pursued by a secret
feeling of embarrassment and uneasiness. I was dissatisfied
with my position, but she imagined that I was dissatisfied
with hers; she was fretting to get out of it, and her eager
wishes allowed no room for quiet planning. Her false position made her behave with inconsistency and to advance
with undue haste. Her mind was clear but limited; the clarity of her intelligence was distorted by the impetuosity of
her nature, and its lack of scope prevented her from seeing
the best approach and understanding subtle shades of
meaning. For the first time she had a purpose, but because
she flung herself after it she missed it. How many humiliations she swallowed without telling me! How often I
blushed for her without having the courage to tell her! Dis-
cretion and moderation have such power over men that I
had seen her more respected by the friends of Count P——,
as his mistress, than she was by her neighbors as heiress
of a large fortune, surrounded by her dependents. Haughty
and suppliant in turn, sometimes courteous, sometimes irritable, she had a certain impetuousness in her words and
actions that destroyed respect, which can only flourish in
calmness.

In pointing out Ellenore's faults in this way I am only
blaming and accusing myself. A word from me would have
calmed her: why was I unable to say this word?

Nevertheless we lived more peacefully together; the distraction gave us relief from our usual thoughts. We were alone together only at intervals, and since we had unlimited confidence in each other (apart from our intimate feelings) we replaced these feelings with observations and facts, and our conversations took on something of their old charm. But this new life soon became a new source of perplexity. Lost in the crowd surrounding Ellenore, I found that I was the object of surprise and censure. The time for deciding the lawsuit was approaching; Ellenore's opponents claimed that she had alienated her father's affection by her numerous dissipations; my presence supported their allegations. Her friends reproached me for harming her cause. They excused her passion for me, but accused me of indelicacy; they said that I was abusing a feeling I ought to have controlled. I alone knew that if I abandoned her I would only draw her after me, and that to follow me she would give up all thought of her fortune and all consideration of prudence. I could not make this secret public, so I appeared to be only a stranger in Ellenore's house who was harmful to the success of the proceedings that were about to decide her fate: by a strange reversal of truth, while I was the victim of her unshakable will, she was pitied as the victim of my power.

A new circumstance arose to complicate this unhappy situation further.

A peculiar and sudden change took place in Ellenore's behavior and manners. Up until now she had appeared to be concerned with me alone; all at once I saw her receive and seek out attentions from the men around her. This woman, so reserved, so cold and retiring, seemed suddenly to change character. She encouraged the affections and even the hopes of a crowd of young men; some of them were attracted by her beauty, and others aspired to her hand, regardless of her past. Her manner with them was of that doubtful but attractive nature that encourages by gentle reproofs, because it indicates indecision rather than indifference, and delay rather than refusal. I learned later from her—and the facts proved it to me—that she was acting according to a false and deplorable scheme. She thought that she could rekindle my love by arousing my jealousy, but she was only raking ashes that were no longer capable of warmth. Perhaps a little feminine vanity was also mingled in this scheme, without her being aware of it. She was hurt by my coldness and wanted to prove to herself that she was still attractive. Perhaps, too, the loneliness in which I had left her heart found some consolation in hearing the expressions of love that I had not used for so long.

Whatever the case, I mistook her motives for some time. I thought that I saw the dawn of my future freedom and congratulated myself on it. Fearing to interrupt by an ill-considered move the important development on which my freedom was to depend, I became gentler and seemed happier. Ellenore took my gentleness for affection, my hope to see her finally happy without me for the desire to make her happy. She was pleased with her stratagem, but she was occasionally alarmed when she noticed that I showed no anxiety. She reproached me for not putting any obstacle in the way of these affairs that apparently threatened to take her from me. I laughed off her accusations, but I did not always manage to pacify her; her character showed through the pretense she had imposed on herself. The scenes began again on a different level, but they were no less stormy. Ellenore blamed me for her errors. She suggested that a single word would bring her completely back to me. Then, offended by my silence, she flung herself into flirtation again with a sort of fury.

Here particularly, I feel, I shall be accused of weakness. I wanted to be free and I could have been so with everyone's approval. Perhaps I ought to have made the break. Ellenore's conduct authorized it and seemed to force my hand. But was I not aware that this conduct was of my doing, and that deep in her heart Ellenore had not ceased to love me? How could I punish her for an imprudence for which I was responsible, and with cold hypocrisy find in this imprudence a pretext to abandon her without pity?

I certainly have no wish to excuse myself, and I condemn myself more severely than another might do in my place, but I can at least give this solemn assurance in my favor: that I never acted from calculation, but was always motivated by true and natural feelings. How is it that with such feelings I have only wrought my own and others' unhappiness?

Society, however, watched me with surprise. My staying with Ellenore could only be explained by a deep attachment to her, but this was belied by my indifference to the relationships she seemed always ready to form. My inexplicable tolerance was attributed to lightness of principle and carelessness of morality, which indicated (it was said) a profoundly egoistic man whom the world had corrupted. These conjectures—as well calculated to make an impression as they were in keeping with the minds that conceived them—were welcomed and repeated. Their rumor finally reached me. I was indignant at this unexpected discovery: as a reward for my long service, I was misunderstood and maligned; for a woman's sake I had neglected all my interests, refused all of life's pleasures, and I stood condemned!

I had a heated argument with Ellenore. A word ensured the disappearance of the crowd of admirers, whom she had only gathered to make me fear her loss. She restricted her society to a few women and a small number of elderly men. An appearance of regularity was restored around us, but we were only more unhappy: Ellenore believed that she had won new rights, and I felt burdened with new chains.

I cannot describe the bitterness and rage that arose out of the new complications in our relationship. Our life was nothing but a perpetual storm. Intimacy lost all its charm, love all its sweetness. We did not even have any more of those fleeting returns of feeling that seem to heal incurable wounds for a brief moment. Truth made itself felt everywhere; to make myself understood, I used the harshest and most pitiless language. I stopped only when I saw Ellenore in tears; and even her tears were nothing but molten lava that fell, drop by drop, into my heart and forced cries from me without being able to force a denial. Then, more than once, I saw her rise, a pale, prophetic figure, and cry, "Adolphe, you do not know the harm you are doing; one day you will find out—you will find out from me, after you have driven me into the grave." Alas! when she spoke like this, why did I not throw my wretched self into the grave before her!

IX

I had not been to Baron T——'s house since my first visit. One morning I received the following note from him:

"The advice that I gave you did not deserve such a long absence. Whatever line of action you take in your own affairs, you are still the son of my dearest friend, and I would still have pleasure in your company, and I would also have a great deal of pleasure in introducing you to a group of friends whose society I can promise you you would enjoy. Allow me to add that the more unusual your mode of life is—and I do not wish to disapprove of it—the more you should dispel ill-founded prejudice by showing yourself in society."

I was grateful for the kindness the older man showed me. I went to see him; Ellenore was not mentioned. The baron kept me for dinner; the only other guests that day were a few moderately intelligent and pleasant men. I was embarrassed at first, but I made an effort to be animated and to talk. I used my intelligence and knowledge to the best of my ability. I saw that I succeeded in winning approval. My self-esteem found a pleasure in this success, which it had long been denied. This pleasure made Baron T——'s society more agreeable to me.

My visits to him increased. He gave me some duties connected with his mission that he thought he could safely entrust to me. Ellenore was surprised at first by this change in my life, but I told her about the baron's friendship with my father, and of the pleasure I felt in consoling my father for my absence by appearing usefully occupied. Poor Ellenore—I write this now with a feeling of remorse—was happier because I seemed more contented, and without much complaint, resigned herself to often spending most of the day apart from me. On his side, when a little confidence had been established between us, the baron reintroduced the subject of Ellenore. I positively intended to speak only good of her, but unconsciously my tone became lighter and more flippant. Sometimes I indicated by general remarks that I recognized the need to extricate myself from her; sometimes I resorted to pleasantry: I would talk laughingly of women and of the difficulty of breaking with them. This conversation amused the elderly minister, whose powers were diminishing but who vaguely remembered that he too in his youth had been plagued by affairs of the heart. In this way, by merely concealing part of what I felt, I deceived everyone in some degree. I deceived Ellenore because I knew that the baron wished to separate us and I did not tell her. I deceived Baron T— because I let him think that I was ready to break my bonds. This duplicity was quite foreign to my real nature, but man degenerates as soon as he entertains a single thought he must constantly conceal.

Until that time I had met at the baron's house only men from his own circle of friends. One day he suggested that I stay for a large reception he was giving for the elector's birthday. "You will meet the loveliest women in Poland," he said. "It is true that you will not find the one you love among them. I am sorry, but there are some women whom one may meet only in their homes." I was painfully affected by this statement. I said nothing, but silently reproached myself for not defending Ellenore—when she would have so warmly defended me if I had been attacked in her presence.

It was a large reception. I was carefully observed, and I heard the names of my father, Ellenore, and the Count of P— spoken in whispers around me. They stopped when I approached, and started again when I moved away. People were obviously telling my story; doubtless everyone had his own version. My position was intolerable; a cold sweat covered my forehead, and I alternately blushed and turned pale.

The baron noticed my embarrassment. He came to me and redoubled his attention and kindness; he sought every occasion to sing my praise, and the influence of his attitude soon compelled others to show me the same regard.

When all the guests had left, Baron T—— said to me, "I should like to speak frankly to you once more. Why do you insist on remaining in a situation that makes you unhappy? What good are you doing to anyone? Do you think nobody knows what goes on between you and Ellenore? Everyone is aware of your bitterness and mutual dissatisfaction. You wrong yourself by your weakness, and no less by your harshness; and as a crowning inconsistency, you are not making this woman happy—and she makes you miserable."

I was still hurt by my recent painful experience. The baron showed me several letters from my father. They indicated a much greater distress than I had supposed. I was badly shaken. The thought that I was prolonging Ellenore's anxieties increased my irresolution. Finally, as if everything were conspiring against her while I hesitated, she herself decided me by her impetuosity. I had been away all day; the baron had kept me after the gathering. It was getting late. A letter was delivered to me in the baron's presence. In his eyes I saw a look of pity for my bondage. Ellenore's letter was full of bitterness. "What!" I said to myself. "Can I not spend a day in freedom, or breathe an hour in peace? She pursues me everywhere as if I were a slave to be brought back to her feet." I became more violent as my weakness increased. "Yes!" I exclaimed. "I promise to break with Ellenore. I shall tell her so myself; you may let my father know in advance."

I left the baron as I spoke. I was oppressed by my words, and hardly believed the promise I had just given.

Ellenore was waiting for me impatiently. By a strange coincidence someone had told her for the first time in my absence of Baron T——'s efforts to separate us. My conversations and jests were reported to her. Her suspicions were aroused, and various circumstances had come to her mind that seemed to confirm them. My sudden connection with a man I had never seen before and his friendship with my father seemed to her incontrovertible proofs. Her anxiety had increased so much in a few hours that I found her fully convinced of what she called my perfidy.

I had come intending to tell her everything. When she accused me—can you believe it?—my only thought was to evade everything. I even denied—yes, I denied that day what I was determined to tell her on the next.

It was late. I left her; I was in a hurry to go to bed to end this long day, and when I was sure it was over, I felt temporarily relieved of an enormous burden.

Next day I arose toward noon, as if I had delayed the crucial moment by delaying the beginning of our interview.

During the night Ellenore had become reassured by her own reflections and by what I had said the day before. She spoke to me of her affairs with such confidence that it was only too obvious that she thought that our lives were indissolubly united. How could I find the words that would thrust her back into solitude?

The time was passing with frightening rapidity. Each minute increased the need for an explanation. Two of the three days I had fixed were almost gone. Baron T—— was expecting me on the day after tomorrow, at the latest. His letter to my father had been sent, and I was going to fail in my promise without having made the slightest effort to fulfill it. I went out, I came back, I took Ellenore's hand, I began a sentence—and immediately cut it short. I watched the sun as it went down toward the horizon. Night came again, again I delayed. I had one day left; an hour would have been enough.

This last day passed like the one before. I wrote to Baron T—— asking for more time, and, acting as weak natures will, I filled my letter with numerous arguments to justify my delay, and to prove that from that very moment my connection with Ellenore could be regarded as broken forever.

X

I passed the following days more calmly. The necessity for
action had been put off indefinitely; it no longer haunted
me like a ghost; I thought I had plenty of time to prepare
Ellenore. I wanted to be gentler and more tender with her
so that she would at least have some memories of friendship. My trouble was now quite different from what it had
been hitherto. I had prayed heaven for an impassable barrier to come between Ellenore and me. This barrier had now
appeared. I gazed at Ellenore as a being I was about to
lose. I was no longer horrified by her unreasonable demands, which had so often seemed intolerable; I already
felt free of them. When I yielded to her now I was easier,
and no longer felt that inward rebellion that had formerly
driven me to ruin everything. I was no longer impatient;
on the contrary I secretly wanted to delay the fatal moment.

Ellenore noticed this more affectionate and tender mood
and became less bitter herself. I sought conversations I had
previously avoided. I took pleasure in loving words that
were once tiresome: they now seemed precious because
each time they were used could be the last.

One evening we separated after talking more gently than
usual. The secret I kept in my heart made me sad, but my
sadness had no violence in it. The uncertainty about the
time of the desired separation enabled me to push the
thought of it to the back of my mind. During the night
I heard an unaccustomed sound in the castle. It was soon
over, and I thought no more about it. But the next morning
I remembered it and wanted to know the cause. I went
toward Ellenore's room. Imagine my astonishment when I
was told that she had had a high fever for twelve hours,
that a doctor, called in by the servants, had declared her

life in danger, and that she had strictly forbidden me to be told or allowed to see her.

I wanted to insist. The doctor himself came out to explain the necessity for not causing her any emotion. He did not know the reason for this prohibition, but attributed it to her wish to spare me any anxiety. In torment I questioned the servants as to what could have plunged her so suddenly into such a dangerous condition. After leaving me the night before she had received a letter from Warsaw, delivered by a man on horseback. When she had opened and read the letter, she had fainted. On her return to consciousness she had flung herself on her bed without a word. One of her maids, alarmed by the distress she had witnessed in her mistress, remained in the room unknown to Ellenore. Toward midnight she had seen her mistress seized with a fit of trembling that shook the bed she was lying on; she wanted to call me, but Ellenore forbade it with such violence and terror that no one dared disobey. A doctor was sent for; Ellenore refused to answer him and still did; she had passed the night muttering disjointed words that no one could understand, often pressing her handkerchief to her mouth as if to keep herself from speaking.

While they were telling me these details, another woman, who had stayed with Ellenore, came rushing in, very frightened. Ellenore appeared to have lost the use of her senses. She could distinguish nothing around her. She cried out several times, she repeated my name, then, terrified, she made a gesture as if to ask that some hateful thing be removed from her sight.

I went into her room and saw two letters at the foot of her bed. One was my letter to Baron T——, the other was from him to Ellenore. I understood only too well the clue to this horrible puzzle. All my efforts to gain time to devote to our last farewells were now turned against the unhappy woman I had hoped to spare. Ellenore had read in my own hand my promises to leave her: these promises had been dictated only by my desire to stay with her longer, and the very strength of this desire had made me repeat and elaborate them. The impartial eye of Baron T—— had

readily detected in each word of these repeated protestations the irresolution they concealed and the ruses of my
own uncertainty. But the cruel man had foreseen only too
well that Ellenore would read them as an irrevocable de-
cree. I went up to her; she looked at me without recognition. I spoke to her; she shivered. "What is that sound?"
she cried. "It is the voice that has injured me." The doctor
saw that my presence increased her delirium, and begged
me to leave. How shall I describe my suffering for the three
long hours that followed? At last the doctor came out. Ellenore had fallen into a deep sleep. He did not despair of
saving her if her fever had gone down when she awoke.

Ellenore slept for a long time. When I was told that she
was awake, I wrote to her asking her to let me see her.
She sent word that I might come. I started to speak, but
she interrupted me. "Do not let me hear a cruel word from
you," she said. "I no longer make any claims or any objections, but the voice I have loved so much, that has echoed in the depths of my heart—do not let it enter my heart
now to tear it to pieces. Adolphe, Adolphe, I have been
violent, I may have offended you—but you cannot know
what I have suffered. Please God you may never know!"

Her agitation became extreme. She put her head against
my hand: it was burning; a terrible spasm disfigured her
features. "In heaven's name, dear Ellenore," I cried, "listen
to me. Yes, I am guilty: that letter . . ." She trembled and
tried to move away. I held her back, and went on. "Weak
and tormented, I yielded for a moment to the pressure of
cruel insistence, but do you not yourself have innumerable
proofs that I cannot desire our separation? I have been dissatisfied, unhappy, and unjust; perhaps you have struggled
too violently against my rebellious fancy and given too
much weight to passing whims that I now despise, but how
could you doubt the depth of my affection? Are not our
souls bound to one another by countless bonds that nothing can break? Do we not have all the past in common?
Can we look back on the three years that are just over
without recalling the feelings we have shared, the pleasures we have enjoyed, and the sorrows we have borne to-

gether? Oh Ellenore, let us begin a new era today, let us recall our hours of love and happiness." She looked at me doubtingly for a while. "Your father," she said finally, "your duty, your family, the things expected of you . . ."

"Yes, of course," I replied. "Sometime, someday perhaps . . ."

She noticed that I was hesitating. "Good heavens!" she exclaimed. "Why did he give me hope only to snatch it from me immediately? Adolphe, thank you for your efforts; they have done me good—so much the more in that they will, I hope, cost you no sacrifice. But I beg you, let us speak no more of the future. Do not reproach yourself for anything, whatever happens. You have been good to me. I have wished for the impossible. Love was my whole life: it could not be all of yours. Take care of me now for a few days more." Tears were streaming from her eyes; her breathing was more relaxed; she leaned her head on my shoulder and said, "This is where I have always wanted to die." I pressed her to my heart, renounced my plans again, and disclaimed my cruel rages. "No," she said, "you must be free and contented."

"How can I be, if you are unhappy?"

"I shall not be unhappy for long, you will not have long to pity me." I thrust away the fears that I believed were imaginary. "No, no, dear Adolphe," she said. "When we have prayed for death for a long time, heaven finally sends us an infallible presentiment to tell us that our prayer has been granted." I swore to her that I would never leave her. "I have always hoped so: now I am sure of it."

It was one of those winter days when the sun seems to illuminate the gray countryside sadly, as if it looked with pity on the earth it no longer warmed. Ellenore suggested that we go out.

"It is very cold," I told her.

"Never mind. I would like to go for a walk with you."

She took my arm. We walked for a long time in silence. She moved with difficulty, leaning almost entirely on me.

"Let us stop for a minute."

"No," she replied. "It gives me pleasure to feel myself still supported by you."

We relapsed into silence again. The sky was clear, but the trees were leafless; no breeze stirred the air; no bird flew through it; all was motionless, and the only sound was the crunching of the frozen grass beneath our feet. "How calm everything is!" said Ellenore. "How nature is resigned! Should not the heart learn resignation too?" She sat down on a stone; suddenly she slipped to her knees and, bowing her head, she held it in her hands. I heard a few words murmured in a whisper. I realized that she was praying. When she finally got up she said, "Let us go in, the cold has affected me, I am afraid I am sick. Say nothing— I am in no condition to understand."

After that day I saw Ellenore grow weaker and begin to decline. I summoned doctors from everywhere to see her. Some told me that the case was incurable, others lulled me with empty hopes. But nature's invisible hand silently and somberly pursued its pitiless task. There were moments when Ellenore seemed to regain her hold on life. It was as if the iron hand that pressed her down were sometimes lifted. She would raise her languid head, her cheeks would fill with slightly brighter color, and her eyes would be animated again, but suddenly in this cruel game of an unknown power the deceptive improvement vanished, before skill could discover the cause. In this way I witnessed her gradual movement toward destruction; I saw etched on that noble and expressive face signs that are the forerunners of death; I witnessed the humiliating and pitiable spectacle of this proud and energetic nature in the throes of countless confused and incoherent motions of physical suffering; in these terrible moments it seemed as if the soul, bruised by the body, was being completely transformed in order to submit with less pain to the organic deterioration.

Only one feeling never changed in Ellenore's heart: this was her affection for me. Her weakness rarely allowed her to speak to me, but she would silently fix her eyes on me, and it seemed then that her eyes were asking me for the life I could no longer give. I was afraid of arousing any strong emotion in her; I invented excuses to go out; I wandered at random through all the places where I had been with her; with tears I watered the stones, the trunks of trees, and everything that recalled her memory.

This was not regret for love, but a sadder and more somber feeling; love identifies itself so completely with the beloved object that it retains some of its magic power even in despair. It struggles against reality and against fate: the ardor of its desire makes it seem stronger than it is and sustains it in the midst of sorrow. Mine was a gloomy and solitary feeling; I could not hope to die with Ellenore: I was going to live without her in this desert of the world, which I had so often longed to cross alone. I had crushed the being who had loved me; I had broken her heart, companion to my own, the heart that had persisted in devoting itself to me with untiring tenderness. Loneliness was already seizing me. Ellenore still breathed, but I could no longer confide my thoughts to her; I was already alone on earth, no longer living in that atmosphere of love she had shed around me; the air I breathed seemed harsher, the faces of the men I met were more indifferent; the whole of nature seemed to be telling me that soon I would cease forever to be loved.

Ellenore's danger suddenly became imminent; unmistakable symptoms announced her approaching end. A priest of her religion warned her that it was near. She begged me to bring her a casket containing many papers; she had several of them burned in her presence, but she seemed to be looking for one she could not find, and she became extremely distressed. I implored her to stop this painful search, during which she had fainted twice. "I will," she replied, "but dear Adolphe, you must grant me this one prayer. Somewhere among my papers you will find a letter addressed to you: burn it without reading it, I implore you in the name of our love, in the name of these last moments that you have made easier for me." I promised; she was calmer. "Now let me devote myself to the duties of religion," she said. "I have many sins to atone for—perhaps

my love for you has been a sin, though I would not have
thought so if it could have made you happy."

I left her; I returned only with her whole household to
take part in the last solemn prayers; kneeling in a corner
of her room, I was sunk in my thoughts for part of the
time; for part of it I watched with involuntary curiosity
all the people who were gathered together—some were terrified, others inattentive; I noticed the strange effect of custom that carries indifference into all ordained rites and
makes us regard the most solemn and terrible ceremonies
as conventional and purely formal things; I heard these men
repeating mechanically the words of death as if they themselves were not bound to play the chief role in a similar
scene someday: as if they themselves would never have to
die. Nevertheless, I was far from despising these practices.
Dare a man in his ignorance call any one of them useless?
They were bringing peace to Ellenore, they were helping
her to cross that terrible barrier toward which we are all
traveling without the ability to foresee what we will feel
then. I am not surprised that man needs a religion; what
astonishes me is that he can ever feel himself strong enough,
or safe enough from misfortune, to dare to reject any of
them; in his weakness I should think that he would be
driven to call upon them all. In the profound darkness that
surrounds us can we afford to ignore a single gleam? In
the middle of the flood that engulfs us dare we refuse to
grasp a single branch?

This mournful ceremony deeply affected Ellenore and
seemed to have tired her. She sank into a fairly peaceful
sleep and woke feeling better. I was alone in the room with
her; we talked occasionally and at long intervals. The doctor who had proved the most skillful in his guesses had
told me that she would not live another twenty-four hours.
I looked in turn at a clock marking the hours, and at Ellenore's face, on which I could see no new change. Each
minute that passed revived my hope, and I began to doubt
the conjectures of a deceitful art. All at once Ellenore
started up with a sudden movement; I restrained her in
my arms; a convulsive trembling shook her body; her eyes

sought me, but in them was a vague terror, as if she were asking mercy of some threatening thing that escaped my sight; she raised herself and then fell back; it was obvious that she was making an effort to escape; she seemed to be struggling with an invisible physical power that was tired of waiting for the fatal moment; it seized and held her down to dispatch her on her deathbed. She finally yielded to the furious force of hostile nature; her limbs collapsed, she seemed to regain a certain amount of consciousness: she wrung my hand, she tried to weep—but there were no more tears, she tried to speak, but there were no more words; as if resigned, she let her head fall on the arm supporting it; her breathing became slower. A few minutes later she was no more.

I stayed motionless for a long time beside the lifeless Ellenore. The belief in her death had not yet penetrated my soul; my eyes gazed at her inanimate body with stupid astonishment. One of her women came in and spread the disastrous news through the house. The clamor around me roused me from the lethargy into which I had been plunged. I got up. It was then that I felt the lacerating grief and all the horror of an irrevocable farewell. All the movement and activity of ordinary life, all the cares and trouble that no longer concerned her, shattered the illusion that I was prolonging—the illusion of thinking that I was still living with Ellenore. I felt the last bond break, and hideous reality came between us forever. The freedom I had longed for weighed on me so heavily! How I craved the dependence that I had so often resented! Until then all my actions had a purpose; with each one I was sure that I was sparing a pain or giving a pleasure; I had complained about it: I had been annoyed that a friendly eye was watching my moves, and that another's happiness was dependent on them. Now nobody watched my actions; nobody cared about them; nobody disputed my time or the hours I kept; no voice called me back when I went out: I was free indeed. I was no longer loved; I was a stranger to everyone.

Ellenore's papers were brought to me as she had ordered; at every line I came across fresh proofs of her love, fresh sacrifices she had made for me and concealed from me. Finally I found the letter that I had promised to burn; I did not recognize it at first: it was not addressed, and it was open. Some words caught my eye in spite of myself. I tried in vain to turn my eyes away, but I could not resist the urge to read it all. I have not the strength to transcribe it. Ellenore had written it after one of the violent scenes before her illness. "Adolphe," she wrote, "why do you attack me so furiously? What is my crime? To love you, and to be unable to live without you. What strange pity makes you lack courage to break the tie that oppresses you and makes you destroy the unhappy creature whom your pity will not let you leave? Why do you refuse me the sad pleasure of believing you to be at least generous? Why do you appear furious and weak? The thought of my suffering haunts you, but the sight of it cannot stop you. What do you want of me? That I leave you? Cannot you see that I have not the strength? It is for you, you who do not love, to find the strength in the heart that is weary of me, and that all my love cannot disarm. You will not give me this strength; but you will make me pine away in tears, you will make me die at your feet. . . . Say but the word," she wrote elsewhere. "Is there a country where I would not follow you? Is there a place where I would not hide to live near you without burdening your life? But no, you do not want it. All the plans that I suggest in fear and trembling (for you have frozen me with fear) you dismiss impatiently. The best I can hope for from you is silence. So much harshness is not in keeping with your character. You are good, your acts are noble and devoted—but what actions can obliterate your words? Those cutting words echo all around me; I hear them at night, they pursue me, they consume me, they ruin everything you do. Must I die, Adolphe? Very well, you shall be satisfied: she shall die, this poor thing whom you have protected, but whom you have struck with repeated blows. She shall die, this tiresome Ellenore whom you cannot endure near you, whom you consider as an obstacle, who prevents you from finding any place on earth that is not wearisome to you; she shall die: you shall walk alone among the crowd you are impatient to join! You shall know the men whom today you thank for their indifference, and perhaps one day, when you are wounded by those arid hearts, you will regret the heart that was at your disposal, that lived by your affection, that would have braved countless dangers to defend you, and that you no longer deign to reward with even a glance."

Jenny

BY PAUL DE KOCK

TRANSLATED BY D. M. AIRD

CHARLES PAUL DE KOCK
1793–1871

De Kock was born in Passy a few months after his father, a Dutch banker, had been guillotined by the revolutionists. After a brief, somewhat desultory education he gave up his job in a bank to achieve overwhelming popularity as a writer. The Brussels edition of his *Works* comprises over a hundred volumes, most of which are available in all the major languages. His phenomenal success may be attributed to a fertile imagination that permitted him to deliver unceasingly the kind of literature that the growing middle class reading public desired: sentimental stories wrapped in eroticism. At times, particularly in his shorter fiction, he observed critically and rather adroitly the *modus vivendi* and worst ills of his generation. Even members of England's cultural elite (Macaulay, Elizabeth Barrett Browning) were fond of him, and Claretie says that when the Catholic aristocrat Chateaubriand, the literary giant of early-nineteenth-century France, visited the Vatican, Pope Gregory XVI's one excited question was: "How is my dear son Paul de Kock [*mio figlio Paolo de Kocko*]?"

ABOUT DE KOCK: Except for Jules Claretie's introduction to *The Works of* CHARLES PAUL DE KOCK (Boston, 1902), Vol. I, pp. xv–xl, there is nothing in English worth while. Old biographies in French are by E. de Mirecourt (Paris, 1856) and T. Trimm (Paris, 1873).

I. THE FLOWER MARKETS

Paris will soon be a vast parterre. The goddess Flora has been spreading her incense, and everywhere altars are being raised to her.

Do you love flowers? They are sold everywhere, and before long, instead of trees—thanks to the gas that consumes their roots—we shall have only roses, jasmine, and sweet-smelling flowers. Perhaps there will be less shade, but what delightful odors!

Francis the First once said, "A court without ladies is like a spring without flowers." Yet during his reign there were not three flower markets in all Paris. To love the fair sex, one must love flowers, for, as you know, we can scarcely speak of one without the other. How many poets have said, "A woman is a flower?" The list is endless.

In days gone by flowers were sold only once a week.

Then, every Wednesday and Saturday, the florists and gardeners of the capital would hawk their fragrant wares on the quay near the Palais de Justice, and early in the morning young men and girls, grocers and grisettes from every section of Paris would come to buy a modest pot of daisies, or perhaps a carnation or a box of myrtle.

The students from the Latin Quarter came too; more, perhaps, to gaze at the pretty girls than to buy bouquets. Then, at about six o'clock, came the ladies of fashion, who sometimes alighted from their carriages to buy a *cactus grandiflores*, or a *rosa centifolia*.

And in the evening, just around closing time, the modest

JENNY

lodger wishing to purchase a pot of myrtle for his window sill might have been seen bargaining, despite the police, who frowned, at that hour, on every pot that met the eye.

Then the gatekeeper would leave his post in charge of an officious neighbor and run to the quay to buy a pot of basil or convolvulus.

Other times, other ways. Yet the Flower Quay is still frequented. In fact, it is considered to be the best of the three markets in the capital, and has a reputation all its own.

At any rate, whenever the girls of the Marais or the housekeepers of the Porte St. Denis think of giving flowers, they do not have to cross half of Paris on foot, or take a bus, to buy a twelve-sou pot of violets for six. Every quarter needs its own market, just as a flower needs its own pot, because, to so many girls who spend their days at work, the sight of a little greenery—of bursting buds and bright, fragrant petals—is sweet relaxation. Flowers are the only luxuries in which the poor indulge; we ought, therefore, to secure them this indulgence at a small price. A luxury that creates even momentary happiness has almost the right to assert its claim as a necessity.

At present, the Marais has its flower markets on the Boulevard St. Martin, in front of the Château d'Eau, and every Thursday, although we cannot go picking, we can choose carnations, jasmines, or dahlias.

From the neighborhood of the Château d'Eau, a cool, refreshing odor spreads over the boulevard. The shade trees that have been planted and transplanted so many times since the Revolution will, perhaps, take root at last.

Poor trees! They are stubborn, as if they wished to punish us for uprooting those that protected and endeared the promenade to our ancestors.

Here benches have been placed at the foot of the sycamores, in hopes that they will soon spread their shady green branches and attract passers-by with facilities for rest.

There are still no dandies or fashion plates to be seen lolling on the seats of Boulevard St. Martin, but there are plenty of children in sailor suits. Eventually it may become a second Boulevard de Gand. As people say, Paris was not built in a day.

But when the weather is good on Mondays and Thursdays, everyone comes, for then the pretty flowers, set off to advantage by their picturesque vendors, make the walk pleasant, and it is always much cleaner than the flower market on the quay.

Then the elegant and fashionable quarter, the neighborhood of bankers and ballet dancers, of dandies and *petites maîtresses,* of social lions, and of rats—the Chaussée d'Antin —has its own flower market, which is located on a high piece of ground next to the Madeleine, and consequently out of carriage reach, and almost always dry.

This market ought to be the best of the three, with the prettiest flowers, the rarest plants, and the loveliest women. But no; on market days—every Wednesday and Saturday —there are seldom many customers, and the amateur finds very little choice. The *petites maîtresses* like flowers well enough, but never purchase any. And they are right—bad habits are hard to break.

On any day of the week you can browse among roses, dahlias, and orange trees, and if, like Jean-Jacques, you think that Paris is a city of noise and smoke and dirt, you would see it changed to a greenhouse full of flowers.

II. THE WRITING MASTER

One Wednesday, about a year ago, when the flower market was at its charming best, and visitors were strolling about the stalls, a little man in a seedy black suit came by.

His wizened old body looked as worn as his coat, and he wore a wig that may have once been blond but had turned red with age. It was threadbare and moth-eaten around the edges and reached no farther than his ears. Tufts of gray hair stuck out on either side, ill-concealed under his dust-brown hat, the brim of which was so small that, seeing him, you might ask yourself, "Could anyone possibly talk to him?"

But despite his shabby attire he was the happiest creature imaginable. His little gray eyes sparkled vivaciously, there was a smile on his lips, and as he walked along, he rubbed his hands together like someone who has just made a good bargain or feels perfectly content with himself.

After a good deal of browsing among the finest plants he went up to a flower girl who was selling cheap little pots of violets, pointed to one, and said:

"How much?"

"Six sous, monsieur."

"What! Six sous? How dare you! I'm an old customer."

"Perhaps you often buy from others, but this is the first time you've come to me."

"Bah! You forget. Why, not a Wednesday or Saturday goes by that I'm not here. I love flowers, and if I had a garden—oh! if I had a garden, it would be paradise! But I have only a window box, and that is not very large. I'll give you two sous for this pot. That's enough, you know."

"Four. Nothing less."

"I've told you, I'm a customer. Every two months I renew my violets. They aren't the most expensive, I know, but I think they are the sweetest. All right, then, here, take your money. I never buy on credit."

"No, monsieur. Four sous. Nothing less."

"If the gentleman won't take it, I will."

The old man glanced up angrily at the newcomer, but his resentment disappeared when he saw a pair of pretty dark eyes and a bright, friendly smile.

There are men who squander their youth in folly, and spend their old age wishing they could squander more.

Now Monsieur Alexandrin (for that was the old man's name) took the pot and presented it to the girl, saying:

"I'm not sorry to lose it, seeing that one flower is about to be united to another."

She smiled.

Compliments are always appreciated, especially when

they are not sought, so, instead of taking the violets, the girl replied:

"Oh, monsieur, I didn't mean to offend you. Perhaps you've taken a liking to this flower. I know there are plenty of others on the quay, but sometimes we become attached to one more than another. You have it, monsieur; I won't buy it."

"No, mademoiselle. I'm only too happy to let you have it, and I trust it is not with the idea of revenge for your offering so much. But, please, mademoiselle, let me carry it for you. It might soil your dress and stain your hands, but I have nothing to worry about, as you can see. I am too old to pursue you, and no one would take me for your sweetheart. Permit me, then, to be your porter; old age, you know, must have its privileges."

The old man shouldered the pot as a soldier does his musket, and the girl could scarcely repress her laughter.

"All right, monsieur," she replied with a gracious look, "providing you carry it to my room. I live on the sixth floor. Remember, I warned you."

"Were it atop the towers of Notre-Dame, or the column of Place Vendôme, atop the Obelisk, or the famed Column of July, I would be honored to accompany you."

As he spoke, Monsieur Alexandrin went through the motions of tipping his hat, but the brim was so fragile he dared not touch it.

The girl started out, followed, or rather elbowed by Monsieur Alexandrin, who sometimes hopped and sometimes skipped so as to avoid looking tired.

The person toward whom he showed such gallantry must have been twenty at the most. She wore a simple cotton dress, neatly pleated, a black apron, a kerchief thrown loosely over her shoulders, and a close-fitting bonnet.

Was she a grisette, a seamstress, a maid, or a shop girl?

It would be hard to say, for, in Paris, people dress so much alike it requires a practiced eye to tell what someone really is at first sight.

The girl crossed Place du Palais, turned up Rue de la Harpe, and then down Rue des Mathurins, where she stopped before a house as old as the quarter itself and entered a dark alley, saying:

"Here we are, sir. Be careful, the stairs are dark and slippery, but once you find the banister, you won't have any trouble."

The old man began to think that perhaps he had carried things a bit too far. Nonetheless he groped along, holding the pot in one hand and feeling his way with the other.

The girl took the lead and walked with the sureness born of habit, while behind her the old man kept bumping into the wall.

"It's a little high, monsieur," she said, turning to her companion, "a hundred and fourteen steps up."

"I didn't count them," he answered, "but I'll be very glad to reach the top."

"Here we are. This is my room."

III. JENNY

She opened the door, entered a neat, plainly furnished room, and hastened to relieve the old man of his burden, then, pulling up a chair, she said:

"Now, monsieur, I hope you will join me for supper. After such a climb you can hardly refuse me. But first, as it is only natural for you to want to know who I am, I shall tell you:

"My name is Jenny Desgrillon, and I am the daughter of honest tradespeople, who taught me to color prints. Three years ago I lost my parents, who on their deathbed recommended me to one of their friends, a Monsieur Benoît, who is a grocer. Monsieur Benoît has a son, Monsieur Fanfan, who has been courting me and wants to marry me, though I must confess, I really don't love him, and care very little for being a grocer's wife. But I do love the stage, and want to be an actress—to play noble characters, and appear in public, be roundly applauded, and wear fine clothes, to be a princess one day, and a peasant the next, one day, English, the next, Polish—to hear a handsome knight say, 'I adore you!' and have poets write me odes, to the tune of 'A Kiss to the Bearer,' or 'The Apothecary's Family.' Ah! That must be true happiness, and I dream of it all the time, even when I'm painting Bluebeards or Tom Thumbs. But how can I become an actress, and make my debut, when I don't know anyone but the Benoîts, who are satisfied to see giantesses and wax dummies? Ah, monsieur, you see I need help and advice, and I appeal to you."

"Mademoiselle!" declared the old man. "Your confidence does me honor. But as one confidence is worth another, I will also tell you who I am.

"My name is Triptolema Erasistrate Alexandrin; my grandfather was a schoolmaster, my father, an author; and, as for myself, I give lessons in writing and versification at twenty-sous per copybook. That's very cheap, for I have a very good hand, but steel pens hurt us very much. Every-one writes with them without any idea of a hairline stroke or a flourish, but even so, I could have earned an easy living, if not for the stage."

"What, monsieur? You wanted to be an actor?"

"No, mademoiselle, not an actor, but an author, a poet, a man of letters. Indeed, I *am* an author. I have written at least thirty pieces, including dramas, vaudevilles, and tragedies—but none of them has been staged. Still, my dear, I am sure that at least one must be a masterpiece. I have not been rejected or ridiculed, but no one will listen to me. Influence and jealousy make directors turn a deaf ear. Nev-ertheless, I keep on writing. I find subjects in the most tri-fling incidents: a carriage that bumps into another, a chim-ney that falls on a passer-by, a policeman running after a thief, a husband who cheats on his wife, or a wife who loves her husband. I send manuscripts to all the theaters, from the Opéra to the Petit Lazary, from Bobino to the Renaissance. In a month or six weeks I may have eight of my plays in rehearsal, and when I saw you, mademoi-selle, smiling so prettily, I said to myself, 'What a charming Abigail for Molière! What a pretty page!' And I won't deny that that thought added much to my desire to carry the flowerpot for you."

"Monsieur, you are an author?"

"As much as one can be without being published."

"Oh, how glad I am that I met you, Monsieur Alexandrin! You will give me elocution lessons and hear me rehearse, and correct my pronunciation."

"Of course, my dear. Besides, I know my authors by heart—Racine, Voltaire, Molière, Picard."

"I only know the pieces by Victor Ducange and Monsieur Scribe," interrupted Jenny, "but I have an excellent memory—I can learn a long part overnight."

"I'll read you my thirty plays, and you can choose a suitable part. Then I'll rehearse you."

Between an author and a tyro Thespian an acquaintanceship is easily formed.

The author was a little too old and the actress too young, but the experience of one may be useful to the other. Both sat down at the table, delighted to have met each other.

All during the meal the lovely Jenny recited scraps from different plays, and old Alexandrin gave her a detailed account of the plots. They both enjoyed hearing themselves talk, and in that respect they are not alone in the world, for such is one of the failings common to man.

When dinner was nearly over, a young man entered the room with a little bag of prunes. It was Monsieur Fanfan Benoît, who came to bestow on Mademoiselle Jenny this token of his affection.

As he entered the apartment, Jenny, who had recently seen *Paul and Virginia* performed at one of the suburban theaters, seized the old writing master by the arm, and, hurrying through the room, took an umbrella and held it over her head to imitate the storm scene in which fair Virginia finds a shelter for her adored Paul.

Monsieur Fanfan was amazed to see Mademoiselle Jenny crouching in the corner of the room with a man, and both under an umbrella. As he drew near, he said:

"Do you think it's raining, mademoiselle?"

In reply the old writing master, who was well versed in his part, drew Jenny to the opposite corner, crying:

"It is Monsieur de la Bourdannaye who would bear you off, Virginia, but no one shall snatch you from my arms."

Monsieur Fanfan was frankly puzzled, but relieved to see that the person hiding under the umbrella with Jenny was an old man, and not a rival.

At last *Paul and Virginia* was at an end, and Jenny came over to Monsieur Fanfan, introduced the old man, and said:

"This is Monsieur Alexandrin, author."

The grocer looked at the threadbare coat and muttered:

"Author. Oh, author! What does an author sell?"

Mademoiselle Jenny burst out laughing.

"Ah, that's a question that savors of the grocery."

"Monsieur," said old Alexandrin, approaching the young man, "an author makes men dream. He makes them laugh or cry. In a word, he amuses them. The worst he can do is to put them to sleep, but even then, he gives enjoyment, for sleep is an excellent thing. Thus you can see, he is a valuable man, a near divinity. Formerly, altars were raised to him. Now he prefers to buy houses. It is less glorious, but there's more substance."

"Ah, they buy houses," replied Fanfan Benoît, his eyes still fixed on the old man's threadbare coat, "then it's a good business. If I had known, I would have taken to it. Never mind, Mademoiselle Jenny, here's a pound of grade-A prunes, courtesy of my father. He asked me to tell you that he expects you to dinner tomorrow, so that we can make plans for the wedding, and running the shop when he retires."

"Monsieur Fanfan," replied Jenny, rolling up various pictures destined to illustrate *Mother Goose*, "if that is why he sent you, he might have saved you the trouble. I don't want you or your prunes; I want to be an actress! Instead of spending my days at a counter, waiting on the neighborhood, I will shine on the stage—I will be ogled, applauded, worshiped, and featured in every paper. My name will be on every poster and billboard. This gentleman, who is in the theater, says I have the makings of a star. He will coach me, and give me lessons. Isn't that better than selling coffee and sugar? So you can be sure I won't marry you."

After this little speech she bundled up her pictures and went out, saying:

"Good day, Monsieur Fanfan. I am going to take in my work. Then I shall buy three scripts. Wait, Monsieur Alexandrin; you will give me my first lesson."

IV. THE DEBUT

Jenny left. The poor grocer was speechless, while the old man kept popping his hand in the bag, saying:

"My dear friend, we must never oppose strong inclinations to an honorable calling. A strong will indicates talent. Look at me, for instance. I was born a man of letters. If I had not been obliged to give lessons for a living, I would be famous. The fine arts! Ah, we must give up everything for the sacred fire. After all, 'Naturam expellas furca, tamen usque recurret.' I beg your pardon—I didn't mean to speak Latin. Your prunes are excellent. I devour them unknowingly, like the contents of a favorite volume."

The young man was too upset to realize that his bag was nearly empty. At last he heaved a sigh, wiped his brow, and cried:

"Let her be happy, that's all I ask. I thought she would enjoy being the head of a prosperous shop, but she must decide for herself. Good day, monsieur."

The old poet was sorry to see the young grocer rush off, especially as they had not yet finished the prunes.

Mademoiselle Jenny soon returned with her several plays. She chose a part, began reciting, and would not let the old man go before he had promised to return the next day.

And he kept his promise. For two weeks he never once failed to call on the fair colorist, who in turn studied vaudevilles and dramas and totally neglected her Cinderellas and Wandering Jews.

"Bravo, mademoiselle! Your progress is astounding. You pronounce better; you have more energy and sentiment! Another year, and you will be ready to make your debut on Rue Chauterine."

"A whole year! But why so long?"

"Take care, my dear. Haste may affect your success."

"Didn't you say I had a charming figure for the stage?"

"Yes, your face and figure are fine, but that's not enough. Beauty means a great deal, but it can't take the place of talent. I could cite numerous examples, but I dislike speaking ill of actresses, especially pretty ones."

Jenny was very self-confident, and began to think that she knew as much as her professor. At about this time old Alexandrin came down with a fever, and was forced to stay in bed.

A month went by, and though he could not go out, he was not bored, but spent his time by the fireplace, writing.

The Muses did not forsake him, for, although they often fail to nourish the body, they do occupy the mind, and those they treat the worst are, nonetheless, happy.

As soon as he could get about, Monsieur Alexandrin headed for Rue de la Harpe. He longed to see his pupil, whom he could not accuse of indifference or ingratitude, for he had never given her his address, and she could not be expected to know where to find him.

He climbed to the sixth floor and knocked.

But instead of Jenny there stood a fat man wearing an apron.

"What do you want?"

"What do I want? Why, to see the young mistress."

"Good Wife, come here a minute. An old gentleman's come to see you. Did you measure him for a pair of pants or a coat in my absence? He certainly needs a new suit."

A woman with plump cheeks came to the door.

"No, don't know him," she said. "Never saw him before. What does he want with me? What is it, monsieur?"

Monsieur Alexandrin was puzzled. He looked at the door, then at the stairs and the old woman, and muttered:

"Isn't this the sixth floor?"

"That's right, monsieur. And this is the Monsieur Witch-man, tailor. What can I do for you?"

"I'm a bit confused. Wasn't this room occupied by a young girl named Jenny, about a month ago?"

"Yes, monsieur. That's when we moved in. Would you like a pair of trousers, a coat, or both?"

"I must admit, a coat or a pair of trousers wouldn't do me any harm, but I'm really looking for Mademoiselle Jenny, the picture colorer."

"We told you, she left here about two weeks ago."

"Can you tell me where she's moved to? She had no creditors, so she must have left an address."

"That's true. She must have left it. Husband, where did you put it?"

"What? You mean the one you gave me? Now I remember; I wrote it on a card—on the back of the queen of diamonds."

"The queen of diamonds! I gave it to Toinette yesterday to play with. She made a nun of it, and put it in the fire."

"You hear, monsieur? Our daughter made a nun of it. I'm sorry, but that needn't prevent me from making you a cheap coat."

"No, monsieur, I don't want anything," said Monsieur Alexandrin, muttering to himself as he went down the stairs.

"Where shall I find her now? Paris is so big! Poor girl, without my lessons, she won't make any more progress. Damn that tailor! Why did he give that card to his child?"

The old man made inquiries in the neighborhood, but in Paris two weeks is like two thousand. Time soon brings changes and reverses, so that someone who has not been seen for two weeks is forgotten, and scarcely a trace is left.

Unable to locate Jenny, the old writing master said to himself:

"Well, this was a pleasant dream, and when something leads you nowhere, you had best forget about it."

Five months rolled on, and the little old man continued to give writing lessons and compose verses for his amusement.

But his passion for the arts did not extinguish his love for flowers. Violets were still his favorites—as he could afford them.

V. THE INVITATION

One day when Monsieur Alexandrin was near Boulevard St. Martin, he remembered that it was Monday, and that there was a flower market nearby. He headed for the Château d'Eau and soon came within sight of the crowds strolling among the pots and boxes of myrtles, carnations, and flowers of the season, as the market women called out their fragrant wares.

He began to follow the crowd, then stopped to breathe in the delightful odors, when he caught sight of a pot of violets and approached the vendor to offer his usual price. When so occupied, a rather coquettishly dressed lady stopped at a stall a few steps away from him and asked the price of a moss rose.

Her voice was so familiar he was startled.

"Jenny!" he cried.

"What, you, my dear Professor?" she said, recognizing him immediately. "Ah, how happy I am to see you! I thought you were dead!"

"No, my dear girl, I assure you I am very much alive. How wonderful to find you here again, among the flowers. In fact, if I had thought about it, I suppose this is the first place I should have looked for you."

"Always gallant, my dear Professor. But I have so many things to tell you. Will you walk me home?"

"With pleasure. I trust you will allow me to carry your purchase, for I see you have bought that rose."

"What! You want to carry it?"

"Yes, I would be delighted to, for I still pretend to be good for something."

"Well, since you are so nice about it, I'll let you. Come with me."

Monsieur Alexandrin took the big beautiful rose tree, which was heavier than he imagined. Sweat trickled down his face, and he could not help thinking to himself, "Six months have made a big change. Fashionable hats, a silk gown, a handsome shawl, and an apartment on the third floor! Hmm. I wonder what has happened?"

Mademoiselle Jenny led him to a neat house on the boulevard, where the stairs were well lighted and scrubbed.

They were soon on the third floor, and the old man was ushered into a small, handsomely furnished apartment.

"There. Make yourself comfortable," said Jenny, taking off her bonnet and shawl. "Now, my dear Professor, we'll have a chat together. In the first place, you must be surprised at my good fortune. And even more so to hear that I am an actress, and perform in one of the neighboring theaters."

"An actress! What? You made your debut and have work?"

"Yes! I play leading roles, both comedy and tragedy."

"Oh dear! I can hardly believe it, but I'm so glad."

"Here's how it happened. A few days after you stopped calling on me——"

"I came down with a fever."

"Poor man! Well, as I couldn't go on the way I was, I told one of my friends about my love for the stage. I knew she was acquainted with an actor who occasionally gave theater parties. She told him about me and introduced us; I took a part, and everyone liked me."

"Ah, so you didn't forget my lessons."

"Apparently not, my dear Professor. Well, I played a second time, and was equally successful. That evening, a newspaperman recommended me to the director of a theater, who asked me to play a third time, so that he might see me. I readily consented, and he was delighted, for he hired me on the spot at a salary of twenty-five hundred francs. Twenty-five hundred francs! I think that's a pretty sum to start with. At any rate, it's better than coloring

Bluebeards and Tom Thumbs. I did what I felt was right: I asked you for elocution lessons, but most important, I rejected Monsieur Fanfan Benoît. I am so happy and contented, that if not for dressing-room gossip and jealous actresses—but I suppose I'll get used to that."

"How wonderful! I would love to see you act."

"Oh, then come tonight. I have a part in a new play. You must come; I have a ticket for you. Just give your name at the door. Look! There's my theater. You can see it from here."

"Thank you, thank you. I'll be there without fail."

"And tomorrow morning we'll have breakfast together. You can tell me how you enjoyed the show, and everything the audience said."

"Of course, my dear. Until tonight, then."

Monsieur Alexandrin left, rubbing his hands with joy and impatient for the evening's entertainment.

VI. THE FAILURE

As soon as he had eaten, the old professor left for the theater, and arrived early. No matter. He would wait for the treat in store.

Finally the doors were opened. He went in, gave his name, and was ushered to a seat near the orchestra. He was the first and only one there.

The audience, however, soon began to arrive, and when he looked about, he thought that he saw a familiar face. It was a young man, not dressed in the latest fashion, who kept glancing about with apparent surprise and reaching in his pockets.

Monsieur Alexandrin at last recognized him as Jenny's suitor, Fanfan Benoît, and he went over to sit beside him, pleased to meet someone with whom he could speak about his pupil.

"Well, young man, do you know who's playing tonight?"

Fanfan looked at the old man for several minutes; then he exclaimed, somewhat audibly:

"Ah! Now I know you. I found you one morning with Mademoiselle Jenny, hiding under an umbrella."

"There you have it. I was her first professor. I discovered she bore the sacred fire."

"Sacred fire?"

"I mean, I recognized her talent, which always leads to success. What are you cracking that way, young man?"

"Almonds and raisins. They help to pass the time between the acts."

"That's very true. They are good, and make the time fly. We are going to see her play, and enjoy her triumph, for I'm told she's well liked here. But how long it takes to start! Give me a few of your raisins, they will amuse me, too."

"Willingly, monsieur. Put your hand in my left pocket."

The old writing master didn't need a second invitation. He plunged his hand into Fanfan's pocket, drew out a handful, and, cracking and swallowing them, resumed the conversation.

"Did you love Mademoiselle Jenny, young man?"

"Yes, monsieur. And I think I still do."

"What? Aren't you sure?"

"Well, monsieur, I try not to be."

This reply was accompanied by a sigh.

Monsieur Alexandrin was touched. He dabbed his eyes with his handkerchief and resumed the conversation.

"You want to forget her! Lovely Jenny . . . Your raisins are excellent. And you would have married her?"

"Yes, monsieur. I was foolish enough to think she would be honored."

" 'Foolish' is a bit too severe, but since you said the word, allow me to say that it would have been selfish of you to prevent her from pursuing a brilliant career. Look how fast she has risen! Her apartment, her furni——"

"Nonsense! Do you think the theater gave her the furniture?"

Monsieur Alexandrin did not reply. The suggestion was

plain enough, and, in order to change the subject, he again plunged his hand into Fanfan's pocket, crying:

"These are delicious. They certainly help to pass the time."

"Well," said Fanfan, "if she is happy—and really talented —perhaps she was right not to marry me, but if——"

"Hush, young man, the curtain's going up."

The play began, but Jenny did not appear until the second act.

She played the role of a farmer's daughter, and her dress became her admirably.

Some said:

"Isn't she beautiful?"

"She doesn't walk well," said others; "she has no poise."

"But she *is* pretty."

Fanfan Benoît said nothing. He could scarcely look at her. As for old Alexandrin, he jumped up from his seat, and from time to time he cried:

"Keep your arms down, and throw your head back. Oh, my Lord! She can't remember what I told her a hundred times. She cranes her neck too much, and how badly she turns herself!"

Jenny got through the first part tolerably, but the new play was bad, and the actress was not good. Sometimes she missed her cues, and sometimes she mumbled when she wished to speak with passion.

The audience began to buzz and ultimately to hiss.

"They're not hissing the actress, but the play."

"Ah! I don't know," replied Fanfan Benoît, "but it seems to me that Mademoiselle Jenny is not at home, either."

In fact, Jenny, who was not used to this reception, became agitated and lost control.

Catcalls issued from all parts of the theater, and the curtain dropped in the midst of a frightful tumult, during which the actress fainted.

Monsieur Alexandrin said no more. The audience rose and left, and Fanfan Benoît accompanied the old professor. Finally, out on the boulevard, he broke the silence.

"Is that what you call success? I, for one, will no longer

be a party to Mademoiselle Jenny's triumph. It wasn't her fault. She had a miserable part."

"It's all one, monsieur. I don't know much about such things, but I think Mademoiselle Jenny stumbled over her lines, and I will never again go to the theater when she plays. Good night, monsieur. I am sorry you ever discovered that Mademoiselle Jenny had the sacred fire."

Fanfan Benoît left Monsieur Alexandrin, and the latter went home, saying:

"She certainly made her appearance too soon. I'm sure she needs coaching for at least another year."

Next morning the old man visited Jenny and found her sad and ill. She served a magnificent breakfast but did not touch a bite, and while the old professor feasted, she overwhelmed him with questions.

"What did they say last night?"

"They said the play was worthless."

"What about me?"

"They said your dress was very pretty. And especially your bonnet. Ah! What a lovely bonnet!"

"What about my acting?"

"They said that when the play is clipped and pared, it may succeed."

"But what of me? You won't answer my question."

"Ah, my dear friend, what could you expect them to say about an actress who played in a flop? They pity her, and they pitied you very much, especially that poor Fanfan Benoît—you know, the one with the prunes."

"What? Was he there?"

"Yes, right beside me. He was going to fight the hissers, but there were too many of them."

"Ah, Monsieur Alexandrin, what an evening! I shall never forget it! I was mortified! I see now that all is not honey on the stage."

"My dear friend, if all were honey on the stage, everyone would become an actor, and there would be no one left to hiss. Take heart, my friend. You must learn to put up with reverses. Now, just between us, you still may need a few lessons. You really do. There are sentiments you feel correctly, but show badly, and on the stage, the most important thing is to make ourselves understood."

Mademoiselle Jenny bit her lips and frowned.

A few minutes later she suddenly rose and said:

"I hope you will excuse me, my dear Monsieur Alexandrin, but I mustn't be late for rehearsal."

"In that case, I must leave you, my dear pupil. When shall I call again, to resume our lessons?"

"I don't quite know. But now I have your address, and shall send for you when I have time."

"Very well. And when I pass by, I shall call on you, if you will allow me."

"Of course. Good-by, Monsieur Alexandrin."

They bowed, and the old man returned home rubbing his hands and flattering himself that his lessons to Mademoiselle Jenny would be good for his stomach, for he was somewhat of a gourmand, a failing common to poets.

A week elapsed, and when Mademoiselle Jenny did not send for him, he decided to call on her himself.

He asked the servant for Mademoiselle Jenny Desgrillon. The servant looked him over carefully and then said that she was not at home.

"I shall come back another day, but be good enough to tell her that Monsieur Alexandrin called, and that he is anxious to hear from her. You understand—anxious."

The servant scarcely deigned to reply. Servants have a habit of being rude to those who wear threadbare coats.

"I'm sure she'll send for me tomorrow," Monsieur Alexandrin told himself, but she did not.

He returned several times to the house of his old friend, and got the usual answer:

"Madame is out," or "Madame is not receiving."

Old Alexandrin was not devoid of pride, so, one day he told the servant indignantly:

"Mademoiselle Jenny ought to always be visible to me, her professor—to me, who directed her first dramatic studies, and would have made of her a Mars, or a Georges, if she had only listened. So tell Mademoiselle Jenny that I shall call on her no more. If she wants to see me, she knows

my address. She can come to my house; no one is com-
promised by calling on me."

In reply, the servant shut the gate in the old man's face.
This time the old author returned home without rubbing
his hands.

"Women!" he muttered. "Cato maintained that wisdom
and reason are beyond you. Catullus says your oaths are
graven on the winds and rippling waves. Henceforth I
agree with them. And with Virgil, who declared, '*Varium
et mutabile semper femina.*' We learn these things by heart,
but the heart soon forgets them."

Weeks and months rolled by without any word from
Jenny. Faithful to his resolve, Monsieur Alexandrin did not
return to her house. Still, he was interested in her, and
whenever he went out, the first thing he did was to look
at the theater bills. He pored over those of the theater
where she had played, and tried to find her name, but always in vain.

"She very seldom plays; perhaps she's gone to another
theater."

He kept checking, but he never found the name of Jenny
Desgrillon.

"She's probably changed her name to something more
striking. Perhaps she thought her own was too simple. Poor
little thing! It's not the name that makes talent, but
the other way around. She ought to have remembered,
though, that the name 'Jenny' brought happiness to the
theater, and that two actresses with that name acquired
fame, and fully gained the approval of a judicious public."

VII. THE ENCOUNTER

Six months went by. Monsieur Alexandrin sometimes
thought of pretty Jenny of Rue de la Harpe, whom he
preferred to the one on Boulevard St. Martin, but he went
less often to read the playbills.

One fine day, after giving several lessons in hair strokes and curlicues, the old writing master was strolling along the boulevards near the Madeleine, and was surprised to see few people at the flower market. True, the quay offers greater variety, but one can always find something to embellish a fruit basket or renew a jardiniere.

He walked around for a long time, admiring the plants, and, as usual, keeping an eye out for violets. But at the Madeleine market common flowers are rare, and he had not found what he was looking for, when an elegant tilbury drew up, and an exquisitely dressed young lady alighted.

She wore a leghorn bonnet that partly concealed her features, and she stopped from time to time before the stalls, although she could not seem to find anything good enough to buy. At length her attention was attracted by a superb camelia, and she went over to ask the price of it. Suddenly old Alexandrin heard a familiar voice, looked up, and there was Jenny!

She also recognized him, and held out her hand, smiling.

"It seems as if we meet in all the flower markets in Paris," she said.

"Yes, that seems to be our fate."

"I'll wager, my dear Professor, that you came here to renew your pot of violets."

"To tell you the truth, I did. And I see you have chosen a superb camelia. Now that our purchases are not the same——"

"My dear Monsieur Alexandrin, please don't be angry with me. I know you have every right to, but I'm terribly sorry. Can you ever forgive me?"

"How can one refuse a pretty woman? Let me carry your camelia; it's my privilege."

"Agreed, providing you take me home in my carriage."

The old man did not reply but took the camelia, which was in a box. It was rather heavy, but self-esteem doubled his strength, and he was proud of still being Mademoiselle Jenny's porter.

Fortunately the tilbury was close at hand. The footman helped them in, and the poor professor hardly knew where he was as he felt himself rolling along in a splendid carriage and seated with a lady wearing feathers, silks, and cashmeres.

They soon stopped before a beautiful house on Rue d'Antin. This time the camelia was carried by a servant, and Monsieur Alexandrin was not at all sorry. He followed Jenny, who ushered him into a splendid apartment one flight up, and after crossing a richly furnished salon they reached a boudoir hung with silks and cashmeres. Jenny motioned to the old man to sit down beside her, on a divan. And he, admiring everything around him, sat only on the edge, muttering, "Oh, how magnificent! How superb! What theater do you belong to now, my dear Jenny?"

"I am no longer called Jenny. My name is now Madame de St. Eugène; it suits me better."

"Madame de St. Eugène! Indeed, that has a ring to it!"

"Besides, I no longer act. I have given up a career in which, in order to win success, we must put up with a thousand bothers and vexations—being the butts of liberal criticism, and petty jealousies. Do you remember, my dear Professor, when I first played?"

"Yes, perfectly. I was seated beside Monsieur Fanfan Benoît, the grocer."

"The next day, when you came to see me, you would not actually tell me that I had played my part badly, but you hinted that I had a lot to learn. Instead of admitting my mistakes, I felt offended—my pride was hurt, and I ordered the servant to tell you, whenever you called, that I was not home."

"On my eleventh visit, I suspected as much."

"Pardon me, Monsieur Alexandrin; flattery had turned my head. I thought I had great talent, when I had none, for I made a second attempt, and was hissed again. Oh! Then I was in despair! I don't know where it would have led me, but just then, I received a visit from a respectable gentleman who was very rich. He had seen me play, and thought me so pretty that he placed his heart and fortune at my feet, providing I left the stage. Goodness! The moment was too well chosen for me to think of refusing, so

I accepted his offer, and ever since then I have occupied this apartment. I have servants and a carriage at my disposal, and my slightest wish is instantly granted."

Monsieur Alexandrin shook his head and replied, "You say you are happy, but you no longer have that fresh, healthy look you had when you lived on the sixth floor on Rue de la Harpe. You look pale and wan, and your eyes are glossy. Forgive me, perhaps I shall offend you again —but I am only telling you what strikes me."

"Oh, that's nothing. Now I spend whole nights at balls and parties. What difference does it make? It's fashionable to be pale, and this way, I am thought charming."

"And your husband, Monsieur de St. Eugène, what does he do?" resumed Monsieur Alexandrin with marked emphasis. "Won't you introduce me to him?"

Jenny smiled and said:

"When Monsieur de St. Eugène is here, I receive no one. But he never arrives before four o'clock; therefore, my dear Alexandrin, you must come and see me in the mornings, and breakfast with me. I will treat you to the nicest delicacies, for I remember you are rather fond of good things."

The old man rose, took up his hat, which he had placed on the floor, and, bowing gravely, said:

"Madame de St. Eugène, I have the honor to wish you good day."

"Are you leaving already, my dear Professor?"

"Yes, Madame de St. Eugène. I have several writing lessons to give. Ah! I ought to have stuck to them, and never given any others."

"But you must come again soon. I am always here, provided you come before four o'clock."

"That will do, Madame de St. Eugène; I'll remember. Please don't trouble yourself."

The old man hastily left the splendid apartment occupied by the beautiful Jenny, saying to himself:

"Oh no, that will not suit me. Now she is following a path I do not like. She has left the stage, for which I fancied she had a decided predilection, but it turns out that her inclination was for plumed bonnets and cashmeres. No,

I won't visit her again. I am a gourmand, I won't deny it; nonetheless, I shall never commit an act of baseness. I must no longer seek the society of Mademoiselle Jenny, now that she has changed her name to Madame de St. Eugène, and has an invisible husband who never goes home until four."

The old man crossed the yard, and was about to leave Jenny's house, when he bumped into a grocer carrying a basket full of groceries.

"Aren't you Monsieur Fanfan Benoît?"

"Yes, and I think I remember you—you're the professor, the author, the——"

"Ah, my dear friend, I've almost given that up. The mind cools with age. But where are you going?"

"To deliver these goods to this house."

"To this house?"

"Yes, monsieur."

"To whom?"

"Oh, to Madame de St. Eugène. She must be a person of quality; she orders the best sugar and coffee."

"What? Madame de St. Eugène? Do you know who she is?"

"No, but she pays ready cash, and that's what counts."

"You won't be so indifferent when I tell you that she is none other than Jenny Desgrillon, the former colorist of Rue de la Harpe, whom you intended to marry!"

"Jenny!" cried Fanfan Benoît, putting down his basket. "Jenny! What, she has become a lady, and made her fortune in so short a time? I see now, Monsieur Alexandrin, that you were right in saying she was possessed of genius, and that it would be better for her to be an actress than a grocer's wife. I never would have been able to provide her with servants and a carriage. She owes you a great deal, but to get so much money, she must at least be at the Opéra."

"No, not at the Opéra," replied the old man, sighing, "she's not at the Opéra. She's left the stage."

"Left the stage! And made her fortune, too? Then a rich man must have married her. Is her husband a peer of France?"

"Her husband! I don't believe she has a husband who is a peer of France, or even a dealer in rabbit skins! I believe—hmm! My dear friend, women—you know, Virgil said, '*Varium et mutabile semper femina*'! And, if I add Catullus and Cato, the result will not be flattering to the ladies."

"Monsieur," said Fanfan Benoît, taking up his basket, "I don't understand Latin, but I do know what you mean. I only hope she is happy, and that her luck may last, but let her do her shopping elsewhere. Good day, monsieur."

The young grocer hurried off, and as Monsieur Alexandrin looked after him, he said to himself:

"He's an honest fellow, that grocer! Yes, he is. In his place I'd have done the same. Only, since he didn't take the coffee to Madame de St. Eugène, he might have offered some to me. No matter, Monsieur Fanfan has spirit; a man oughtn't to supply a woman with sugar who has treated him with disdain."

The old professor now returned home, determined not to visit the Chaussée d'Antin again, nor to shop for flowers in the market near the Madeleine.

VIII. THE FUNERAL

Time waits for no one, treating rich and poor alike; time is the perpetual motion.

Monsieur Alexandrin still cultivated the Muses, which profited him little, but now there was no one to share his passion for the theater, and he often thought of Jenny.

"I am sure she would still listen to me with pleasure," he said to himself, "for she *was* very friendly the last time I saw her, and her fortune did not make her snub me. But no, I can't go to see her: her society is no longer fit for me."

As he said this, the old professor still thought of his former pupil. At his age man is not inconstant in his affections —a new passion does not suddenly chase away an old one.

He did his utmost to remain firm in his resolution, but every day it became weaker.

"Perhaps I am being too hard on her," he would say. "She was so kind to me the last time I saw her. Then, too, she frankly acknowledged her errors! That's something we don't often meet with. Besides, if she turned out badly and gave up her calling, am I not somewhat to blame? Wasn't I the first to flatter her love for the stage? Ah, it was very wrong of me, if I wash my hands of her . . . No, no. That I do not keep the society of Madame de St. Eugène is perfectly right, but not to go, even once, to see kind Jenny, that would be ungrateful. I must pay her a visit."

One morning Monsieur Alexandrin dusted off his hat and coat and started off for Rue d'Antin. Six months had elapsed since he had seen Jenny.

When the old man arrived, he didn't see the house but was sure that he would recognize it when he did. He examined every door carefully until he came to one that looked familiar, and saw that it was draped in black.

A hearse was parked in front of it, and as he passed, he took off his hat but went on. He could not seem to find the house he was looking for and, retracing his steps, came back to the hearse, and felt depressed. He quickly passed by, still trying to find the house, but in vain. He tried again, and found himself close to the house draped in mourning, convinced that Jenny's house must be on that side, and he had an idea.

"Can it be the one in black?"

The more he looked, the more he seemed to remember, and approached it, saying:

"After all, what's so surprising about someone dying in the house she lives in? In Paris, so many people lodge under one roof, that often one dies on the second floor, another is married on the first, and a child is born on the third."

He entered the gateway where the coffin lay, and went to the concierge.

"Madame," he said, "if I am not mistaken, doesn't a

young lady live here, by the name of Madame de St. Eugène?"

"Yes, monsieur," the woman said, looking at him strangely, "she did."

"Has she left? You must know her address."

"Are you a relative, monsieur?"

"No, only a friend. Why do you ask?"

"Ah, monsieur! To tell you the truth, the person you seek no longer occupies the first floor. She is—she's there!"

The concierge pointed to the bier in the gateway.

"Is it possible?" cried the old professor, carrying his handkerchief to his eyes. "What. Kind Jenny! So pretty, and so young!"

"Alas, monsieur, she died yesterday. For some time back she had had a cold, and neglected it. She wouldn't take care of herself; she went to balls, and never liked to stay home. She was always out. Then, about a month ago, she took to her bed, and never again rose from it!"

"Poor Jenny!" murmured the old man. "Ah, I knew it! At least I can pay my last respects."

The body was put in the hearse. Monsieur Alexandrin followed, and looked around for the other mourners, but there was no one else. Soon they arrived at the church. A marriage was being performed in the adjoining chapel—that of Fanfan Benoît.

Monsieur Alexandrin saw the newlyweds about to pass him by. He knelt and hid his face in his hat, wishing to spare the young grocer. The writing master followed Jenny to her final resting place. The tomb was set off by a small railing, with a little space for flowers. The old man returned the following day with a pot of violets and said:

"Poor Jenny! This is how we met! Now, whenever I buy violets, I shall bring them here."

The Scientist and the Crocodile

BY JOSEPH MÉRY

TRANSLATED BY MARTIN NOZICK

JOSEPH MÉRY
1798-1865

Méry was born in Aygalades and studied in Marseilles and at the Aix Law School. After a brief sojourn in Constantinople and a hike through Italy he returned home to start a liberal newspaper, which succeeded in landing him in jail for three months. Arriving in Paris in 1824, he collaborated with Auguste Barthélemy in writing poems (*Les Sidiennes* [1825], *La Velléliade* [1826]) which satirized the Restoration, Louis Philippe, and religion, until Barthélemy became reconciled with the status quo in 1833. Méry then translated *The Æneid*, prepared librettos for Rossini's *Semiramis* and Verdi's *Don Carlos*, wrote vaudevilles and plays, including three in collaboration with Gérard de Nerval: *Chariot d'Enfant* (1850), *L'Imagier de Harlem* (1851), and *Paris à Pekin*, which was never produced. He also wrote a series of "nocturnal" short stories set against backgrounds almost totally unknown to him: *Les Nuits anglaises*, *Les Nuits italiennes*, *Les Nuits espagnoles*, *Les Nuits d'Orient*, and other truculent tales full of verve and spicy satire, notably "La Chasse au chastre" (1853) and "The Scientist and the Crocodile" (1860), here included.

ABOUT MÉRY: Nothing in English and very little in French: E. de Mirecourt, *Méry* (Paris, 1854), and Georges Benoist, "Gérard de Nerval and Joseph Méry," *Revue d'Histoire Littérarire de la France*, Paris, 1930, Année 37, pp. 177–95.

This title sounds like the beginning of a fable, but the story I am going to relate is true.

The city of Belfast, Ireland, is full of scientists: science runs through its streets as wit through ours.

When I got to Belfast, I was immediately struck by the general appearance of the passers-by; every face looked like a geometric figure, just as in Paris everyone in the street seems to be straight out of a vaudeville act at the Gymnase, the Variétés, or the Palais-Royal, complete with song and dance.

Mr. Adamson, one of the innumerable scientists who keep to the right on the streets of Belfast, was not only wealthy but learned, and yet he was unhappy. Every morning, on rising, he pondered this question: Why did the famous explorer Bruce not discover the Isle of Meroë?

Men find their unhappiness in one obsession or another.

I once knew a very honorable man who wasted away with grief over having been turned down by the National Guard in 1830 "for unfitness for military service." He was told that the rifle could be held in the right hand only, even if he had two left hands.

Mr. Adamson studied Bruce's map, from the mountains of the Moon to Hermopolis, and could not find the peninsula that the trustworthy Herodotus had seen as clearly as I see you.

This anxiety was undermining the solemn Irishman's health.

One day he provided himself with a pair of Dublin hose and set sail for Egypt by way of the St. George Canal, the Channel, France, and the Mediterranean.

Along the way he had eyes for nothing. Bruce's peninsula absorbed his entire attention.

He came to the Nile, paid no heed to the Pyramids, an extraordinary discourtesy that seemed to make no difference at all to those stoic monuments, and after a few hours in Cairo he went on to the ruins of Karnak.

He barely glanced at the majestic colossi of Memnon, the Ozymandias crypts, the hypogea of Sesostris, the pylons of Isis, the obelisks of Luxor, and all the marvels of the Thebaid.

As he made his way up the Nile he passed Latopolis, Elethya, Apollinopolis, Ombos, and Syena known today by the unattractive name of Aswan. The ruins of these ancient cities never once excited his enthusiasm; they were really quite offensive to the Egypt of Sesostris.

One day the heat of noon—a natural phenomenon in the tropics—was so great that the learned Adamson yielded to the call of the cool waters of the Nile and for the first time in his dedicated life decided to take a swim in the holy river.

He looked around him with great care and saw not a living soul.

The desert was living up to its name.

Not a single statue of Isis, Ibis, Anubis, or Serapis was in sight. The Nile flowed along in religious silence and on its left bank bathed the magnificent, anonymous ruins that rose up along rocky paths to ancient Elephantine.

Made confident by the solitude and absence of policemen, Adamson plunged into the living waters of the Nile, but only after having carefully arranged his clothes and boots on the barren shore.

The scientist gave thanks to Mother Nature for having provided such a cool river in the midst of burning sands.

The delight he took in his swim is beyond the ken of science, and his thoughts traveled back to the first swimming lessons he had received as a child on the banks of the Kingstown. Then he flung caution to the winds and swam recklessly out.

While disporting himself like a sweet-water Triton, he grew aware of a menacing stir and beheld quite near him, on the surface of the water, a pair of gaping jaws adorned with leonine teeth and topped by flaming eyes.

Immediately—and yet already too late—the scientist remembered a fable that begins: *Egyptian dogs keep on running as they drink from the Nile, for they are afraid of crocodiles.*

"Oh wise dogs!" he exclaimed, and, madly flapping his hands and feet, he made a desperate effort to reach a little sandy island, a reef for boats but salvation for swimmers.

As a matter of fact, he was being followed by a most beautiful specimen of a crocodile; a colossal, amphibian lizard, more ferocious than a Bengal tiger or an Atlas lion.

It was swimming toward the scientist, who, although emaciated by study, would still prove a tasty morsel for the ravenous appetite of a hungry crocodile.

Adamson reached the shore with the crocodile at his heels; he imagined he could feel its hot breath on his soles, a terrifying contrast to his cool bath.

It was the breath that spurred him on.

He touched ground, but just as he was about to rejoice he remembered that crocodiles are amphibian. Spying a delicate palm tree, standing alone on the reef, he flung his arms about the trunk and clambered to the top with the agility of a squirrel.

Had Adamson belonged to the large class of unqualified scientists—the type with protuberant bellies—he would have been lost; happily, at the age of twenty, he had solved fifteen Euclidian propositions, a concentrated effort that had trimmed him down and made him fit for climbing palm trees.

Adamson settled down as best he could on that part of the tree where branches and leaves stretch, mount, fall, and interlace according to their respective whims, and, having found a firm support for his feet, looked down upon the Nile.

For a moment he blinked with terror: the crocodile was coming out of the water, shaking the shiny scales of its carapace, and crawling on, like a fish converted into a quadruped, toward the base of the palm tree.

The scientist racked his brain for what Pliny and Saavers had written about crocodiles and he thought that he recollected they said that such animals could scale palm trees.

"Oh, my Lord!" he exclaimed. "I hope that in this case my fellow-scientists have been as wrong as they are wont to be."

Suddenly he experienced another shudder of horror: in the *Belfast Review* he had published a paper that claimed that crocodiles could scale trees like cats.

If only he could burn the article! But it was too late, all of Belfast had read his report, it had been translated into Arabic, and nobody in the Orient, not even in Crocodipolis, had challenged him.

The ferocious amphibian reached the foot of the tree and evinced great joy when he discovered the swimmer up among the leaves; the animal circled back and forth, looked up again, and then stopped in his tracks; since it was absolutely impossible to take the fort by assault, he would stage a blockade.

At this point let us pay tribute to the true scientific spirit. Despite the preoccupations of the moment, Adamson was overcome by a wave of justifiable anguish; true, in writing his paper, he had committed an error in natural history, but he was resolved never to correct it even if he escaped this predicament alive. The article had been written with conviction; it proved that crocodiles could climb palm trees, and as such it was a contribution to science and beyond retraction even if Mr. Adamson managed to avoid the clutches of *one* crocodile unable to scale a palm tree on the Nile.

A scientist must have unshakable convictions.

The crocodile's position had taken an alarming turn. His blockade showed a profound knowledge of strategy. Now another contribution could be made to scientific lore: namely, that crocodiles do not climb, they blockade.

This was material for another paper that, without refuting the first, would credit animal intelligence with greater craftiness than ever before.

Stretched out in all its enormous length, the crocodile basked in the sun like a lizard; it showed no impatience as it waited for the scientist to descend, and the wriggling of its tail recorded the extent of the joy aroused in it by the mere thought of the inevitable feast.

As for the scientist, he was studying the habits of the beast, but, having completed his observations, he again began to tremble like a dying man hanging from a lion's jaws.

During a blockade an hour is two hundred and forty minutes long, but it passes like any other; time in its swiftness often moves on crutches, but it keeps on moving nevertheless.

The sun went down exactly as it had done the evening before; night fell after a very brief twilight and the dying rays of the sun revealed to the blockaded scientist a crocodile in sinister, horizontal motionlessness.

Rummaging through his memory for some comparable occurrence to afford him hope or consolation, Adamson stumbled across his fellow-countryman Robinson Crusoe, a native of York who, after his shipwreck, had spent a night in a tree as a measure of precaution.

The tree that had given him shelter had probably been a palm tree; it was therefore possible, if difficult, to live on the top of one.

Robinson Crusoe even says he slept.

Besides, at English inns one often finds beds as hard as a treetop, a reflection that helped assuage the bitter anguish of the unfortunate Belfast scientist.

Adamson slept very little during that first long night; he had several short but touching dreams: he dreamed that he was seated before the academicians of Belfast, reading them a paper to prove that crocodiles were no more real than sphinxes, and that the Egyptians had invented the fictitious animal.

At the very end of the dream Adamson could swear that

he felt a dew of crocodile tears on his cheeks; he awoke with a start and almost fell from the top of the palm tree onto the tail of the sleeping dragon.

This taught him to be more careful, and he forced himself to stay awake by keeping his eyelids open with his fingers.

The things one will not do to stay alive!

As the sun rose Adamson saw, to his despair, that everything was *in statu quo.*

However, the crocodile no longer covered the terrain occupied the previous evening; during the night the famished beast had trapped innocent fish that had come down the White Nile and he had comforted himself with a midnight snack like a glutton at the former charterhouse of Villeneuve-lès-Avignon, where the meager and *ichthyophile* cooking had made such spectacular progress.

The edge of the little island was littered with a debris of bloody fishbones, a sad sight for the scientist; because, he told himself, the blockade will never come to an end and from sheer undernourishment I shall fall into my voracious enemy's mouth.

He knew that he was quite right and the realization made his hair stand on end.

His stomach, an organ quite independent from his mind, had its own inexorable requirements and was clamoring not only for breakfast but for a second meal to make up for the night before.

The rumble of hunger made its way up to Adamson's ears and would not be silenced.

Had there been two scientists in danger of dying of hunger, they would have fallen back on precedents established during sieges and shipwrecks; the stronger would have devoured the weaker and so at least one devotee of science would have been preserved.

But Adamson was alone and with justifiable terror he knew that famine had joined hands with blockade, just as had happened in Genoa under Massena.

Among other things, our scientist was ignorant of the fact that palm trees yield exquisite, plump fruit on which the Arabs have subsisted comfortably since Adam, the first farmer in Araby.

But then a ray of the morning sun that had slipped in among the massive leaves disclosed thick clumps of dates to the famished scientist.

In Belfast, Adamson breakfasted on a slice of beef and two helpings of York ham, washed down with port; here he had to give up such delightful gastronomical habits and be content with what he could get, manna from the desert.

After breakfast a strange thought struck him; he recalled the remark made in the Egyptian book *Sethos* by a scientist who held that crocodiles are the natural avengers of all the outrages perpetrated on Egypt by the barbarians.

That seems reasonable, he thought, for if crocodiles do not exist to avenge outrages, what are the horrible beasts good for?

His conscience reproved him for all the disrespect implicit in his failure to hail the pyramidal shades of the Pharaohs and the colossi of the divine Ozymandias during his trip through Egypt.

But he could still fall back upon the last resort of all great criminals about to die: he could repent. And he vowed that if he escaped the avenging crocodile, he would kiss the toes of Memnon, the tenor who sings a cavatina at sunrise.

A vow always helps to calm the spirit. He looked down upon the Cerberus-like beast in the hope that his promise had had some effect. The monster was still on guard; he seemed completely unaware of any vows.

A burning thirst tore at the scientist's breast—another effect of the blockade! Dates make one very thirsty.

Where could he find water? Beneath the feet of the unhappy Tantalus flowed a broad river, and yet he was dying of thirst. The Nile made ironic noises; it was content to cool the air but it would not offer a single drop of water to the parched lips of the unhappy prisoner.

Comparing himself to his fellow-countryman, Robinson Crusoe, he concluded that the latter had enjoyed every advantage over him.

True, Robinson Crusoe had spent the night in a tree, but the next morning he had come down; he had killed some parrots and transformed them into mock chicken fricassee; he had drunk clear water and rum; he had strolled beneath a parasol; he had built himself a shelter; he had encountered no crocodiles, and he had found himself a Man Friday.

"Oh happy Robinson Crusoe!" murmured the scientist. "Oh happy islander, both king and subject! And yet the ingrate had dared to complain! . . . I'd like to see him up here in this palm tree!"

One is compelled to agree that Robinson Crusoe's laments were insults to Divine Providence.

That's how men are, they always complain of their misfortunes. But was Adamson more reasonable when he denounced his fellow-countryman from York? Alas, no. Perched on his palm tree, he was unaware that that very day, at that very hour, the unfortunate French scientist Adolphe Petit, was being devoured by a crocodile, before the ruins of Ombos!

Men should really cease complaining about their fate.

Just then a slight mist covered the sun and Adamson experienced a momentary joy; he was hoping for a good downpour and was already preparing the hollows of his hands to lap up the dew of heaven in an hydraulic orgy.

His joy was short-lived.

He recalled the wretched inscription: *"limite delle pioggie,"* or the rain limits that the courageous explorer Rossignol, Belzoni's friend, had put on his map of the Nile.

Adamson's palm tree was inexorably situated in a latitude that glazes the sky but never moistens it.

To quench the thirst of his imagination, he recited a passage from the *Jerusalem Delivered* in which Tasso describes how the crusaders drank miraculous rain water out of their helmets after the long hardships of a leaden sky.

These verses, although recited in Anglicized Italian, made his mouth water.

The crocodile seemed to sense the sufferings of the Belfast Tantalus, for as he drank from the carafes of the Nile he cast sly, oblique glances at the palm tree.

Savage beasts are capable of the most insufferable jokes.

Adamson felt quite disgusted, a reaction that only served to aggravate his thirst.

He let his gaze wander over the Nile in the hope of descrying some sailboat or canoe and sending up a cry of distress, but such hope was illusory in these treacherous parts, *situated on the slopes of rapids,* as Bruce says.

He was alone in a deathlike silence, and all he could see were blackened ruins crowned here and there by ibises as motionless as exclamation marks.

Despite himself the scientist's thoughts went back to Robinson Crusoe.

"True, he was a castaway," he told himself, "but he was wrong to rebel against a misfortune that seems so minor to me. Besides, he was no fool. He made himself bread, a parasol, apparel, and even a pipe. Necessity made him ingenious. Had he been in this palm tree, he would even have found water. But let's see, how would he have gone about it?"

For a long time he pondered on how he could follow in the inventive footsteps of Robinson Crusoe, but the inner flame of his thoughts ended up by burning his tongue; there were hot coals in his mouth, and he was so desperate he would have sold his soul to the devil for a drop of water.

And the calm, majestic waters of the Nile kept rolling by.

Oh, necessity, mother of invention, you never abandon Robinson Crusoe's disciples!

The scientist clapped his hands, as if applauding himself. He had discovered a hydraulic technique!

How little men need to be happy! Here we have a man perched on a palm tree, a dying man about to fall into the gaping mouth of a crocodile, and yet he finds some reason for rejoicing because he has invented a strange way of treating his lips to a bit of brackish Nile water!

Adamson, proud of competing with his fellow-countryman from York, immediately set to work: he tore some rather long branches off the tree, tied them together at both ends with some threads ripped from the trunk and rolled between his teeth and lips. Then, when the crocodile took a short stroll to take care of his amphibian needs, Adamson let his sucking pump down slowly onto the river edge, where the spongy leaves left loose at the lower tip of the contraption were able to absorb a good deal of water. This vegetable-fiber cord was then pulled up with great care and two burning lips fastened themselves on the leaves saturated with sweet, twice-sweet, water.

Never had a gourmet at a Parisian banquet derived a more voluptuous thrill from a glass filled by the scarlet Naiad flowing by Bordeaux.

Our scientist laughed with delight, like a schoolboy; and since he had nothing better to do, he started his experiment all over again, surrendering himself completely to all the excesses of intemperance in a desire to pay his parched lungs a debt long due.

Tantalus had never thought of such a device.

Adamson was especially delighted at having mystified his crocodile. Really, the monster deserved to be outwitted.

Having satisfied two of the basic needs of his life, Adamson was assailed by the memory of the discomfort he had suffered during the treacherous, cold, wet hours of the previous night. As a swimmer, he had not missed his clothing; in the tropical heat of the day he had felt no need for covering, but now he had to think about protecting himself against the rigors of night.

And so, like Robinson Crusoe, the scientist started looking about for some decent apparel.

"Suppose some vessel, sent from heaven to save me, were to pass by, how could I face the public?" considered the judicious scholar.

After due thought Adamson plucked from his lofty recess a number of enormous leaves and, squatting like a tailor, put himself together a vegetable overcoat that, if not in the height of fashion, could at least boast of a certain primitive picturesqueness.

Two leaves sufficed for a not inelegant nightcap that was certainly no worse than the awful hats we wear by day.

The author of all these ingenious discoveries showed his

self-satisfaction by throwing his arms around himself: nature had provided shelter, clothing, food, and drink.

Adamson thought himself very fortunate; now, from the height of his palm tree he could look down upon Robinson Crusoe with disdain.

As he reflected happily upon his good fortune, he perceived the crocodile at the foot of the tree. The beast seemed to be in the power of some evil thought.

Yes, the crocodile had been thinking too.

Since he could not take the palm tree by force or through blockade, he would try to knock it down. The beast's enormous teeth went to work gnawing away with fierce determination at the base of the tree. It was as if he were saying, "This has gone far enough."

And Adamson trembled as he heard the snapping of a monstrous jaw against the base of his residence.

He had the happy idea of commending himself to St. Simeon Stylites, the anchorite of the pillar.

A crocodile's molars and incisors are so arranged that they cannot injure the base of a palm tree; the beast can gnaw only sideways; he grazes the surface but does not penetrate deeply.

That is how Mother Nature sees to it that her palm trees give shelter to wretches pursued by crocodiles.

The scientist, however, was not aware of the organic peculiarity—the maxillary impotence—of the scaly sapper. Pliny and Saavers mention this reassuring fact, but at the moment the chapters they wrote on crocodiles could not be consulted.

Adamson looked down upon the base of operations, but since he was too far up and too ill-situated to appreciate the true situation, he expected his lifesaving tree to collapse at any moment. His hair curled under his leafy turban at the idea of being hurled right into the beast's mouth and then being shoved farther down in bloody installments, as into a scaly tomb, without even an epitaph to announce the virtues of the deceased to the posterity of Belfast.

After the crocodile had worked away for several hours, his jaws became somewhat discouraged and he resorted to another expedient: battering away at the tree with his mighty tail.

The tree held firm, but the shocks were not reassuring to the scientist; he was being treated to a sort of extended earthquake as his leafy shelter was tossed about in convulsive waves.

Every once in a while, a bunch of dates broke off a branch and fell down upon the crocodile's scales; like a besieger hit by a projectile hurled from the ramparts the beast redoubled his fierce efforts.

The falling of the dates increased Adamson's terror: what would happen to him if his entire stock of food disappeared the same way?

Never did a man experience such anguish, and our scientist, convinced that life was not worth the price he was paying, decided to hurl himself down from his roof and find surcease in death.

Obsessed by this desperate idea, he stood straight up on the summit of his tree, pushed aside the branches that might break his fall, put one foot out, but energetically kept the other one back and did not jump.

A virtuous thought kept him from the abyss; Adamson had no family, no wife, no children, no nephews; he was therefore obliged to keep himself carefully alive as the only representative of the Adamsons on earth.

A man is always ingenious when it is a matter of coming to terms with despair. If he has a family and children, he wishes to stay alive for their sake; if he is alone on earth, he wishes to keep alive as a service to himself and to avoid *complete annihilation*. "*Non omnis moriar*," says the Latin poet.

Adamson was very grateful to himself for having taken such a heroic stand; he even accused himself of cowardliness for having momentarily entertained the idea of serving himself up as pabulum for a voracious amphibian monster; having done his duty, he again sat down on his vegetable armchair and took the most minute precautions to prevent himself from falling.

Who shall ever plumb the human heart, especially the heart of a scientist?

And would you believe it? After recovering from his terrors our palm-tree hermit began to derive a rather strange pleasure from the spectacle of the crocodile working madly away at a tree trunk firmly incrusted in rock.

The undulations of the tree, at first so alarming, now made Adamson feel as if he were on a swing; he smiled paternally down upon the beast's efforts, directed English epigrams at him, and called him *goose, rascal, naughty boy.*

The sharp accents that accompanied these insults irritated the monster into answering them with a rattle of scales that sounded rather harmonious to the ear of the Belfast scientist.

There was no doubt. The tree was unshakable. Adamson had won.

He recalled Seneca's comments on how one can construct an edifice of happiness in any situation of life, and he resolved to construct his own.

He could foresee a happy future.

What was missing? The climate was good, the food frugal but healthy, the solitude delightful; there was an abundance of sweet water, and someday he might even catch some Ethiopian pigeons on the wing and roast them in the sun.

As for recreation, there was a marvelous river below, mysterious ruins, an amusing crocodile, in short, everything necessary to make the hours pleasant.

In addition, in his leisure time, he might do some serious work in preparing manuscripts on the antiquity of the countries that spread out before him and extended to the Emerald mountains and the hills of Ajas, immense solitudes broken by the ruins of the temples of Jupiter and Apollo, between Berenice and Nechesia.

Elated over these new ideas, he gave serious thought to making his lodgings as comfortable as possible.

He divided his shelter into three separate and distinct rooms with partitions of leaves; as he passed from one room to another, he enjoyed a bit of exercise and reveled in the

pleasures of ownership. In his study there were several
reams of palm leaves on which he could write as on vellum
with the aid of a bark stiletto.

His dining room abounded in fresh and dried dates that
fell right into his mouth.

The hydraulic pump, which he had perfected, had its
special corner. There was only one thing missing: a pair
of gloves.

Happiness is never complete.

The days broke pure and serene; at dawn, he would listen to the desert and enjoy the cavatina of the colossus
of Memnon: every morning he had his evening at the opera.

Next he would peer down at the crocodile and when he
felt quite pleased with him he would drop some rotten
dates, which the monster gulped down greedily, adding to
the merriment of the solemn Adamson.

Between meals he would give himself up to study and
meditation; he would open the library of his memory, and,
as he read Herodotus, he would be transported to the Labyrinth, to the shores of Lake Moeris, or to Arsinoë, the province of roses.

On one occasion he followed the Emperor Hadrian up
the banks of the Nile to the city of Antinous.

When a profound thought flashed through his brain, he
would record it on papyrus and took extreme pleasure in
reading it over twenty times.

During his brief strolls along a horizontal branch, he took
pleasure in gazing upon the distant valley of Cambyses and
shed a tear for the wise but unhappy Egyptians so cruelly
decimated by the cruel, stupid Persians.

Before going to sleep he would give himself some lessons
in astronomy from the splendid constellations so dear to the
Chaldeans and to the sculptors of the zodiac of Tentyris.

Never did a jealous neighbor spy upon his doings or gossip about him; never did a newspaper refer to him; never
did a policeman stop him with his stick; never did a tax
collector demand his due.

He was as free as the air in his room, and he laughed

at all the sarcasms the misanthrope Alceste had hurled at humanity.

"Why didn't Alceste take refuge on a pillar like St. Simeon Stylites or in some palm tree like me?" he asked himself. "He would have spared himself much worry and heartache."

And now let us leave our treetop anchorite for a moment and go down to the left bank of the Nile where, to Adamson's misfortune, a new episode in this story is to take place.

Mr. Darlingle, the learned English botanist, was seeking yellow lotus on the deserted banks of the Nile.

Herodotus had seen yellow lotus; but Herodotus had been privileged to see such nonexistent things as two pyramids six hundred feet high in the center of Lake Moeris. He might very well, then, have seen yellow lotus.

True, yellow lotus has disappeared since the time of Herodotus, a fact that impels conscientious botanists to keep on looking for it.

That is why Mr. Darlingle was making his way across the Lybian chain, rummaging in all crevices suspected of concealing his lotus.

Two Arabs, armed with rifles, accompanied him.

There are things that, when encountered in the desert, stagger the imagination.

The explorer Caillaud tells us that he was overcome with amazement when he discovered the forty Pyramids of the Meroë peninsula. But Caillaud had little reason to be overwhelmed on that occasion. One's terror, however, would be completely justified if, in the middle of the Sahara, one came across a little isolated shop and the sign "Reading Room."

Therefore, Darlingle was perfectly within his rights when he uttered a cry of horror on the left bank of the Nile.

He had just spied two boots, one erect and proud, the other languidly bent as if tired after a long rest.

There is nothing silly about two boots awaiting the porter outside a hotel room, but the reactions they inspire on a deserted bank of the Nile are beyond words. One utters a cry and recoils in horror.

Mercury's two serpents would be less terrifying.

We should also add that the clothing that had been abandoned on the bank of the Nile had disappeared, either swept away by the river current or devoured by some omnivorous crocodile that had chanced to pass by.

Only the boots remained, a little to one side on a rocky pedestal.

Now you can fully sympathize with the fright of the English botanist.

First he thought that the two examples of footgear were a freak of nature, twin outcroppings of Lybian rock; but as he drew closer he recognized the authenticity of the leather and retreated in fear just as he would have done in the presence of a ghost betrayed only by its shoes.

The two faithful Arabs, native of Ombos, had never in their lives seen any boots; caught up in the botanist's panic, they fired valiantly at the two leather stalks, which fell, pierced by four bullets.

Such an execution could not restore Darlingle's equanimity, yet he was grateful to the Arabs for their devotion and thanked them with an expressive gesture.

The botanist turned his attention again to the supine boots; in their new position they seemed even more out of keeping with the surrounding desert.

At the top of his palm tree Adamson heard the shots and shuddered; among savages the sound of weapons always signifies the presence of civilized men.

He left his bedroom, entered the vestibule, pushed aside some leaves that impeded his view of the east, and saw three men standing on the bank of the Nile.

His first reaction came in the form of a sharp curse hurled at the intruders who would disturb his solitude and meditations, but then human weakness won out and he decided to catch the attention of the three men with distress signals.

He cut a long palm branch, stripped it of all its leaves except those at one end, and waved it above the tree with one hand while with the other he hurled bunches of dates —the only projectiles available—down into the Nile.

The botanist, surrounded by a silence known only to aeronauts, was attracted by a slight noise from the river caused by a hail of dates. This time he experienced even a greater surprise than before.

The boots were forgotten; now he saw a palm tree waving an enormous feather duster without the aid of the slightest breeze. Infinite joy followed upon the initial moment of surprise. That phenomenal palm tree was worth all the yellow lotus in the world.

Opening his travel diary, Darlingle hastened to record the discovery and wrote:

> *In Upper Egypt, there is a sort of palm tree that has the properties of the aloe; the aloe, however, after hurling its stem twenty feet above the ground, holds it motionless, while the palm tree of Upper Egypt waves its upper trunk vertically with an amazing regularity of movement.*
>
> *We have named this tree the Darlingle palm.*

Having written, the botanist drew a sketch of the palm tree and for lack of any other public at the moment he showed it to the two Arabs.

These children of the desert, with their lynx eyes, had just discovered a human form beneath the thick foliage of the island palm. With gestures they pointed it out to the botanist, who, completely involved in the happiness of his discovery and the beauty of his sketch, understood nothing of the Arabs' agitation. He could think of nothing but the sensation the Darlingle palm would create in the world of science.

But the Arabs kept on pointing and Darlingle, despite his self-absorption, was finally compelled to follow the direction of their index fingers.

Their pantomime was as clear as words.

"Look," they said, "look at that little island and you will see a human being on top of the palm tree; he is signaling us that he is in danger and we should rescue him."

Darlingle stretched out his little spyglass, shrugged his shoulders like a man making a polite concession, then looked carelessly at the Darlingle palm. . . .

This was his third surprise in one hour, but this one canceled out the other two.

He had distinctly seen a face, an English face, staring out between two branches, and a hand brandishing a naked branch crowned with a bunch of fronds.

He put his spyglass away sadly, reread his notes, gazed again at his sketch, and, after a bit of reflection, like Brutus debating with himself whether to destroy his two children or let them live, he decided on the latter course of action.

"What is written is written," he said. "I shall not cut out a single word. Besides, since the aloe exists, the Darlingle palm could very well have existed had nature found it useful; I find it useful and therefore stand by it."

Having made his decision, he conferred with the Arabs: now they had to find some sort of vessel to rescue the traveler in distress. One of the Arabs made a suggestion that was adopted.

They started out for Aswan, situated some miles away in the desert, and after two scorching hours and a rapid dash over sand dunes they reached the village, which in Herodotus's time had been a city.

Mr. Darlingle sought out a fisherman and pointed to a gold piece and a boat in unequivocal pantomime.

They set the boat afloat, and the botanist, indicating the direction of the river, said proudly as if the fisherman could understand:

"To the island of the Darlingle palm!"

It would have been enough to point. They went down the Nile.

The island of the Darlingle palm was soon on the horizon and as they approached it, the lynx-eyed Arabs manifested a certain uneasiness and exchanged signs of understanding.

After a quarter of an hour there was no longer any doubt: they had actually seen an enormous crocodile prowling around the palm tree.

When they told the botanist of their discovery, the latter

was treated to his fourth surprise of the day, and trembled with cold at forty degrees Réaumur.

Yet it must be said to his credit that he repressed his fear lest he compromise the dignity of England's explorers in the eyes of Arabia Deserta. He hid his fright—a fright not at all unnatural in a botanist, who is more in the habit of dealing with plants than tangling with amphibian monsters of the Nile.

The Arabs were carrying on a quiet conversation with each other, like people quite accustomed to hunting crocodiles. They loaded their guns again with English bullets, which are always safety-patented and infallible; they sought out firm support for their feet and told the man who was rowing to be extra careful in his movements.

The crocodile saw the little boat come nearer and could not decide whether it was prey or peril; he was prepared for defense or flight, depending on the number of attackers.

Lying at the edge of the river, as motionless as a stuffed animal, he kept his mouth wide open to gobble up the first one who dared come at him.

Both Arabs were very well acquainted with the ways of such beasts and took their positions in the front of the boat; they cocked their weapons, uttered one syllable together, and two shots fused into one.

The bullets entered the only vulnerable side, the open mouth, and then traversed the entire inner length.

The beast shook his head with comic contortions that provoked outright merriment from the upper gallery of the palm tree; then, vomiting torrents of black blood on the sand, he shut his tear-filled eyes and moved no more.

Adamson adjusted the disorder of his vegetable toilette, automatically looked about for his gloves, and, finding none, let himself down with utmost care to prevent tearing his overcoat and to spare his compatriot any undue shock—for even from afar he had recognized him as a fellow-countryman by his hair and gloves.

Arabs are by nature solemn, but their solemnity changed to wild laughter at the sight of Adamson's garb.

The botanist himself, reassured by the crocodile's death,

bit his lips to spare his fellow-countryman the spectacle of English hilarity, quite unseemly on such an occasion.

The botanist and the scientist shook hands, as Englishmen do, and told each other their stories. Adamson begged Darlingle to order the Arabs to desist from their immoderate laughter; otherwise he should complain to his consul.

Then Darlingle had an idea even more generous than St. Martin's; he removed his gray duck overcoat and handed it to his compatriot.

Adamson took it, drew away, made the proper arrangements and buttoned up tightly.

They put the crocodile crosswise at the back of the boat, as a conversation piece, and for a while Adamson even entertained the idea of going down the shore to retrieve his boots.

The departure was a solemn one.

Since Lord Byron's time the English have been in the habit of saluting islands or continents they leave forever. Adamson saluted his palm tree; he even embraced it and shed a few tears upon its bark. Then he collected all the leaves he had used as furniture or for other domestic purposes.

These precious relics were meant for the National Gallery at Charing Cross. In the name of the city of London, Mr. Darlingle thanked the scientist and could not pass up the opportunity of delivering an hour-long speech on the very spot where the gift was so generously made.

For his part, Adamson was very kind toward the botanist; in the name of science he thanked him for the precious discovery of the Darlingle palm, which added another member to the great family of palm trees; he even promised to write an article for the *Belfast Review* to prove that this palm tree, newly discovered through the indefatigable zeal of Mr. Darlingle, belonged to the so-called improviser species of Ceylon aloes.

The Arabs watched and listened with amazed eyes as these two Englishmen spoke on and on in the middle of the desert, under a sun that baked one's scalp and made it smoke like meat on the grill.

Then they went overland to the village of Aswan, where Adamson found a complete Arab outfit and hospitality worthy of the times of Abraham and Jacob. From that moment on the scientist and the botanist became the closest of friends.

The one forgot about his Meroë peninsula, the other about his yellow lotus; they longed simply for consulships somewhere in India; their obvious qualifications would certainly not be overlooked by the English government.

They therefore took advantage of the departure of the first caravan, crossed the desert, and got to Cairo. Strangely enough, although the danger was over, Adamson did not forget the vow he had made. He kissed the sacred toes of the colossus of Ozymandias, and when he caught sight of the Pyramids, he saluted them most graciously. At Alexandria the two friends caught the steamer for Malta and soon landed on that English island, the flower of the world, *fior del mondo,* as the Maltese say.

There Darlingle and Adamson divided the work; Adamson wrote an admirable article for the *Malta Times* on the fearless botanist-explorer Darlingle, who had discovered the Darlingle palm at the risk of life and limb and had killed two black reptiles of the cobra-capel species.

The article was illustrated with a woodcut showing the new tree waving its fronds in the air. For his part, Darlingle told the world of Mr. Adamson's dangerous expedition, of how he had ventured above the third cataract, had corrected Bruce's errors, and had killed two crocodiles by means of electricity.

Both reports preceded their authors to London.

The *First Clerk* summoned them immediately to Whitehall and congratulated them on their discoveries.

But that was not all.

They were awarded a pension of five hundred pounds and given consulships at two of the best residences in India.

A reproduction of the Darlingle palm was added to the Zoological Garden collection and the body of the electrocuted crocodile was hung from the ceiling of one of the halls of the Charing Cross gallery.

This is how things in this world happen—or almost happen.

Those who have reflected on mankind will not be surprised by the end of this true story.

Today Adamson represents England in Chandernagor; he has a superb house on the Ganges, six elephants in his stables, ten servants, and a beautiful Creole wife. He lives as luxuriously as a nabob, but very often during those long days when he has nothing to do, he thinks back nostalgically upon the quiet life he had led in his leafy rooms on the island palm. He misses the stirring sight of the amphibian monster; he misses his burning thirst so deliciously quenched with a few drops of water.

Boredom, which is a spiritual thirst, sometimes takes such violent hold of him that he is ready to leave his elephants, his mansion, his wife, and go back to that palm tree for a fortnight.

If the governor grants Adamson a leave of absence, that is precisely what he will do.

Can it be, then, that misfortune is happiness? If that were so, it would explain why one never finds happiness in this world.

Let us think about it.

Physiology of a General Lover

BY FRÉDÉRIC SOULIÉ

TRANSLATED BY D. M. AIRD

FRÉDÉRIC SOULIÉ
1800–47

Soulié was born at Foix, studied in Nantes and Poitiers, and later took up law in Paris. His *Amours françaises* (1824), a collection of verse, passed unnoticed, but his play *Roméo et Juliette* (1828) was such a hit that he was encouraged to devote more time to his creative writing (he was then manager of a sawmill). He tried his hand at fiction, becoming a worthy competitor of Sue and Alexandre Dumas with his historical romances *Le Comte de Toulouse, Vicomte de Béziers, Diane de Chivry,* and the spectacular *Mémoires du diable,* all written during the 1830's. However his shorter fiction, such as "Physiology of a General Lover [Le Lion amoureux]," shows him perhaps in a better light, as a keen observer of Parisian manners, and the intermittences of the heart.

ABOUT SOULIÉ: Harold March, *Frédéric Soulié. Novelist and Dramatist of the* ROMANTIC PERIOD, Yale University Press, 1931.

I. STERNY

The name of "*lion,*" applied to numerous individuals in France, has now become so common it would be useless for us to enter into a long explanation to convince our readers that we do not mean the terrible king of the forest, or the obedient slave of Van Amburgh. This species at one time bore several epithets—those of "*muguet,*"[1] "*homme de bonne fortune,*"[2] "dandy," "fashionable,"—but at the present period the most familiar one is that of "*lion.*"

Why, may we ask, are they called *lions?* Is it because they are the kings of that portion of society termed the *beau monde?* Is it because, like the lion in the fable, they claim the four quarters of the prey that others have seized? I cannot tell, but I will endeavor to sketch the physiology of one, and then I will leave you to guess for yourselves.

The *lion* is in general a sprightly fellow who has passed from the state of infancy to that of manhood. The desire to be thought young has for some years been abandoned, for among them youth is as much despised as old age; in fact the *lion* has *never* been a young man, for there is nothing he despises more than the lovesick youth of eighteen. He is a lover of the fair sex, of wine, and gaming, but remember, that *liking* for woman is not to be called *love,* for this passion admits of no other, while the lion adds to the three mentioned—that is to say, when it is in his power

[1] lily of the valley
[2] man of good fortune

—a strong passion for horses. They, unlike the lover, who is happy in the esteem of her he loves, must attract the attention of all, and have their mistresses for the same end as they have their carriages—to make a display in the eyes of the world. The windows of the Café de Paris are always crowded with them, because this establishment is situated in the most public part of the capital. They make no great pretense of being drunkards, yet they always seem to have emptied a number of bottles, which makes a material difference to the host.

The lions are, for the most part, ignorant of love, although they claim the privilege of speaking in the most familiar terms with all the pretty girls they meet—from the ballet dancer of the opera to the *grisette*, who toils by day to make herself attractive by night. They have a foot in the higher circles of society, and a hand in the lower: are desperate enemies of the worthy mechanic, who, loving, cannot declare his passion, but sits in inward bliss, gazing on the object of his affection. The lion, on the contrary, without feeling the pains and pleasures of the soft, yet bitter passion, is not backward in declaring his love, and practices to best advantage the language of the eyes, which, *he* says, speaks the true feelings of the heart.

But it is too much to bother us this way with discussions. Tell us your story, inventor of news—out with it!—let the drama begin, and let the scenes pass before our eyes. You are fit for nothing else. If you do not amuse us, we will rail against you today; if you please us, the critics will be at you tomorrow. Alas! Since it must be so, let us begin, in the name of all that is good, but I assure you I have lost both my courage and my confidence. So much watching, so much fatigue, and so many hours of study; so much of our heart, and so much of our health, in order to reach a mean corner in the temple of fame; and all this in misery, bearing the buffets of some, and the slanderous tongues of others. No one ever tells us to stop—that our labor has been great. No, no; the poor minstrel has not sung his last lay; he must string his instrument and begin anew.

A few days ago, about the hour of twelve, a lion of fash-

ionable mien descended from his carriage, and entered the
Café de Paris. His appearance, for two good reasons, excited much astonishment: the first, because he was superbly
dressed; the second, because he asked for his breakfast like
a man who was in a hurry and who had some business of
importance to transact. One of his companions looked
searchingly at him—he did not, however, make use of his
eyeglass—and said:

"Where the deuce are you going, Sterny?"

"To a wedding," the young man replied.

"What fool's going to get married?" the interrogator demanded.

At this question a half-dozen heads were lifted up, looks
were exchanged, eyes were raised to the ceiling, and each
person asked himself the question, What fool is going to get
married?

Sterny, on seeing this pantomime, speedily replied, with
an indifferent air:

"Nobody, gentlemen—nobody; it's a private affair."

"And when will you be free?"

"I cannot tell you," Sterny replied, "but I will make my
escape as soon as the church ceremony is over, after which
I shall no longer be required."

"Must you then go?"

"Yes. I am the groom's witness?"

"The groom's witness!" was repeated on all sides.

"Yes," Sterny replied, seeing the astonishment that was
depicted on all countenances. "*Yes*, I am to be the witness
of a godson of my father's. The old fellow has sent me a
letter, asking me to do him the honor, as the good young
man who is about to be married will be pleased, and consider it a great honor. I have told you all, now," Sterny
added, rising. "Finish your breakfasts in peace. I shall be
with you in the evening."

As he was going out, one of his comrades cried:

"Where is your marriage to be held?"

"My faith!" Sterny replied. "You know as much as I do.
I was to be at the bride's, Rue St. Martin, at twelve
o'clock; it is now a quarter past. Good day."

He left; and although this affair was of little or no importance, it was the subject of a somewhat long conversation.

"The old Marquis de Sterny," said the son of a wealthy valet, who had a great respect for hereditary titles, "the old Marquis of Sterny still retains the habits of the ancient nobility, and the office our friend has to perform is of a rather pleasing nature, but, in spite of his great name, he will not be able to appreciate it, and instead of being good and affable to those poor people, making them happy and comfortable, he will appear before them with a haughty and derisive air; nevertheless——"

"Nevertheless," said an eighty-year-old *ex-beau* whose right to the title of lion had often been contested. He was elegantly dressed, very tall, and exceedingly ugly—a kind of wealthy chiropodist who called every woman he met his *petite.* "Nevertheless," he said, "it may be very amusing; pretty women are to be found in the lower, as well as in the higher, ranks of life."

"Pretty," cried a genuine lion, who was a strong supporter of the fine arts, "yes, but they are tradespeople."

"Ah, gentlemen," replied the son of the valet, "the ancient nobility used to hold the working classes in great esteem."

"Poppycock!" replied the lion artiste. "The working classes in former times! Ah, that is easily conceived; young girls, who knew nothing; women, who knew little more, engrossed in the pious duties of the family, for whom the pleasures of the world, the arts, and literature, were far beyond their reach; who looked upon a young man of the court as a serpent of the Book of Genesis: to penetrate into this life, to throw into disorder, to play with the ignorant, to astonish them, as we do children, when we tell them fairy tales, might have been very amusing—and I can easily account for the passion of the Maréchal de Richelieu for Madame Micherlin. But how different the working people of today! Most of them gifted with a sort of education they make use of with incredible impertinence, determined not to be astonished at anything; virtuosi and prodigies, who play the sonatas of Steibelt, and who, condemning Rossini and Meyerbeer, decide in favor of the *Postillon de Lonjumeau;* bluestockings, who read Madame Sand as a study, but who devour Paul de Kock with delight; artists, who get their portraits taken by Monsieur Dubuffe; women, in fact, who give their opinions on the regulation of taxes, and the immortality of the soul. It is truly heart-sickening, and I can easily comprehend Sterny's ennui; the women will be looking at him as they would at a wild beast, and God knows whether they will not measure him with the yardstick of some short-legged counter skipper, who has composed twelve verses in honor of the marriage—who will carve at table—sing during the dessert—dance all night—and be proclaimed the most amiable man of the company."

Thereupon the lion lighted his cigar, sat down upon a chair, pulled another near him, placed it between his legs, and began to look down on the people who were passing. The other lions resorted to occupations of a similar nature, and Léonce Sterny was no longer the topic of conversation.

II. LISE

Young Sterny came to Rue St. Martin. He had no appointment that day, no hunting excursion, no woods to explore, and therefore thought nothing about what pleasure he might have had, but entered the house of Monsieur Laloine, feather dealer, thinking only of performing his father's commission. They were waiting for him when he arrived. He was introduced to the bridegroom and bride, who had not the courage to look at the marquis, then to the parents, and he saw that the young people were all embarrassed when he greeted or spoke to them. He looked around the room, trying to find someone to converse with, but, seeing no likely candidate, retired to a corner of the room. While they were busy preparing for their departure, a young girl entered, calling out:

"I told you I would have my gown changed, before your great marquis arrived."

"Lise!" said Monsieur Laloine reproachfully. The rest of the company was stupefied. The glance that Monsieur Laloine directed toward Sterny, showed his young daughter the indiscretion of her conduct, and she colored up to the eyes; such a blush our lion had never before witnessed.

"Pardon, Father!" she said. "I was not aware that he was here."

Monsieur Laloine then approached Sterny and said, in a parental tone:

"You must excuse her, sir; she is only a child of sixteen, who does not yet know how to behave herself."

Sterny gazed upon the "child" for she was beautiful as an angel, and muttered in astonishment:

"Is she, also, your daughter?"

"Yes, Monsieur le Marquis."

"Ah, well," Sterny said, "have the kindness to introduce me to her, so that I may excuse myself for being so late."

"Never mind," Monsieur Laloine replied; "you must pay no attention to that young miss."

But Sterny was not of that opinion—he had never seen anyone so lovely.

At last they set out for the mayor's; Sterny went into the coach with the bride, her mother, and a male relative. It was fortunate that the distance was not great, for these four were very much embarrassed. The relative, to begin the conversation, said:

"What do you think, sir, of the sugar question?"

Sterny had never given it a thought. He replied coldly:

"Sir, I am in favor of the planters."

"I understand," his interrogator said bitterly, "the progress of national industry frightens you; but the French government will ruin everything."

So this worthy continued speaking till they reached the mayor's, without giving any other person an opportunity of putting in a word. Sterny thought no longer of the beautiful Lise, and began to find his task disagreeable. As he alighted from his carriage, he saw the young girl spring from the coach she had come in, her face glowing with delight. An incident then took place that perhaps gave rise to this little story: Lise took the arm of a tall, rawboned young man who had the honor of being best man, and on being called from behind to go and arrange a flower in the young girl's headdress, which had come in contact with the top of the carriage, she left her escort, who, as he waited for her return, remained motionless, with his arm crooked, ready to do his duty: no sooner had Lise performed her task than someone at the head of the procession called the youthful clown. Sterny was then left by the side of Lise, who, on giving a finishing touch to her friend's coiffure, took hold of the first arm she met, which was the marquis's, saying:

"Come, let's hurry."

On seeing Sterny's countenance Lise gave a faint scream and tried to withdraw her arm, but he prevented her, saying smilingly:

"Since chance has given me your arm, I hope you will allow me to retain it."

"Excuse me, sir," Lise replied, "I am the bridesmaid—I cannot; Monsieur Tirlot would be angry."

"What! Is that Monsieur Tirlot?"

"Yes," Lise replied. "He is the 'man of honor,' and therefore claims the privilege——"

"It is a privilege I intend disputing by sword or pistol," the young lion said, in a significant manner.

Lise looked at him in astonishment and replied in agitation:

"If it must be so, sir—come; I will tell him that such was my desire."

From the way Lise spoke Sterny saw that she had taken what he had said in earnest, and that she was convinced that he would kill the best man if he dared make any objection. Sterny and Lise were the last in the procession, and as soon as they entered the magisterial hall, the young girl said:

"Monsieur Tirlot left me on the road, and if it had not been for Monsieur le Marquis, to whom I am much obliged for his politeness, I should have been forced to come by myself."

As the mayor had not yet arrived, Sterny sat down by the side of Lise. He scarcely knew what to say, and his presence evidently much embarrassed her.

"Such a day as this," Sterny said, "causes the hearts of young people to beat."

Lise remained silent.

"A remarkable day, this."

Still the same silence.

"And such a day will soon be yours, Lise."

"Ah!" she said. "It is very inconsiderate of the mayor to keep us waiting so long."

Sterny saw that his advances were meeting with very little success. He sat for some minutes admiring with pleasure the marvelous regularity of her features, the gracefulness of her white neck, which was neither too long nor too short; and then he felt, for the first time in his life, a pleasure far sweeter than he had ever derived from the society of ladies of fortune. He, however, was not discouraged, and, profiting by her words, he said caressingly:

"You speak very lightly of so worthy a magistrate! You must know that it is he who in reality is to marry your sister. The ceremony at the church is only a form."

At these words Lise raised her eyes and fixed them upon him in astonishment, drew back a little, then looked downward, and said:

"I know, sir, that there are men who think so, but I will never be the wife of anyone who will not wed me in the presence of his Maker."

"Ah!" Sterny thought to himself. "The girl is pious, but she is handsome; therefore I must have another trial."

"But this oath," he said, "will not be of much service to you, for your husband is sure not to do all that you require of him."

"I expect he will," Lise said dryly.

"Ah!" Sterny said, smiling. "You are truly despotic."

"Oh, quite so," she replied with her former carelessness.

"But are you aware that it is very wrong?" Sterny said with a serious expression.

"What is that you say?" she replied, laughing in his face. "You are, at all events, not the person who will have to suffer."

"That will not prevent me from pitying the man you will someday tyrannize over."

"But I am sure he will not complain; that will satisfy me."

"Has he told you so?" Sterny inquired.

"No, but I am sure of it," Lise said.

"He loves you, then?"

"Who?" Lise inquired in astonishment.

"Why," Sterny replied, "your future husband—the slave who will be so happy in his chains."

"Do I know him?"

"You said that you were sure——"

"Ah!" Lise said. "I am sure that I shall love him; I am sure that he will be an honest man; and as I shall be a virtuous woman, I hope he will be happy."

This was said with so much sincerity and truth that Sterny believed in the faith of the young girl, and said, with conviction:

"You are right; he will be so."

"Ah!" Lise said, rising. "Here's the mayor."

The mayor entered, and the ceremony began; oaths were taken on both sides, and all went into the private office to sign their names. When it was Sterny's turn, he did exactly as the others, but on handing the pen to the next person he was surprised to see Lise toss her head with an air of displeasure. Was it because he had signed the "Marquis de Sterny?" But the omission of his title would not have been very agreeable to Prosper Gobillon, who was desirous of having such a distinguished witness. Had he signed before his turn, or taken more space than was necessary? Sterny, who prided himself on etiquette, was at a loss to ascertain what had given rise to the young girl's displeasure, and wished to know how he had offended her. He remained standing for some time in the office, his eyes fixed on Lise, then on the persons who signed after him, who seemed to do exactly as he had done, without offending her. Then it was her turn, and as the clerk handed her a pen, she said in a mocking tone:

"Wait, please, till I take off my glove."

And when it was off, she signed, with a hand perhaps the whitest and smallest that Sterny had ever seen. He then perceived his error, and said to himself:

"The little thing has her points of delicacy. What does a glove more or a glove less signify to the sanctity of an oath, or to the signing of a contract? Nothing, surely; yet it seems that the naked hand uplifted to heaven evinces greater sincerity of heart."

Sterny was lost in reflection until they were preparing to leave. Monsieur Tirlot, best man, and consequently master of the ceremonies, went to tell the coachman to draw up, while Sterny offered his arm to Lise, which she immediately took, without observing that she had forgotten to put on her glove. The young marquis walked by her side, his head inclined, and his eyes fixed on the little white hand resting so softly on his arm. He had never seen such a hand; it was so beautifully made, and her fingers were so exquisitely tapered. His eyes at length fell on a medallion, upon which was a small gold plate, with an inscription that he in vain tried to read.

While he was so occupied, Lise, seemingly content with her own thoughts, began tapping her fingers, and ultimately finished by beating a galop upon the arm of her companion. At this moment Sterny looked at Lise, who, on noticing his attention, gazed at him, her expression full of mockery.

"It appears that mademoiselle is a musician," Sterny said.

"Why, sir?"

"Because," Sterny replied, "you have been playing a most beautiful galop upon my arm."

Lise blushed and withdrew her arm, saying, in a half-audible voice:

"Oh pardon, sir! I have forgotten to put on my glove."

"Just as I forgot to take it off," Sterny replied; "you see that everyone is liable to mistakes."

Lise did not reply. The steps of a carriage were lowered
before her; she mounted them so hurriedly that Sterny got
a glimpse of her foot, so straight, so little, surmounted by
the most delicately formed ankle imaginable! He was about
to place himself beside her, but, seeing her mother, he
turned around and said to the coachman:

"Shut the door, and follow the other carriages."

No sooner was Sterny seated in the carriage with Madame Laloine than she said:

"What have you done with Lise?"

"I saw her into a carriage," Sterny replied.

"With whom?" demanded the prudent mother.

"By herself, Madame."

"How! Alone!" Madame Laloine exclaimed in astonishment.

"Yes, Madame, she unthinkingly made a mistake, and
went into my carriage."

"Ah!" Madame Laloine said. "I don't know what's the
matter with her; ever since this morning she has been as
giddy-headed as anyone could be."

"It is my cabriolet," the young marquis added modestly,
"and there are only two seats. I dared not——"

Madame Laloine thanked Sterny for his kindness, and
after a few moments' silence said:

"I think she will be weary by this time."

Sterny thought within himself that she would not be so
lonely as her mother imagined.

In fact Lise was at first astonished to find herself alone,
but was not sorry, as Sterny's words and looks had embarrassed her. She thought of all that had happened—her
naked arm—of the observations he had made—of her imprudence in going into the carriage of a marquis, and, as
if in answer, she tossed her pretty head, saying:

"Oh, what do I care?"

Now she began to examine the rich silk that ornamented
the carriage; she sat on one side, then on the other, to enjoy the soft flexibility of the cushions; she lifted up one of
the windows, to see how thick the glass was, then, smiling
at the idea of her own ease and comfort, it struck her that

the carriages of the great ladies she had seen in the Champs Elysées were similarly made, and without thinking, as many young people would have done, that she might someday have one of her own, she began to imitate the nonchalance with which those ladies seat themselves in the corner of their equipages, and who look with an air of superiority on the passers-by. Pressing with her white shoulders and fresh cheek the soft silk, which seemed, from its elasticity, to caress her, and pretending that she perceived some of her friends, she bit her underlip in the midst of a smile, moved her hand slightly in one direction, and graciously inclined her head in another. She then thought that if the handsome marquis were on horseback by her side, how graceful her salutation would be! Now she saw Sterny at the carriage door, offering her his hand to help her alight. She started, and blushed at the idea of being caught in such a ridiculous position. On descending, Sterny demanded laughingly:

"Whom were you saluting with so pleasant a look, and so sweet a smile?"

She hid her face in shame and appeared agitated. When she entered the church, Sterny plainly saw that she paid little attention to the ceremony that was going on. Lise neither gave a side glance at the countenance of the husband or the peculiarly embarrassed deportment of the fair spouse, nor did she watch with curiosity to see if the ring passed the second joint, which indicates submission. She was praying; her heart was struck with remorse, and she was fervently asking God to pardon her mistakes. Her prayer was answered, for at last she rose, evincing both fortitude and happiness. Sterny looked at her in surprise, as she approached him, saying, in a changed tone from that in which she had previously spoken to him:

"This wedding must be very tiresome to you, sir."

"Tiresome!" Sterny replied. "Why should it be?"

"Because it is neither in accordance with your habits nor your pleasures, but it is now nearly over."

Till then, Sterny, in spite of the solicitations of Prosper Gobillon and Monsieur Laloine, had determined to leave as

soon as he had signed his name at the church, but what
Lise said had the same effect as telling him good-by. Having no relish for leaving in that manner, he replied:

"I assure you, Mademoiselle, that it is not at all tiresome
to me, but if my presence is so to you, you must scold your
brother-in-law. It was for *him* that I came."

Lise did not reply but hid herself among her young companions, and Sterny went forward to sign his name.

"Look, look!" said a young girl, touching Lise on the
shoulder. "He has taken off his glove this time."

Sterny, who heard the exclamation, lifted his head, and
his eyes met those of Lise. The young girl felt, as by instinct, that there was something between her and the marquis that ought not to be, and so much did this thought
afflict her that, when it was her turn to sign, her eyes were
full of tears and her hand trembled. And when her mother,
who was by her side, asked her what the matter was, she
replied:

"Oh, nothing! It was just an idea that crossed my mind."
Then, profiting by her mother's alarm, she took hold of her
arm, saying, with the greatest simplicity:

"I must go home, Mother, in the same carriage with you."

"Yes, you shall, my poor Lise," the good lady said, em-
bracing her.

Léonce, at this moment, struck with the beautiful expression of the young girl's countenance, said to himself:

"Ah! I shall go to the dinner, and nothing shall prevent
me from dancing with that beautiful creature this evening."

Lise looked searchingly at the handsome marquis, and
her bosom heaved as he got into his carriage, which soon
afterward rolled rapidly away from her.

III.   THE MEDAL

Seated in the coach beside her mother, she, for the first
time since morning, felt herself at ease, and began speak-

ing of the beautiful outfit she had for the ball. In the midst
of the conversation, on putting her hand to her throat, she
cried:

"Oh, Mamma! I've lost my medal! Oh dear! Oh dear! Yes,
I had it, I'm sure."

"Perhaps," her mother said, "you dropped it at the
mayor's, either in the church or the carriage."

"Oh," Lise exclaimed, "I hope not!"

"Why?" the mother said. "The marquis will find it and
bring it to us."

"Is he coming again?"

"He promised he would," the mother replied.

Lise ceased speaking and became pensive. She thought
no longer of her handsome gown, her pretty shoes, and
kid gloves, or of her beauty, or the effect her appearance
would produce in the ballroom, but she was of that age
and of that character when sad thoughts are of short dura-
tion, for she had scarcely reached home when she threw
aside her vague fears, crying:

"Ah, but no; I must be happy today."

And without further reflection she determined to amuse
herself at the expense of the handsome marquis, for he was
only a young man, like those who were around her.

As for Sterny, as soon as he was alone, his resolution of
returning began to shake. Notwithstanding the good opinion he had of himself, he thought that there was very little
chance of making a conquest of the charming Lise, for today could not, for him, bring a tomorrow. What excuse
could he find, after the nuptials, for being received at the
feather merchant's? And if he were given the gate, what a
fine fix would he be in! It would be much better for him
to write a note, begging to be excused, and to dine at the
Café de Paris, instead of going to the Cadran Bleu, where
the nuptial feast was to be held.

While Sterny reasoned thus, the image of Lise was ever
before his eyes, and it was so beautiful, so graceful, so full
of charms. Who could describe the sweet thoughts that
flashed through his mind as he reflected on that rare beauty?
To excite her love for him, to take her from her family, to

fight with one of her brothers, to be subjected to a lawsuit, to be publicly spoken of in the newspapers, to be condemned for seduction by the courts and pardoned by the people, to whom the marvelous beauty of the girl would plead a sufficient excuse for committing the crime, to gain in this conquest a renown that would vex and shame his companions—this appeared to him very tempting; but as soon as he had measured the obstacles and counted the difficulties, he banished the idea, not because it was immoral, but impractical. At length he decided to stay home and abandon the project, when he saw on the opposite cushion a gold medal attached to a chain of plaited hair. He took it up, recognized it as the one that Lise had worn around her neck, and read the following inscription:

What we wish, we can do

"Well!" the lion said to himself. "If this motto is true, I must succeed."

In a state of indecision he reached his own house, where he found five of his friends warmly discussing the impropriety of allowing government horses to compete in the races of the Champ-de-Mars.

The arrival of Sterny put an end to the discussion. On his appearing the tall dandy, Lingart, of whom we have previously spoken, cried out, burying his chin in his cravat:

"Ah! Ah! Monsieur Aymar."

"Well," said Aymar de Rabut, the lion artiste, "I lose."

"How, in heaven's name," cried Marinet, the son of the valet, "do you make wagers with that tall stock-jobber? You are well aware of his instinct for making profitable bargains and wagers, and that if he is concerned in what appears a bad speculation, he is sure to come off the winner."

"Yes, it is true I am somewhat lucky," Lingart said, screwing his mustachios in seeming contentment.

"What is all this about?" Sterny demanded.

"Only," Lingart said, "that we dine at the Rocher de Cancale, and that the dinner is to be at the expense of Aymar de Rabut."

"You have laid a wager, then?" Sterny said, pricking up

his ears like a war horse on hearing the sound of a trumpet.

"Yes," Aymar de Rabut replied. "I do not know how it was, but for more than an hour I maintained that the marriage would be tiresome to you, that you would be disgusted with men, women, and children, and it turns out that I was the one who wagered that you'd stay to both the dinner and the ball. Lingart bet that you wouldn't and that we'd have you with us tonight."

"But I tell you," Marinet cried, "that if you were going to sue Lingart for a hundred louis, and he did not wish to pay them, he would prove to you that you owe him ten thousand francs, as plainly as two and two are four."

"Nonsense," exclaimed Lingart. "Do you think it's so plain that two and two makes four?"

At this remark they all looked at each other, as if Lingart had been guilty of a piece of foolery, but he added, with an arrogance that surprised them all:

"Well, see if you can prove to me that two and two makes four."

"This savors of buffoonery," Marinet replied.

"Well," Lingart said, "if this is buffoonery, I'll bet twenty-five thousand louis that none of you can prove to me that two and two makes four."

"What!" said Aymar de Rabut. "You require proof?"

He stopped, and Lingart replied triumphantly:

"Well, what do you say?"

He waited for an answer and, receiving none, said haughtily:

"Go and order our dinner, and——"

"And," Sterny said, interrupting him, "let it be a splendid one; Lingart is doing the honors."

"How do you figure that?" said the speculator.

"Because Aymar has won. I return to dinner, and I intend to go to the ball."

"You simply want to make me lose," said Lingart.

At these words Sterny reflected, and said:

"I cancel the bet."

"Why?" asked Lingart.

"Because when I entered," Sterny replied, "I had not decided, nor do I know whether I should yet have done so, if you had not spoken of it."

"And what has made you decide so suddenly?"

"Nothing," Sterny replied. "Only I cannot do otherwise."

"Why so?" Lingart demanded.

"Ah," Sterny replied laughingly, "this is as difficult to explain as it is to prove that two and two makes four."

"Nevertheless, you at first doubted it."

"You are becoming tiresome, Lingart," Sterny said, "with your discussions."

"He is practicing for the Chamber of Deputies," Marinet said with a smile.

Lingart, who had given thirty thousand francs for three votes in the last election, bit his lips, shrugged his shoulders, and allowed the conversation to turn upon something else. At last a debutante of the opera became the theme of conversation. Aymar spoke of her beautiful feet and graceful shoulders, while Marinet praised her bright eyes and fine expression. Sterny had seen her the previous evening, had admired her beauty as well as her performance, but now that he drew a comparison between her and Lise, he saw nothing pretty in the former, while the latter filled him with delight. What would his companions say on seeing this paragon of perfection? What would be their exclamations on seeing one so perfect in form, so naturally graceful? The feather merchant's daughter became every instant more beautiful in Sterny's eyes, and, by a strange freak of his mind, he began to repent of the idea he had formed of seducing her. Six o'clock struck; Sterny rose, bade his companions good night, and hurried to the Cadran Bleu.

IV. THE DINNER

Love is a strange passion—sudden—irresistible—that strikes the heart at the sight of an unknown being—a strong passion that penetrates the soul with imperceptible progression —a feeling that absorbs all others, that changes the dim eye to a bright one, the uncouth voice to the softest notes of music—that, in fact, blinds the enamored party, for he can see no imperfections.

When Sterny entered, no one had arrived but the newly-weds and Monsieur Laloine, who were superintending the arrangements for the festival. Prosper wished Monsieur Laloine to remain with the marquis, but Sterny did not want to stand on ceremony, but to attend to their affairs as if he were not present. Perhaps you may ask, Is it actually Léonce Sterny, a lion who knows well the advantages of arriving late, who arrives early and sits down to the table like a shopkeeper or a literary man when invited to the houses of the rich? Indeed it is really Léonce Sterny, one of the most furious of his band. But do you know what he did in the host's absence? He went to the table, read the place cards, in order to find out where his seat was, and, seeing that it was between that of Madame Laloine and another lady, unknown to him, he changed his for Monsieur Tirlot's, who had been destined to sit by the side of Lise. Picture to yourself the handsome marquis, trembling with fear, like a child when putting his finger in a bowl of cream, for fear he would be discovered; look at him turning suddenly toward the wall, as the waiter enters, pretending to admire an old engraving of Æneas carrying his father, Anchises, then, as soon as the servant disappears, finishing his expert maneuver.

He succeeded, however, and for some time was very uneasy about the trick he had played. Monsieur Laloine entered, and went to see if the seats and place cards were properly arranged, but as soon as Sterny saw his intention, he went up to him, spoke about ostrich feathers, contrasted them with those of peacocks and other birds, and Laloine, taking for granted that all was right, was delighted with the marquis, who laughed and chatted, who asked for snuff, found it excellent, and complimented him on his good arrangements and better taste. A carriage arrives. The marquis sends Monsieur Laloine to give his hand to the ladies.

Laloine runs to the door, finds that it is a lady and gentleman who ask for a private dining room, returns, and Sterny makes a long rigmarole speech upon the morality of private dining rooms.

What is the matter with him? what does he want? I told you before that love is incompatible with reason, for, behold our lion putting himself to a great deal of trouble—for what, you may ask? Why, to be seated near a little girl.

Success gained by stratagem atones, in the eyes of many, for the worst of actions; then Sterny should be excused, for he succeeded. The company arrived. Sterny stood at the door that opened upon the dining room, assured that Lise would not pass without speaking. At last she entered with her mother and sister, when the former said kindly:

"What, Monsieur le Marquis, so soon?"

Sterny replied, looking meaningly in Lise's face, said:

"One fault in a day is quite enough."

The countenance of Lise crimsoned; she felt the reproach and retired, displeased, into a corner of the room, determined to have as little as possible to say to the marquis.

A somewhat amusing scene took place as the seats were being taken around the table. Sterny, who knew his, went to install himself behind his chair, while Lise was searching for hers on the other side.

"Over there," Prosper cried, pointing to the side where Sterny was, but on observing the marquis he appeared much surprised.

Prosper then exchanged looks with Monsieur Laloine, who bit his lips in a manner that seemed to say:

"My son-in-law is certainly a fool."

On the other hand, Madame Laloine, who had calculated upon being by the side of the marquis, looked at Monsieur Tirlot with an air of astonishment, while he, proud of the honor that had been conferred upon him, sat down in seeming delight. Lise advanced timidly, scarcely knowing what to do, for she had seen the exchanging of looks and shared in the general confusion. As for Sterny, his eyes fixed upon the ceiling, he saw nothing, and appeared totally ignorant of what was going on. His embarrassment, however, terminated, for he heard Monsieur Laloine say to his daughter:

"Come, Lise, go and sit down."

The manner in which these words were pronounced revealed a forced resignation to Gobillon's awkwardness. While Sterny moved his chair to make room for Lise, she greeted him so dryly that he guessed she was aware that it was not her brother-in-law who had made the mistake. From the first sentence he said, he foresaw that Lise had determined to answer him only in monosyllables, but he had two hours before him, and that was more than was necessary to make her change her resolution. At first he left her to herself, and directed his attention to the fat gentleman who was seated on the other side of her, he being no other than the honorable silk mercer who had entertained him in the morning with his long speech on the sugar question. Sterny renewed the discussion, when each of the opponents was obliged to speak either by inclining before or behind Lise, who at last became so annoyed that she could not keep from fidgeting and thus revealing her impatience, but Sterny had no pity: he tormented his opponent to such a degree that Monsieur Laloine, seeing their conversation grow so animated, exclaimed:

"What have you been talking about, gentlemen?"

"Beetroot and sugar cane," Lise replied sullenly.

"Ah!" Monsieur Laloine exclaimed, delighted that the question was of so innocent a nature.

Sterny, imagining that it was the moment for attack, addressed his companion:

"Indeed, sir, I am afraid that our conversation has been tiresome to mademoiselle; we will resume our discussion some other time."

"Willingly," replied the mercer, who perceived that he had allowed the first course to be nearly over without touching anything, and who appeared willing to make up for lost time.

Lise, however, made no reply, and the silk mercer said:

"Is your mother not right, Mademoiselle Lise, in saying that men have lost all their gallantry? Look at the two of us, sitting beside a pretty young girl, and we can find nothing better to speak of than politics. But for me, there is an excuse; I am a father, and have forgotten all. You, sir, though being a young gentleman, ought to have many fine things to say."

Then find something, you fool! thought Sterny, who, seeing Lise, scarcely knew what to say. At last he offered her a glass of wine, which she accepted with thanks. A silence ensued.

"There now!" the lion said to himself. "I am becoming as stupid as a Negro. It's high time to start the attack."

"It is very strange, Mademoiselle," Sterny said, "it is truly unfortunate, that, having had the honor of seeing you only twice, I should have unwittingly displeased you three or four times."

"Me, sir!" Lise replied in astonishment.

"Yes, you. First of all, this morning, for being late; then at the mayor's, for not taking off my glove; and here, perhaps," he added whisperingly, "for arriving too soon, and——"

"And——" Lise said, looking him in the face.

"And," Sterny added with a winning smile, "for stealing Monsieur Tirlot's seat."

Lise blushed, and smiled; she was pleased, for flattery has momentary gratifications even for the most stoic. The marquis had played a trick, in schoolboy fashion, to be near her, and that afforded her pleasure. Lise did not think of the marquis's purposes, nor of the end he had in view, for she was too innocent to entertain an idea of seduction. Shortly after, however, the smile that graced her countenance gave way to sudden embarrassment, and she said to herself:

"He intends to amuse himself with me."

"I see very plainly," Sterny said, "that I have displeased you, in taking this seat."

"Oh, sir," Lise exclaimed, tossing her head, "it matters little to me who took it."

Sterny laughed, then said, rather impertinently:

"I don't believe it—I am sure you would prefer Monsieur Tirlot by your side."

Lise remained silent.

"Is Monsieur Tirlot a relation of yours?" Sterny asked.

"No, sir."

"Is he a friend?"

"No, sir," she again replied, coldly.

"He is, then, one of Prosper's?"

"Yes, sir."

"So much the better," Sterny said, "for Monsieur Tirlot, knowing that I am Prosper's friend, will more readily forgive the error I have committed."

"Oh!" said Lise. "You are not Prosper's friend."

"Why not? He is a young man I like very much, and would willingly render him any service that is in my power."

"I don't doubt it," Lise replied, "but that's not what I mean."

"I am also sure," Sterny said, "that he respects me very much."

"I am sure of it, but still, you know that you are not friends."

"Why?" Sterny demanded.

"Because," Lise replied, "you are Monsieur le Marquis de Sterny, and he is Prosper Gobillon, feather merchant."

"It is very wrong of you to say so," Sterny said.

"Why?" Lise demanded.

"Is it not as much as to say that the title I bear makes me proud, haughty, and impertinent?"

"Ah, sir."

"Is it not saying," Sterny added, "that I do not render justice to the honor and worth of those individuals who have not a similar title? It is almost enough to make me regret having been brought up in what is called the higher circles, for you seem to assert we no longer live in an age when worth is due to merit."

Ah, ah, lion, what have you made of your crest of nobility? What, what! Speaking freely the sentiments of *Le Constitutionnel,* and as if you meant them? Where now are your friends to laugh at you, as you would have done at them, if they had uttered such a sentiment?

Lise, from the serious manner in which Sterny had spoken, said, in an affected tone:

"I thank you, sir, on Prosper's account, for what you have said; I am sure it will make him happy when I tell him."

"Oh," Sterny replied, "Prosper has known me for a very long time. We knew each other in childhood, and he is not like you—he does not take me for a dandy or a lion."

"A lion! What is that?" Lise said laughingly.

"Oh," Sterny replied, "lions are beings of this world who imagine themselves wise and witty because they laugh at all others, despise everything that is not suited to their taste, and have no other occupation save that of doing nothing."

"Ah," Lise said, "I know what you mean, but I pray you to understand that I have not so bad an opinion of you."

"Not *quite* so bad," Sterny said, "but not very favorable."

"I cannot tell you—I do not know," Lise said hesitatingly.

"Ah, you must give me an answer; do give me your opinion of me."

Lise hesitated, then, looking Sterny in the face with an expression of infantile malice, said:

"Well, I will do so, if you will tell me the reason why you took Monsieur Tirlot's seat."

Sterny was somewhat embarrassed at this demand. He hesitated, then replied:

"Indeed, I cannot tell you."

At these words Lise burst into a fit of laughter, which drew the eyes of all the company upon her.

"What is the matter with you, Lise?" Monsieur Laloine shouted out.

"It is," Lise said, still laughing, "because Monsieur le Marquis——"

"Oh!" Sterny whispered, full of fear that Lise would relate the trick he had played. "For heaven's sake do not betray me!"

"What is the matter?" was again shouted out.

"Oh, nothing at all—an idea," she replied.

"Come, come, Lise!" the mother exclaimed, frowning on her daughter for her indiscretion.

"Let her laugh," Monsieur Laloine said, "it becomes her age—she will be serious soon enough."

Lise had already become so, and was reflecting on her conduct, when Sterny said to her in a low voice:

"I thank you for having kept my secret."

"Oh, it is nothing."

"Still, I went to a lot of trouble." Then he related, in an amusing manner, his fears of being caught when the best man entered, and how he had diverted the attention of her father.

Lise listened, half laughing, half vexed, and finally said:

"And you did all this without being able to give a reason."

"I could do so, but I dare not give it to you," Sterny replied with emotion.

"What! To me?"

"Yes—to you."

"You are making fun of me."

"Do you want me to tell you?"

"I don't know; that depends upon what you have to say. Ah, no," she added, "I don't want to know."

She guessed all, but that was not enough for our lion; he wanted to speak, for he enjoyed holding her attention.

"This morning, when——"

"Stop, stop," Lise exclaimed, interrupting him. "Monsieur Tirlot is going to sing."

"He is a ridiculous fellow, that Monsieur Tirlot," Sterny said, displeased at being interrupted when about to begin his declaration.

"Ridiculous!" Lise said. "Why so, Monsieur?"

"Because I don't like him," Sterny replied.

"Why not?"

Sterny smiled and said, "First, because he is the best man and had the privilege of walking with you this morning."

"It seems to me," Lise said, in laughing, "that he did not profit much by it."

"And then, because his seat was next to yours."

"And he has taken good care to keep it."

"And lastly," Sterny added, "because he is going to dance with you first."

"He has forgotten to ask me," Lise replied.

"In that case, I must have that pleasure. I should like to deprive him of everything."

"How! Deprive him of everything?" Lise inquired.

"Yes," Sterny said gaily. "I delight in robbing him, and if I were by his side, I would eat from his plate, and drink the wine he had poured out for himself."

"Ah, poor Monsieur Tirlot!" said Lise, pleased by the marquis's attentions.

"We are going to dance the first quadrille together, aren't we, Lise?"

"I suppose I must," said the young girl, smiling.

"As for this Monsieur Tirlot," Sterny added, elated at his success, "I should like even to rob him of his song."

"That would be difficult," Lise said. "Look, he is going to begin."

"Never mind," Sterny whispered, "I'll compete for the prize."

"Indeed!" Lise said in astonishment.

"You'll see!"

Monsieur Tirlot began. He sang four verses, which were tolerably good, both as to measure and rhyme, and which introduced Monsieur and Madame Laloine, and the newly-weds, Monsieur and Madame Gobillon. Monsieur Tirlot triumphed, for he received the loud acclamations of all present. Lise was highly delighted, and while applauding, she repented of having deprived him of his *contredanse*. Sterny, however, was in a good mood; he gently touched Lise's elbow, saying, "Announce that I am going to sing."

Lise rose, held forth her pretty hand, and everyone fell silent, but when she said that Monsieur le Marquis was about to sing, all were astonished, and showed their delight at his condescension.

"Pardon, ladies and gentlemen," Sterny said on rising, "it is not a song; it is only a verse, to complete the spirited *chanson* of Monsieur Tirlot."

Monsieur Tirlot leaned forward, and there was a great round of applause. Then Sterny looked at Monsieur and Madame Laloine and sang:

> *The sacred right to make men glad*
> *Is so sublime, it prompts God's will*

Then, glancing at Prosper Gobillon and his wife:

> *And like yourselves, when two are wed,*
> *With happiness your task is filled.*

At Monsieur and Madame Laloine:

> *But still the right of blessedness*
> *For you has not outdone its share.*

Then, turning toward Lise:

> *For, seeing Lise, we all admit*
> *She'll make a bride beyond compare.*

Oh, Marquis, what a disgrace! Improvising verse at the table, and at the nuptials of a feather merchant's daughter. Oh, lion! where now are your haughty look, your head raised in pride, and your lip bearing the expression of scorn? Sterny had no time to think, for scarcely had he finished his verse when the room resounded with *bravos* and expressions of delight. Lise, who did not expect such a conclusion, blushed, and hid her face by bending her head, and Madame Laloine, in going to kiss her daughter, said:

"It is true, Monsieur Tirlot, you forgot my Lise."

Monsieur Laloine stretched his hand to Sterny, saying with warmth of heart:

"Thank you, Monsieur le Marquis, thank you."

The mother expressed her gratitude to Sterny, and congratulations were heard on all sides. At last the company rose, and Monsieur Gobillon cried out:

"To the hall—the ball is about to begin."

Sterny offered his arm to Lise; she took it, and he felt that her hand trembled. She was confused and embarrassed, yet she seemed to be pleased.

"You are not angry with me, Lise," Sterny said, "on account of the verse I sang?"

"Oh no," she said softly. "It made my father and mother so happy."

"And how did you like it?"

"Oh, very much; it was very pretty," Lise replied, casting her eyes downward.

She then begged to be excused for a moment, as she wished to speak to a few of her friends who had come to the ball, and who had just been told the reason of the applause that had shaken the walls of the Cadran Bleu. As Lise approached they demanded:

"Is it true that the handsome marquis composed a verse on you?"

If the question had been asked in ridicule, most probably Lise would have denied it, but the "handsome marquis" was pronounced with so much envy she replied with affectation:

"Yes, it is true."

"It seems you have made a conquest of him," said one of nature's less-favored children.

"Why not?"

"And, without doubt, he has made one of you?" another demanded.

"Who knows?" Lise said, thinking that her friends were very impertinent.

"And," said another, "in order to refuse dancing with him, I will go and engage myself for the whole evening."

"Oh, don't bother; these blue-bloods never dance."

"Sometimes they do," said Sterny, who had stealthily approached them. He held out his hand to Lise, saying with a respectful air:

"Mademoiselle has not forgotten her promise of dancing the first quadrille with me."

"No, sir, no," Lise muttered, holding out her hand. It was trembling, and Sterny pressed it.

V. THE BALL

Sterny, hurried, as it were, from one step to another, by the charms of Lise, and perhaps delighted with his own success, hadn't time to reflect on all he had done, for, had he had but a moment of leisure, he would have been astounded and frightened to think how much he had deviated from his usual habits.

The orchestra gave the signal for the dance, and Sterny, with Lise by his side, took his place. She was pretty; yes, beautiful as the angels seen in dreams, and at that moment, trembling beside him, she seemed lovelier than ever. Sterny wished to speak, but his voice faltered; Lise tried to reply but her voice faltered too. They went through the dance this way, and not until he led her to her seat did it strike him that he was about to be separated from her. Then he whispered:

"Do you waltz?"

"Oh no, sir, no!" Lise replied with evident pleasure. "But won't you dance with anyone else?"

"Only with you, Lise," said Sterny.

"At least with my sister—please!"

"With the bride? You are right; thank you for reminding me."

"Thank you for consenting," Lise replied with a complacent smile.

Sterny left her with her mother and went into another room. Despite himself he was happy. And for what? For having disturbed the mind of a young girl! Poor triumph for a man who had caused the wealthiest and most artful women to tremble under his gaze. Don't ask Sterny why he was happy; he would not be able to tell you, for that strange emotion was as new to him as it was to Lise, and he never thought of examining it, or struggling against it. He tried to stay away from the room where Lise was, but unconsciously he went to the door and looked in. She was dancing, but her heart was not in it; her head was slightly inclined, and from time to time she cast a furtive glance. Whom was she seeking? Sterny was afraid that it was not he, but when she saw that he was present, she no longer looked about. He felt happy at seeing this—a happiness so great that it made him fearful. He asked himself why, and blushed.

"Ah," he said to himself, "I'm getting childish! How ridiculous! Devil take me, if I am not tipsy. It's not possible."

And to assure himself that he was not the sort of man who would allow a passion for a child to govern him, he again bent his looks on Lise. She was dancing with a fine young man, as handsome as our lion, and who spoke to her with an air of ease and politeness. At this sight a revolution took place in Sterny's bosom and he felt assured that nothing could give him an advantage over his rival. This chagrin increased when he saw an expression of happiness and tranquillity beaming in the countenance of Lise. The poor girl, on finding that Sterny's look was fixed upon her, felt happy and proud—an ecstasy she no longer dreaded, for he was no longer by her side; the contact of his hand, the sound of his voice, no longer made her tremble. A strange doubt pierced the heart of Sterny. He said to himself:

"Is it possible that this girl can be of the *arrière boutique?* Ah! Truly, this is too ambitious, my fair one! You are handsome, but your pretensions are somewhat extravagant."

As these thoughts passed through Sterny's mind, his countenance took on an expression of haughtiness and disdain, and Lise, having glanced at him, was so frightened she turned pale, and her eyes, which were fixed on him, seemed to say:

"Oh, what is the matter? What have I done to you?"

She no longer heard the fine compliments of her dancing partner and made three successive mistakes in the dance.

Sterny saw everything, and wondered if this was a trick. He had no inclination to become the dupe of a tradesman's daughter; therefore, as soon as the dance was finished, he assumed a confident and indifferent air and approached Lise and her mother.

"Excuse me," he said to Madame Laloine, without looking at Lise, "please forgive my thoughtlessness, Madame. On my way home I found this chain. It must belong to one of your guests, and I had completely forgotten about it."

At the words "one of your guests," Lise gave Sterny a look that seemed to say, "Didn't you know it was mine?"

Madame Laloine thanked him, then said to Lise, "You see, I was right, Monsieur le Marquis did bring it to you."

"Ah, it belongs to mademoiselle," Sterny said coldly, in presenting it with a haughty air.

"Yes," Lise said, looking at Sterny as if to say, "Am I, then, a child?"

"Give it to me, Lise," the mother said. "I will put it around your neck."

"Later," Lise said impatiently, and while rolling it up in her handkerchief she became pale, and her lips trembled. Sterny, satisfied with his maneuver, said, with affected politeness:

"Mademoiselle has not forgotten that she is to dance a galop with me?"

"I do not know," Lise replied with a melancholy air, "but if Mamma wishes . . ."

"With Monsieur le Marquis? . . . Certainly, certainly," said Madame Laloine.

The musicians began, and Lise gave her hand to Sterny.

"Why," Sterny said as they were walking, "why did you not put your chain around your neck? I suppose it is a keepsake."

"Ah yes," she replied, casting her eyes up to heaven, "it serves to make me mindful."

"And," Sterny asked, "do you believe in the inscription 'What we wish, we can do'?"

"Yes, sir, until now I have had reason to, and," she added, "I trust I always shall. But we are not dancing, sir."

Sterny threw one arm around the lovely girl and took hold of the hand in which she held her talisman. They danced then—he, devouring her with his looks, and she,

with downcast eyes and a melancholy expression. Suddenly
a tear splashed down her cheek. Sterny, on observing this,
felt uneasy and led her to a corner of the room, saying,
"Have I offended you, Mademoiselle?"

"No, sir, no!"

"But why are you weeping?"

"I am not weeping, sir."

"Come now, Mademoiselle," said Sterny with an air of
frankness, "I don't know of anything I have said or done
to offend you, but if I have, I sincerely beg your pardon,
for, I assure you, such was never my intention."

"Oh, sir, pay no attention to what I say or do. You must
know that, from childhood, being always weak and suffering, I have been much indulged, and among other weaknesses that I have is a foolish susceptibility."

"But how have I wounded that susceptibility?"

"Oh, do not ask me, sir," Lise said, then she added, in
apparent trouble, "Let us continue the dance, I pray you."

The galop ended, and Sterny conducted Lise, as before,
to her mother's side. At that moment Monsieur Tirlot came
to claim his privilege of dancing with the bridesmaid, but
she said:

"Not yet, Monsieur Tirlot; I've caught a chill."

Sterny looked at Lise; she was pale, and her lips trembled
convulsively. Her mother, on seeing her, was much alarmed,
and said:

"Come with me, my child."

The poor girl left the room, leaning on her mother's arm.

"What is the matter with her?" Sterny demanded, addressing himself to Monsieur Tirlot.

"Good gracious!" Tirlot said with a pitiful look. "Always
the same thing—those frightful palpitations of the heart.
The least fatigue hurts her, and a little excitement is enough
to kill her."

"To kill her!" Sterny said to himself. "And what have
I done? When I looked at her with disdain—when I told
her mother of the medallion I knew belonged to her, and
which, although she knew I had it, she never asked for!
Perhaps I wounded her sensitive heart, and turned her joy

to misery. Ah, poor girl, poor child! Oh, if I had thought so! How foolish I've been! how unmanly my conduct!"

To play with the vanity of a little seamstress might be very amusing, but to hurt the feelings of such a lovely child was truly criminal. Sterny heaped curses on his own head and kept accusing himself of being a brute. Thus it was with the purest motives of friendship that he remained at the door of the room where Lise had taken refuge with her mother. Soon afterward she left the room. She was still pale but appeared calm and resigned, and when she saw the alarmed looks of Sterny, she raised her hand gently to her bosom, showing him the gold medallion, which had just been suspended around her neck; the gesture signified "What we wish, we can do."

The smile that accompanied this movement was so sweet, so resigned, that it touched his heart. Lise was then suffering, and had suffered much, and all for him—all on his account. He wanted to beg her pardon, but, as she would no longer dance, he had no opportunity of doing so, and therefore showed his contrition by appearing before her with a sad and thoughtful countenance. At last he became restless; the people who surrounded him were tiresome—not, as he might have considered, the next day, on account of their ridiculous appearance, but because they looked at him as if they penetrated the secrets of his heart. This idea at length so influenced him that he was upon the point of leaving, but he could not think of going away without first obtaining the pardon of that weak and gentle creature whom he had caused to suffer so much. He went to Madame Laloine, and said with a grave air:

"If I had been but an ordinary guest at this nuptial feast, Madame, I should have considered myself at liberty to retire without ceremony; but I was Prosper's witness, and I pray you to accept my thanks for having admitted into your family an honest man, who, it may almost be said, belonged to mine."

"I thank you, sir," Madame Laloine said with emotion, while Lise looked at him with tenderness, "I thank you, sir, for it is only your friendship for Prosper that could have induced you to make use of such flattering words to people as humble as ourselves."

"I assure you, Madame, that from the kindness I have experienced, you and your family shall ever have a claim to my esteem and gratitude."

In saying this he turned toward Lise and bowed, without casting his eyes upon her. He did not then see the radiant smile that lighted her countenance, but he saw that she made an involuntary movement with her hand, as if to take his, and to thank him.

He left, and did not look back until he had reached the other end of the room. Lise had her hand resting upon her bosom, and was looking after him; he fixed his eyes upon her, and she did not withdraw hers from him. They thus looked at each other for some time, both forgetting where they were—both trying to read each other's heart. Madame Laloine spoke to her daughter, who seemed to be awaking from a dream, but, before answering, a slight movement of the head had, as it were, said to Sterny:

"Farewell, and thank you!"

VI. THE DEATH OF LISE

The lion left; he was half mad, confused, and stunned. He tried to rally, but couldn't, for the image of Lise was before him, saying in all her candor and purity, "Wretch! Why such behavior? Why insult one you know to be good and holy, because she smiled at her own happiness?" Sterny became restless in his carriage; he looked around to see if there were yet a trace left of Lise; but no; he once had the medallion, but without being asked—to be impertinent —he had returned it to her mother.

In a state of fury, cursing himself for his own stupidity, he arrived at the club of the lions. He hesitated, then went upstairs, saying to himself:

"If that booby, Lingart, makes one foolish remark, I'll

strike him!" He then sat down at the gambling table, lost
five hundred louis, offended all present by his ill-temper,
entered his own house at daybreak, and thought as little of
the money he had lost as of his last mistress.

"I shall see Lise again," he said. "I must see her—but
how?"

However, when a few hours of rest had calmed his mind,
he thought more seriously, perhaps, than he had ever done
before. He was in love—he felt it; he was not ashamed of
his passion, but he was afraid of it. To seduce Lise would
be base and ungenerous. "For," he said to himself, "she
would love me, if I wished; she would love me, I am sure,
and her love would be so ardent that, if I did not marry
her, I might break her heart. That must not be! Well," he
added, "I remember that when I was a child, and very ill,
my mother took me to church, and, placing me on my knees
before the Virgin Mary, made me repeat after her, 'Holy
Virgin, who witnessed the death of thy Son, save me for
the sake of my mother!' That image I supplicated has been
graven on my heart as something sacred and ineffaceable,
and of which I have never spoken, lest I might be insulted.
Lise will be to me like a keepsake—a celestial image, of
which I had a glimpse, and whose form I will keep in the
sanctuary of my soul! Ah, if Lise were not what she is, if
she were a queen, I would risk my life to win her; I would
dare everything, in thinking of the words she carried near
her heart, 'What we wish, we can do.' But she is a feather
merchant's daughter, and I cannot stoop so low! No. I must
think no more of her. No! No!"

To accomplish this end, Sterny went to the Opéra, and
with that success that always attended his efforts made a
conquest of the dancer who had excited the admiration of
his companions. One evening, when seated in one of the
boxes of the Théâtre Français, he recognized two women
who were staring at him: one was Prosper's wife—the other,
Lise.

"Look at those girls in the box across from us!" said the
dancer. "Do you know them?"

"No," Sterny said, blushing while telling the lie.

"Then why are you sitting in back of the box? I think you are afraid."

"Away with your jealousies!" Sterny said, and, looking out of his box, he saw Lise, who was obviously talking about him. Suddenly she lifted her head and, meeting his gaze, she withdrew her eyes, being apparently much agitated. Sterny did not greet her, but rose to leave.

"If you leave my box, I'll make a scene," the dancer said angrily.

He was hesitating whether to go to Lise, when his mistress added:

"If you go to her box, I'll scratch her eyes out."

Sterny was fit to be tied, but kept his temper. But when he took her home, he broke everything he could lay hands on, for, as he would not beat her, he was determined to do her all the harm he could by destroying her belongings, and went home in a fury.

The next day he called on Monsieur Laloine and was told that no one was home, that the family had gone to the country. "What a fool I am!" he said to himself on hearing this. "If I saw her again, I would again have a palpitating heart, and the next day she would amuse herself, while I—I'm going mad!"

Two weeks went by and our lion, by dint of indulging in the most extravagant excesses, had all but succeeded in forgetting Lise. Nevertheless, at times, her mild and pensive countenance seemed to appear before him, but it was pale, deathlike, and distracted. She seemed staring at him with a look of despair, as if reproaching him for bringing upon himself his own ruin and hers. That image appeared before him, even in his sleep, and in his dreams he saw it watching over him like a guardian angel.

One morning the servant knocked at his door and announced that someone by the name of Gobillon wished to speak with him. Sterny had been thinking of Lise all night. He started up and said:

"Show him up immediately!"

"Why, what is the matter?" Sterny said, on seeing

Prosper's sorrowful appearance. "You seem very sad for a newly married man."

"It is on account of the grief at home: you remember poor Lise?"

"Lise!" exclaimed Sterny.

Prosper showed him the crepe that was on his hat.

"Dead!" the marquis uttered.

"Dead, and now a saint in heaven."

"Oh my God! My God!" Sterny exclaimed in a fit of despair. "Dead without having seen her again! Dead!"

"Alas, it is so," Prosper said. "I have been to her funeral, and have come to perform her dying wish."

"Her dying wish?"

"Listen, Monsieur le Marquis, you must not think ill of the poor child, for, although she was excitable, she had a good heart. The night she died my wife and I were at her bedside. Lise wanted to speak to me in private, and when we were alone, she asked me to unfasten the chain of hair she wore around her neck. I did so. Then she asked me to come closer. 'Prosper,' she said, 'give this to the Marquis de Sterny. Tell him not to be fickle and cruel to others, as he has been to me. I send him this present, for one day he will be a good and distinguished man—I am sure of it.' She then put this medallion into my hand, and an hour later she died, murmuring, 'What we wish, we can do . . . except to be loved, to be loved . . .' Then she died."

Sterny fell on his knees, and received this token of pure and innocent love. For some time the tears flowed copiously from his eyes, but not until he was calm did Prosper leave him.

Sterny remained home all that day, nor was he at home to any of his friends. All were surprised, and their astonishment increased when they heard that he was about to leave France for a long time, and most probably they would have thought he was deranged, had they seen him, the morning before he left, kneeling at the tomb of Lise, offering up a sincere and fervent prayer to his Maker.

Kernok, the Corsair

BY EUGÈNE SUE

TRANSLATED BY D. M. AIRD

EUGÈNE SUE
1804–57

Sue was the son of the surgeon-in-chief to the Imperial Guards in Napoleon's Russian campaign (1812). His godparents were Prince Eugène de Beauharnais and the Empress Joséphine. More interested in gaiety than scholarship, he got through the Lycée Bonaparte and the school of medicine only because of his father's stern guidance. In 1825 he shipped in the *Breslau* as surgeon, but when on his father's death he inherited a vast fortune, he retired to write sea novels: *Atar-Gull* (1830), *Plik et Plok* (1831), *Salamandre* (1832), *La Vigie de Koatven* (1833), which met with some success. Later he attained world recognition and huge profits when under the influence of Fourier and other Socialists he turned to the sensational depiction of city slums and the working class, in the serialized novels *The Mysteries of Paris* (1842–43), *The Wandering Jew* (1845–47), and *The Mysteries of the People, or a Proletarian Family across the Ages* (1849–56). These "masterpieces" won him admirers (Balzac, Dostoyevsky), as well as critics (Marx, Engels), and the title of "Fenimore Cooper of French fiction." Although he was a titanic figure a century ago, whose name stood high in literary history, his books are difficult to find today. "Kernok, the Corsair," an episode from *Plik et Plok* published separately in the periodical *La Mode* in 1830 and much admired by Balzac, illustrates some of Sue's characteristic features: his imagination, power of observation, and melodramatic effects.

ABOUT SUE: J. Forster, *Some French and Spanish Men of Genius*, London, 1891; G. Saintsbury, *History of the French Novel*, London, 1917; in French: a biography by Paul Ginisty (Paris, 1929), and a critical dissertation by Nora Atkinson (Paris, 1929).

I. THE SKINNER AND THE SORCERESS

It was a cold dark night in November. The wind was blowing fiercely from the northwest, and the granite rocks that bound the coast of Pampoul were lashed by the billowy ocean, their jagged summits now disappearing beneath the waves, now rising above the dazzling foam.

Between two rocks, sheltered from the fury of the storm, stood a miserable-looking cabin whose approach was rendered loathsome by the heaps of bones, skins, and offal of animals that were scattered about, which plainly announced that the proprietor of this abode was a skinner.

The hut door was open, and a woman with a hamper in her hand appeared, enveloped in a black mantle that left no part of her exposed, save a yellow wrinkled face that was partly concealed by her long gray locks.

"Pen-Ouet! Pen-Ouet!" she cried in an angry tone. "By St. Paul, don't you know that this is the hour when evil spirits wander on the shore?"

There was no answer, and nothing was heard but the howling of the tempest, which now redoubled its fury.

"Pen-Ouet!" she cried again.

Pen-Ouet, an idiot boy, at last heard the voice of his mother. He was squatting beside a heap of bones, which he was busy piling up in the most fantastic manner imaginable. Rising with an air of discontent, like a child who is loath to leave his play, he returned to the cabin carrying with him the well-polished skull of a horse, with which he was much delighted, for, by the introduction of several

pebbles, whenever he shook the skull it produced a pleasing sound.

"Come in, accursed creature!" cried his mother, pushing
him so violently that his head, striking against the wall,
bled profusely. The idiot burst into a horselaugh, wiped
the wound with his long black hair, and then went and
squatted by the fire.

"Ivonne, Ivonne! Think of your soul, instead of shedding
the blood of your son!" shouted the skinner, who was on
his knees, apparently in profound meditation. "Don't you
hear?"

"I hear the voice of the tempest, and the noise of the
waves lashing against this rock."

"Say, rather, the voices of the departed! By St. Jean! this
is a day of death! And the drowned . . ." (here he
paused) "may bring to our door the Kariquel-ancon, with
its white sheets and its red tears!" he added in a low, trembling voice.[1]

"Tush! What have we to fear? Haven't we Pen-Ouet, with
us! And don't you know that evil spirits never approach a
roof that shelters an idiot?"

"Then, why have I had, ever since the last shipwreck—
since the lugger that came along our coast was deceived
by our false signals—why, I ask, have I had, ever since, a
burning fever, and such frightful dreams? In vain have I
drunk at midnight of the fountain of Krignoëk, nothing can
cool me, or banish my fears! Ah, Ivonne! Ivonne! It was
your fault!"

"Always afraid! Don't we have to live? Hasn't your work
made you obnoxious to everyone in Saint-Pol? Aren't we
forbidden to enter the church? And isn't it hard for us to
get the bakers to sell us their bread? Pen-Ouet, poor
idiot, never goes to town without coming back covered with
bruises. Why, if they dared, they would hunt us like wolves,
on the mountains of Arnes, and because by scavenging the
coast we avail ourselves of what Teus [the evil spirit of the
tempest] sends us, you must go down on your knees like a

[1] Kariquel-ancon, according to popular tradition, is the carriage
of death, which is said to be drawn by skeletons.

sacristan, and turn as pale as a girl who meets Teus's Arpouliek, with two-three heads and his flashing eye!"

"Ivonne!"

"Yes, you are more timid than a Cournaille!" she added, greatly exasperated.

This is the bitterest insult that can be offered to a Leonais, so the skinner started up and gripped his wife by the throat.

"Yes!" she shouted. "More cowardly than a child of the plain."

The rage of the skinner had no bounds; he seized an ax, and Ivonne armed herself with a knife.

The idiot laughed loudly and shook the horse's skull, thereby producing a strange, hollow sound.

Fortunately a knock was heard at the door; otherwise mischief would have ensued.

"Open the door, I say. Damnation!" cried a rude voice. "The northeastern is strong enough to unhorn a bullock! Open the door!"

The skinner dropped his ax, and Ivonne, adjusting her dress, cast a fierce look on her husband.

"Who can it be at this hour of the night?" said the skinner, approaching the window and looking out.

II. KERNOK

It was the brave and worthy Kernok who knocked at the door; a brave and daring fellow he was, as you will see.

Born at Plougasnou, at fifteen he left his paternal roof, embarking on board a slaver, where he soon became expert in his chosen profession. There was not a powder monkey more active, nor sailor more intrepid, than Kernok, few had so piercing an eye for discovering land under a fog, and none could reef a topsail with more dexterity or grace. And how generous was his disposition! If an officer carelessly laid his purse aside, Kernok was sure to show his dexterity in picking it up, but he always shared its contents with his comrades, as he did also with the captain's rum, whenever it came within his reach.

His tenderness and humanity, too, were most exemplary. How often, on a voyage from Africa to the Caribbean, when the Negroes—their limbs stiffened with the cold and damp of the hold—were unable to crawl on deck to inhale the fresh air; how often, I say, did young Kernok restore warmth to their shivering frames by making them keep step to the sound of the lash! This conduct used even to call forth the approbation of Monsieur Durand, the gunner, surgeon, and carpenter of the brigantine, who truly remarked, that none under the superintendence of Kernok was ever afflicted with that drowsiness and torpor that affected the others. On the contrary, whenever they caught sight of the lash, they were seized with a fit of nervous excitement, which Monsieur Durand considered exceedingly salutary.

Kernok soon obtained the confidence and esteem of the captain of the slaver, who, capable of appreciating his rare qualities, grew fond of him, instructed him in the theory of his profession, and one fine morning, when in as fine a humor, he promoted him to second-in-command.

The young sailor proved himself, by his courage and intrepidity, worthy of promotion. He found out such an advantageous method of stowing away the Negroes, that the vessel, which had hitherto only carried two hundred, was, by his ingenuity, made to carry three. This he accomplished by politely requesting them to lie close together on their sides, instead of lolling about on their backs like so many pashas.

From that day the captain predicted that his protégé would fulfill a high destiny. God knows whether this prediction has been verified!

A few years rolled on. They were sailing, one evening, with a fair wind, toward the coast of Africa. Kernok's worthy captain, having made somewhat free with the rum, was in excellent humor and, seating himself at the cabin window, began to amuse himself, now observing the progress of the thick clouds of smoke that rose curling from his mouth, now watching the swift motion of the vessel, which every moment brought him nearer to his native land.

Then he thought of the beautiful plains of Normandy and fancied he saw, gilded by the rays of the setting sun, the thatched cottage in which he first drew breath; the clear streamlet that ran murmuring by; his wife, his mother, and his little children, who were anxious for his return— longing for the pretty birds and beautiful dresses he was wont to bring with him from distant climes.

Poor fellow! He fancied he saw all this, and his pipe, which long use had rendered as black as a raven, dropped from his mouth, his eyes became moistened with tears, his heart throbbed violently, and by degrees his imagination, aided a little, perhaps, by the rum, gave to this bright vision an appearance of reality, and the worthy captain, taking the ocean for the smiling plain he sighed after, thought he would have a loll upon the sward, leaped upon the cabin window, and fell into the sea.

Some say that an invisible hand pushed him, and that the wake of the vessel was for a moment tinged with blood!

One thing is certain; he was seen no more.

At the time the brigantine was off the Cape Verde Islands. The sea was running high, the wind blowing fresh, so the helmsman heard nothing, but Kernok, who had gone to give the captain an account of the vessel's course, discovered the accident, to which, in all probability, he was no stranger.

Kernok was one of those strong-minded men who are inaccessible to the mean considerations some silly people term pity or gratitude, so, when he appeared on deck, there was not the slightest trace of emotion visible on his countenance. "The captain's drowned," he said calmly, addressing the boatswain's mate; "it's a pity, for he was . . ." We refrain from giving the epithet, which felicitously terminated his laconic funeral oration. Then, fixing his eyes on the steersman, he added:

"The command of the vessel falls to me, as second in rank; therefore, change the course. Instead of going south-east, put the head of the vessel to northwest, and steer for Nantes or St. Malo."

The fact is, Kernok had often, but in vain, endeavored to persuade the deceased captain to abandon the slave trade; not from any motive of philanthropy; oh, no; but from a motive much more powerful in the eyes of a rational man.

"Captain," Kernok used to say, "you do not gain, at the most, more than three hundred per cent on the money you advance, whereas, if I were in your place—if I were master —look—I would gain as much—aye, more—without advancing a penny. Your vessel sails like a goldonis. Fit her out as a privateer; I will answer for the crew; only allow me to act, and I promise that the song of the bold pirate will resound at every capture we make."

The eloquence of Kernok could not move the captain, for he was a sagacious dog, and was well aware that, whoever embraced this noble profession in peaceful times, was sure, sooner, or later, to finish his career by dangling at the yardarm. So the obdurate captain fell into the sea by *accident*.

When Kernok reached Nantes, the brigantine was soon fitted out in the way he so much desired; a crew was speedily secured, the vessel armed, and, with a proud heart, Kernok saw himself about to enter on his favorite project.

Providence seemed to smile on his exertions, for, soon afterward, war was declared between England and France. Kernok having procured a suitable crew, he put out to sea, captured a three-masted merchantman, and carried his prize to St. Pol de Léon.

What more can I say? Fortune always favored him; he took many prizes from the English; and the money thus acquired vanished rapidly in the taverns of St. Pol; and, on the night he disturbed the respectable family of the skinner, he was about to put out to sea again, in order to recruit his exhausted finances.

"Damn it, open up, I say!" he swore, nearly shaking the door off its hinges. A few moments later it opened.

III. FORTUNETELLING

Kernok entered the hut, took off his oilskin jacket, shook his hat, which was dripping wet, then threw himself on a crazy bench by the fireside.

The corsair was about thirty years of age. His bulky, square form, bespoke great strength, and his sunburned features, black hair, and large whiskers gave him a somewhat stern and savage appearance. Yet he would have been deemed rather handsome, had it not been for the extraordinary motion of his eyebrows, which twitched at every impulse of his mind. His dress resembled that of a common sailor, save that he wore two golden anchors embossed on his jacket collar, and had a large cutlass fastened to his belt, with a red silken cord.

The skinner and his wife, eying the stranger with fear and suspicion, waited anxiously to hear the object of his visit, but Kernok appeared only to think of warming himself, and as he picked up some pieces of wood to throw on the fire, he said, "Ah, these belong to some vessel you have lured to her doom! Ah, if ever the *Sparrow Hawk*——"

"What do you mean?" interrupted Ivonne.

The corsair raised his head and looked disdainfully, without uttering a word, then, stretching his legs across the fireplace as freely as if he had been in one of the taverns of St. Pol, he said:

"You are Pen-Hap, the skinner, are you not, my good fellow? And you," said he, addressing Ivonne, "are the sorceress of the coast of Pampoul?"

Then, eying the idiot with an air of disgust, he added:

"As to this monster, if you were to take him to a meeting of witches, he would frighten the devil himself. He, however, resembles you, my good dame; and I fancy, if I had him for the figurehead of my vessel, the dolphins would never play and frolic again under her prow."

The features of Ivonne became distorted with passion.

"Come, my pretty hostess," resumed the corsair, "don't be angry; here's something," said he, shaking his purse, "that will soon appease you, for I require your assistance, as well as that of Monsieur."

This harangue and, above all, the word "Monsieur" were pronounced with an air so evidently contemptuous that it required the sight of a well-lined purse, and Kernok's broad shoulders and iron-tipped stick, to prevent the worthy couple from giving vent to their growing rage.

"Not," he added, "that I believe in your spells. When I was a child, the witches made me tremble, but now, I care as little about them as I do about a broken oar. *She,* however, wants me to have my fortune told before we go to sea again. Come now, madame. Are you ready?"

At the word "Madame" the sorceress made a horrible grimace.

"I will not stay here, Ivonne, this is the day of the dead! Wife, Wife, you will cause our ruin, you will bring down the vengeance of heaven on us!" exclaimed the skinner as he left the house in terror.

"The devil catch him!" exclaimed Kernok, pushing her toward the door. "Run after him, you old screech owl! He knows the coast better than any pilot of the Isle of Batz. Away with you, you witch, for I want his assistance."

"Do you come here to insult those you wish to serve?" cried Ivonne. "Leave off, leave off, or you shall learn nothing from me.

"What is it you want?"

Kernok shrugged his shoulders with an air of indifference. "To know the past and the future; nothing but that, my worthy dame, which is as easy as it is to sail ten knots an hour in the teeth of the wind!"

"Your hand."

"There! Read away, my old dame, but I have about as much faith in the predictions of our steersman, who, when burning salt and gunpowder, pretends that he can tell what sort of weather it will be by the color of the flame. I place more reliance on my cutlass, for, when I say thou shalt die, this blade makes my predictions come true better than all your——"

"Silence!" cried Ivonne.

While Kernok was expressing his skepticism, the sorceress was examining the lines of his hand. She fixed her piercing gray eyes on him, then placed her finger on his brow.

Kernok started at her touch.

"Ah," she said with a hideous laugh, "you tremble already."

"Tremble, hag, tremble! Do you think I can bear the touch of your cursed finger without shuddering? But if it were a soft, plump hand, you would see that——"

He stopped, and lowered his eyes before her fixed and earnest gaze.

"Silence!" she exclaimed, then her head fell upon her breast, and she seemed absorbed in a profound reverie. At intervals her teeth chattered, and her whole frame shook convulsively.

The dying embers of the fire shed a reddish light over the room, the rays of which fell upon the frightful misshapen head of the idiot as he lay asleep in a corner, while nothing was seen of the sorceress save her black mantle and long gray locks. The tempest was moaning outside, and everything conspired to render this scene truly appalling.

Kernok felt a slight shudder pass through his frame with the rapidity of lightning. The superstition of his childhood gradually resumed its sway, and his features lost their air of sneering incredulously, large drops of sweat gathered on his forehead, and his hand automatically sought his dagger, which he drew from its scabbard.

"The devil choke Melie!" cried he. "And me too, fool that I am for humoring her silly scruples. What! Shall I allow myself to be frightened by the mummeries that are used to scare women and children? Come, devil's bride! Quick, for I must be off. Do you hear?" he added, shaking her violently.

The sorceress did not reply, nor did she offer any resistance.

The corsair's heart beat violently.

"Will you speak?" he said, raising her head.

It remained in the position in which he had placed it, but the eyes were fixed and glazed. His hair now stood erect, and he seemed fascinated and subdued by a power that was superior to his strength.

"Kernok," at length said the sorceress faintly, "throw, throw away that dagger; there is blood on it! The blood of *her* and of *him!*" She smiled hideously and, placing her finger on her neck, added, "You struck her here; still, she lives. But that is not all; where is the captain of the slaver?"

Kernok's dagger fell at his feet; he drew his hand across his burning brow, and leaned, for support, against the cabin wall.

The sorceress continued:

"That you threw your benefactor into the sea after stabbing him is true. Your soul will go to Teus's. To strike Melie, without killing her, is also true; to stab her, who, to follow you, left that beautiful country where the deadliest poisons grow—where the serpents, by the light of the moon, twine themselves together in sport—where the traveler hears with terror the howl of the hyena—and where the bite of the red viper is followed by the agonies of death!"

Here the sorceress writhed her body, like one in frightful convulsions.

"Enough! Enough!" cried the terrified corsair.

"You have raised your hand against your benefactor and your mistress; their blood is on your head! Your days are numbered. Pen-Ouet!" she cried in a deep voice.

At that sound the idiot, who was apparently asleep, rose and went to his mother, who, taking hold of his hands, placed her brow against his, and said:

"Pen-Ouet, he asks how long Teus's will permit him to live? Answer, in the name of Teus's."

The idiot uttered a wild cry, appeared to reflect for a moment, then struck the horse's skull on the ground thirteen times.

"Five, ten, thirteen!" said his mother. "You have thirteen days longer to live! Do you hear? And may Teus's drive your body, livid and cold, with glazed eyes and foaming at the mouth, upon our coast! Thirteen days, and your soul will be in the hands of Teus's!"

"But what of her? Tell me!" exclaimed Kernok in agitation.

"What of her? Why, you have only paid me for yourself. Well, I will be generous."

Then, placing her finger on her forehead, and reflecting for a moment, she said:

"She, too, will be cold and lifeless, with teeth clenched, and foaming at the mouth. Yes, you will be a beautiful pair! Please Teus's, I shall see you with a rock for your bed, the billowy ocean for curtains, the croak of the raven for your nuptial song, and the flaming eye of Teus's for your bridal torch!"

Kernok fell senseless on the floor, and the cabin resounded with shouts of laughter.

A knock was now heard at the door, and a sweet voice called out, "Kernok, my dear Kernok!"

These words produced a magical effect on the corsair; he opened his eyes, looked around him with fear and astonishment and, rising, said:

"Where am I? Have I been dreaming? No, it's too real, you witch!"

"Kernok, my dear Kernok," again said the soft voice.

"She here!" exclaimed the corsair, rushing to the door. "Come! let's leave this place!" he said as he bore her rapidly away.

They proceeded along the coast and soon were on the road leading to St. Pol.

IV. THE *SPARROW HAWK*

The fog that hung over the neighborhood of the little port of Pampoul gradually disappeared, and the sun's red disk was seen high above the horizon. At first the little town of St. Pol, with its towering steeples, was only a blur in the mist that rose from the water, but it soon became more visible, when the pale rays of a November sun had dissipated the damp morning air.

On the right was the Isle of Kalot, to the left the mill and the church steeple of Plougasnou, while in the distance appeared the coast of Tréguier, terminated by huge rocks that reached as far as the eye could see.

It was seldom that any but small vessels were seen in the pretty bay of Pampoul. Therefore, the *Sparrow Hawk* towered high above the ignoble crowd of luggers, sloops, and shallops that surrounded it.

The *Sparrow Hawk* was certainly a fine-looking vessel. Who could help admiring the delicate rigging, the elegant sloping of its sails, the beautiful flag as it fluttered in the breeze, the studding sails, as graceful as the wings of a swan, and the brass cannon that bristled on each side?

But if you admire the *Sparrow Hawk* as it lies at anchor, what would you say if you saw it flying after some unfortunate merchantman? Never did foaming courser bound so fleetly—never did swallow skim the water so swiftly, as the beautiful brigantine in a fresh breeze, her sails set, glided over the surface of the ocean!

The *Sparrow Hawk,* as it lay slumbering at anchor, was certainly a beauty!

There were only a few men on board: just the boatswain, six seamen, and a cabin boy. The boatswain, who was a man of about fifty, was hastily pacing the deck, and the restless motion of the protuberance on his left cheek denoted that he was biting his quid in no very amiable mood. The cabin boy was standing watching this fatal prognostic with great anxiety, for the boatswain's quid was, to the crew, a sort of barometer that indicated unerringly the variations of his temper, and, according to the boy's observations, there was, at this time, every appearance of squally weather.

"Thunder and lightning!" exclaimed the boatswain. "What can be keeping him? What wind has drifted him away? Where is he? Ten o'clock, and not on board! His fool of a wife, too, must needs set off in the middle of the night to seek him. To lose such a fine breeze as this! A thousand curses!"

The boy, impatient at the length of this soliloquy, had twice tried to interrupt it, but he was deterred each time by the ominous restlessness of the tobacco in the cheek of his superior. At length, after a great effort, he ventured to say:

"Breakfast is ready, Master Zeli."

"Ah! it's you, Grain-o'-Salt, is it? What brings you here, cursed monkey? Do you wish your hide tanned, eh? Answer. What do you want, imp of hell?"

At this torrent of abuse the boy assumed the gravity of a stoic. He was well accustomed to the freaks of his superior's temper.

Grain-o'-Salt again uttered, though in an exceedingly submissive tone:

"Breakfast is——"

"Oh, breakfast!" interrupted the boatswain, delighted at having found an object on which to vent his fury. "Here, impudent dog!"

These words were accompanied by a box on the ear, and a kick that made the lad disappear through the hatchway as if by magic.

On reaching the bottom of the hold the poor lad, who had miraculously escaped breaking his neck, muttered, "Ah, the quid never deceives. No, no; I could easily see the humor that Master Zeli was in; yes, and I felt its effects, too. Then," he added after a few moments' silence, with an air of satisfaction, "it was lucky for me, however, that I fell on my feet; it's better than if I had fallen on my head, surely."

Having consoled himself with this philosophic reflection, he went to see about breakfast.

V. THE RETURN

Although Zeli had partly vented his anger on Grain-o'-Salt, he continued pacing the deck, and casting his eyes from time to time up to heaven, while he muttered something, that was impossible to be mistaken for a pious invocation. Suddenly he stopped, seized a spyglass, and, looking toward the jetty, exclaimed:

"How fortunate! Here he is, at last! Yes, it's he. What sweeps of the oar! Come along, my lads, make haste, and we may yet be in time to save the tide."

Master Zeli never thought of the difficulty of making himself heard out of gunshot reach, but continued encouraging, by voice and gesture, the sailors who were bringing Kernok and his fair companion on board.

As the boat neared the brig, the boatswain's whistle was heard, and a few moments afterward Kernok leaped lightly on board the brigantine.

Zeli was surprised at the agitated and pale looks of his commander, who had returned bareheaded and without his dagger, his clothes in the utmost disorder, and his whole appearance showing that something extraordinary had taken place. He, therefore, instead of upbraiding his captain with the length of his absence, approached him with an air of respectful solicitude.

Kernok's keen eye searched every corner of the vessel to see if all was in order, then, looking at Zeli, he demanded, in an imperious tone:

"When will the tide serve?"

"At two o'clock, Captain."

"If the breeze holds up, we'll be under way by that time. Order the flag to be hoisted, fire off the signal gun, weigh anchor, and when you're ready, let me know. Where's the lieutenant, and the rest of the crew?"

"Ashore, Captain."

"Send off a boat in search of them. Whoever is not on board at two o'clock shall have twenty lashes and eight days in irons. Lose no time."

Zeli had never seen Kernok in so stern a mood before; therefore, instead of, as he was wont to do, making a host of objections to his captain's orders, he promptly set about executing them.

Kernok, having attentively observed the direction of the wind, made a sign to his companion, who followed him to the cabin.

This was the person who had sought the corsair in the den of the sorceress, and whose soft voice had given utterance to the words "Kernok, my dear Kernok!"

Her features were exquisitely fine; she had large eyes veiled by long silken lashes, and beautiful auburn hair that clustered beneath her bonnet; her form was slender and graceful, her step light and free, and the hue of her countenance seemed deepened by the rays of the tropical sun. Indeed, it was from that burning clime that Kernok had brought his companion, who was a beautiful young colored girl.

Poor Melie! To follow her lover, she had left Martinique and its plantations, her friends, and her home; she would have made any sacrifice for him, even to the little purse containing the heart of a dove and the teeth of a serpent—a potent charm!—which would protect her from injury as long as it remained in her possession.

Judge, then, if Melie loved her Kernok! And Kernok, in return, was passionately fond of Melie, for he had christened his favorite gun after her, and he never fired a bullet from it without thinking of his mistress. But the strongest proof of the pirate's love was a deep scar on her neck, occasioned by a slash he had given her with a knife in a fit of jealousy. Now, as the violence of jealousy is the best test of the force of love, it is evident that the corsair must have been strongly attached to Melie, and that for her time must have flown sweetly by, in company with her mild lord.

On entering the cabin Kernok threw himself on a chair,

and, as if to avoid some fatal vision, he concealed his face in his hands.

Melie approached him timidly and, throwing herself on her knees, took hold of his hand, saying:

"Dear Kernok, what ails you? Your head is feverish!"

The corsair started, raised his head, and smiled, then, throwing his arms around her neck, he embraced her affectionately, but when his lips happened to touch the fatal scar, he exclaimed:

"Perdition seize me! Where did that accursed sorceress learn——"

He then approached the cabin window, but, as if repulsed by an invisible power, he turned away in horror, then threw himself dejectedly on the bedside. His red and fiery eyes, after remaining fixed for some time, gradually closed, as he yielded to the fatigue and agitation of the previous night. Melie, her cheeks wet with tears, gently lifted his head, placed it on her bosom, the soft heavings of which soon lulled him to sleep; then she parted the black hair that shaded the broad forehead of her lover, now kissing him, now passing her slim fingers through his bushy eyebrows, which were contracted even in his sleep.

"Captain," said Zeli, entering the cabin, "anchor is weighed."

Melie pointed to Kernok as he lay asleep, and signed to Zeli not to disturb him, but Zeli, faithful to the order he had received, repeated in a still louder tone:

"Captain, the anchor is weighed, and we wait your orders."

"What? Who is it?" cried Kernok, disengaging himself from the arms of Melie.

"The anchor is weighed, Captain."

"Fool! Who gave that order?"

"Yourself, Captain."

"I!"

"Yes, on coming on board about two hours ago."

Kernok looked at Melie, who inclined her head and smiled, as if confirming the assertion of Zeli.

"Yes, yes, I remember," he finally said, pressing his brow

with his hand; "it's all right. I'll be on deck presently. The wind hasn't fallen, has it?"

"No, Captain, on the contrary, it blows fresher."

"Look sharp, then, and get everything ready," said Kernok in a milder tone, and Zeli, perceiving that his captain's agitation had calmed down, could not refrain from putting in a "But, Cap——"

"Are you going to begin with your ifs and your buts? Take care, or I'll break your head with the trumpet!"

Zeli said no more but secured his retreat as quickly as possible.

"Be calm, my dear Kernok," said Melie timidly. "Do you feel better now?"

"Yes, yes; these two hours' sleep have chased away the foolish thoughts that accursed sorceress put into my head. Come, the breeze is freshening; we must leave port. There is no use in remaining here, when there are three-masters in the channel, galleys in the Bay of Biscay, and rich prizes in the Straits of Gibraltar!"

"How! Sail on a Friday?"

"Listen to what I'm going to say, my sweet one! I ought to chastise you for teasing me to go and hear the ravings of a fool! I, however, pardon you, but let me have no more of such trash, or else——"

"Were her predictions, then, unfavorable?" interrupted Melie.

"I care nothing about her predictions. Only, I know this, that the first time I am at Pampoul I will pay the old hag a visit she will not readily forget. May the lightning blast me if I demolish not her cursed den, and leave her back of as many colors as the rainbow!"

"Don't talk thus of a woman with second sight. And oh! For mercy's sake, do not sail today! A black and white dolphin has been seen near the vessel, uttering piercing cries. That, you know, is an unlucky omen."

In saying this Melie threw herself at the feet of Kernok, who listened to her patiently for a few minutes, but, growing tired of her importunities, he pushed her away with violence, seized his speaking trumpet, and hurried on deck.

VI. SETTING SAIL

When Kernok appeared, not a sound was heard. At last, Zeli's whistle, long and loud, reached the ears of the crew, then the words "Shall we unfurl our sails, Captain?"

"Not yet; get all hands on deck."

The boatswain's whistle was again heard, and fifty-two men and five boys appeared, forming two lines, their heads upright, and their arms hanging by their sides.

These brave fellows did not exactly possess the candid and open air of young collegians. Oh no! It was evident, from their weather-beaten faces, on which the passions had plowed their deepest furrows, that the life led by these honest fellows was somewhat stormy and precarious.

Then, what a strange, motley crew! Nearly every nation in the world had its representative among them—France, Russia, England, Germany, Spain, Italy, America, Egypt, and even a representative of China whom Kernok had decoyed on board at Manilla! Yet this crew, although heterogeneous, lived in perfect harmony together, owing to the rigorous discipline their captain had established among them.

"Call the roll," shouted Kernok.

The roll was called, and a man named Lescoet, a countryman of the captain's, was missing.

"Mark him down, twenty lashes and eight days in irons," said Kernok, who then mounted the quarter-deck and spoke in the following terms:

"We set out once more, my lads. We have roosted here long enough. Our pockets are empty, but our powder magazine is full; our cannons are as open in the mouth as ever, and are willing and ready to speak. With this stiff nor'-wester, we can pay a visit to the Straits of Gibraltar, and, if St. Nicholas aids us, by heavens, my lads, we'll return with our pockets lined, to drink the wine of Pampoul, and dance with the pretty girls of St. Pol."

"Hurrah! Hurrah!" shouted the crew in exultation.

"Hoist the mainsail!" shouted Kernok in a stentorian voice, and the order was scarcely given when it was accomplished.

After a few other orders that were promptly given and speedily obeyed the brigantine readily yielded to the impulse of the breeze—the large sails filling gradually and the wind whistling among the cordage. Pampoul, and the coast of Tréguier, receded from the view of the sailors, who gazed at the land as earnestly as if they were taking their last farewell of France.

"Larboard! Larboard!" suddenly shouted Zeli in terror.

"What is the matter?" demanded Kernok.

"It is Lescoet, who joins us in a boat, which we would have run over like a nutshell, had I not sung out."

Lescoet jumped on board and approached the captain with a downcast look.

"Why so late?"

"My old mother was dying, and I stayed to close her eyes."

"Indeed!" said Kernok. Then, turning to the lieutenant, he added, "Square your account with this dutiful son."

Lescoet was then led forward by Zeli, who said:

"You and I, my lad, have a bone to pick."

"I understand you; how many?" said Lescoet, turning pale.

"Oh, you will not be stripped for a trifle, depend upon it; you can count them. I'll warrant that you will not be cheated."

"I'll have my revenge."

"Oh, that's always said at first, but when it's over, it's no more thought of than yesterday's gale. Come, my lad, make haste, for I see the captain is getting impatient, and perhaps he might take it into his head to give me a taste of the same sauce."

Lescoet was stripped, and Zeli, receiving a signal from the captain, began his operation.

Up to the sixth lash he stood firm, but at the seventh his courage abandoned him; and well it might, for each stroke was vigorously dealt, leaving long, blue-red lines and ultimately causing the blood to spurt in all directions.

Monsieur Durand, the surgeon-carpenter, approached, felt the pulse of poor Lescoet, and, shrugging his shoulders, made a significant sign to Master Zeli, who willingly set to work again.

In giving the last lash Zeli pronounced the word "twenty" with an air of satisfaction mixed with regret, like a young girl, when giving the last of her promised kisses to her lover, or, if you prefer the simile, like a banker counting his last pile of crowns.

"Now," said Kernok, "clap a good plaster of gunpowder and vinegar on his back, and there will be nothing seen of these scratches tomorrow." Then, turning to the lieutenant, he added, "Keep the head of the brigantine to the southwest, and if you fall in with a sail, come and tell me."

He then descended to the cabin to rejoin Melie.

VII. CARLOS AND ANITA

It was still mild and serene, and a three-masted vessel called the *San Pablo*, which was off the Straits of Gibraltar, had all her sails set to catch the breeze. She had come from Peru, was bound for Lisbon, and carried English colors, being ignorant of the war that had broken out between France and England.

Don Carlos Toscano, a rich merchant of Lima, had freighted the *San Pablo* at Callao, and he and his wife occupied the captain's apartment, which was furnished with everything that could contribute to luxury, elegance, and splendor.

The air was calm, the sky clear, and the sea so smooth and unruffled that, but for the slight motion of the vessel, one might have believed he was on land.

Carlos, seated on a rich sofa, was gazing on his wife, who was holding a guitar in her hand.

"Bravo, bravo! Anita," cried he. "Never was the song of love sung more sweetly."

"Because," replied she, "it was never felt more sincerely, my dear."

"It will last, too," said Carlos.

"For life!" said Anita with fervor.

Their lips met, and Carlos pressed her fondly to his breast; the guitar fell at their feet, causing a melodious sound, like the dying note of an organ.

Carlos cast on his wife one of those passionate glances of love that thrill the soul with delight: and she, fascinated by his keen looks, fell gently at his feet, and rested her head against his knees, so that her beautiful face was nearly veiled by her long dark tresses, through which her eyes sparkled, like stars in the midst of a somber sky.

"She is mine!" thought Carlos. "Mine, mine forever! For we will grow old together, wrinkles will furrow that soft face, and these dark locks will become silvery," said he, pressing his fingers through her glossy hair. "On some beautiful evening, in autumn, surrounded by her grandchildren, she will expire, and her last words will be, 'I come to thee, my Carlos.' Yes, for I shall die first, but, what happy days shall we pass together before that time! Young and strong, and rich and happy, with a pure conscience, we shall again see our own beautiful Andalusia, Cordova, and its Alhambra, with its richly sculptured porticos, and our lovely villa, with its orangeries and its marble fountains!"

"And my father," exclaimed the young girl, for Carlos had spoken the greater portion of his reverie aloud, "and the house where I was born, and the green lattice I used to open so often when you were passing by, and the old church of San Juan, where, when I was at prayer, you first whispered in my ear, 'My dear Anita, I love thee!' The Virgin heard my prayer, for, at that moment, I was beseeching her to grant me thy love. We must return thanks to her at Notre Dame for having blessed our union."

"Oh, how happy and smiling is the future for us! How tranquil! How——"

She could not finish the sentence; a cannon shot came whizzing into the cabin, cracked her skull, and cut the body of Carlos in two!

VIII.   THE PRIZE

"Bravo! Admirably aimed! See, Master Zeli, the ball entered below the taffrail, and found its way out of one of the portholes on the starboard side. Bravo, Melie!" cried Kernok, patting the gun that bore that name, and had fired at the *San Pablo,* because she had not speedily hoisted her flag.

This was the shot that killed Carlos and his wife.

"Ah, how lucky," resumed Kernok, when he saw the English flag hoisted. "An Englishman! And the dog has the impudence to own it, without having a gun on board. Zeli, Zeli," cried he, in a voice of thunder, "get the oars shipped immediately, and we'll be alongside of her in half an hour. Lieutenant, send the men to their guns, and see that everything's got ready for boarding." Then, jumping on one of the guns, he added, "If I am not mistaken, my lads, that three-master is from the South Seas, and from her build is either Portuguese or Spanish, under English colors —ignorant, no doubt that war has been declared between France and England. However, that's not our affair. That dog there ought to have piastres in its stomach; we shall soon see, my lads. Spread out thy wings, my brave *Sparrow Hawk,* then thou shalt soon show thy talons." He then went below and locked the cabin door on Melie, who was fast asleep.

The captain of the unfortunate *San Pablo,* recognizing the character of the brigantine, had hoisted the English flag, hoping to place himself under its protection, but when he observed the preparations that were going forward on

board the *Sparrow Hawk,* and saw that vessel rapidly gaining ground on him, all his hopes vanished. Flight was impossible, for the faint breeze, which they had had up to
this time, was succeeded by a dead calm. Defense was also
out of the question, for what could the two miserable guns
of the *San Pablo* do against the twenty that opened their
frightful mouths on board the *Sparrow Hawk?* The prudent
Spaniard, therefore, hove to, and ordered his crew to fall
on their knees and pray for the assistance of San Pablo, who
could not fail to manifest his power in their favor on so
momentous an occasion.

The crew, following the example of the captain, fell on
their knees, and commenced repeating their paternosters,
but the *Sparrow Hawk* kept gaining on them.

The Virgin was then appealed to, but with no better success, for the terrible voice of Kernok rang in the ears of the
Spaniards.

"Oh, oh!" said the corsair. "She has brought to, and has
struck her flag. She's ours, my lads. Zeli, lower, and man
the longboat, and I'll go and have a chat with the captain."

Kernok then thrust a pair of pistols into his belt, seized
a cutlass, and jumped into the boat.

"If this should be a trick of the three-master," he cried
to the lieutenant, "if she makes the slightest resistance,
come to close quarters."

Ten minutes elapsed. Kernok jumped on board the *San
Pablo,* a pistol in each hand, and his cutlass between his
teeth. At the sight of the Spaniards, who were on their
knees before a rude image of St. Paul, beating their breasts
violently, the cutlass fell from Kernok's mouth, and he burst
into a fit of laughter. The Spanish captain, kissing a relic,
was murmuring, "*San Pablo, ora pro nobis!*" San Pablo,
alas, did not hear him.

"Come, come, finish your mummeries, old croaker, and
show me the way to your nest!"

"*Señor, no entiendo!*" replied the unfortunate Spaniard,
trembling.

"True, you don't understand French," said Kernok.
"Well," he added—for the corsair knew just as much of ev-

ery language as his profession required—"*El dinero, compadre*—your money, old man."

The Spaniard again muttered, "*No entiendo*," but Kernok, having exhausted his stock of Spanish, changed the dialogue into pantomime by presenting the muzzle of his pistol, which was instantly understood, for the poor fellow heaved a heavy sigh, and made a sign for the pirate to follow him.

To reach the locker, Kernok was obliged to pass through the cabin, on the floor of which lay the bleeding remains of Carlos and Anita.

The poor Spaniard turned his head away, and drew his hand across his eyes to wipe away a tear.

"*Morbleu!*" said Kernok, pushing the bodies with his feet. "This is the work of Melie, but it can't be helped. *El dinero, amigo, el dinero*—that's the stuff, my worthy fellow."

When Kernok was shown the hoards of money—about a hundred barrels, on each of which was written, "20,000 piastres"—a strange feeling came over him.

"Is it possible?" cried he. And in his joy he embraced everyone around him, captain, lieutenant, sailors, and powder monkeys—even the remnants of the once-happy Anita.

Two hours later the last barrel was transported on board the *Sparrow Hawk,* and the crew of the *San Pablo,* including the captain, were all made fast to the deck, in different parts of the vessel.

"Now, my lads," said Kernok, addressing his crew, "I shall give you this evening a *nopces et festin,* and if you behave yourselves, something else that will astonish you."

"Oh, Captain," replied Zeli facetiously, "we'll be as prudent as young maidens."

IX. THE ORGY

"Wine, wine, sacrebleu!"

Bottles are broken, decanters are smashed, and songs and

oaths resound on every side. Now is heard the heavy fall of a drunken pirate, now the hiccuping of those who, holding their glasses in one hand, cling to the tables for support with the other.

"More wine, I say, cursed monkey, more wine, or I'll break your head!"

Some of them wrestle, foot to foot and front to front; they clasp each other, struggle; one falls—a bone is broken, and laughter and imprecations follow. Others, again, insensible, blood streaming from their temples, are lying at the feet of those who join in the loud bacchanal song, and some, in the last stage of drunkenness, amuse themselves by crushing between two balls the hands of their dead-drunk comrades.

The deck is red, either with blood or wine. What does it matter? Time flies on board the *Sparrow Hawk*, for there folly and delight abound! Go on—enjoy life, for it is short; for who knows if you will see tomorrow? Amuse yourselves, seize pleasure, my brave fellows, whenever it is within your reach, for it may be your last opportunity.

Not that frail, modest pleasure, with wings of gold and azure, that resembles a mild and timid girl shaking her fair and beautiful locks before the mirrors of a boudoir—not that pleasure that demands a cup of ice-cooled liquor—nor that of the Sybarite, who asks only to be surrounded by flowers and perfumes, beauty and harmony, and exquisite and delicate wine. Oh no! It is that robust and athletic pleasure, with the eye of a satyr and the laugh of a demon —that which haunts taverns and gaming houses, drinks till dead-drunk, writhes and tears, and deals blows of death, and then, bawling and swearing, rolls and groans amid the surrounding wreck and confusion.

It was night, and the tables, which had been placed on deck for the purpose of celebrating Kernok's lucky capture, were brilliantly lighted up by lanterns that were suspended from the rigging.

The feast ended, amusement succeeded. The powder monkey, Grain-o'-Salt, daubed himself from head to foot with tar, and, to carry out the fun, rolled himself in a sack of feathers, from which he emerged like a wingless bird. Then, hopping and skipping about, encouraged by the applause of the crew, and stimulated by the lash of Master Zeli, his capers were antic and ludicrous. A German, perhaps the most mischievous fellow of the whole crew, to crown the merriment, approached Grain-o'-Salt, holding a lighted torch behind his back, which he dexterously applied to a tuft of oakum that gracefully balanced itself on Grain-o'-Salt's brow. In an instant the feathery mantle was in a blaze, and the boy ran, amid the shouts and laughter of the crew, screaming frightfully.

One of them, however—a compassionate soul, no doubt, for there are such to be found everywhere—seized the boy and threw him overboard, saying, "I'll soon extinguish him."

Fortunately Grain-o'-Salt could swim like a fish and, being pleased with his bath, he prolonged it by swimming around the vessel, after which he clambered up to one of the portholes, saying, with his accustomed stoicism, "That's better than being burned alive."

Shortly after this the sound of a pistol, followed by a shriek, proceeded from the cabin. Zeli rushed to see what it was, which proved to be nothing, or just the merest trifle in the world.

Kernok, being excited by grog and boasting of his skill as a marksman, exclaimed:

"I'll wager you, my dear, that at the first fire I will strike the knife out of your hand."

Melie did not doubt her lover's skill, but, not caring to test it, she eluded his proposition.

"Coward!" cried Kernok. "Well, to teach you better, I'll take your glass from you," and, seizing a pistol, he fired it, and shattered the glass to pieces.

When Zeli entered, Kernok was still holding the pistol in his hand and laughing immoderately at the terror of Melie, who, pale and trembling, had taken refuge in a corner of the cabin.

"Well, Zeli, my old sea wolf," said Kernok, "are your dames on deck, amusing themselves?"

"You may rely on that, Captain; but they are anxious to see your promised surprise."

"Ah, that's true!" said Kernok. He then whispered in the ear of Zeli, who opened his wide mouth, saying:

"What! You will——"

"Certainly. Will that not be a surprise?"

"Oh, a famous one, and a droll one, to boot. I'll be off, then, Captain."

Kernok then mounted on deck, accompanied by Melie. Both were greeted with loud shouts of joy.

A rocket ascended from the *San Pablo,* and, after describing a curve in the air, it descended in a shower of sparks.

"Captain, do you see that rocket?" said the lieutenant.

"Yes, I understand it. Come, my lads, push the grog about, hand me a glass, and give one to my wife."

Melie was half inclined to refuse, but how resist the attentions of her mild companion?

"Here's long life to the brave comrades of the captain of the *Sparrow Hawk,*" said Kernok, emptying his glass.

"Hurrah!" responded the crew with a loud and sonorous shout.

The orgy was now at its height. The sailors, holding each other by the hand, were dancing wildly around the deck, and singing vociferously snatches of songs, remarkable for their intemperance and obscenity.

Zeli returned from the *San Pablo,* bringing with him the ten men Kernok had left in charge of the vessel. There now remained on board the Spanish frigate only the poor Spaniards, who were bound hand and foot on deck. A second rocket ascended from the *San Pablo.*

"All's right, Captain," said Zeli, "the match has caught——"

"All right," interrupted Kernok. Then, addressing the crew, he said:

"I promised you a surprise, my lads, if you behaved yourselves with propriety. Your prudence and moderation have far exceeded my expectations; such conduct shall not go unrewarded. You see that the Spanish vessel, rigged and fitted out as she is, is worth at least thirty thousand piastres. Well, my lads, I'll give forty thousand for her out of my share of the prize money, just to have the pleasure of treating my crew to the most splendid fireworks ever witnessed, accompanied by the most exquisite music. The signal is given; now take your places."

Those of the crew who were able clambered up the rigging, in order to have a full view of this spectacle.

When the second rocket had ascended from the San Pablo, the fire began to display itself. This was the surprise Kernok had promised. He had sent Zeli on board the Spanish vessel to arrange combustible materials in her hold and to see that her unfortunate crew, who were ignorant of what awaited them, were all secured.

The night was dark, the air calm, and the sea as smooth as glass. At first there arose from the San Pablo a thick smoke, accompanied by myriads of sparks that, when the unfortunate Spaniards discovered their doom, were followed by frightful shrieks that rent the air.

"Do you hear that?" said Kernok. The music begins.

"Their pipes, Captain, are devilishly out of tune," said Zeli. The smoke heightening in color became a lively red. At last it assumed the appearance of a long column of fire that rose and, curling in the air, cast upon the waters a long reflection the color of blood.

"Hurrah!" cried the crew of the brigantine.

The fire rapidly increased; the flames, rising from the three hatchways at the same time, met and spread out over the deck like an immense red curtain, above which appeared the dark rigging and masts of the San Pablo.

The cries of the poor Spaniards, in the midst of this furnace, became so heart-rending that the pirates set up a savage yell to drown the voices of their unhappy victims.

The fire caught the rigging and cordage, and when at its height two of the masts fell on deck with a fearful crash. The cries of the Spaniards were heard no more. Suddenly the flame burst out at the side of the San Pablo, through a large hole it had made; the mainmast fell on the same side, caused her to lurch: the water rushed into the hold, and gradually she sank, leaving for a moment her mizzenmast blazing above the waters, then nothing.

"That was quick!" said Kernok.

"Long live Captain Kernok!" cried Zeli.

This was answered by a loud hurrah! And the weary pirates threw themselves on deck. Kernok, too, went to enjoy a little repose in his cabin, with the secret satisfaction of an opulent man who retires to his chamber after a sumptuous feast.

When Kernok was dropping to sleep, he murmured to himself, "They ought to be satisfied; a three-hundred-ton vessel, and three dozen Spaniards! I think I have behaved handsomely. They mustn't expect it too often. It's all very well now and then, for, after all, a little amusement is necessary."

X. THE CHASE

Everybody was asleep on board the *Sparrow Hawk,* save Melie, who, disturbed by vague apprehensions, was sitting on a deck. It was still dark; but a pale streak of light on the horizon announced the approach of daylight. Large and brilliant wreaths of gold soon lit up the sky, and the stars grew pale and vanished as the sun appeared, rising slowly out of the still blue waters of the ocean, which it seemed to cover with a purple veil.

It was still calm, and the brigantine lay near the place where she had been the day before. Melie, musing with her face in her hands, sat on the quarter-deck. When she raised her head, it was dawn, and, looking around her, she shuddered with horror and disgust. The deck was strewn with ropes, pots, broken glasses, and staved casks, from which wine and brandy were flowing. Here a sleeping sailor lay clutching the neck of a bottle; there a pirate, with his head through the wheel of the rudder, so that at the least movement his skull might be caved in.

Melie blessed providence for watching so carefully over the honest fellows who lay asleep on the deck of the brigantine, for if a storm had arisen during the night, the *Sparrow Hawk*, Kernok, his crew, and the piastres, would have all been lost! Melie knew this, and felt a desire to pray. She went on her knees and turned her eyes toward the vapory blue horizon, and, shading her eyes with her hand, she stood for a moment, then her features assumed an expression of alarm and she ran to Kernok's cabin.

"How foolish you are, Melie," said the corsair, going on deck with a heavy step. "If you woke me up for nothing——"

"Here," interrupted Melie, handing him a spyglass.

"By heavens, you're right! A thousand devils!" He now rubbed the glass, to make sure it was no optical illusion, and it was not!

This discovery was followed by a volley round of the most frightful oaths a pirate can muster.

Then he seized a handspike and went around, now striking the deck, now some sailor as he lay asleep. Soon the men all stood rubbing their eyes, their heads, and their backs, and asking each other what was the matter.

"The matter!" cried Kernok. "Why, you sleepy rascals, there's an English cutter bearing down on us full sail! And with the breeze in her favor!"

Every eye was now turned in the direction in which Kernok was pointing.

"Eight, ten, fifteen portholes!" he cried. "And thirty guns besides. Zeli," he added, "get the oars shipped and man all stations." Then, taking up a speaking trumpet, he shouted:

"All hands on deck! Man your stations! Stretch every inch of canvas! Now, my lads, row away; if we can only catch the breeze, we have nothing to fear. Think of the piastres we have on board! Then choose whether you'll go to the hulks or return, with full pockets, to drink and dance with the girls of St. Pol."

The crew knew that they were rowing for their lives, so they rowed for all they were worth.

Kernok, however, did not deceive himself respecting the

speed of his vessel. He too plainly foresaw that the English cutter, having the wind in her favor, had a great advantage over the *Sparrow Hawk,* therefore, like a prudent captain, he ordered everything to be prepared for action, and attended to the execution of this order with surprising zeal and activity.

The cutter kept gaining on the *Sparrow Hawk.* Kernok sent for Melie. "Go down in the hold," he said, "and don't stir. Come, no tears! Kiss me, and make sure you don't let me see you until the dance is over."

Melie turned pale as death.

"Kernok, let me stay with you!" she said, throwing her arms around him. He felt his heart throb for a moment, then pushed her away, saying:

"Come, leave me, I tell you!"

"I want to protect you," she said, clinging to his knees.

"Zeli," cried the pirate, "take this fool below."

As the boatswain was about to place his rude hands upon her, she sprang to Kernok's side. "At least," she said, "take this talisman; it will protect your life in battle. It was given to me by my grandmother. Take it. Believe me, its magic power is stronger than fate."

"Take her away!" cried Kernok. "Don't you hear me, Zeli?"

"If you should be killed, I will not survive you. There, my life is no longer protected," added Melie, throwing the talisman from her.

"She is a good, kind girl!" said Kernok as he watched two of the sailors place her in a chair to lower her into the hold.

The cutter was coming closer and closer.

"Captain," said Zeli, "the Englishman is gaining on us."

"Do you think I can't see that, you old fool? Our oars are of no use, they only tire the men; unship them, load the guns, and haul out the grappling irons. We'll fight with our topsails set, for under them the *Sparrow Hawk* always shows her talons to the best advantage."

These orders were instantly executed, and Kernok addressed his crew as follows: "Now, my lads, here's a strong-ribbed cutter, so close to us that we have no chance of escape; besides, we haven't a breath of wind. If we're taken we'll be sent to the hulks, and if we surrender, it will amount to the same thing. So, lads, we're in for a fight, and if we're lucky, we may, as the curate said, retire with our breeches. The *Sparrow Hawk* beat a three-master, after two hours' hard fighting, on the coast of Sicily; why should she be afraid of a cutter with a blue flag? Remember the piastres, my lads—the piastres, or the hulks!"

The effect of this speech was decisive; the crew shouted simultaneously, "Hurrah! Death to the English!"

The cutter had by this time come so close that her rigging was quite visible.

Suddenly there was a puff of smoke, a flash, and a loud report, and a shot whizzed past the bowsprit of the *Sparrow Hawk*.

"She wants to see our flag!"

"What shall we hoist?" asked Zeli.

"This," said Kernok, turning over a sailor's old tarry jacket with his foot. "We must be gallant."

"It's a rum 'un," said Zeli, and the old jacket fluttered at the top of the halyards.

This pleasantry did not appear to be well received on board the cutter, for two cannon balls, almost at the same moment, cut their way through the *Sparrow Hawk's* rigging.

"Oh, oh, the lovely creature is getting rusty!" said Kernok. "Now, Melie," he continued as he pointed his favorite gun, "let's hear what you have to say to this English dame."

"Bravo!" he cried when the smoke had cleared away and he had seen the effect of his shot. "See, Zeli, her jib is already in ribbons; that looks good, my boy, but when the *Sparrow Hawk* tickles her sides with her grappling claws, you'll see how she'll laugh."

"Hurrah!" shouted the crew.

The cutter did not reply to the corsair's shot, but quickly repaired her damages, and still bore down on the brigantine.

The two vessels were soon so close that the pirates could hear the English officers giving their orders.

"Now, my lads," said Kernok, jumping on the quarter-deck, "to your guns, and mind you don't fire till I order you."

XI. THE COMBAT

"Send shot, Master Durand!" "We've sprung a leak, Master Durand." "See, how my head bleeds, Master Durand!"

Thus was the name of this worthy functionary, who served as gunner, surgeon, and carpenter of the *Sparrow Hawk*, and now it rang out above the noise and tumult of the struggle. The *Sparrow Hawk* creaked and trembled in every joint, as if its timbers were coming asunder.

"Send shot, Master Durand!" "The leak!" "My leg!" was repeated, amid bustle and confusion.

"Sacrebleu! Wait an instant; I can't do everything at once; shot to send above—a leak to stop below—a head to bandage here—a leg to set there; I must begin with what is most urgent, and then I'll attend to you, grunters that you are; but what's the good of you now? You're as useless as a mast without sails!"

"Shot! I need more shot, Master Durand!"

"Shot! Why, if you play that tune a quarter of an hour longer, we won't have a single one left. Here, my lads, take care of these, for they are the last."

Durand then seized his calking utensils and hurried away to stop the leak.

"Ohhh!" cried Zeli. His right leg was shattered, and the other shot away.

Around him the rest of the wounded lay moaning, waiting until Master Durand could quit the mallet for the knife.

"Ohhh, my throat's on fire!" continued Zeli. "I can't move. What happened? Have our guns stopped firing?"

On the contrary, the firing was going on brisker than ever, but Zeli's hearing was growing weak at the approach of death.

"Oh, how I'm so cold and thirsty," he repeated. Then, turning to a fellow-sufferer, he exclaimed, "What, you, my Polish friend? What makes you stretch out like that? How ugly the rascal is! Look at his white eyes!"

The Pole was expiring in the last throes of agony.

"Durand, my old cock!" cried Zeli. "Come here and look at my leg!"

"Just a minute; another blow, and the damage will be no worse than an oar stroke in the water. Now, then, it's your turn. Oh, you've had it!"

Zeli tried to smile.

"Why, where's your other leg?"

"Still on deck; but help me rid of this one—it's weighing me down. Ohhh, give me a drink!"

Durand examined Zeli's leg, shook his head, and said: "Your number's up."

"Nonsense! Are you sure?"

"Quite sure."

"Then, if you're a good fellow, you'll take my pistol and put me out of misery."

"I was just about to suggest it."

"Thank you."

"Do you want to make a will?"

"No. But here's my watch—give it to Grain-o'-Salt."

"Well, go on."

"Ah! I forgot. If the captain escapes peppering, tell him from me that he's a brave commander."

"I won't forget."

"You think, then, there's no chance for me?"

"On my honor! You may be sure I wouldn't jest this way with a friend."

"That's true, but it's provoking, for all that. How cold it is! I can scarcely speak; my tongue feels as heavy as a lump of lead; good-by, comrade—your hand once more—are you ready?"

"Yes."

"Mind, don't miss me. Fire!"

Zeli's earthly career terminated.

Monsieur Durand would, perhaps, have liked to finish

all his operations in the same style, but his other patients, frightened at the violence of the remedy that had succeeded so well with Master Zeli, preferred the plasters of oakum and grease that the wise doctor applied indiscriminately to all his patients, with these consoling words to the dying, "What odds? When we die, there's an end of us; our next voyage would have been a rough one, with a cold winter; and wine not worth drinking," and a host of other kind sayings designed to soothe the last moments of the poor pirates, who had all the anxiety attendant on quitting an honorable existence, without exactly knowing the coast on which they were next to steer.

Monsieur Durand was rudely interrupted in the discharge of his spiritual and temporal duties by Grain-o'-Salt falling, like a bomb, in the midst of his patients.

"Have you come here to molest me, scoundrel?" said the doctor, accompanying this demand with a blow that might have felled an ox.

"No, Master Durand, I've come for shot; we've just fired the last we had, and the English cutter still holds out; but we've given her a shaving. By-the-bye, I forgot I had lost a finger; look here, Master Durand."

"Do you think I'm going to lose my time in looking at your scratch, you rascal?"

"Thank you, Master Durand; it's better than being short an arm. But look—here's another patient for you."

This was a wounded man they were lowering from the deck with a rope, which, not being properly fastened, slipped, and the poor fellow fell and, groaning, expired.

"Another one speedily cured!" said Durand, whose mind was absorbed in striving to devise a remedy for the want of shot.

"Shot! Shot! I say," cried several voices in accents of terror.

"Damn it! We must do something, even if we have to load our guns with cabin boys!" said Durand, hurrying on deck.

Grain-o'-Salt followed him, without knowing whether the intention the surgeon had expressed of using him as a projectile was a joke or not, but said, "I'd like that better than going to the hulks."

XII. VICTORY

"Shot! Let's have shot, or we'll go to the bottom like dogs!" cried Kernok as soon as Durand appeared on deck.

"Not a one left," said the doctor, grinding his teeth with rage.

"Hell and fury! We can't even give them a proper reception," said Kernok, thrusting Durand aside.

In fact the cutter, though horribly mutilated, was bearing straight down on them.

"By all the saints of the calendar," cried Kernok, "help me now, or I'll tear down every chapel on the coast of Pampoul!"

It appeared that the saints, whom Kernok appealed to so energetically, were favorably disposed toward him, for no sooner had he uttered this strange invocation than, struck with an idea, he shouted joyfully, "The piastres, my lads! The piastres! Let us load our guns with them. The English like money; they'll get it."

This idea electrified the crew, and three barrels of silver were soon brought on deck.

"Hurrah! Death to the English!" shouted the nineteen pirates who were still in fighting condition.

"They can't say we're misers," cried one.

"We're fighting with a lady. Silver shot! How gallant!" said another.

The guns were hardly loaded when the cutter made an attempt to run her bowsprit afoul of the *Sparrow Hawk's* rigging, but Kernok, by a skillful maneuver, got to windward, and then drifted down on her.

The cutter, too, had exhausted all her ammunition, and during the two-hour battle had also performed prodigies of valor.

One of the pirates fired his piece without orders.

"Dog!" cried Kernok, leveling him at his feet with a blow from an ax.

At this moment the two vessels touched each other. The English were standing, their boarding axes in their hands, ready to jump into the brigantine.

All was silent on board the *Sparrow Hawk.*

"Away! Away!" cried the English captain, a fine young man, about twenty-five, who, having had both his legs shot off, had caused himself to be placed in a barrel of bran, to stop the bleeding, and that he might be enabled to command to the last moment.

"Away! Away!" he repeated.

"Fire!" shouted Kernok.

The English sprang forward, and twelve of the *Sparrow Hawk's* guns vomited a shower of piastres full in their faces.

"Hurrah!" cried the pirates.

When the smoke had cleared away, there was not an Englishman to be seen; some of them had fallen into the sea, others back on the deck of the cutter, and all were either killed or frightfully mutilated.

The cries of battle were followed by a gloomy and imposing silence. The eighteen pirates—the sole survivors—isolated in the middle of the ocean, and surrounded with dead bodies, could not look on each other without a feeling of terror.

Kernok himself fixed his eyes, in a sort of stupor, on the trunk of the English captain, which was now further disfigured by the loss of an arm, his fair hair was soaked in blood, and there was a smile on his lips; his last thought was, no doubt, of her who, when she heard of his glorious death, would clothe herself in robes of mourning.

Kernok seemed calm and cheerful. His sailors looked at each other in stupid amazement, then cried, "Long live Captain Kernok and the *Sparrow Hawk!*"

"Hurrah, my lads!" replied Kernok. "You see the *Sparrow Hawk* has a hard beak, but we must now think of repairing our damages. According to my calculation, we must be somewhere near the Azores. The breeze is freshening, my

lads; come, get the deck washed. As to the wounded," said
he thoughtfully, "let them be taken on board the cutter,
Master Durand."

"To——" said the doctor, looking inquiringly.

"You'll find out!" replied Kernok darkly.

Durand went to execute the captain's order, murmuring
to himself, "What's he going to do with them? This doesn't
look good!"

"Come here, boy," said Kernok to Grain-o'-Salt, who was
wiping, with a sorrowful look, the watch that Zeli had be-
queathed to him, which was covered with blood. When the
boy raised his head, the tears were running down his
cheeks; he advanced to the terrible captain without the
slightest fear; one idea had entire possession of his mind—
he was thinking of Zeli, to whom he was devotedly attached.

"Go below, and tell my wife that she may come and
embrace me. Do you hear?" said Kernok.

"Yes, Captain," replied Grain-o'-Salt, and a large tear
ran down his cheek and fell on the watch. He then quickly
disappeared by the main hatchway in search of Melie, and
a few minutes later returned on deck, but Melie was not
with him.

"Where is my wife, blockhead?"

"She is, Captain——"

"She's what? Out with it, you rascal?"

"She's in the hold, Captain."

"I know that well enough, you scoundrel. Why doesn't
she come on deck?"

"Because she's dead, Captain."

"Dead!" exclaimed Kernok, turning pale, while, for the
first time in his life, a look of sorrow and anguish passed
over his countenance.

"Yes, Captain, killed by a shot that struck us below
watermark, and, what is curious, your wife's body has
stopped up the hole, and prevented us from going to the
bottom."

Kernok rushed into the hold, and stood dry-eyed and
clenching his fists, gazing on Melie's body.

Poor Melie! Even her death was useful to her lover!

Kernok remained with her for about two hours, during which time he completely assuaged his grief, for, when he again appeared on deck, his countenance was calm and placid.

"Why can't we stay on the *Sparrow Hawk*, Master Durand?" asked several of the wounded.

"I don't know, my lads; perhaps it's because the air is better here; a change of air does a sick man good."

"But, Master Durand, they're taking the cutter's masts and yards to the brigantine. How can we sail?"

"Perhaps by steam," replied the doctor, who could not resist the pleasure of uttering a joke.

"What! Are you going to leave us, Master Durand? And you, too, comrades?" said the poor fellows as they saw the surgeon and a few of the crew jump into a boat to return to the brigantine.

"Yes," said a Parisian who had lost an arm, and had a bullet lodged in his spine, "it's pretty certain that they've sent us here for a change of air."

"Why?"

"To perish! So they can have our share of the prize. If they had an ounce of decency, they'd make a hole in the bottom and put us out of our misery at once, instead of leaving us here to devour one another, like a lot of sharks, for I've just heard that there are no provisions on board the cutter, which was one of the reasons she chased us. It's rotten to die so rich. With my share of the prize, I'd have a wonderful time in Paris. God! The Ambigu, Vauxhall, and the girls! Ah, what a time! I'll be up the spout before you could fasten a jacket. My legs are already done for."

Here his voice grew faint, and five minutes later he was dead.

The Parisian had guessed rightly. It would be impossible to describe the curses that were heaped on Kernok and his crew. Every one swore in his own language, and the uproar was enough to wake a prebendary, but the men were too far gone to help themselves. Some of them, viewing their fate in all its horror, ended their sufferings by crawling to the edge of the vessel and dropping overboard.

"Your orders are executed, Captain," said Durand on returning to the brigantine.

"We are once more fitted out," replied Kernok. "The breeze is freshening from the south. With this mizzen for a mainsail, and these topgallants instead of topsails, we can force our passage."

"Are we to leave these poor devils?" said Durand, pointing to the cutter.

"Yes," replied Kernok.

"It's not a very delicate proceeding."

"True. Do you know what provisions we have left, resulting from your revel, savages?"

"No."

"Well, we have just one barrel of biscuits, three casks of water, and one of rum; in three days, scoundrels, you got through the provisions destined for three months."

"It was your fault, as much as ours."

"It can't be helped now. We have about eight hundred leagues to go, and eighteen men to feed, who must be looked to first, for they are able to work."

"Then those on board the cutter must either set to and eat one another or die like dogs, for the poor devils will be hungry tomorrow."

"Let them! It's better it should be they, who are half dead already, than we, who have still some cable to run out."

The sailors, having heard this conversation, began to murmur.

"We won't abandon our comrades," they said.

Kernok fixed his eagle glance on them, and, taking up his battle-ax, said:

"You won't, won't you?"

All were silent.

"Do you know," continued he, "that we are eight hundred leagues from land, which will take at least fifteen days to reach, and that, if we were to keep the wounded on board, we would soon be without water?"

"That's true," replied the surgeon; "the wounded always drink like fishes."

"And," resumed the captain, "when we are without water and biscuits, do you imagine that St. Kernok would send us any? We would be obliged to eat each other's flesh, and drink each other's blood, as they'll have to do. How would you like that, lascars that you are? Whereas, if we try to reach the coast of Bordeaux, we may, like good citizens, spend the rest of our lives in France, with our prize money, which will not be any the less for having theirs joined to it."

This argument lulled all their scruples.

"In short," continued Kernok, "it must be so, because I have determined on it, do you understand that? And the first that opens his mouth to grumble again, I'll close it for him with the hilt of my dagger. So now get ready, and we'll run to the northward."

The eighteen survivors still aboard the *Sparrow Hawk* silently obeyed the captain, and cast a last look at their poor comrades, who rent the air with their cries when they saw the brigantine leave them.

After a long and stormy passage the *Sparrow Hawk* cast anchor, and moored in the bay of Pampoul.

XIII. THE TWO FRIENDS

The Golden Anchor at Plonezoch is certainly an excellent inn. Before it stand two fine oak trees, spreading their branches over nicely polished tables, which always have an inviting look, and, as the Golden Anchor is on the main road, it commands, on a fine July morning, especially on a market day, a full view of as stirring and as animated a scene as one can imagine.

Two honest-looking fellows, admirers of this beautiful locality, were seated at one of the tables, chatting on a variety of subjects, and it looked as if their conversation had lasted a considerable time, for they had a goodly number of empty bottles before them.

One of them was a ugly man of about sixty, with large white whiskers that contrasted strongly with his sunburned skin. He had on an immense and grotesquely fashioned blue coat, large drill trousers, and a scarlet waistcoat, with anchor buttons on it, which was five or six inches too short for him. An immense well-starched shirt collar rose high above his ears, silver buckles sparkled on his shoes, and a glazed hat, sitting jauntily on one side of his head, gave him a careless appearance, rather at variance with his advanced age! It appeared, however, from the restraint visible in his manners, that he was in full costume for the occasion.

His friend was simply attired and appeared to be a good deal younger. His dress consisted of a cloth jacket and trousers, and a black cravat, negligently tied, so as to display a sinewy neck, which supported a joyous, open countenance.

"It will be," said the younger, knocking the ashes out of his pipe and sighing heavily, "twenty years come St. Saturnin since our poor brigantine anchored for the last time in the bay of Pampoul, under the command of the late Monsieur Kernok."

"How quickly the time passes!" replied his companion, tossing off a glass of brandy. "It seems like only yesterday, doesn't it, Grain-o'-Salt? When we're by ourselves, I always call you Grain-o'-Salt because it reminds me of our happy days."

"Confound it! Don't put yourself under any restraint, Monsieur Durand; you are privileged; besides, you were a friend of poor Kernok," he added with a sigh.

"It can't be helped, my boy; we must all slip our cables when the time comes, as I used to say to my patients, and——"

"Yes, yes, I know, Master Durand," interrupted Grain-o'-Salt, afraid that the ex-gunner, carpenter, and surgeon of the brigantine was about to start telling of his triple exploits, "but my heart aches when I think that, only a year ago, we used to amuse ourselves at his farm, and smoke our pipes together."

"That's true, Grain-o'-Salt. God in heaven! What a man he was! How beloved in the whole neighborhood! If an unfortunate sailor applied to him, he was sure to be relieved immediately. In fact, during the whole twenty years he lived there, everybody spoke of his charity. And how respectable he looked, with his long white hair and his brown coat! and wasn't he the picture of good temper, when he carried the old gunner's children on his back! There was only one thing I had to reproach him with—he was too fond of the clergy."

"Oh, that was because he was churchwarden, Master Durand. But that was only to kill time. When robed in his large gown on the fete days of the parish, wasn't he the spitten image of St. Jean du Doigt?"

"I preferred seeing him on the quarter-deck, with his battle-ax in hand," replied Durand, emptying his glass.

"And in the procession, Master Durand, with his wax taper, which, despite everything, he would always carry, like a sword. But what vexed the curate most was his chewing during mass, and spitting among the people. How provoking it was that all his property should go to the government because he didn't make a will! I was at St. Pol when the accident happened, but you, I believe, were present, Master Durand?"

"Yes, my boy, I was there. It was about eight o'clock in the morning when they came to tell me that there was a smell of fire proceeding from Kernok's chamber. None of them had courage to venture into the room, so I went in, and, well, it unnerves me to think of it!"

After swallowing a glass of brandy, he continued: "Went in, and saw the body of my old friend, covered from head to foot with a blue flame. I threw some water on him; it was no use. You seem surprised, Grain-o'-Salt. I wasn't; I predicted it."

"What, Master Durand!"

"Yes, I used to say to him, 'My old friend, immediate combustion is certain to put an end to your existence.'"

"But," said Grain-o'-Salt, "aren't you afraid of meeting the same fate?"

"Oh, it's different with me, my boy; I always dilute my brandy with a little gin. He, the old lascar, used to gulp his in its raw state. By-the-bye, Grain-o'-Salt, I believe it's about time for us to go to the chapel and hear the Mass we've paid for the good of our poor old friend's soul."

Grain-o'-Salt drew out a large silver watch, saying, "You're right. Do you remember that watch, Master Durand?"

"Do I know it? Ah yes. Poor Zeli gave it to me, the day the *Sparrow Hawk* fought the English cutter, saying, "Give this to Grain-o'-Salt. Good-by, old friend; don't miss me.' Damn it! When I think of that now, it makes me feel worse than I did then."

Grain-o'-Salt paid the check, and the two friends walked, arm in arm, to the chapel of St. Jean du Doigt.

XIV. MASS FOR THE DEAD

The clock of St. Jean's had just announced the hour at which the service for the soul of the late Nicholas Kernok was to commence, and the whole population of the district, by whom the worthy old man was almost adored, had left their work and were now waiting at the church door to pay their last tribute to the memory of their departed benefactor.

Grain-o'-Salt and Master Durand arrived just as the church door was opened, and were respectfully greeted by the crowd. The sun joyously darted its golden rays through the stained-glass windows, and the light fell, checkered with a thousand hues, on the pew that Kernok, decked in his robes of office, used to occupy on solemn occasions. Alas! How calm and dignified was his demeanor! How skillfully he would hide his chewing from the eyes of the curate! How piously he would close his eyes, as if in prayer, when the sermon made him a little drowsy!

Monsieur Karadeuc, the officiating priest, now rose amid profound silence and began to speak.

"My dear brethren, *'Apprehendi te ab extremis terrae et a longinquis ejus vocavi te; elegi te, et non abjeci te; ne limeas, quia ego tecum sum.'"*

As the audience was composed of Bretons, not well versed in the classics, this exordium did not produce a great effect.

"This, my brethren, means, 'I have taken thee by the hand, to bring thee from the extremities of the earth. I have called thee from the most distant places; I have chosen thee, and I have not rejected thee; fear nothing, for I come to thee!' Now, my brethren, these words are applicable to the late worthy and virtuous Monsieur Kernok, whose loss we all so deeply deplore."

Here Master Durand nudged Grain-o'-Salt, who placed his finger by the side of his nose and smiled.

"Alas, my brethren," resumed the curate, "Monsieur Kernok was a lamb removed from the fold to distant climes, and providence took him by the hand."

"What a lamb!" said Grain-o'-Salt with suppressed laughter.

The preacher continued:

"Providence, my brethren, also said to him, *'Elegi, non abjeci te.* I have chosen thee, and have not rejected thee, although thy life had been one of agitation.' Yes, my brethren, his life was agitated, but, after sailing on a stormy sea, the poop of his skiff reached a shore of peace and repose."

"Poop!" said Durand disdainfully. "It's the prow, you mean, Father."

The preacher looked indignantly at Durand, and again said:

"Yes, the poop of his skiff reached, at last, a shore of peace and repose, where, under the fostering care of this worthy and virtuous man, the flowers of charity and religion sprang up and blossomed around him. Therefore, my brethren, join with me in thanking the King of kings for

having bound the brow of him, whose loss we so much regret, with the garland of eternity."

"Amen!" responded the congregation.

"I say, Grain-o'-Salt, picture to yourself Kernok's brow
being bound with the garland of eternity!"

The curate descended, and proceeded, followed by all,
to the cemetery, where the remains of Kernok reposed.

The countenance of Grain-o'-Salt became sad and mournful. In his two hands he held his hat, while Durand, with
one hand pressed the arm of his companion, and with the
other wiped the tears from his eyes.

The curate muttered a prayer, which was repeated by
the assistants on their bended knees. All then retired, save
Durand and Grain-o'-Salt, who, long after the sun had disappeared behind the mountains, were still seen seated pen-
sively by the corsair's tomb.

Gaspard de la Nuit

BY ALOYSIUS BERTRAND

TRANSLATED BY ANGEL FLORES

ALOYSIUS BERTRAND
1807–41

Bertrand was born at Ceva, in the Piedmont, where his French father was captain of the garrison, but he spent most of his life in Dijon. His work first appeared in print in the local *Le Provincial*, but after this paper ceased publication he moved to Paris. When he read his poems at Charles Nodier's Sunday evenings, the literary critic Sainte-Beuve and the publisher Victor Pavie heard them and were favorably impressed. But he never saw publication of his only book, *Gaspard de la Nuit*, which though ready for the press in 1836 did not appear until a year after his death of tuberculosis in a Paris hospital, and then only thanks to Sainte-Beuve's unflagging interest. Twenty years later, after *Gaspard de la Nuit* had been forgotten, Charles Baudelaire, the greatest poet of the age, confessed that he had learned from it to write his prose poems.

ABOUT BERTRAND: The best biography is in French, by Cargill L. B. Sprietsma, Paris, Campion, 1926. There is an essay in English in Arthur Ransome, *Portraits and Speculations*, London, Macmillan, 1913.

HAARLEM

When from Amsterdam the gold cock crows then
the gold hen of Haarlem will lay.

—THE ANNALS OF NOSTRADAMUS

Haarlem, that admirable genre painting that sums up the
entire Flemish school, Haarlem painted by Jan Breughel,
Peeter Neef, David Teniers, and Paul Rembrandt.

The canal with its trembling blue waters, and the church
with its flamboyant gold wheel-window; the stoël, that
stone balcony, with laundry drying in the sun, and the
roofs, green with clinging hop vines.

And the storks, high overhead, flapping their wings
round the town clocks, with necks outstretched, gathering
raindrops in their beaks.

And the carefree burgomaster patting his double chin,
and the florist pining away with love, his eyes fixed on a
tulip.

And the gypsy absorbed in her mandolin and the old man
making music on his Rommelpot, and the boy puffing air
into a bladder.

And the drinkers smoking in the one-eyed coffeehouse,
and the maidservant at the hotel hanging a dead pheasant
out the window.

THE FIVE FINGERS OF THE HAND

*A decent family which has never gone bankrupt
and none of whose members have ever been hung.*
　　　　　—THE RELATIVES OF JEAN DE NIVELLE

The thumb is that sharp-tongued rogue, a fat Flemish
tavern-keeper who smokes by his door under a bock-beer
sign.

The forefinger is his wife, a virago as wizened as a cod-
fish, who starts off the day by slapping the face of her
maid, of whom she is jealous, and fondling the bottle, with
which she has fallen in love.

The middle finger is their son, a lad roughhewn by an
ax, who might have become a soldier had he not been a
brewer, or a horse had he not been a man.

The ring finger is their daughter, as vivacious and pro-
vocative as a Molière heroine who sells her lace to the
ladies and her smiles to the gentlemen.

And the pinkie is the Benjamin of the family, a whining
brat who forever clings to his mother's apron strings like an
infant hanging from the tusk of an ogress.

The five fingers of the hand are the most fabulous five-
leaf gillyflower that has ever adorned the flower beds of
the noble city of Haarlem.

THE TOWER OF NESLE

*At the Tower of Nesle there was once a guard-
room used at night by the patrol on duty.*
　　　　　—BRANTOME

"Jack of spades!"
"Queen of hearts! I win!"

And the tough soldier who had lost banged the table so hard he sent the stakes flying to the floor.

Just then, however, Sir Hughes, the provost, spat on the iron brazier and grimaced like a miscreant who has swallowed a spider while eating his soup.

"Ugh! Do the sausage makers scald their hogs at midnight? By God, a boatload of hay is burning on the Seine!"

The fire, at first a mere sprite somewhere off in the fog, soon kicked up a devilish row, drawing the cannon and any number of harquebuses along the water's edge.

A huge crowd of punsters, cripples, and nighthawks now hastened to the river front and danced jigs before the spiral of flame and smoke.

And the fire reddened both the Tower of Nesle, whence the night watch came with their carbines on their shoulder, and the Tower of the Louvre, from one of whose windows the king and queen saw all without being seen.

THE GOTHIC ROOM

Nox et solitudo plenae sunt diabolo.
—THE FATHERS OF THE CHURCH

Once I murmured at night: The earth is an embalmed calyx, whose pistil and stamens are the moon and stars.

And with eyes heavy with sleep, I closed the window which the cross of calvary encrusted black in the yellow aureole of the stained-glass windows.

Yet, if it were not midnight—the blazoned time of devils and dragons!—when the gnome gets drunk on the oil from my lamp!

If only it were the wet-nurse humming monotonous lullabies as she rocks a stillborn baby in my father's cuirass!

If only it were a Hessian foot soldier's skeleton sandwiched in the woodwork and banging with his forehead and elbows and knees!

If only it were my grandfather stepping down from his

worm-eaten picture frame to dip his gauntlet in the holy
water of the font!

But it is Scarbo who comes to bite my neck and who,
to cauterize my bleeding wound, sticks into it his iron finger red-hot from the furnace!

SCARBO

My God, grant me at the hour of death the
prayers of a priest, a linen shroud, a sprucewood
bier, and a dry place.—THE MARSHALL'S LITANIES

That night Scarbo muttered in my ear: "Whether you
die absolved or damned, your shroud shall be a cobweb
and I shall inter the spider with you!"

"Oh! For a shroud," I replied, my eyes red from so much
weeping, "give me at least an aspen leaf in which the lake
breeze will rock me."

"No!" chuckled the dwarf cheerily, "you should be fodder
for the horn-beetle who hunts at evening the gnats dazzled
by the setting sun!"

"Do you prefer then," I answered still weeping, "do you
prefer that I be sucked by a tarantula with an elephant's
trunk?"

"Well," he added, "console yourself: your shroud will be
of strips of gold-studded snakeskin and I shall bind you like
a mummy.

"And from the shadowy crypt of Saint Benigne where I
shall set you standing by the wall, you shall listen at your
leisure to infants weeping in limbo."

THE MADMAN

*One carolus gold piece, or else, if you like, a
golden lamb.*—FROM A MS. IN THE KING'S LIBRARY

The moon was combing her hair with a large-toothed
ebony comb that sent silver showers of fireflies over the
hills, the meadows, and the wood.

On my roof sat Scarbo, a gnome of immense treasure,
sifting, to the cry of the weather vane, ducats and florins
that hopped about rhythmically as the counterfeit coins fell
and cluttered the street.

How the madman giggled, each night, roaming the
empty city, with one eye on the moon, and the other slit
open!

"Deuce take the moon!" he growled, gathering the devil's
coins. "I shall buy the pillory to warm myself in the sun!"

But it was still the moon, the moon about to sleep. And
in my hollow Scarbo worked quietly striking ducats and
florins from the machine.

While lost in the night, a snail, with horns erect, sought
its way over my luminous stained-glass windows.

MOONLIGHT

*Awake, ye sleepy heads,
And pray for the dead.*
                    —THE NIGHT CRIER'S CRY

Oh! how sweet it is, as the hour trembles in the belfry, to
watch the moon whose nose is like a carolus of gold!

Two lepers lamented beneath my window, a dog howled
at the crossroads, and the cricket in my hearth prophesied
in undertones.

But soon my ear questioned naught but a deep silence. The lepers had stepped inside their hovel keeping time to the blows Jacquemart was showering on his wife.

The dog had taken to his heels before the halberds of the watch rusty with rain and stiff from the cold north-wind.

And the cricket had gone to sleep as soon as the last spark had flickered its last in the ashes of the fireplace.

And, to myself—so incoherent is the fever!—it seemed that the moon, wrinkling her face, had stuck out her tongue like a hanged man.

Emilie

BY GÉRARD DE NERVAL

TRANSLATED BY WILLIAM M. DAVIS

GÉRARD DE NERVAL
1808–55

The Parisian Gérard Labrunie, who early became known as "Gérard de Nerval," was perhaps the only really romantic poet to come out of France. At the age of twenty he translated *Faust*. He took part in the boisterous première of Hugo's *Hernani* in 1830. And in 1836 he fell deeply in love with a musical-comedy actress. When she rejected him for another man he felt it to be "the most anguishing, the most terrible blow that Destiny can deal a soul" and, in the end, he went mad. From 1842, the year of her death, until the cold winter's dawn in 1855 when he was found hanging from the window bars of a Paris flophouse that had refused to admit him, Nerval's life and work were suffused with his sense of personal tragedy. He tried hopelessly to recapture time past: reliving his blissful adolescence in *Sylvie* (1853); re-creating from his dreams an incantatory world in *Aurélia* (1853); and fusing, as in his group of sonnets, *Les Chimères* (1853), the lugubrious climate of madness with flashes of genius and shades of Swedenborgian occultism.

ABOUT NERVAL: S. A. Rhodes, *Gérard de Nerval*, N.Y., Philosophical Library, 1951; see also Angel Flores, *An Anthology of French Poetry from Nerval to Valéry*, N.Y., Doubleday Anchor Books, 1958.

"No one really knows the story of Lieutenant Desroches, who was killed last year at the battle of Hambergen, two months after his wedding. If it was suicide, may God forgive him! But surely a man who died defending his country deserves to have his actions given a better name than that, whatever his intentions."

"Which brings us back," said the doctor, "to the question of compromising with conscience. Desroches was a philosopher who had had enough of life. He didn't want to die a useless death, so he plunged bravely into battle and killed as many Germans as he could, saying, 'This is the best I can do. Now I'm content to die.' And as he took the blow that killed him he shouted, 'Vive l'Empereur!' Ten soldiers from his company will tell you the same thing."

"It was no less a suicide for that," said Arthur. "Still, it wouldn't have been right to deny him church burial."

"In that case, you underrate the self-sacrifice of Curtius. That young Roman knight may have been ruined by gambling, unlucky in love, and tired of living, who knows? But there must be something fine about a man who when he has made up his mind to leave this world, makes his death useful to others. So you can't call Desroches a suicide, for suicide is no less than the supreme act of egoism, which is the only reason men condemn it. . . . What are you thinking about, Arthur?"

"About what you were just saying—that Desroches killed as many Germans as he could before he died."

"Well?"

"Well, those fine fellows will give a pretty poor account-
ing of the lieutenant's glorious death before God. And you
must admit, this *suicide* looks very much like *homicide*."

"Oh, but who would think of that? The Germans are our
enemies."

"But does a man who has made up his mind to die have
enemies? At that moment, all feelings of nationality disappear, and I doubt if one thinks of any country but the next
world, or of any emperor but God. But here's the abbé,
listening to us without a word. Still, I hope he approves
of what I'm saying. Come now, Father, give us your opinion, and try to reconcile us. It's a knotty question, and the
story of Desroches, or rather what the doctor and I think
we know of it, appears to be every bit as involved as our
discussion."

"Yes," said the doctor, "I've heard that Desroches was
greatly distressed by his last wound—the one that disfigured
him so badly—and that perhaps he surprised his young
bride wincing or making fun of him. Philosophers are easily
offended. At any rate, he died, and willingly."

"Willingly, if you must, but don't call death in battle
suicide. It only adds to the confusion. You die in battle
because someone kills you, not because you want to die."

"Then . . . do you suppose it's fate?"

"My turn," said the priest, who had been collecting his
thoughts during this discussion. "Perhaps you will think it
strange of me to object to your paradoxes and suppo-
sitions. . . ."

"Go right ahead, by all means. You probably know more
about it than we do. You've been living at Bitche for a long
time now, and we've been told that Desroches knew you.
Perhaps you were even his confessor."

"In that case, I should have to keep silent. Unfortunately,
I wasn't, but I assure you, he died like a Christian, and I
shall tell you how and why, so that you will think of him
as a gentleman and a soldier who died a timely death for
humanity and for himself, according to the will of God.

"Desroches joined a regiment when he was only fourteen, at a time when most of our men were getting killed on the frontier, and our Army of the Republic was drafting children. He was as weak and slender as a girl, and it distressed his comrades to see his young shoulders sink under the weight of his gun. You must have heard the story of how permission was obtained from the captain to have it cut down six inches. With his weapon thus suited to his strength, Desroches did splendidly in Flanders; later on, he was sent to Hagenau, where we, or rather you, had been fighting for so long.

"At the time of which I am going to speak, Desroches was at the height of his powers, and as regimental ensign-bearer, he served far in advance of his rank, for he was practically the only man to survive two reinforcements. He had just been made a lieutenant when, twenty-seven months ago, at Bergheim, he led a bayonet charge and received a Prussian saber cut straight across the face. The wound was ghastly. The field surgeons, who had often joked with him because he had come through thirty battles without a scratch, frowned when he was brought in. 'If he lives,' they said, 'he'll lose his wits or go mad.'

"The lieutenant was sent to Metz to recover, and many miles went by before he regained consciousness. It took five or six months in a decent bed, with the best of care, before he could sit up, and another hundred days before he could open one eye and see. Soon tonics were prescribed, then sunlight and movement, and finally, short walks. One morning, supported by two companions, he set out all giddy and trembling for the Quai St. Vincent, which adjoins the military hospital, and there they sat him in the noonday sun, under the lime trees, at the edge of the promenade: the poor fellow thought he was seeing the light of day for the very first time.

"Soon he could walk by himself, and every morning he came to sit on the same bench. His head was a mass of black taffeta bandages that all but covered his face, and as he passed, he could always count on a friendly greeting from the men, and a gesture of deep sympathy from the women. From this, however, he derived little comfort.

"But once seated on his bench, he forgot his misfortune and thought only of how lucky he was to be alive after such a shock, and in such pleasant surroundings. Before him, the old fortress—a ruin since the time of Louis XVI— spread its dilapidated ramparts, the flowering lime trees cast shadows on his head, and at his feet, in the valley that dipped away from the promenade, the Moselle, overflowing its banks, kept the meadows of St. Symphorien green and fertile between its two arms. Then came the isle of St. Saulcy, with its powder magazine, and its shady trees and cottages, and finally, the foamy white falls of the Moselle, its course sparkling in the sunlight. Then, as far as he could see, the Vosges Mountains rose up bluish and misty in broad daylight, and he gazed at them with ever-increasing delight, his heart gladdened by the thought that there lay his country—not conquered land, but true French soil, while these rich new provinces he had fought for were fickle beauties, like those of a love won yesterday, and gone tomorrow.

"In the early days of June, the heat was intense, and as the bench Desroches had chosen was well in the shade, one day two women came and sat down beside him. He greeted them calmly and continued to gaze at the horizon, but his appearance inspired so much interest they could not resist the temptation to ply him with sympathetic questions. One of the two was well advanced in age, and proved to be the aunt of the other, whose name was Emilie. The older woman earned her living by doing gilt embroidery on silk or velvet. When Desroches replied to their questions with questions of his own, the aunt informed him that Emilie had left Hagenau to keep her company, that she embroidered for churches, and that she had been an orphan for some time.

"The next day, the bench was similarly occupied, and by the end of the week, its three occupants were fast friends. Desroches, in spite of his weakness and humiliation at the attentions the girl lavished on him as if he were a harmless old man, felt lighthearted, and more like rejoicing at his good fortune than being distressed by it. Then, on his return to the hospital, he remembered his ghastly wound, and his scarecrow appearance, which caused him many hours of despair, though he had become almost used to it.

"Desroches had not dared remove the useless bandages, or look at himself in a mirror. Now the thought of doing so frightened him more than ever. Nevertheless, he ventured to lift up one corner of the dressing, and found beneath it a scar that was slightly pink, but by no means too repulsive. On further examination, he found that the various parts of his face had been sewn together fairly well, and that his eyes were as healthy and clear as ever. Of course, a few scraps of eyebrow were missing, but that was nothing! The slanting scar across his face, from forehead to ear was . . . well, it was a sword cut received at Bergheim, and nothing could be finer, as many a song has said.

"Desroches was astonished to find that he was so presentable after the long months during which he seemed a virtual stranger to himself. He cleverly concealed the hair that had turned gray on the wounded side under the abundant black on the left, drew his mustache out as far as it would go over the line of the scar, and on the following day, put on his new uniform and set out triumphantly for the park. Those who passed him on the way failed to recognize this sprightly young officer with tilted shako and a sword that jauntily slapped his thigh.

"He was the first to arrive at the bench by the lime trees, and sat down with his customary deliberation, although he was profoundly agitated and much paler than usual, despite the approval of his mirror.

"The two ladies were not long in arriving, but they suddenly turned and walked away at the sight of the smart-looking officer sitting on their accustomed bench. Desroches was deeply moved.

" 'What!' he cried. 'Don't you recognize me?'

"You mustn't think this is the prelude to a tale of pity turned to love, like the plot of some contemporary opera. The lieutenant now had serious intentions. Glad to find himself once more considered eligible, he hastened to reassure the two ladies, who seemed disposed to continue their friendship. Their reserve gave way before his forthright declarations. Besides, the match was suitable from every point of view: Desroches had a little property near Épinal, while Emilie's parents had left her a small house at Hagenau, which she rented as a restaurant, and received an income of five or six hundred francs, half of which she gave to her brother Wilhelm, chief clerk to the notary at Schennberg.

"When the arrangements had been completed, it was decided that the wedding should take place at Hagenau, which was Emilie's real home, for she had come to Metz only to be with her aunt, and it was agreed that she should return there afterward. Emilie was delighted at the prospect of seeing her brother again, and more than once Desroches's astonishment was aroused by the fact that the young man was not in uniform, like his contemporaries. He was told he had been excused on account of poor health, and Desroches was full of sympathy for him.

"So one day the prospective bride and groom and the aunt set out together for Hagenau. They took places in the public carriage that changes horses at Bitche. In those days, it was simply a ramshackle stagecoach made of leather and wickerwork. As you know, the road leads through beautiful country. Desroches, who had only been along it in uniform, sword in hand, with three or four thousand other men, was now able to enjoy the solitude, the hills in their mantle of dark green foliage, and the fantastic shape of rocks that cut the skyline. The fertile uplands of St. Avold, the factories of Saarguemines, and the thickly wooded copses of Limblingue, where poplar, ash, and pine display their varying banks of foliage, ranging from gray to dark green . . . you know what delightful scenery it is.

"As soon as they arrived at Bitche, they stopped at the Dragon, and Desroches sent for me at the fort. I went at once to join him, met his new family, and complimented the young lady, whose rare beauty and charm impressed me greatly. It was easy to see that she was very much in love with her future husband. The three of them lunched with me right here, where we're sitting, and several officers who were old friends of Desroches came to the inn and begged him to dine with them at the restaurant near the fort, where the staff took their meals. So it was agreed that the ladies should retire early, and that the lieutenant should devote his last evening as a bachelor to his friends.

"The dinner was lively; everyone enjoyed his share of the happiness and gaiety Desroches had brought with him. They all spoke rapturously of Egypt and Italy, and complained bitterly of the hard luck that kept so many good soldiers cooped up on the frontier.

" 'Yes,' grumbled some of the officers, 'the monotony is getting on our nerves. We're stifling here. We might as well be off on a ship somewhere as live without fighting or distractions of any kind, or any chance of promotion. *The fort is impregnable.* That's what Napoleon said when he passed through here to rejoin his forces in Germany. About all we have here is a chance to die of boredom.'

" 'Alas, my friends,' replied Desroches, 'it was hardly more amusing in my time. When I was stationed here, I had the same complaints. I got my commission by tramping in army boots down every highway and byway, and knew only three things: military drill, the direction of the wind, and the kind of grammar you learn from the village schoolmaster. So, when I was made second lieutenant and sent to Bitche with the second battalion of the Cher, I looked upon my stay here as an excellent opportunity for some real uninterrupted study. With this in mind, I assembled a collection of books, maps, and charts. I had studied tactics, and learned German without any trouble, for nothing else was spoken in this good French country. This way, the time—so tedious for you who have so much less to learn—seemed to pass all too quickly. At night I retired into a little stone room under the spiral of the main staircase. There I lit my lamp and worked, with all the loopholes carefully stopped, and on just such a night . . .'

"Here, Desroches paused a moment, drew his hand over his eyes, emptied his glass, and went on without finishing his sentence.

" 'You all know,' he said, 'the little path that leads up

here from the plain—the one they've made impassable by
blowing up a huge rock and not filling up the pit. Well,
it was always fatal to hostile troops attacking the fort. No
sooner did the poor devils start climbing up than they were
raked by four twenty-fours that swept the whole length of
the path. I suppose they're still there.'

" 'You must have distinguished yourself,' said one of the
colonels. 'Wasn't that the place you won your promotion?'

" 'Yes, Colonel, and that was where I killed the first and
only man I ever struck down in hand-to-hand fighting.
That's why it always distresses me to see this fort.'

" 'What!' they cried. 'After twenty years in service, fifteen
pitched battles, and perhaps fifty skirmishes, you expect us
to believe you've killed only one man?'

" 'I didn't say that, gentlemen; of the ten thousand cartridges I've rammed into my gun, for all I know, half may
have missed the mark. But at Bitche, I give you my word,
my hand was first stained with the blood of an enemy, and
my arm first drove the cruel point of my sword into a human breast—till it quivered to the hilt.'

" 'It's true,' interrupted one of the officers, 'a soldier does
lots of killing, but hardly ever feels it. Gunfire isn't really
execution; it's only the intention to kill. As for bayonets,
they play only a small part in the most dangerous charges;
ground is held or lost without close personal combat. Guns
clash, then disengage when resistance gives way. Take the
cavalry, for instance. They really fight hand to hand.'

" 'And so,' replied Desroches, 'just as you never forget
the last look of a man you kill in a duel, his death rattle,
or the sound of his fall, so I bear with me, almost in remorse—yes, laugh at me if you will—the pale, dreadful sight
of the Prussian sergeant I killed in the little powder magazine of this fort.'

"Everyone fell silent, and Desroches went on:

" 'It was night, and as I just explained, I was working.
At two o'clock everyone was asleep except the sentinels.
They patrolled in complete silence, so that any sound was
suspicious. However, I kept hearing some kind of protracted
movement in the gallery below my room. Then someone

bumped against a door, and it creaked. I ran out into the corridor and listened. I called to the sentry in a low voice —no answer. I hurried to alert the gunners, threw on my uniform, grabbed my naked sword, and ran in the direction of the noise. About thirty of us arrived at once at the place where the galleries converge, and in the dim lantern light, we recognized the Prussians. A traitor had let them in through the postern gate. They dashed forward in great confusion, and catching sight of us, fired a few shots, which produced terrific detonations under those low, shadowy ceilings.

" 'So there we were, face to face, with more of us pouring in all the time. We could hardly move, but a six- to eight-foot space still divided us. We French were so surprised, and the Prussians so disappointed, that no one thought of entering the lists. But this hesitation was only momentary.

" 'Extra torches and lanterns lit the scene—some of the gunners had hung theirs on the walls, and a kind of old-fashioned fighting took place. I was in the front line, face to face with a tall Prussian sergeant covered with stripes and decorations. He had a gun, but there was such a crush he could hardly move it. Alas! How well I remember! I don't know if he even intended to resist me; I lunged at him, and thrust my sword into his noble heart, then his eyes opened horribly, he tried to clench his fists, and he toppled backward into the arms of his comrades.

" 'I don't remember what happened next; later, I found myself in the courtyard, drenched with blood. The Prussians had retreated through the postern gate, and our gun-fire followed them back to their encampment!'

"When Desroches had finished speaking, there was a long silence, and then they spoke of other things. The look of sadness worn by these soldiers after hearing of this seemingly ordinary misfortune was very curious, when you come to think of it—and you could tell just how much a man's life is worth—even a German life, doctor—by examining the faces of those professional killers."

"I agree," replied the doctor, slightly taken aback, "bloodshed is a terrible thing, no matter what causes it.

Still, Desroches did nothing wrong—he was simply defending himself."

"Who knows?" muttered Arthur.

"A while ago, Doctor, you spoke of compromising with conscience. Tell us now, wasn't this sergeant's death a bit like murder? Can we be sure the Prussian would have killed Desroches?"

"But that's war. Who's to blame?"

"All right, that's war. But we kill men at three hundred paces in the darkness—men we don't know and who can't see us; we face these men we don't hate, and slaughter them with anger blazing in our eyes. Then we pat ourselves on the back and feel proud. And we call ourselves honorable, and Christians.

"It was time for bed, and Desroches himself was the first to forget his dismal story, for, from the little room he had been given, he could see a certain window through the trees, where a night lamp was burning. There lay his future happiness, and when, in the middle of the night, he was awakened by the watchman making his round, he was oppressed and a little frightened by the thought that in case of danger his courage would no longer electrify him into action. The next day, before the morning gun was fired, the captain of the guard opened a door for him and he found the two ladies waiting near the outer fortification. I accompanied them as far as Neunhoffen, and they went on to Hagenau to be married at the Registry Office, after which they were to return to Metz for the religious ceremony.

"Emilie's brother Wilhelm welcomed Desroches cordially enough, and the two brothers-in-law proceeded to take each other's measure. Wilhelm was of medium height, but well built. His blond hair was already very thin, as if he had been weakened by too much study or some great sorrow, and he wore blue glasses, for, as he said, his eyes were so weak that the least light pained him. Desroches had brought a bundle of papers with him, to which the young law student gave his careful attention, and then Wilhelm, in turn, produced the title deeds to his family property, insisting that Desroches should examine them. But he was dealing with a man who was trusting, unselfish, and in love, so the inspection did not last long. This attitude seemed to flatter Wilhelm somewhat, so he began taking Desroches's arm as they walked, offered him the use of one of his best pipes, and took him to see all his friends in Hagenau.

"This involved much smoking and drinking, and after ten introductions, Desroches begged for mercy. From then on he was allowed to spend his evenings alone with his fiancée.

"A few days later, the two lovers of the promenade bench were wed by the mayor of Hagenau. This worthy functionary, who must have been burgomaster before the French Revolution, had often held Emilie in his arms when she was a young child. He himself may even have registered her birth, and on the day before the wedding he had whispered to her, 'Why don't you marry a good German?'

"Emilie appeared to give little thought to such distinctions. Even Wilhelm had become reconciled to the lieutenant's mustache, for, to tell the truth, at first there had been a decided coolness between them. But Desroches had made great concessions—Wilhelm, a few, for his sister's sake—and with Emilie's good aunt to pacify and smooth things over at every interview, there was perfect agreement between them, and Wilhelm embraced his brother-in-law most cordially after the marriage contract had been signed. Before nine in the morning, everything was in order, so the four of them set out for Metz that same day. By six o'clock in the evening, the coach drew up before the Dragon at Bitche.

"Travel is none too easy in this country of woodland and interlacing streams; there are at least ten hills for every mile you go, and the coach shakes up its passengers pretty badly. This was probably the main reason for the young bride's discomfort on arriving at the inn. Her aunt and Desroches stayed in her room with her, while Wilhelm, who was famished, went down to the little dining room where the officers dined at eight.

"This time no one knew of Desroches's arrival, and the

soldiers of the garrison had spent a field-day in the Hus-
poletden woods. Desroches was determined not to leave
his wife that evening, and told the landlady not to mention
his name to a soul. The three of them stood at the window,
watching the soldiers go back into the fort, and later, as
it grew darker, they saw the men, dressed in fatigues, lining
up in front of the canteen for their army bread and goat's-
milk cheese.

"Wilhelm, meanwhile, trying to pass the time and forget
his hunger, had lit his pipe and was lolling near the door-
way, where he could breathe in both the tobacco smoke
and the smell of the cooking. At the sight of this middle-
class traveler with his cap pulled down to his ears and his
blue glasses fastened on the kitchen, the officers took it that
he would dine with them and looked forward to meeting
him. Perhaps he had come from a distance, was clever, or
had some news. That would be a stroke of luck. On the
other hand, if he came from the district, and maintained
a stupid silence, they could enjoy poking fun at him.

"A second lieutenant from the military school approached
Wilhelm and questioned him with exaggerated politeness.

" 'Good evening, sir. Have you any news from Paris?'

" 'No, sir, have you?' he replied quietly.

" 'Good Lord, sir, we never leave Bitche. How would we
ever get any?'

" 'And I, sir, never leave my office.'

" 'Are you in the Engineers?'

"This quip, aimed at Wilhelm's glasses, delighted the
other officer.

" 'I am clerk to a notary, sir.'

" 'Really? That's odd, at your age.'

" 'Do you wish to see my passport, sir?'

" 'Of course not.'

" 'Very well. Just tell me you're not trying to make a fool
of me, and I'll answer all your questions.'

"The officers became more serious, and the lieutenant
went on:

" 'I asked you, with no ill intentions, if you were in the
Engineers, because you wear glasses. Don't you know that

the officers in that corps are the only ones who have the
right to wear them?'

" 'And I suppose that proves I'm in the army, as you say.'

" 'But everyone's a soldier these days. You're not twenty-
five yet; you must be in the army, or else you are rich, you
have an income of fifteen or twenty thousand francs, and
your parents have made sacrifices for you, in which case
you wouldn't take the dinner at a place like this.'

"Wilhelm shook out his pipe and said, 'I don't know, sir,
whether you have the right to question me like this, but
I'll answer you explicitly. I have no income; I am simply a
clerk to a notary, as I told you. I was excused from the
service on account of my eyes. In short, I'm nearsighted.'

"This declaration was greeted by peals of laughter.

" 'My dear fellow,' cried Captain Vallier, slapping him
on the back. 'You're quite right. As the proverb says, *Better a live coward than a dead hero!*'

"Wilhelm turned crimson. 'I'm not a coward, Captain,
and I'll prove it whenever you like. What's more, my papers
are in order, and if you are a recruiting officer, I'll be glad
to show them to you.'

" 'Enough!' cried several of the officers, 'let him alone,
Vallier; he's a peaceful fellow with a perfect right to eat
here.'

" 'Yes, of course,' said the captain, 'let's sit down and eat.
I meant no harm, young man. Don't worry—I'm not the
recruiting doctor and this isn't the recruiting room. And
just to show you there are no hard feelings, how's about
sharing a wing of this tough old bird they'd like us to think
is a chicken?'

" 'No, thank you,' said Wilhelm, whose appetite had vanished. 'One of those trout at the end of the table will be
enough for me.' And he motioned to the servant girl to
bring him the dish.

" 'Are they trout, really?' said the captain to Wilhelm,
who had taken off his glasses to eat. 'By God, you've got
better eyesight than I have. Look here, frankly you could
handle a gun as well as the next man . . . but you have
influence, and know how to use it. Quite right, too. You

love peace and quiet. And why not? But if I were you, it would make my blood boil to read the army bulletin and hear about young men my own age getting killed in Germany. Perhaps you aren't French?'

" 'No,' said Wilhelm, with an effort that, however, brought him great satisfaction. 'I was born at Hagenau; I'm not French, I'm German.'

" 'German? But Hagenau is on this side of the Rhine frontier. It's one of the finest villages in the French Empire, province of the Lower Rhine. Look at the map!'

" 'I'm from Hagenau, I tell you. Ten years ago it was German; today it's French. But I shall always be German, just as you would always be French if your country ever belonged to Germany.'

" 'Those are dangerous things you're saying, young man. Be careful.'

" 'I may be wrong,' Wilhelm continued impetuously, 'and no doubt it would be wiser to keep them to myself, since I can't change them. But you yourself have carried things so far, that I must justify myself at all costs, or be taken for a coward. And now you know the reason that, to my mind, warrants my eagerness to make use of a real infirmity, though perhaps it would not stand in the way of someone who really wanted to defend his country. I must admit, I feel no hatred for the people you are fighting. If I had been forced to march against them, I suppose I, too, might be helping to lay waste and burn German fields and cities, and slaughter my own countrymen—former countrymen, if you prefer. And who knows?—perhaps even slay my own flesh and blood, or some friend of my father's, in some group of pretended enemies. Surely you can see that it's far better for me to busy myself with documents in a notary's office at Hagenau. And besides, there's been enough bloodshed in my family. My father gave his to the last drop, you see, and I——'

" 'Your father was a soldier?' interrupted Captain Vallier.

" 'My father was a soldier in the Prussian army and for a long time he defended the territory you occupy today. He was killed in the last attack on the fort at Bitche.'

"At these words, everyone pricked up his ears, and lost interest in refuting the nonsense about Wilhelm's nationality.

" 'Was it in '93?'

" 'In '93, on the seventeenth of November. My father had left Sirmasen the day before to rejoin his company. I know he told my mother that by means of a daring plan the fort would be taken without firing a shot. Twenty-four hours later he was brought back to us, dying. He expired on the doorstep, after he had made me swear to stay with my mother. She followed him two weeks later.

" 'Afterward I learned that that night the sword of a young soldier had pierced his breast, and thus fell one of the finest grenadiers in Prince Hohenlohe's army.'

" 'But we've heard about that,' said the major.

" 'Yes,' said Captain Vallier, 'that's the story of the Prussian sergeant killed by Desroches.'

" 'Desroches!' cried Wilhelm. 'Do you mean Lieutenant Desroches?'

" 'Oh no, no,' replied one of the officers hastily, realizing they were on the brink of some terrible revelation, 'the Desroches we meant was a light infantryman from this garrison who was killed four years ago, the first time he went into action.'

" 'Ah, he's dead,' said Wilhelm, mopping the sweat from his brow.

"A few minutes later the officers saluted and withdrew. Desroches watched their departure from his window upstairs, and then came down to the dining room, where he found his brother-in-law sitting at the long table with his head in his hands.

" 'Hmm . . . Asleep already? Well, I'd like some supper. My wife's finally got to sleep, and I'm famished. Let's have a glass of wine. It'll rouse us a bit, and you can keep me company.'

" 'No, I have a headache,' said Wilhelm. 'I'm going up to my room. By the way, those gentlemen told me some interesting things about the fort. Why don't you take me up there tomorrow?'

" 'Of course.'

" 'Fine. I'll wake you in the morning.'

"After supper, Desroches went up to Wilhelm's room, where a bed had been prepared for him, for he would sleep alone until the religious ceremony had been performed. Wilhelm lay awake all night, sometimes weeping silently, and sometimes glaring furiously at Desroches, who smiled in his dreams.

"What we call presentiment is very much like the pilot-fish that swim ahead of an enormous half-blind whale to bring it news of jagged rocks and sandy bottoms. We go through life so mechanically that some of our fellow be-ings, who are heedless by nature, would run afoul or be dashed to bits without a moment's thought of God, if noth-ing ever ruffled the surface of their happiness. Some take warning from the raven's flight; others, for no apparent rea-son; and yet others proceed with the greatest care if they have had some sinister dream. Such is presentiment. 'You are going to be in danger,' says the dream. 'Watch out,' cries the raven. 'Be sad,' whispers the brain.

"Toward the end of the night, Desroches had a peculiar dream. He was in a cave beneath the earth. A white shadow was following him, and its garments kept brushing against his heels. When he turned upon it, the figure drew back. Finally, it retreated so far he could see nothing but a little white speck. Presently this speck began to grow. It became luminous and filled the whole grotto with light. Then it went out. A slight noise was heard, and Wilhelm entered the room, wearing his hat and a long blue cloak.

"Desroches woke up with a start. 'Good Lord! Have you been out already this morning?'

" 'You must get up,' replied Wilhelm.

" 'But will they let us in at the fort?'

" 'Of course. Everyone but the guards is out drilling.'

" 'Already? Very well. I'll be with you in a moment. Just give me time to say good morning to my wife.'

" 'She's quite all right, I've seen her. Don't concern your-self.'

"Desroches was rather surprised at this reply, but he put

it down to impatience and gave in once more to this fraternal authority that he would soon be able to shake off.

"On their way to the fort, he looked back at a window in the inn, and thought, 'Emilie is probably asleep.' But the curtain fluttered and was drawn across the window, and Desroches thought he saw someone step back into the room to avoid being seen.

"They had no trouble gaining entrance to the fort. A disabled captain, who had not dined at the inn the night before, was in command of the outpost. Desroches asked for a lantern and proceeded to guide his silent companion from room to room.

"After stopping at several points of interest to which Wilhelm paid little attention, he asked, 'Aren't you going to show me the underground passages?'

" 'Certainly, if you like, but I assure you it won't be very pleasant. The dampness down there is terrible. The gunpowder is stored under the left wing and we can't get in without a special pass. On the right, are the water mains and raw saltpeter, and in the center, the countermines and galleries. Do you know what a vault is like?'

" 'Never mind. I'm curious to see where so many sinister encounters took place, and where you yourself, I am told, were once in mortal danger.'

" 'He won't spare me a single vault,' thought Desroches. 'This way, then, Brother; this gallery leads to the postern.'

"The light from the lantern flickered dismally on the musty walls, and glinted here and there on rusty sword blades and gun barrels.

" 'What weapons are these?' asked Wilhelm.

" 'Spoils from the Prussians killed in the last attack. My friends hung them here as trophies.'

" 'Then several Prussians were killed here?'

" 'A great many, where these passages meet.'

" 'Didn't you kill a sergeant here, a tall elderly man with a red mustache?'

" 'Yes, did I tell you about it?'

" 'No, but at dinner last night I was told of that exploit . . . you so modestly kept from us.'

" 'What's the matter, Brother? Why are you so pale?'

" 'Don't call me Brother, but enemy! Look, I am a Prussian! I am the son of the sergeant you murdered!'

" 'Murdered!'

" 'Or killed! Does it matter? See, here's where your sword went in.'

"Wilhelm threw back his cloak and pointed to a tear in his father's green uniform, which he had reverently kept and was now wearing.

" 'You—the son of that sergeant! For God's sake, tell me you're only joking!'

" 'Joking! Who would make jokes about a frightful deed like that? My father was killed here; his noble blood reddened these stones; perhaps this was his very sword! Come now, take another, and give me my revenge. . . . Come, this is no duel, it's German against Frenchman! En garde!'

" 'My dear Wilhelm, have you lost your mind? Put down that rusty sword. You want to kill me—is it really my fault?'

" 'You have a chance to kill me, too. Come on, defend yourself!'

" 'Wilhelm! Kill me as I am, unarmed. I'm going mad; my head's spinning. Wilhelm! I did what every soldier has to do. Just think! And besides, I'm your sister's husband— she loves me. Oh no! It's impossible!'

" 'My sister! . . . Yes, and that's the best reason there is why one of us has to die! My sister! She knows everything, and will never again set eyes on the man who made her an orphan. Your parting from her yesterday was final.'

"Desroches uttered a cry of rage and rushed at Wilhelm to disarm him; the struggle was a lengthy one; for the younger man answered Desroches's shaking with a strength born of fury and desperation.

" 'Give me that saber, you idiot! Give it to me!' Desroches cried. 'I refuse to be killed by a madman!'

" 'Go ahead,' Wilhelm retorted, choking with rage. 'Kill the son in the same gallery. And the son's a German too! A German!'

"At that moment footsteps were heard and Desroches let go. Wilhelm was at the end of his strength.

"Those footsteps were mine, gentlemen. Emilie had come to the presbytery and told me everything. The poor child wished to put herself under the protection of the Church. I kept back the words of pity that rose to my lips, and when she asked me whether she could continue to love her father's murderer, I said nothing. She understood, shook my hand, and left in tears. I had a hunch, and followed her to the inn, where she was told that her brother and husband had gone together to the fortress, and, suspecting the awful truth, I arrived in time to prevent these two men, maddened by rage and grief, from enacting a further tragedy.

"Although disarmed, Wilhelm refused to listen to Desroches's pleading; he was beaten, but his eyes still blazed with anger.

"I reproached him for his obstinacy. 'You alone,' I said, 'make the dead cry out for vengeance, and you alone would be the cause of this dreadful thing. Aren't you a Christian? Do you want to trespass on God's justice? Are you prepared to go through life with a murder on your hands? Atonement will be made, you may be sure of that, but it's not for us to force it.'

"Desroches shook my hand and said, 'Emilie knows everything. I will never see her again. But I know what I must do to give her her freedom.'

"'What are you saying?' I cried. 'Do you mean suicide?'

"At this word, Wilhelm got up and took Desroches's hand.

"'No!' he said. 'I was wrong. I am the only offender. I should have borne my suffering in silence.'

"I shan't describe the agony we all went through on that fateful morning; I used every religious and philosophical argument I knew, but could find no way out of that cruel situation. A separation was inevitable, in any case, but what grounds for it could be stated in court? Not only would it be painful for all concerned, but there was a political danger in letting it be known.

"I devoted myself to the task of defeating Desroches's sinister intentions and creating in his mind a religious antipathy to the crime of suicide. As you know, the poor fellow had been schooled in eighteenth-century materialism. Since his wound, however, his ideas had changed considerably and he had become one of those half-skeptical Christians—we've seen so many—who have concluded a little religion can't do any harm, and even consult a priest in case there may be a God! It was a vague belief like this that enabled him to listen to my comforting words.

"A few days went by. Wilhelm and his sister had not left the inn, for Emilie's health had not withstood the shock. Desroches stayed at the presbytery with me and spent his days reading the pious books I lent him. One day he went alone to the fort, and spent several hours there; on his return he showed me a sheet of paper with his name on it —his appointment as captain in a regiment that was about to rejoin the Partouneaux division.

"In about a month's time we received news of his strange and glorious death. Whatever may be said of the mad frenzy that drove him into battle, one felt sure that his bravery was a splendid example to the whole battalion, which had sustained heavy losses in the first charge."

When the story was over, the listeners remained silent, their minds absorbed by what they had heard of the life and death of this man. Then the priest rose from his seat and said, "If you have no objection to a change in the direction of our evening walk, gentlemen, we can follow this line of poplars glowing in the sunset, and I will take you to the Butte-aux-Lierres. From there we can see the cross of the convent where Madame Desroches withdrew."

The Anatomist

BY PETRUS BOREL

TRANSLATED BY ROSETTE C. LAMONT

PETRUS BOREL
1809-59

Petrus Borel was the twelfth child of an ironmonger. Born in Lyons, he studied at local religious schools and at fourteen was apprenticed to an architect in Paris, but his real interests were literary and political. He attended Nodier's Sunday evenings (where he met Aloysius Bertrand and Gérard de Nerval), championed romanticism at *Hernani's* première, and fought with the republicans during the 1830 Revolution. Emulating Byronic heroes and calling themselves *Jeunes France* and, later, *Bouzingos* (Noisemakers), Borel and his friends attacked all the established institutions of philistinism, particularly church, school, and academy, in the pages of his short-lived "La Liberté." His literary career began with a promising book of poems, *Rhapsodies* (1831); this was followed by a collection of short stories, *Champavert* (1833), in which "The Anatomist" appeared. As a collection the book is uneven, and in some places melodramatic, but the stories demonstrate Borel's originality and sense of humor. He contributed to sundry periodicals, translated *Robinson Crusoe* (1836), wrote a rambling two-volume novel, *Mme. Putiphar* (1839), and edited several journals. He also planned to found a publishing house, with Gérard de Nerval, but, in dire poverty and desperation, was forced to sail for Algeria as "Inspector of Colonization," a post that Théophile Gautier obtained for him in 1846. There, after wrangling for years with the civil and military authorities, he was dismissed for "inefficiency," and found little satisfaction in anything thereafter except his marriage to young Gabrielle Claye, by whom he had a son. Two years after the child's birth he died, in circumstances that remain mysterious. Some authorities have attributed his end to sunstroke, others to starvation.

ABOUT BOREL: Enid Starkie, *Petrus Borel the Lycanthrope*, New York, New Directions, 1954.

I. CHALYBARIUM

At that hour of nightly peace when cities look like ceme-
teries only one narrow, crooked street in Madrid was still
alive, an obscure artery that still pulsed with feverish violence. This somnambulant street of the slumbering city was
called Country House Lane. At one end of it rose a rich
dwelling, inhabited by a foreigner, a Fleming. Lights shining from within the brightly illuminated house projected
obliquely the outline of its stained-glass windows upon the
dark façade of the house opposite, so that in the darkness
it seemed to be strewn with maws of furnaces, with fiery
nets and golden webs.

The inner gate of this mansion was wide open and revealed a high, rib-vaulted portal, with its drop keystone,
at the foot of a great stone stairway, with openwork balus-
trades as delicate as the ivory of a fan, and all strewn with
sweet-smelling flowers.

A few halberdiers paced back and forth at the entrance.

At rare intervals, when the shouts of the mob at the outer
gates died down, the soft strains of an orchestra reached
the bottom of the stairs and re-echoed against the sonorous
vault.

The whole palace was feasting, but a crowd of common-
ers howled and banged at the outer gates, like knaves, and
stood on the parvis steps.

Now frightful hurrahs, now tittering and the sound of
hidden weapons: passing from one group to another, these

noises rose and subsided like peals of satanic laughter borne by stormy clouds.

"The doctor has chosen a good wedding day indeed. Saturday, the Feast of the Sabbath. A sorcerer could do no better," said a toothless old hag crouching in the opening of a wicket.

"True enough, my love, and by the God I worship, if all his dead clients came to the wedding, the lot of them would make a ring around Madrid."

"Imagine what would happen," the old woman started again, "if all the poor Castilians plucked clean by this hangman should appear, God help them, and come to reclaim their skins?"

"I've been told," said a little man with a beard, who was buried in the crowd and had to stand on tiptoe, "that he often dines on chops that didn't come from the butcher's."

"It's true! It's true!"

"No, no, it's false!" cried a tall young man leaning against a window. "Not true in the least! Why don't you ask Rivadeneyra, the butcher?"

"Silence! Will you keep quiet?" cried still louder a man in a brown cape with his hat pulled over his eyes. "Don't you recognize him? It's Enrique Zapata, the apprentice skinner! Hangman and executioner stick together. I'll bet if we searched his doublet, we'd find a hand or a leg."

"To think that old corpse eater is marrying a beautiful young bride!" said the old woman. "If I were King Philip, I'd prevent that ogre from——"

"Don't you realize," said the man in the brown cape, "that Philip II protects this Flemish dog? Why, even yesterday, Torrijos, the baker of La Cebada, disappeared, and you can be sure that he'll fatten the wedding cake. It's a disgrace! We must put an end to it!"

"It's foolish of the king to protect him. He ought to be burned alive!" hissed the crowd.

"Kill him!" shouted the angry crowd, hurling invectives at the halberdiers who held them at bay.

"Let him die!" echoed the mysterious young man in the brown cape.

"Death!" shouted the monks, raising their crucifixes and stirring up the crowd. "Kill him! Burn down the house!"

Suddenly the storm broke. Men shouting, "Kill him! Kill him!" rushed against the gate. A monk, brandishing a torch, led the onslaught. But the halberdiers, supported by Enrique Zapata and several students, forced them to retreat. Then the noise increased. The people drummed on kettles; the sound of bells mingled with the clash of naked blades and became a deafening, flailing thunder, an almost homicidal symphony.

II. SALTATIO, TURBA, MORS

Cordial banter seemed to be the order of the day within the palace, where no one paid heed to the rioting outside, particularly since the prevailing custom of the time was to greet the union of an old man and a young bride with such a clatter.

The bride's dancing partner, a dashing knight, had just made his appearance in the midst of the festivities, and the young couple seemed to be more interested in the whispered comments they exchanged than in the dance. At the other end of the ballroom the bridegroom was paying court to a pretty young cousin.

The ballroom opened onto a balcony that overhung the courtyard; and was full of guests. Ladies, knights, old people, and dueñas, ostensibly out for a breath of cool night air, came to give free rein to their lashing tongues. It was a concert of voices, high-pitched and low, grating or cackling, and a collection of pretty faces, and features convulsed with raucous laughter.

"Who is that handsome knight the bride is making eyes at?"

"Señorita, you are cruel!"

"Ha, ha, ha! Look at Don Vesalius over there, preening himself in his crimson hose and black doublet! Gad! Don't the legs in his boots look like quills in an inkwell? Watch him cavort with rosy, plump Amalia de Cárdenas. Doesn't he look like Milord Saturnus?"

"Or like Death leading Life in a dance?"

"Holbein's dance."

"Tell me, Olivares, what will he give her?"

"An anatomy lesson."

"Something to talk about, that's all."

"Thanks for the bride."

"Now that the saraband is over, watch him kiss the hand of our cousin Amalia."

"This isn't a middle-class wedding, but a brilliant *sarao.*"

"But where's the bride?"

"And where's the handsome knight?"

"Don Vesalius is looking for her, all flustered. *Busca, busca, perro viejo!*"

"Go ask him, Olivares, the one who's known as a sorcerer, what María's doing."

"Friend, let's not jump between the devil and the deep blue sea!"

The dance resumed. Vesalius again asked Amalia de Cárdenas, who made a face and laughed behind his back.

The bride was no longer in the ballroom, nor the brown cape in the cloakroom, and, in a dark corridor, steps were heard, and this:

"Cover yourself with this cape, María. Let's leave quickly!"

"Alderán, I can't!"

"And I can't leave you to be the prey of Vesalius. No! You belong to me. In my absence you betrayed me. I was told, and hurried here this very morning, mingled with the crowd, and now that I have you alone to myself again and ask you to follow me, you refuse! Oh no, María, don't delude yourself. Come, there's still time! Break this ignominious tie, and we shall be happy! I will be yours, yours alone, and forever. Come, María!"

"Alderán, my family has imposed this yoke on me, and I will bear it. But you will always be my lover and I will be your love! What does this man matter? What is he? Another valet, a curtain to veil our secret love. Now leave me, leave me, adieu!"

"So you refuse, María, then go; let this old man defile you! Carry out your wish—I'll carry out mine! Go!" And, pushing her out of his arms, he watched her run from the gallery back into the ballroom.

For a moment Alderán paused, deep in thought. He cursed and stamped his foot, then, suddenly, he vanished in the night.

Meanwhile the crowd outside had swollen like the waters of a pond in a violent storm. The tumult grew more and more intense, and the revelry more frightful. The rabble had regained some of its audacity and, drawing closer, laughed in the face of the halberdiers. Curses and shouts of death rose again. They threw stones at the windows and painted walls with ox blood and dung. Suddenly the crowd parted to make way for an unkempt woman who howled like a dog at the moon. It was La Torrija, the baker's wife, who was calling for her husband, and revenge.

"It's La Torrija, the baker's wife," they were saying on all sides. Now the crowd fell silent, and La Torrija sobbed and howled.

Then the man in the brown cape climbed up the stairs and shouted:

"Friends, let's treat him as he deserves! Whoever doesn't follow me is a coward! Death to Vesalius the sorcerer!"

The crowd replied by hurling stones at the windows and the halberdiers, who retreated as far as the stairs.

The multitude invaded the portal, threw itself against the halberdiers' spikes, seizing and breaking them, climbed the stairs and started breaking down the door of the great hall when a gallop was heard in the distance. Run, the constables! Seized with panic, the rabble scattered down the stairs. Some ran into the corridors, others jumped out the windows. A few brave men took their stand alone.

"By order of the king, disperse!"

"Death to the Fleming!"

"In the name of the king, disperse!"

Then the constables entered the porch on horseback, a rain of furnishings greeted them, and they answered with a volley of shots that felled the most courageous. The man in the brown cape uttered a cry and raised his hand to his side. The healthy and wounded took flight. Five corpses lay on the ground.

Suddenly the palace and the street grew dark. The watch dragged off the bodies of the vanquished, and the trembling guests escaped through the back way.

Only in Vesalius's wing two windows still gleamed in the darkness.

III. QUOD LEGIT NON POTEST

Through the broken panels of the living-room door María had witnessed the fall of the man in the brown cape struck by a bullet, and she had fainted at the sound of his piercing cry. She had then been carried to her room and on a sofa she lay motionless for a long time. Vesalius, kneeling beside her, tearful and trembling, covered her hands and forehead with kisses.

"How do you feel now, María, my love?"

"Better—but what of the fighting? Has it died down?"

"Yes, that ugly mob has been tamed. What can they have against me? Peaceful and retiring, I spend my days studying anatomy for the good of humanity, the progress of science, and the greater glory of God. They ask for my head; they think I'm a sorcerer. Whenever someone disappears, it is I, Vesalius, who must have seized him for my experiments. The masses will always be ugly and stupid! Dumb and ungrateful! This is the fate in store for those

who give their lives to them! For men who point the way
or bring a new message. They crucified Jesus and laughed
at Columbus. The mob will always be ugly and stupid,
dumb and ungrateful!"

"Banish these dark thoughts, Vesalius. But frankly this
clash won't make them love you."

"What do I care if they love me, as long as you do,
María? You love me, don't you, just a little?"

"How can you still ask such a question?"

"I know I'm old, María, and when you're old you have
doubts. I know I can't make pretty speeches, and that,
broken by long vigils, I've grown as thin as the skeletons
in my workroom, but my heart is young and ardent! I bring
you no rancid passion, but a new soul in an old skin. I have
met many women in my time, María, but I swear to you,
none ever kindled such a flame! Did I have to reach de-
crepitude to know love in all its violence? María, accustom
your eyes to the rough coffer imprisoning my youthful soul!
The sap is boiling under the bark of the centenary oak."

María then threw her arms around his neck, pressed her
lips to his bald head, and covered his white beard with
kisses. Vesalius wept with joy.

Bedtime! A time of ecstasy, throbbing with shame and
delight! A time that fuses beings, wakes and drowns desire! Bedtime, yielding lies or beauty! Hour too often full
of contrasts! Often fateful hour!

The bride gracefully threw off her wedding gown and
her jewels; the rose seemed to shed its casing; she was a
Castilian beauty such as one sees in dreams!

Vesalius awkwardly removed his festive attire, unveiled
his ugly frame and looked like a mummy unwinding its
wrappings.

Suddenly the lamp was blown out, and the curtain rings
grated on their rods. A profound peace fell over the house,
now and again tumultuously interrupted, yet no one heard
María utter the cry . . .

Then, far into the night, caresses and kisses given but
not answered, and murmurs and complaints, while the

learned professor of anatomy trembled, and kept saying:

"Oh, don't think it's weakness, María! The violence of my love for you is what tires me, your beauty shames me, and it seems that I am touching something holy. I love you so much, María! I love you so much! But don't think it's weakness! In the morning I'll show you in twenty authors, you'll see in Mundinus, Galianus, Gonthierus Andernaci, my master, and chief physician of Francis I of France, you'll see that, on the contrary, it's potency and excessive love! I love you madly, María!"

It is to be believed that this excess of love did not die down, for only a few days later María moved into an isolated apartment in another wing of the house, accompanied by the professor's devoted housekeeper whom he had metamorphosed into a dueña for his spouse. The owl did not see his dove except at mealtimes, when they treated each other with the coldness and elaborate politeness of utter strangers.

Once more Vesalius was betrothed to science. Engrossed in research, he went from the laboratory to the amphitheater, from the amphitheater to the laboratory.

Young men and women, ready for marriage, here is the lesson to be drawn from this: if your passions are ardent, never marry a doctor of philosophy, a member of the Academy of Inscriptions and Belles Lettres, or an immortal of the Academy of Forty Chairs and its irrepressible Dictionary.

IV. NIDUS ADULTERATUS

About four or five years had gone by when Doña María, who, against her custom, had not appeared at table for several days, sent for Vesalius, her husband. He went to her quarters at once, and found her stretched out on her bed, wan, weak, with deep circles under her eyes, and a lackluster voice. Vesalius pulled up a chair and sat down. María, feeling a warm breath on her forehead, opened her eyes and, recognizing Andrea Vesalius, heaved a deep, agonized sigh.

"Andrea, you are my lord and master," she began. "Every moment I grow weaker; soon I shall stand at the feet of God and be judged. And I am impure! I have sinned against you, Vesalius! But the sinner begs forgiveness. You are a wise, learned man, my spouse and my master, do not grow wrathful! Let me bare my soul to you."

"Señora, you are not as ill as you seem to think. Your imagination is——"

"No, a patient is his own best doctor. Something in me proclaims that the end is at hand. You are my husband, and my good lord; listen and find forgiveness in your heart for perhaps I'm not entirely to blame. We both took an oath at the altar and both of us have been faithless to it; I, because I was young and too full of life, and you, because your hair turned white from study, and your body grew weary from work. Misery! What misery! To be reduced to cursing one's youth! If you only knew what it is to be a woman, if you only felt what she feels, Vesalius, I know you would forgive me. Listen calmly: I have committed adultery and been guilty of vile betrayal. I am steeped in crime, Andrea! I have brought my lovers into your house, made them drunk on your wine, gorged them with food from your table; and while you were immersed in study, or asleep, I laughed with them, mocking you. Our filthy iniquity scorned your kindness—you were our private laughingstock. It's unspeakable! My very deathbed still quivers with our lust. God calls me, and I am dying! Oh, don't reject my plea!"

Her voice was stifled with a sob. Then, after a moment of silence, she started again:

"Already I have been bitterly, horribly punished. How repulsive an adulterous woman must be! She must be vile and loathsome! Since our union, Vesalius, I have had three lovers, but I possessed each one only once. When after the assiduous pursuit I yielded to their obsession, when I allowed them to have their will, and shared this bed with them . . . Yes, a guilty wife must be repulsive! In the

morning, when I awoke, I was alone! And I never saw them
again! Never! Is any punishment worse than that? Crime
is linked to punishment; crime calls for torture! Andrea, be
merciful, let me obtain the remission of my sins! I loved
the last one, insanely, boundlessly! His loss is killing me;
abandoned by him I perish! Now I have said all. In the
name of Our Lady of Atocha, in the name of San Isidro
Labrador, in the name of San Andrés, your patron saint—
forgive this weak creature who has offended you. Let your
blessing purify her. Oh, forgive her, for she is close to
death!"

And, seizing his hand, she covered it with kisses and
tears of repentance. Vesalius snatched it away, pushed back
his seat, and said in a voice quivering with intensity:

"Rise, María; follow me!"

"I am faint. I cannot."

"I told you to follow me!"

María struggled to get up, slipped on a dressing gown,
and hobbled along behind Vesalius, who went down the
main stairway, crossed the courtyard, and opened a low
door, pierced with slits, which led into a small building,
its large windows solidly encased in stone. The small iron
door slammed shut behind them, and the bolts on the inside screeched in their rings.

V. OPIFICINA

Now we find ourselves in Vesalius's workshop, or laboratory, a large, square chamber, with a vaulted ceiling, stone
walls, and a stone floor. The entire furnishings consisted
of a few dirty, greasy tables, a couple of workbenches, two
or three vats, a cupboard, and a few chests. Several cal-
drons were scattered about near the fireplace, whose wide
mantel descended directly from the vault, and a kettle of
boiling water hung over the hot fire. The workbenches were
loaded down with pieces of cadavers; one might trample

on scraps of flesh or amputated limbs, and, crossing the room, the professor crushed under his sandals pieces of muscle and cartilage. A skeleton hung up against the door which, when stirred, creaked like the wooden candles on candlemakers' signs on cold, windy nights. The vaulted ceiling and the walls were covered with bones, coal rakes, skeletons, and carcasses (some human, but mostly those of monkeys and pigs, the animals closest in structure to human osteology), which had served Vesalius in his studies, for it may be said that he was the first to make a real science of anatomy, and to dare to dissect cadavers, even of orthodox Christians, and work on them publicly. Not much earlier, around 1315, Mundinus, a professor at the University of Bologna, had offered the novel spectacle of three dissected corpses. But the audacious scandal had never been repeated. The Church formally forbade such practices as sacrilegious. Mundinus himself, frightened by the new edict of Boniface VII, took no advantage of his findings. Among the ancients, contact with a corpse, or even the sight of one, was supposed to pollute the viewer to such an extent that only a series of lustral ablutions, or other forms of expiation could erase the stigma. In the Middle Ages, to dissect a creature made in God's image was held to be an act of impiety worthy of the scaffold.

VI.   ENODATIO

"What do you want of me here in your laboratory, Vesalius?" said María, weeping. "What do you want of me? I can't stay; the stink of these corpses is choking me. Open the door and let me out! I can't stand it!"

"I don't care. Now listen to me: you've had three lovers, right?"

"Yes, My Lord."

"You made them drunk on my wine, right?"

"Yes, My Lord."

"Well, the wine was not pure. Your dueña mixed it with opium, a powerful narcotic, and you slept deep and long, didn't you?"

"Yes, My Lord, and when I awoke I was alone."

"Alone, right?"

"Yes, My Lord, and I never saw them again."

"Never! Now come and see!"

And, gripping her by the arm, he dragged her to the back of the room. There, in a chest he opened, hung a complete skeleton, white as ivory, with all its natural articulations.

"Do you recognize this man?"

"What, these bones?"

"Do you recall this doublet and brown cape?"

"Yes, My Lord, it belongs to the knight Alderán."

"Look closely, and you will see the handsome knight who danced with you so gallantly at our wedding."

"Alderán!" María uttered a shriek that could have brought back the dead.

"At least, señora, you see that everything profits science." Then he turned to her coldly and said, "Science is much obliged to you."

And with a scornful, jeering laugh he steered her toward a kind of reliquary, or cage, enclosed in glass, that revealed a human skeleton amazingly preserved; the arteries were filled with a red liquid, and the veins with blue fluid; the bony frame seemed to be encased in fine silk netting; it was easy to distinguish the body; tufts of beard and hair still adhered in some places.

"This one, señora, remember? Look at his handsome beard and blond hair."

"Fernando! You killed him?"

"Till now, having never dissected any living bodies, we have had only vague, imperfect notions of the circulation of the blood, but thanks to you, señora, Vesalius has been able to lift many veils, and acquire eternal glory."

Then, seizing her by the hair, he dragged her toward a huge chest, and with some effort lifted the lid. Still holding her, he bent down toward the opening.

"Look here now! This is your last, isn't it?"

Within the chest pieces of flesh were immersed in jars containing alcohol.

"Pedro, Pedro . . . You killed him, too?"

"Yes, him too!"

Then with a hideous cry that was her death rattle, María toppled to the floor. The next day a procession issued from the palace.

The gravediggers who lowered the coffin into the vault of Santa María la Mayor remarked to each other that it was heavy, and that as it reached bottom, it made a sound unlike the sound of a body.

And the following night, through the slits in the low door, one might have seen Andrea Vesalius, in his laboratory, dissecting a beautiful corpse, that of a young woman whose blond hair streamed down to the floor.

VII. AFFABULATIO

In the midst of the opulent court of Madrid, gorged with the world's treasures brought back by Christopher Columbus, and which powerfully dominated all Europe, Andrea Vesalius basked in glory, rich and highly esteemed. Caught between the Inquisition and Philip II, he favored the study of anatomy as much as possible, when an accusation brought him a series of misfortunes.

During the public autopsy of a nobleman the heart seemed to palpitate under the scalpel. The vindictive Inquisition, accusing him of homicide, asked for the death penalty, and only with the greatest difficulty could the king prevail upon it to commute the sentence to a pilgrimage to the Holy Land. Vesalius made his way to Palestine in the company of Malatesta, leader of the Venetian armies.

After braving the many perils of the voyage, on his return, he was shipwrecked on the shore of Zante, where he died of hunger on October 15, 1565.

At the time, he had just been appointed by the republic of Venice to teach at the University of Padua, which the same year had lost his disciple, Gabriel Falloppe, who died before his time.

If one is to believe Boerhave and Albinus, Andrea Vesalius perished a victim of his eternal derision of the Spanish monks, their ignorance, their costume and their way of life, and of the Inquisition, which grasps any opportunity to rid itself of a discomforting scientist.

The great work of Andrea Vesalius, *De humani corporis fabrica* (*On the structure of the human body*), was published in Basel in 1562, illustrated with plates attributed to a friend of his, named Titian.

The War with the Turcomans

BY JOSEPH ARTHUR,
COMTE DE GOBINEAU

TRANSLATED BY J. LEWIS MAY

JOSEPH ARTHUR, COMTE DE GOBINEAU
1816–82

Joseph Arthur, Comte de Gobineau, was born in Ville d'Avray, near Paris, on Bastille Day, "an anniversary he was to deplore all his life." After receiving his education in France and Switzerland, he became private secretary to Alexis de Tocqueville. For some years after 1855 he was envoy to Teheran, a post that stimulated his interest in Oriental languages and literatures; later he was to return to Persia as ambassador. He traveled widely during his years in the diplomatic service, and on his retirement once again began his wanderings, spending some time with his friend Richard Wagner and finally dying, like Wagner, in Italy. Most of Gobineau's writings dealt with history and philosophy. In 1853 he published Part I of *The Inequality of Human Races*, which was to become one of the nazis' sacred books. He also composed a treatise on the religions and philosophies of Central Asia and brought together his biographical sketches of Savonarola, Cesar Borgia, Michelangelo, and other figures of that time in a book he entitled *The Renaissance*. He is best known today for his memorable letters, his novel, *The Pleiads* (1874), which reflects Stendhal's influence, and his *Asiatic Tales* (1876), a nineteenth-century masterpiece in which "The War with the Turcomans" appeared.

ABOUT GOBINEAU: Arnold H. Rowbotham, *The Literary Works of Count de Gobineau*, Paris, Champion, 1929; Gerald M. Spring, *The Vitalism of Count de Gobineau*, New York, Institute of French Studies, 1932; Alexis de Tocqueville, *The European Revolution & Correspondence with Gobineau*, New York, Doubleday Anchor Books, 1959.

My name is Ghulam Hussein but, as that was my grand-father's name, and as, of course, my parents, in speaking of him, always referred to him as "Aga," that is to say, "My Lord," I came to be called Aga out of respect for the head of the family, whose name was not to be taken in vain. So that is what I am called, Aga, just like the innumerable compatriots I have in the world who answer to the name Aga for the same reason, namely, that their grandfathers, like them, called themselves Ali, Hassan, Muhammad, or whatever it might be. Aga, then, I am. In course of time, and when fortune smiled on me, that is to say, when I had a fairly presentable coat to put on, and a few *shahis* in my pocket, I thought it behoved me to confer on myself the title of "Beg." Aga Beg doesn't sound so bad. Unfortunately I have usually had such ill luck that my title of Beg has had to be dropped, time and again, owing to my sorry external appearance. When that happened, I became Baba Aga, "Uncle Aga." I made the best of it. Since circumstances in which, I must confess, my own will played no part, permitted me to visit the tomb of the Imams, in the holy city of Mashad, and to partake of the soup supplied by the mosque as often as I felt inclined, it appeared to me natural, to say the least of it, to adorn myself with the title of Mashadi, that is to say, pilgrim of Mashad. A thing like that imparts an air of staidness and dignity to a man. Thus, I have been fortunate enough to be generally known as Baba Mashadi Aga, or, preferably to my mind,

Mashadi Aga Beg. Howbeit, God orders all things as he pleases.

I was born in a little village of the Khamseh, a province that marches with Azerbaijan. My village lies at the foot of the mountains, in a delightful little valley abounding in murmuring streams that flow across the wide fields, purling with contentment and leaping merrily over the shining pebbles. Their banks are thick with willows, whose foliage is so green and lively that it does one good to behold it, and countless birds nest in these willows and make such a stir and to-do as fills one's heart with joy. There is no pleasanter thing in the world than to sit at one's ease beneath these cool shades and enjoy a good pipe, with its fragrant aroma. We grew a lot of wheat; we also had rice fields and crops of dwarf cotton whose delicate stems were completely protected against the summer heats by castor-oil plants disposed quincunx-fashion; their broad leaves spreading a parasol over the white, flaky blossoms of their companions. A *mustofi*, a counselor of state of Teheran, a wealthy and highly esteemed worthy named Abdal-Hamid Khan, drew the rent of the village. He looked after us most carefully, so that we had nothing to fear from the governor of Khamseh, or from anyone else. We lived in a state of absolute contentment.

As for myself, I confess that working in the fields did not appeal to me. I liked eating grapes, melons, and apricots much better than growing them. So it came about that, when I was barely fifteen, I took up a profession that suited me a great deal better than farm work. I went in for hunting and shooting. I brought down partridges, guinea fowl, grouse; I went hunting the deer and the gazelle in the mountains; now and again, I knocked over a hare, but I didn't care much about hares; they indulge the disagreeable habit of feeding on carrion, and no one cares much about eating them, and, since there is very little sale for them, it is a waste of powder and shot to shoot them. As time went on, I pushed farther and farther afield, descending into the very heart of the Ghilan forests. From the excellent marksmen of that country, I learned never to miss

my aim, and this gave me, as it gave them, a deal of confidence when our quarry was a tiger or a panther. They
are fine beasts and their skins fetch a good price. I should,
then, have gone on, perfectly well contented with my lot,
taking pleasure in my work and getting a fair amount of
money out of it (though of course I said nothing about
that to my father and mother) if, all of a sudden, I had
not gone and fallen in love. That ruined everything. God
ordains all things!

I had a little cousin of fourteen whose name was Leila.
I greatly liked meeting her, and I met her very often. As
we had a host of things to say to each other and, therefore,
did not want to be interrupted, we fixed on a delightful
trysting-place under the willows that fringed the principal
stream, just where they grow the thickest, and there we
would linger for hours, quite oblivious of the flight of time.
At first I was very happy, but I thought such a lot about
Leila that I was impatient and fidgety when I did not see
her, and I would rush about all over the place to try and
find her. Thus it was that I was let into a secret, a secret
that plunged me into the deepest gloom. I found out that
I was not the only one she was meeting.

She was so artless, so charming, so kind and so soft-
hearted I never for a moment suspected that she was playing me false. I should have died if I had thought that.
However, I was much disturbed to find that there were
others who could interest and amuse, or at least distract her,
and, after wondering, over and over again, whether I should
pocket my pride and tell her all my troubles, and finally
deciding that I definitely would *not,* I went and blurted
out the whole thing to her.

"Thou seest, child of my uncle," I cried one day, weeping
hot tears, "my life is ebbing away, and in a few days they
will be carrying my corpse to the cemetery. Thou dost dally
with Hassan, hobnob with Kerim, sport with Sulaiman, and
I have got a strong impression that thou hast made an appointment with Abdullah. I know, of course, there's no
harm in it, and that they are just as much thy cousins as
I am, and that thou art incapable of breaking the promise

thou gavest me when thou didst swear to love me and me
alone, and that thou dost not wish to give me pain. But all
the same, I am suffering, breathing my last, dying, dead
and buried, and thou wilt never see me again. O Leila, my
dear, my heart, my treasure, have compassion on thy slave,
for he is exceeding sad."

As I said these words, I wept more bitterly than ever,
I began to shout aloud, I flung down my cap, I banged
myself violently on the head, and I rolled about on the
ground.

Leila displayed great emotion at the sight of my despair.
She flung her arms about my neck and kissed me on the
eyes.

"Forgive me, light of my life," said she. "I have done
wrong, but I swear by all that is holy, by Ali, by the Imams,
by the Prophet, by thy head, that I will never do it again,
and as a guarantee that I will keep my word, go and ask
of my father my hand in marriage. I want no other master
than thee, and I will be thine all the days of my life."

Then she began kissing me again more passionately than
ever. Unquestionably, I was very much in love with her,
but I had never told her I had any money because I was
afraid she would want it, and, sooner or later, wheedle it
out of me. Now, if I went and asked my uncle to consent
to my marrying her, I should inevitably have to tell my
father, my mother and the whole clan, to say nothing of
her, all about my little nest egg. In that case, where should
I be? Ruined, lost, destroyed! On the other hand, I was
extremely anxious to marry Leila and so become the happiest man imaginable, whether in this world or the next.
Furthermore, I should have nothing else to fear from the
flirtatious activities of Hassan, Kerim, Sulaiman, and Abdullah, who, as things were, had got me roasting, so to speak,
on a slow fire. All the same, I did *not* want to part with
my money, and I was in such a desperate quandary about
the whole thing I started weeping again more copiously
than ever, clasping Leila in my arms in an agony of distress. Thinking that she was the one and only cause of my
trouble, she said:

"My soul, why dost thou go on grieving thus, when thou knowest that I am to be thine for ever?"

So sweetly and softly did her voice steal into my heart I began to lose my head.

"Why?" I answered. "Why, because I am so poor that I owe for the very clothes on my back. I swear by thy head that I have not been able to pay for them, though they are certainly not worth a penny more than five *sahabgrans*. That being so, how in the world am I going to pay thy father the dowry he will expect from me? Of course, if he would agree to accept a promissory note . . . Dost think that would be out of the question?"

"Most certainly I do," answered Leila, shaking her head. "How canst thou expect father to hand over a pretty girl like me for nothing? Be reasonable."

So saying, she fell to gazing at the water, absent-mindedly plucking, every now and again, one of the tiny blossoms that blew amid the grasses on the river's brink. At the same time she put on such a pretty little pout I simply didn't know what to do with myself. However, I had the sense to reply:

"It is indeed a dreadful thing. Alas, I have not a penny in the world!"

"Is that a fact?" she said, and, throwing her arms about my neck, she gazed at me in such a way, holding her head a little on one side, that, somehow or other, I can't tell how, I completely lost my head.

"I've got thirty *tomans* in gold," I gasped. "They're buried in the ground two feet from where we are," and I pointed to the tree trunk at the foot of which I had secreted my treasure.

She burst out laughing. As for me, a cold sweat came out on my forehead.

"O *liar!*" she cried, kissing me on the eyes. "How little thou dost love me! How I had to beg and pray to get the truth out of thee! Now go and see my father, and ask him for me. Promise him seven *tomans*, but only give him five. Tell him thou wilt let him have the other two later on. He will never see them. Leave it to me to get two of the five back again. I will bring them to thee without fail; so, when the whole thing is settled up, I shall not have cost thee more than three *tomans*. Now, canst thou see how much I love thee?"

I was overjoyed at this conclusion to the matter and hurried away to seek out my uncle. After two days of haggling, with a wealth of prayers, solemn promises, and tears on my part, I prevailed at last and married my beloved Leila. She was so charming, she had such consummate skill in getting her own way (I afterward learned how she managed this, and whence she derived this irresistible power of hers) that when, a few days after the wedding, Leila persuaded me to go and settle down with her at Zanjan, chief town of the province, she contrived somehow to get a superb ass out of her father and, more than that, she lifted a lovely carpet from him without so much as a by-your-leave. There are no two ways about it, she is a pearl among women.

We had only just settled down in our new house, where, thanks to the twenty-five *tomans* I had got over, we were beginning to have a good time, since Leila loved gaiety and I was the last man to shun it, when who should put in an appearance but Kerim, one of those cousins of hers, of whom I had previously been so jealous. To start with, I had a twinge or two of the old uneasiness again, but my wife laughed me out of that so completely that I too saw the funny side of it. Besides, Kerim was such a pleasant fellow. I took a tremendous fancy to him, and, the fact is, he deserved it, for I never saw such a thoroughgoing joker in all my life. He had always got some yarn to tell that made me laugh enough to kill myself. We used to spend a good part of the night sitting up drinking *raki* together, and at last, at my urgent invitation, he came and took up his abode with us.

For three weeks this arrangement worked swimmingly. Then my temper took a turn for the worse. There were things I did not like about it all. What were they? Well, I could not exactly put my finger on them, but somehow Leila began to pall, and I began to wonder what on earth it was that had made me so mad about her. One day I found out. It happened when I was mending my cap, the lining of which had become unstitched. In it I was amazed to discover a little packet consisting of some silk thread, wool and cotton of different colors, all mixed up with a lock of hair, the same color as my wife's. At once I recognized the talisman that had been holding me in thrall. I quickly disposed of these sinister objects and when I put on my cap again, my ideas had taken a totally different direction, and I concerned myself no more about Leila than I should have about the veriest stranger. On the other hand, I felt greatly distressed about my thirty *tomans*, which were now nearly all gone; and that made me moody and morose. Leila noticed this, and made up to me with all sorts of little coquettish advances that left me absolutely cold, as of course they were bound to do, seeing that I was no longer under the influence of her spells. At last she flew into a rage. Kerim joined in, and there was a regular squabble. I don't quite know what I said, or what my cousin said, but, drawing my *gama*, I tried to land him a good whack across the shoulders. He was too quick for me and, brandishing his own weapon, brought it down with such force on to my head that my blood began to flow in torrents. Hearing Leila's piercing shrieks, the neighbors came running in and, on their heels, the police. They were for clapping hands on the unhappy Kerim with a view to dragging him off to the lockup, when I shouted:

"In God, for God, and by God, don't touch him! He is my cousin; he is the son of my aunt! He is my friend, and the light of my eyes! He has got a perfect right to shed my blood, if he so desires."

I loved Kerim; I loved him infinitely more than I loved Leila, and I should have been distressed if any ill had befallen him over a stupid affair that, I take it, we were perfectly free to settle between us. I spoke with such depth of feeling that, although the blood was streaming down my face, they all calmed down at last, and went away and left us. Kerim bound up my wound, Leila lending a hand.

Then we kissed each other, all three of us. After which I lay down and went to sleep.

Next day I was sent for by the *katkhoda*, or district magistrate, who informed me that I had been put on the register of men selected for military service. I might have expected something of the kind. No one knew me at Zanjan; I was a complete stranger there, and there was no one to take my part. How was I to help being among the first to fall into the sort of hole into which everyone was naturally anxious to shove me, in order that he himself, or someone belonging to him, might keep out of it. I attempted to protest and to put up a case for exemption, but, without moving a muscle, the *katkhoda* had me bound to the *falakah.* They flung me on my back. Two *farrashin,* taking hold of the pole at each end, held me feet uppermost. A couple of truculent warders brandished, each, a handful of birch rods with which they struck a series of violent blows. They hit the pole because, in the act of falling, I had managed to tip them a *sahabgran* apiece.

All the same, I now realized beyond all doubt what I had to expect if I displayed any further reluctance to embrace my lot. It then occurred to me that I hadn't a penny to bless myself with, nor a single thing to my name. Very likely it was irksome to "right wheel" and "left wheel," and go through all those idiotic maneuvers of the infantry, but then it occurred to me that, after all, there might be some perquisites and compensations about the job of which, for the time being, I was ignorant. Meantime, there was, as I told myself, one outstanding fact and that was that there was no escaping my destiny, and, as my destiny was to be a soldier, I might as well accept the inevitable and make the best of it.

When Leila heard what had happened to me, she uttered fearful cries, beat her face and chest, and tore her hair. I did my best to comfort her, and Kerim, too, used his best endeavors to the same end. At last she listened to reason, and, seeing that she was a little calmer, I addressed her as follows:

"Light of my eyes, the whole company of the prophets,

Imams, saints, angels and God Himself, bear witness that I cannot live without thee, and, if I had not thee, I swear by thy head that I should be as good as dead, aye, far worse than dead. Dismal, however, as my plight now is, my thoughts are solely for thee and for thy happiness, and, since leave thee I must, what is going to become of thee? The best thing, in my opinion, would be for thee to resume thy freedom, and mayest thou find a husband less unfortunate than I!"

"Dear Aga," she answered with a kiss, "the same infinite love thou hast for me, I, too, nourish in my heart for the dear and adorable husband that is mine; and since, as a natural result of women being more devoted in their attachments than men, I am more disposed than thou canst possibly be, to sacrifice myself. I think that, however much it costs me, I had better give thee back thy freedom. As for me, my fate is sealed. I shall abide here weeping until there is not a tear left in my poor body, then I shall give up the ghost."

At this lugubrious announcement Kerim and I began groaning in unison. We might have been seen, the three of us, squatting on the rug, facing one another, with a blue glass decanter of raki between us and our three cups, lolling our heads from side to side and moaning most mournfully, punctuating our groans at intervals with such ejaculations as "*Ya Ali! Ya Hassan! Ya Hussain!* O my eyes! O my life! I am dead!" Then we would kiss and start sobbing again louder than ever. The truth is that we adored each other, Leila and I, and God Almighty never created, never could create, a more affectionate, more devoted wife. Ah yes! Ah yes! 'Tis the very truth, and I cannot help weeping anew when I think of it all.

Next morning, my beloved spouse and I called betimes on the mullah and had the deed of divorce drawn up. Then, after bidding me the tenderest of farewells, she went back home again. As for me, I betook myself straight to the bazaar and made for a shop kept by an Armenian who sold raki, where I knew I was sure to find Kerim. For three days past I had had something on my mind that, though I had plenty of other things to worry about, caused me particular anxiety.

"Kerim," I said, "this day I have it in mind to call on my sultan, that is to say, on my captain. I am given to understand that he is a very punctilious person and a great stickler for etiquette. Now, if I go and make my bow in this spotty, out-at-elbow old rig that I now have on, he will not look favorably upon me, and such an inauspicious start might harm my military career. That being so, I am going to ask you to lend me your new *kulijeh,* just for this special occasion."

"My poor Aga," answered Kerim, "I cannot, alas, do what thou dost ask. I have got a big thing on today; I'm getting married and as I wish to cut a decent figure before my friends, I absolutely must have on my best clothes. Besides, I think a tremendous lot of my *kulijeh;* it is made of yellow Hamadan, edged with a charming border of Kandahar silk. It is one of Baba Taher's creations, Baba Taher, who works for all the best people in the province, and he told me himself he had never turned out anything more perfect in his life. I have, therefore, decided, as soon as the wedding is over, to pawn my *kulijeh,* because I have no cash today, and shall have plenty of debts tomorrow. So, even to oblige thee, I cannot part with my solitary asset."

"Oh, very well then," said I, relapsing into the deepest dudgeon (for I was completely obsessed by the *kulijeh* and could think of nothing else), "I am lost, ruined, without a friend in the world to care a straw about my troubles."

These bitter words went home. My friend was moved. He tried reasoning with me. He said everything he could think of to console me, and continued to plead his wedding, his notorious poverty, and I know not what besides. But at last, seeing how upset I was, he gave way, and said consolingly:

"If only I could absolutely rely on thy returning my *kulijeh* in an hour from now."

"What wilt thou that I swear by?" I asked, all on fire with excitement.

"Dost thou promise to return it?"

"Immediately; under the hour. Just give me time to put in an appearance and get back. By thy head! By my eyes! By Leila's life! By my salvation! Let me burn like a cursed dog through all eternity if thou hast not thy garment back before even thou dost wish it."

"It is agreed. Come!"

He led me into his room, and there I beheld the magnificent vestment. It was yellow. It was superb. I was entranced. I slipped it on hurriedly. Kerim protested that its like was not to be seen anywhere on earth, that the tailor was a marvel, and that he would certainly pay him one of these days, out of sheer gratitude.

"But," he added, "if thou hast any self-respect, thou canst not wear such a robe with those dowdy old blue linen breeches. Stay a moment, here are my red silk shalwars, absolutely new."

I soon had those on too. I looked like a prince, and I rushed out of the house. For two hours I sauntered about the bazaars. The women kept ogling me. I was in the seventh heaven. I ran up against two other fellows who, like me, had to join up. We went and had a nip of something to cheer us up, at a place kept by a Jew. They were leaving that same evening for Teheran to join their unit. I decided to go with them; so, having borrowed some clothes from one of them, and the rest from the other, I carefully folded up my sumptuous costume, and then, when the Jew had his back turned, we bolted for the door, slipped out into the street, and finally got to the city gate. Then, laughing like lunatics at our mad quips and jests, we crossed over into the desert and went on tramping half through the night.

The journey was a very merry, very happy one, and I began to find that a soldier's life suited me. One of my two companions, Rustam Beg, was a *vekil*, or sergeant major. He suggested that I should place myself under his orders, a proposal I readily embraced.

"Look, Brother," said he, "foolish people think it is a

poverty-stricken job, this soldiering. Do not believe it. The
only people who get left in this world are the duffers. Thou
art not such a one. Nor am I. Nor is Khurshid here. Dost
thou know any trade?"

"I am a hunter."

"A hunter! Not much doing in that line at Teheran. Be a
mason. Our friend Khurshid here is a blacksmith. Myself,
I am a wool carder. Give me a quarter of thy pay; the
sultan will take half, being the captain; every now and then,
thou wilt give a bit to the *naib*, or lieutenant. He is not
very bright, but he is not ill-disposed. The colonel, naturally, takes the rest and thou wilt live like a king on what
thou wilt earn."

"Do masons earn much at Teheran?"

"They earn a bit, but over and above all that, there are
many ways of making one's life pleasant, as I will show
thee."

He did show me, on that very journey, and a highly di-
verting business it was. As he had on him his *vekil's* commission, we made out, in one of the villages, that we were
tax collectors. The peasants were completely duped, and,
after a good deal of discussion, they made us a little present
so that we should not put up the rates on them and should
give them a fortnight's rebate besides. To this we assented,
and departed overwhelmed with blessings. After playing
one or two similar tricks, all of which ministered to our
profit, our amusement, and our reputation, we made our
entry into the capital by way of the Shimiran Gate, and
proceeded, one fine morning, to report to our *serhang,*
Colonel Mehdi Khan.

We made a profound obeisance to the great man as he
was crossing the courtyard of his house. The *vekil,* who
was already acquainted with him, presented us, Khurshid
and myself, and commended, in well chosen terms, our
bravery, our submissiveness, and our devotion to our leader.
The colonel appeared delighted with us, and with a few
kind words sent us away to barracks, where I was straight-
away incorporated into the 2nd Regiment of the Khamseh.

It is certainly true that, in some respects, a soldier's existence is the reverse of gay. It is not that losing one's pay is of any great importance. After all, since the vizirs prey on the generals, I confess that it seems natural enough for the latter to take it out of the colonels, that they in turn should batten on the majors, and the majors on their subalterns and soldiers. It is for these last to think out ways of subsistence for themselves, and thank God no one forbids that. But the worst is that a good many of the instructors are Europeans, and everyone knows that these Feringhis, or some of them, have no equals for brutality and ineptitude. They are always preaching about upright dealing and integrity and pretending that they ask for nothing better than that the men should be paid with regularity. That would be right enough, so far as it goes, but then, in return, they would like to make regular beasts of burden of us. That would be a horrible fate, and, frankly, if they were to succeed in their designs, life would not be worth living. They would like, for example, to make us live in barracks, to sleep there every night, to let us in, and let us out, at any hours they liked to fix. With this sort of thing, men would become absolute machines. They would have to get leave to breathe, and even the breath of life would be rationed. God does not wish that. Then again they would like to bring us all, the whole lot of us without distinction, down on to the plain, summer and winter, in the broiling sun or pelting rain, to do—what *do* you think? Why, move our legs up and down, wave our arms about and twist our heads now to the right, now to the left. *Wallah! Billah! Tallah!* Not one of them could explain what earthly good these absurd antics could possibly do. I don't mind saying that, when I see one of these gentlemen coming, I make myself scarce, because one can never tell what mad fit is going to take them next. Luckily heaven, who made them very brutal, made them also very stupid, so that, as a general rule, one can tell them any old yarn and they will believe it. Glory be to God for giving the Muhammadan this weapon of defense!

For my part, I saw right away what these European in-

structors were like, and I gave them a wide berth from the
start. As my friend the *vekil* had been careful to put in a
word for me to the sultan, I never had to do any of this
drill, as they call it, and as far as I was concerned, life was
quite bearable. Our regiment had come to take the place
of the Sulaimanieh, which had been ordered to Shiraz, and
I happened to belong to a detachment quartered in one of
the posts in the bazaar. These dogs of Europeans, God's
curse be on them, insist on the posts being relieved every
day, and on the replaced men being sent back to barracks.
They concentrate all their ingenuity in trying to find out
ways of making the soldier's life a misery. Fortunately, the
colonel had no wish to be constantly bothered and disturbed, so the upshot was: once in the *corps de garde,* always in it! You could make yourself at home, and there
you were, not for twenty-four hours, but for two or three
years sometimes; anyhow, for as long as the regiment was
on garrison duty in the town.

Our post was not at all badly situated. It was at the
corner of two avenues of the bazaar. The building consisted
of a single room for the *naib,* and a sort of large hall for
the men. There were no windows, only just a single door
that opened onto a wooden gallery running alongside the
street, the whole being raised some three feet above ground
level. Hard by our building there were a number of shops,
all displaying their alluring wares. To start with, there was
a fruiterer, with his grapes, his melons and his cantaloupes,
piled up in pyramids, or hanging festoon-wise above the
customers' heads. A case of dried figs stood in one corner,
and the worthy proprietor would always allow us to take
a picking out of it when, of an evening, we went in to have
a chat with him about various matters of interest. A little
farther along there was a butcher who sold first-rate mutton, but, for one joint he got paid for, I verily believe there
were four whose disappearance remained for him an un-
fathomable enigma. Not a day passed but he would bewail
the depredations of which he was perpetually the victim,
but as, every now and again, we brought him in a thief
who owned up to his misdeed, returned the stolen article

and begged for forgiveness, he never did us the injustice
to lay the suspicion on us. I still remember with emotion a
cookshop proprietor whose ovens exhaled perfumes that
would have done honor to Paradise. He had a way of cooking *kebabs* that was absolutely unequaled. Every bit of
meat was grilled to such a nicety, and so well steeped in
the fragrant essence of laurel leaves and thyme, that you
thought a portion of heaven itself was melting in your
mouth. But one of the great attractions of our station was
the storyteller who had set up in the courtyard of a ruined
house. Every day, before a wonder-stricken audience palpitating with curiosity, he told tales of fairies, genii, princes
and princesses, of valiant heroes, the whole enmeshed in
a tissue of poesy so sweet to the ear that you came away
with your head well-nigh turned. Many and many an hour
did I spend there, filled with a delight I can find no words
to express.

Well then, it amounts to this, that life in a *corps de garde*
is full of charm. Our *naib*, a handsome fellow, never put in
an appearance. Not only did he give up all his pay to his
superiors, but he made them handsome presents in addition, so that he might have leave to engage himself as a
pishkedmet, or footman, in a big house, an occupation that
brought him in a great deal more than his army pay. The
vekil, my friend, went off every morning. I can see him
now in his voluminous breeches that had once been white,
his red canvas coat all out at the elbows, his belt of nondescript hue, his calamitous hat, and a long staff in his
hand. He was off to practice his profession of wool carder,
and was frequently away for a whole week. The rest of us,
who had nowhere else to sleep, usually got back to the post
somewhere between midnight and two in the morning. As
a rule, however, we were all up and away again by eight or
nine in the morning, all, that is to say, but one or two who
for some reason or another elected to stay behind and look
after the place. It is, of course, a matter of common knowledge that soldiers on sentry duty answer absolutely no purpose but to present arms to the bigwigs who happen to
pass by. That we did with great regularity. From a long

way off, whenever some high and mighty personage on horseback, attended by a numerous retinue, hove in sight along one of the avenues leading to our post, all the shop-keepers shouted to us as loudly as they could. Our detach-ment, nominally about twenty strong, could never muster more than about four or five, and they, naturally enough, would be engrossed in conversation, if they were not fast asleep. Often enough, there was nobody there at all. In that case, there shot out from every shop substitutes who snatched up our rifles from wherever we had chucked them, formed up smartly in line, one of them pretending to be the *vekil,* another the *naib,* and, at the proper moment, the whole lot presented arms with a portentous and most European gravity. The personage bowed his acknowledg-ments, and the whole thing was in order. I recall with de-light that excellent *corps de garde,* those wonderful neigh-bors, the happy days that then were mine, and now, in my old age, I wish I could light again upon so pleasant a re-treat. *Inshallah! Inshallah!*

I do not wish to give the idea that I stuck much closer to the post than did the others. On the *vekil's* advice I had become a mason, and I certainly was making a bit of money, but what paid me a great deal better than money *making,* was money *lending.* Kerim's magnificent coat, which I promptly sold to an old-clothes man, put me in funds, and I started advancing money to my friends and acquaintances, who soon began to swarm about me like ants. I lent only very small sums at a time, and I stipulated for prompt repayment. It was absolutely necessary to ob-serve these precautions, and they were rewarded with con-siderable success. However, I did have some bad debts, too, and, to offset these, I raised some loans on my own account that I did not invariably repay. Taking things all around, I estimate that I was never seriously out of pocket. Mean-while, I went out of my way to ingratiate myself with my superiors. I called now and again on the colonel; I made a good deal of fuss of the major; I think I may say I was on friendly terms with the sultan; the *naib* made me his confidant; I sedulously kept on the right side of the *vekil,* and frequently made him little presents. All this relieved me from the necessity of ever presenting myself at the barracks, nor did I once turn up to drill. All my free time I spent in pursuit of business or pleasure, and no one ever interfered. I admit that I had a liking for the taverns run by Jews and Armenians. One day, I was passing along by the King's College; I thought I would go and take a look inside. There, in the garden, I heard the learned Mullah Aga Teherani giving a lecture. I was greatly impressed. From that day forth I became deeply interested in metaphysics and I was often to be seen among the audiences of this sublime professor. The company was both numerous and distinguished. There were students, soldiers like myself, nomad horsemen, noblemen and respectable burgesses. We discussed the nature of the soul and God's relation to man. It was all most delightful. I now began to frequent the society of learned and estimable people. I contrived to make acquaintance with certain grave and taciturn personages who initiated me into doctrines of far-reaching import, and I began to understand what I had hitherto but imperfectly realized, namely that the whole world was out of joint. There is no denying that empires are governed by an abominable lot of rogues, and that if you put a bullet through their heads, every man jack of them, you would only be giving them what they deserved. But what good would that do? Their successors would be worse still. Glory be to God, Who, for reasons unknown to us, has ordained that evil and stupidity should govern the universe.

There were also times, and they occurred pretty frequently, when my thoughts reverted to my dear Leila and my good friend Kerim. On such occasions my eyes filled with tears. But this did not last long. I soon returned to my debtors and creditors, to my boon companions, and to the philosophy of Mullah Aga Teherani, and I submitted absolutely to the will of the Supreme Being, who orders all things according to His pleasure.

For a whole year things went on like this, that is to say, very pleasantly. I am now an old soldier, and I can sol-

emnly affirm that I never saw anything more satisfactorily
run.

One night, about ten o'clock—I had been absent three
whole days—I turned up at the guardhouse and was amazed
to find almost all my comrades there, as well as the *naib*
himself. They were sitting on the floor in a circle. A blue
lamp shed a dim and uncertain light upon their faces and
figures, but I saw that they were all bathed in tears. The
one who was weeping the most bitterly of all was the *naib*.

"Good health be yours, Excellency," I said. "But what is
the matter?"

"Disaster has fallen upon the regiment," replied the officer with a sob. "The august governor has decreed the ex-
termination of the Turcoman nation, and we are under orders to leave tomorrow for Mashad."

At this announcement my heart sank, and I did what the
rest were doing; I sat down and wept. The Turcomans, as
everybody knows, are a terrible race. They are for ever carrying out forays, *japao* they call them, on the provinces of
Iran the Well-Guarded that march with their frontiers, and
they carry off the unfortunate peasantry by the hundred.
They take them and sell them to the Uzbeks of Khiva and
Bokhara. I deem it perfectly reasonable that the august
Government should have decided to wipe out these robbers
to the last man, but it was singularly perverse of them to
select our regiment for the task. We spent a good part of
the night bewailing our lot; however, as all our lamenta-
tions did nothing to improve matters, we finally began to
laugh, and we were all in excellent humor when at break of
day the men of the Damghan Regiment arrived to relieve
us. We picked up our rifles, and, after a solid hour spent
in saying good-by to our friends and neighbors, we quitted
the town and proceeded to link up with the rest of the regiment, which was drawn up in line of battle in front of the
Dowlat Gate. Then it was that I heard we were to be re-
viewed by the king himself. There were four regiments in
all. Their nominal strength was about a thousand each, but,
actually they numbered from three to four hundred each.
They consisted of our own battalion, the second Khamseh,

an Ispahan regiment, a regiment from Kum, and the first Radabils. Then there were two batteries of artillery, and about a thousand horse, Silsupoms, Kakavands, and Alavends. They presented a magnificent spectacle. Our red and white uniforms contrasted bravely with the blue and white of the other regiments. Our officers wore tight-fitting breeches with gold stripes, and orange, sky-blue, and pink *kulijehs*. Then there appeared successively on the scene the *mirpendi,* or divisional commander, with his suite; the Amir Tuman, commanding a force twice the size, with a large body of horse; the Sipeh-Salar, still more numerously attended, and, finally, the King of Kings himself, the ministers, all the leading pillars of state, and a host of servingmen. It was a gorgeous scene. The rolling of the drums was terrific; the European band played stately airs, while the rank and file, carrying their outlandish instruments, swayed to and fro as they stood playing their part; the flutes and tambourines of the artillery, with its teams of camels, screamed and rattled. The mob of men, women, and children who thronged around us on all sides were wild with delight, and we ourselves proudly joined in the general rejoicing.

Suddenly the king, having taken up his position, together with the lords of state, on a lofty eminence, orders were given that the *tamash* officers were to advance at the double on both flanks. It is a curious fact that the Europeans, whose languages are as absurd as the European mind, have had the good luck to borrow from us this highly expressive and uniquely graphic word; only, being unable to pronounce it properly, the fools call it "État Major." *Tamasha,* as everybody knows, signifies all that lends splendor to a scene, and is the only sensible thing I've ever noticed about European tactics. Anyhow it must be admitted that it is very charming. Some handsome young men in the smartest of uniforms, mounted on fine horses, go galloping about in every direction, as hard as they can. They go and they come, they wheel about, and off they go again. It is delightful to see them. They are never allowed to ride at a trot, because that would spoil the effect. It is a grand idea. God be praised for it!

When the king had spent some time looking at these maneuvers, it was decided to show him how it was intended to deal with the Turcomans. With that object in view a mine had been prepared, which they now proceeded to blow up. Unfortunately, they did not allow sufficient time for all the soldiers to be warned of the danger, and to withdraw to a safe distance. As a consequence three or four were killed. Except for this misadventure, the whole thing went like clockwork, and everybody was vastly entertained. Then three balloons were sent up amid tremendous applause, and, finally, infantry, cavalry, and artillery marched past before the king. At night the army was ordered to set forth immediately. It did so two days later.

The first week all went well. The regiment made its way along the foothills of the mountains in a northeasterly direction. We were to pick up our general, our colonel, the major, and most of the captains, after a two months' march, at Mashad or some other place. We ourselves were all privates, except for three or four sultans, the *naibs,* and our *vekils.* We pushed on in good heart. Each day we started about two in the morning, arriving about midday at some place or other where water was to be had, and there we settled ourselves in. The column moved forward in small groups, everyone linking up, if he wanted to, with his friends. If we got tired, we just fell out, had a spell of sleep, and then fell in again. With us, according to the usual custom, we had a long train of asses carrying our baggage, victuals for those who had any, together with our rifles and our cartridge pouches, for you can well suppose that no one was fool enough to clutter himself up with his arms while on the march. Why should he? Some of the officers had as many as ten or a dozen asses of their own, but a couple of privates in our company had twenty. They had purchased them at Teheran just before starting, and I had gone shares with them, for they had got an idea for putting them to profitable account.

These twenty asses were laden with rice and butter.

When we reached the *manzil,* that is to say, the halting place, we unloaded our rice and butter, and even a modicum of *tombeki,* and we sold the lot at no small profit. Whatever we liked to ask, buyers were always forthcoming, and we did very well out of it all, for people simply had to come to us. If they hadn't, they would have found themselves pretty hard up for food after the first day or two.

It is well known that in the great valleys in Persia, the valleys through which our men had to march, the villages are few and far between. The peasants were not such fools as to go and plant themselves just where troops had to march. They would not have had a minute's peace, and would sooner or later have died of hunger, not to mention a hundred and one minor inconveniences they would have had to endure. For this reason they established themselves far away from the main roads, and the result was that they were not always accessible. But the troops were not fools either. On arriving at the *manzil,* those who had any knowledge of the country told us all they knew. Then, any men who were not too fatigued after the march went out to see what they could pick up. This sometimes meant putting in another twenty to twenty-five miles, out and back. But the prospect of adding to our store kept us going. It was necessary to take the villagers on the hop, and that was not always an easy matter. These confounded peasants, devil take them, are just about as cunning as they make them. If they got sight of us a long way off, the whole lot of them, men, women and children, would fly away with all possible speed, taking with them all they had, to the very last rag. When this sort of thing happened, the houses, when we reached them, were nothing but four bare walls, with not a scrap of anything to take away. There was nothing, in that case, but just to tramp back again, more weary and footsore than ever, only to be greeted with the jeers and derisive laughter of our companions. But when our luck was in, and we were able to catch hold of the villagers, my word, didn't we lay about us, striking right and left without mercy. Then we came back with corn, rice, sheep, and poultry. But that wasn't often. Sometimes, too, we came up against uncouth, churlish people, more numerous than ourselves. They would snipe at us with their rifles and we should have to run for it, counting ourselves lucky if we got away alive. When you're in a hole like that it's a case of running hell-for-leather, and devil take the hindmost.

It would be unfair not to mention that the august Government had given out that we should be fed like fighting cocks throughout the campaign. But no one believed it. That is the kind of thing august governments always promise but are never able to perform. The general officer commanding is not the sort of person to go spending money he can keep in his pocket on providing good meals for his men. Well, to cut a long story short, at the end of a fortnight, when we had no more rice to sell, my two partners and I shut up shop. You wouldn't have found two paltry loaves if you had searched through the whole regiment. So we started eating the donkeys. I never fell in with more ferocious specimens than the peasants of the Khorassan. They live in fortified villages. When a poor devil of a soldier gets anywhere near, they shut their gates, mount the ramparts and, if you don't take care to show a clean pair of heels, you'll get a packet of lead in your inside. They never miss. May the sires and grandsires of these murderous devils burn everlastingly in hell's deepest pit, with nothing to mitigate their pain. *Inshallah! Inshallah! Inshallah!*

We started, I say, to eat the donkeys. Poor devils! I forgot to tell you that there were not many left. As there was nothing for them to eat, they began dying one after another, and their dead bodies marked the way we had come. The few we had managed to keep alive, at the cost of infinite trouble, were in a pretty poor way. Whenever we reached a station, we had to go miles into the mountains to look for grass to give them. Moreover they were exhausted with fatigue. True, we began to relieve them of our rifles and packs, which we left lying in the desert, though we tried to keep our personal belongings to the very last. Anything we particularly valued we had to hump onto our own backs. What was truly frightful was the lack of water. More than half the day had to be spent in digging holes in the ground to try and find a little. When we were lucky, we used to bring to light a drop or two of brackish mud we endeavored to clarify as best we could by filtering it through a bit of cloth. At last we found ourselves with nothing to eat but grass, and not much of that. Many did as the donkeys did. They died. All this did not stop us singing. If you're going to give way to despair about things that are part of life itself, better not be born at all. Besides, with a little patience, everything can be put to rights. And the proof of that is that the remnants of the regiment did succeed in reaching Mashad.

No doubt we were not in the best of trim when we made our entry into the Holy City. The major came out to meet us, with a group of officers and a crowd of people selling food of every description. We paid pretty stiff prices for what they let us have. The fact is we were so famished that we hadn't got the heart to do much haggling over prices. You don't know what it's like, if you've never been through it. You haven't the faintest notion of what it feels like to have a boiled sheep's head suddenly thrust under your nose. We ate heartily, and the good food brought gladness once more to our hearts. The major called us a lot of dirty dogs because we had lost our rifles, but he had some others served out to us, which he borrowed for the purpose from the Khorassan Regiment. And then, as we clubbed together to make him a little present, harmony was soon restored between him and ourselves. It was arranged that he should send in a favorable report of our conduct to the colonel. In order to make the latter a present we passed the hat again and realized ten *tomans,* or thereabouts. These matters having been duly settled, our formal entry into Mashad was fixed for the following day.

At the appointed hour the drummers of the other regiments that had already arrived in the city came and took up their station at the head of our column. This was a necessary measure as we had thrown away our drums at the same time as our rifles. A large group of officers mounted on horses that had been raked together from somewhere or other, took up a position behind the drummers, and then we came along in as good order as possible. We might have numbered as many as two or three hundred. The towns-folk surveyed us with a certain amount of indifference. For a month past they had been treated to a whole series of ceremonial entries, and they saw nothing particularly at-tractive about them. We were assigned a camping space, but, as the ground was swampy, everyone went off to shift for himself, trusting to find a billet, and whatever else he needed, in the city.

For my own part, I made a beeline for the mosque of the Holy Imams. My devotional instincts led me thither, but there was also the subsidiary idea that I might come in for a portion of the soup they dole out to the needy, and needy I had some right to call myself. The wide world knows no more entrancing sight than the venerable mosque at Mashad. Its great dome, its sumptuous and imposing gateway, the elegant clock towers by which it is flanked, the whole structure adorned from top to bottom with tiles enameled in blue, yellow, and black, its superb courtyard with its spacious pool for ablutions—you are transported on the wings of wonder and admiration at the sight of it. From morning till night multitudes of pilgrims, from Iran, Turke-stan, from the heart of India, and from the far-off regions of Rum come bringing to Imam Riza (glory be to his name) an incessant tribute of genuflections, prayers, gifts, and alms. Its sacred precincts are perpetually filled with a noisy throng; troops of poor folk come thither for the food the mullahs make ready for them every day. They would gladly die rather than forgo the privileges of the mosque. I made my way with feelings of veneration and emotion through the several groups, and, as I was cautiously inquiring of one of the gatekeepers, with an immense white turban, where I ought to go to secure my part of the share-out, the aforesaid worthy and venerable turban, or rather the head that carried it, displayed a physiognomy eloquent first of surprise and then of joy, and a wide mouth, opening in the midst of an enormous black beard, while a pair of jet-black eyes sparkled with delight, began to utter cries of satisfaction.

"The Holy Imams be blessed! 'Tis thou! 'Tis thy very self! Baba Aga!"

"Myself in person," I replied, looking fixedly at my interlocutor. Then, after a moment's hesitation, I recognized him beyond a doubt.

"*Wallah! Billah! Tallah!*" I exclaimed. "'Tis thou, my cousin Sulaiman?"

"The same, my friend, my kinsman, light of my eyes! What hast thou done with our Leila?"

"Alas!" I said. "She is dead!"

"Oh! My God, what a blow!"

"Dead she is," I went on in sorrowing tones, "else what should I be doing here? I am a captain in the 2nd Khamseh Regiment, and right glad I am to see thee again."

It occurred to me to tell Sulaiman that Leila was dead because I did not much like talking to him about her, and wanted to pass on to some other topic as soon as possible. But he would not let me.

"Merciful God!" he cried. "Dead! Leila dead! And thou didst let her die, wretch that thou art? Didst thou not know that I loved but her in the whole world, and that she never loved anyone in the world but me?"

"Anyone but thee!" I shouted in a towering rage. "Anyone but thee! That's rather a tall story, that is! Why, if that be so, didst thou not marry her?"

"Because I had nothing, absolutely nothing to my name. But on the very day of her marriage, she swore she would divorce thee and come to me as soon as ever I could get a decent home together. That is why I went off, why I came here and got a job as one of the gatekeepers of this mosque. I was just going to let her know how things were with me, when thou dost come to afflict me with this terrible and unexpected news!" Wherewith he started wailing and weeping and swaying his head from side to side. I had a good mind to strike him a blow in the face (for I was anything but pleased at what he had just told me), when it

fortunately occurred to me that it was now very much more
Kerim's business than it was mine, so I just remarked:

"Poor Leila, she loved us both dearly. Ah, what a terrible
thing that she should have died!"

Hearing my words, Sulaiman fell into my arms. "My
friend, my cousin," he cried, "we two shall never console
ourselves. Come home with me. Thou shalt be my guest,
and, so long as thou art in Mashad, thou shalt have everything I have got."

I was deeply touched by this kind gesture on the part
of dear Sulaiman, whom I had always loved from the bottom of my heart, and, seeing him so grief-stricken, I sincerely entered into his sorrow and mingled my tears with
his. We went out through the courtyard, and he introduced
me to any mullahs we chanced to meet on the way.

"This," he told them, "is my cousin, Aga Khan, a major
in the Khamseh Regiment, a hero like those of yore. Neither
Rustam nor Afrasiab was his equal in valor. Come and take
a cup of tea with us and confer a signal honor on my humble
dwelling."

I stayed a fortnight at Mullah Sulaiman's. It was an interlude, a very brief interlude, of pure delight. During that
time the remnants of the various regiments were assembled. Most of them were in no better case than ours, which
is not to be wondered at after such a long march. Shoes
were served out, at least to some of us, and we were given
rifles, or at any rate, implements that looked like rifles.
When we were all more or less equipped, we learned, one
fine morning, that the order to depart had been given and
that the regiment was to march on Merw. I wasn't any too
pleased. It meant, this time, penetrating right into the very
thick of the Turcoman hordes, and God only knew what
might happen. I spent a very gloomy evening with Mullah
Sulaiman. He did his best to cheer me, the dear fellow,
and poured me out endless cups of tea, with lots of sugar
in it. We also drank a glass or two of raki. Again he began
harping upon Leila, and made me go over all the details
of the poor child's death for what, I should think, must
have been the tenth time. It did occur to me once that

I ought, perhaps, to undeceive him, but as I had been at pains to give him such a circumstantial account of the matter, it seemed on the whole better to stick to that, rather than to bewilder him by telling him something different. Poor dear; he had been so kind to me that it gave me a sort of melancholy pleasure, seeing the mood I was in, to recall a number of details, bethinking me, in this latest version, of several things that had hitherto escaped me, the upshot of which was that, before she breathed her last, the dear creature whom we were both mourning had spoken of him in terms of the warmest affection. I cannot go so far as to say that my stories were wholly false; for I had such excellent reason to grow tearful about myself and the rest of us that it was perfectly easy for me to give a sad and touching turn to my discourse, and I can truly say that I spoke from a full heart. Sulaiman and I mingled our tears once more, and, toward morning, when I bade him farewell, I promised him with all my heart that I would never forget him, and it will be noted that I have kept my word. He, on his part, embraced me with genuine affection. I then went and rejoined my comrades. The regiment began the march, and I with it, in the ranks, side by side with my *vekil*.

There were a great many of us. I saw some of the cavalry pass by; they were tribesmen from the south and the west. They looked pretty good in themselves, better than we did, but their horses were underfed and not good for much. The generals stayed behind, at Mashad. That, it would seem, is a matter of absolute necessity because operations can be directed from afar much more effectively than from close at hand. The colonels followed the example of the generals, no doubt for the same reason. On the whole, we had few officers with us above the rank of captain, and that is quite as it should be, seeing that officers are not intended to fight, but only to receive the men's pay. Nearly all the leaders were nomad horsemen. These latter did come along with us, but, as everybody knows, they are uncouth, rough fellows, who care for nothing but fighting. The artillery had been sent on ahead.

We had been marching for three days; the rain was coming down in torrents, and it was bitterly cold. We marched
with difficulty over swampy ground. Those who managed
to avoid slipping, sometimes sank in up to their knees. Wide
channels full of slimy water had constantly to be negoti-
ated, and that was no easy matter. My shoes I had already
lost, and, like my companions, by dint of falling into quag-
mires, getting waist-deep into water, and scrambling on all
fours up steep banks, I was plastered with mud, and so wet
I was shivering with cold. All of a sudden, we heard the
sound of guns. Our column halted abruptly.

We heard guns. There were several discharges. Then
they ceased. There was a brief silence. Then, suddenly, a
train of artillery came thundering right into the midst of
us. Some of our men were run over. Those who could got
out of the way. The guns went lurching and bumping along
and finally came to a standstill. Some went into the mud,
some into the water. The gunners cut the traces of the
horses and away they went like the wind. It was a shock,
a whirlwind, a wild melee, and it was all over in a flash.
We hadn't had time to recover our wits when, a second
or two later, the men in the front line observed a cloud
of horsemen making swiftly in our direction. From every
throat the cry went up, "The Turcomans, the Turcomans!
Fire!" I was at my wits' end and knew not what to make
of it. I saw a few men rush off behind the gunners, instead
of using their rifles. I was going to follow suit, when the
vekil caught me by the arm and shouted into my ear amid
the uproar, "Stop where you are, Aga Beg! Whoever runs
away today is done for!"

He was right, absolutely, the good old *vekil*, and my own
eyes bore instant witness to the fact. I saw, as plainly as
I see you now, the mass of cavalry to which I had just
alluded, split up as if by magic, into innumerable detach-
ments, which, scouring across the plain and avoiding all
obstacles with the skill of men well up in the lie of the
land, were wheeling about, enveloping and cutting off the
fugitives, crushing them with blows, seizing their arms, and
taking prisoners by the hundred.

"Look, boys look!" shouted the *vekil* again. "That's what you're in for, that's what we are all in for, unless we can manage to keep together. Come on, then! Keep your ground, stand firm! Now then! Fire!"

There were about fifty of us all told. The frightful spectacle unfolded before our eyes lent such force to the sergeant's exhortations that, when a pack of these cursed desperadoes began to make for us, our men promptly formed a square and let go at them with might and main. We reloaded and let them have a second dose, and a third, and a fourth. Holy Imams! We saw a tidy few of these heretics, these cursed dogs, these partisans of Abubakr, Omar, and Osman, bite the dust. May they burn everlastingly in hellfire, the monsters! We toppled them over, I can tell you, and that put us into such good heart that, at the command of the *vekil*, and without breaking formation, we started to move forward, determined, since the enemy had stopped short and showed no further signs of coming on, to go and attack them on their own ground. They hesitated a moment, faltered, and finally fled. Meanwhile, however, other bands of Turcomans continued to harry the fugitives, rounding them up, killing some, beating up others, and dragging away such as were able to walk. We uttered shouts of triumph. "*Allah! Allah! Ya Ali! Ya Hassan! Ya Hussain!*" We felt on the top of the world. We had won our deliverance, and were afraid of nothing!

In point of fact we were extraordinarily lucky. We were about fifty strong, and we had proved that some thirty of our rifles were in working order. True, mine was nothing to boast of; to start with, it had no flint, and then the barrel had a crack in it. But all the same it was a good weapon as I proved later on. I had fixed on the bayonet, which had no socket, with a stout piece of string. It kept in place marvelously well and all I was waiting for was a chance to use it.

Others, I don't mind telling you, took a leaf out of our book. We saw, some little distance off, three or four groups of soldiers blazing away for all they were worth, and the Turcomans hadn't the pluck to come on. Moreover, a troop of some three or four hundred horse had made a spirited charge, recovered some of the prisoners, and captured a gun. Unfortunately no one knew what had become of the gunners and their caissons. We, therefore, heaved the thing into a ditch. For a whole hour we saw the Turcomans, a long way off, still taking some of our men prisoner. Then our several groups began to coalesce and we made out that, altogether, we might number some seven or eight hundred; not much that, out of the six or seven thousand that had started from Mashad. However, it was something, and, when we came to take stock of the situation, considering what fearful lions we were, we didn't doubt for a moment that we should be able to get back to a position where the Turcomans would be unable to take any more prisoners. We were in such high fettle that nothing seemed too hard for us to tackle.

Our leader turned out to be the young *bashi* of the horsemen, a Kurd called Rezi Khan, a tall, handsome man with a short black beard, blazing eyes, and magnificently equipped. So blithe was he that his high spirits seemed to communicate themselves to his very horse, so that man and beast seemed to flash and scintillate at every movement. There was also one Abdal-Rahim, of the Bakhtiaris, a fine, strapping fellow with shoulders like an elephant.

"Boys! Boys!" quoth he. "You are regular Rustams and Iskandars. We will wipe out this Turcoman rabble to the last man!" We were thrilled, and starting singing. The infantry had two commanders, a lieutenant, who was unknown to me, and our own *vekil*. Said that brave fellow:

"What we could do with now is some victuals and some powder!"

It was borne in upon us that we were dying of hunger. However, there was a remedy for that. We all started tearing up grass from the plain. A portion of it was kept in reserve for the horses. With the rest, we decided to make soup. But the rain kept falling in torrents, and as there was no wood, we found it extremely difficult to light a fire. We might have done it with dry grass. There was no end of withered grass to be had, but the trouble was it was sodden with rain. So we had no choice but to eat our portion of grass just as it was. It wasn't good, but our stomachs were filled and they ceased to rattle. As for the powder, that wasn't so easy. When we left Mashad, we had hardly any powder served out to us, and that the generals had sold. And now, when we simply had to have some, it was a problem. We collected a few cartridges from the dead bodies. We had about three hundred rifles that would go off, and, when we had finally sized things up, we found there were about three rounds for each rifle. Rezi Khan gave strict orders to everyone that we were not to fire till he gave the word. But we were in such a gleeful mood that some of us fired off their rounds just to celebrate our victory. After all, it didn't matter much; we had some first-rate bayonets. By a very happy coincidence we discovered, not far away, a sort of entrenched camp, built by the pagans in olden days. It was foursquare, with stone ramparts, and it was situated in the middle of a sort of marsh. We went and got into it, to spend the night. It was a good thing we did so, for, at daybreak, the Turcomans returned. They greatly outnumbered us, and, if they had fallen on us again in the open country, we should have had a pretty hot time of it.

From behind our walls we blazed away at the enemy, and killed a few of them. Stung to fury at this, they dismounted and swarmed like ants up our mounds of stones. Thereupon, we fell on them with the bayonet, with Rezi Khan at our head. We gave them such a rough handling that, after putting up a fight for ten minutes, they turned and fled. Unfortunately Rezi Khan and the great Bakhtiari, who had fought like tigers, were both of them killed. As for me, I got a knife wound in the arm. But, God is great! It was but a scratch.

But see what ruffians these Turcomans are. They ran away, but they didn't run far. They came back almost at once, and started prancing around our walls. They had noticed, it seems, that we hadn't done much shooting, and they now perceived, readily enough, that we weren't doing any at all, and for a very good reason; we had no more powder left, not a grain, not an atom. God knows full well what he doeth!

Our enemies decided, therefore, on a fresh assault, and some of them again transformed themselves into infantry. Behold them now, crawling up the slope of our fortress like ants. We made a sortie, led by the *vekil*. Again we routed them. We slew a dozen, and the rest took to flight. Then their cavalry charged. We just had time to scurry back to our hole, and, looking forth, we saw the head of our *vekil*, on the point of a lance, bobbing up and down among the Turcomans.

Ah, I mustn't forget to mention that we were perished with cold the previous night. We hadn't a dry stitch on our miserable bodies, and it was still raining. With nothing but a little wet grass in our insides, it was impossible for us to keep up our strength. As for me, I suffered greatly, and about sixty of our men succumbed, we didn't know why or wherefore. The All High and Merciful God willed it so.

That night the weather was again very bad. The only thing we could do was to huddle as close as possible to one another, so as to give ourselves some sort of idea of what warmth was like. However, toward morning the sky cleared. It was bitterly cold. We were expecting an attack. The lieutenant had given up the ghost.

It was not until midday that the Turcomans put in an appearance. But they kept at a safe distance. In the evening they took heart and approached to within rifle range, making a circuit of our entrenchments. Then they withdrew.

The night robbed us of still more men. We were now not more than four hundred strong, and there was no one to lead us. But we knew what had to be done, and, if we had been attacked we should again have given the miscreants a good taste of the bayonet. We were, however, in a very debilitated condition.

It was getting near the hour of the prayer of Asr, and the declining sun was nearing the horizon, when, in the distance, we descried bands of Turcomans approaching in

greater numbers than on any of the preceding days. Everyone struggled to his feet with what strength he had left, and
picked up his rifle. To our great surprise, however, the entire body came to a halt a long way off. Then four or five
cavalrymen detached themselves from the main force and
came riding toward us, making friendly signs and indicating as plainly as they could that they desired to parley.

A good many of our men were for rushing out upon
them and cutting off their heads. But what good would
that have done? I pointed this out, and so did some of the
others, and, after a lengthy discussion, everybody came
around to my view. So we went forth to meet these sons
of dogs, and, bowing low before them, ushered them back
within our own lines. Everyone sat upon the ground forming a circle around the newcomers, whom we caused to be
seated on horsecloths.

Wallah! Billah! Tallah! There was a big difference between us and them. We looked like phantoms that had been
rolled in the mud and soaked in the waters of misery. They,
on the other hand, were well clad and wrapped in furs,
with gleaming arms and splendid headgear. When they
were duly seated, I, having been authorized to open the
discussion, said to the swine:

"May all be well with you!"

"And with you," they replied.

"We trust," I went on, "that Your Excellencies are enjoying the most perfect health, and that your hearts' desires may all be fulfilled both in this world and the next."

"The kindness of Your Excellencies is infinite," replied
the most elderly of the Turcomans. He was a tall old man
with a diminutive nose, a face as round as a pumpkin, with
bristles sticking out here and there upon his chin, and eyes
shaped like the crescent moon when she is lying on her back.

"What commands are Your Excellencies pleased to convey to us?" I asked.

"Nay," said the old Turcoman, "'tis we who come to
lay a request before Your Highnesses. You know that we
are but poor family men, hard-working tillers of the soil,
slaves of the King of Kings, and servants of Iran the Well-

Guarded. For generations we have done all that in us lies
to convince the August Government of our overflowing affection. Unfortunately we are very poor, our wives and our
children are crying out for very hunger, the lands we cul-
tivate do not yield the wherewithal to nourish them, and,
if we did not do a little profitable business now and again
in the slave market, we should have to die of want, we and
our dear ones. Wherefore, then, persecute us?"

"Everything Your Excellencies have just propounded is
the most absolute truth," I answered. "As for us, we are
the humblest of soldiers. If we have been sent here, we
know not why, and now, already overwhelmed by what
Your Excellencies have said, we venture to ask you to permit us to return to Mashad, whence we set out."

On this the Turcoman bowed in the most friendly manner, and replied:

"Would to heaven that were possible. My companions
and I are quite ready to offer you our horses, and to beg
you to accept innumerable tokens of our friendship. But
judge, yourselves, of our melancholy situation. The August
Government has attacked us without cause, us, who never
harmed anybody, and, besides that, victuals are scarce. You
have nothing to eat. As for ourselves, we have hardly
touched a bit of food for a week. Now, come with us. You
will be well treated. We will not sell you, either at Bokhara
or at Khiva. We will keep you with us, and if your friends
are disposed to ransom you, we shall be ready to agree to
the most moderate of terms. Would it not be better to come
and to await your deliverance beneath our tents, beside a
good fire, than to risk death from starvation?"

The old Turcoman had the appearance of an honest fellow. His comrades began talking to us about new bread,
cream cheeses, and roast mutton. We were all of us deeply
impressed. Suddenly, as by a common impulse, we all
threw away our rifles, and, the ambassadors having risen
to their feet, we followed them with perfect willingness.

On arriving with them at the place where the horsemen
were stationed, we were given a charming reception. We
were placed in the midst of the throng and, as we marched

along, we chatted freely with our masters, who seemed to us a very decent lot. Every now and again, it is true, one or other of us got a stinger with a whip, but that was only because the particular individual wasn't moving fast enough. For the rest, everything went off perfectly well, except that, for beings as worn out as we were, it was a bit hard to have to keep going for eight hours, over sticky ground, before we got to the camp to which they were taking us.

Their women and children came out to meet us. This was our most trying moment. Apparently there were in the crowd some women who had become widows a few days before, we having slain their husbands, and then there were mothers who were indignant at what we had done to their sons. In every country in the world women are a spiteful race, but these were regular devils. The least they would have done to us, if they could have had their way, was to have torn us to pieces with their nails. The children would have liked nothing better than to do the same, and, by way of giving us something to go on with, they greeted us with yells and a volley of stones. Luckily the men did not appear at all disposed to acquiesce in our discomfiture. Half grumbling, half laughing, and dealing the furies a shrewd blow, now here, now there, they managed to get us into the camp, and to make it impossible for our foes and their little auxiliaries, if not to insult us (which we didn't mind at all) at all events to shed our blood. When we were all assembled in the square, they counted us and told us that anyone who attempted to escape would at once be put to death. After that announcement we were distributed among the cavalrymen who had captured us, and whose slaves we now became. Thus, for instance, one man acquired ten prisoners, another five, another two. As for myself, I was assigned to quite a young fellow, who immediately took me off to his abode. My master was not badly off; I could see that when I entered his tent. This tent was of the kind known as *alaljiks*. It was made with separate compartments and with walls of trelliswork covered with thick felt. The floor was of wood, and was cov-

ered with rugs. There were three or four chests painted
in divers colors, and a big bed with cushions, and, in the
middle of the tent, a stove that gave out an agreeable
warmth. In this charming habitation I perceived a young
woman. She was giving suck to an infant. I bowed to her
deferentially. She was undoubtedly my mistress, but she
took not the slightest notice of me, and only just glanced
at her husband. I will tell you here and now what the Turcoman women are like. Nothing very interesting. They are
ugly enough to scare the devil. Take that young woman
in the tent. I afterward learned that she was one of the
beauties of the place. I shouldn't have even guessed it if
I hadn't been told. She looked like a hulking porter from
Tabriz. She had wide, flat shoulders, a great big head, tiny
eyes, prominent cheekbones, a mouth like a baker's oven, a
flat forehead and a couple of mountains on her chest. And
I've seen some worse still. As a class these women are stupid, spiteful, and brutish, fit only for hard work. They are
indeed made to work like mules; and quite right, too.

The master said to his lady, "Put the child down, and
give me some supper." The lady obeyed immediately. She
began to rattle about the plates and dishes, and signed to
me to follow her outside the tent. I obeyed with alacrity,
as I had an idea that zeal might get me into her good
books. She conducted me into a sort of shed that did duty
for a kitchen, where something or other, I didn't know what,
was stewing in a saucepan. She made a sign I didn't understand. Without attempting to explain she picked up a stick
and dealt me a whack on the head. "Here," I said to myself, "is a species of monster who isn't going to make life
very easy for me."

I was wrong. She was a thoroughly sound woman. True,
she often hit me. She was very particular, and wanted everything just so, but she fed me well, and, when she got
to know me a little better, she became more communica-
tive, and, more than once, I managed to deceive her, without her ever finding me out. When she was in a friendly
mood, she would burst out laughing and say, "You Iran

people, you haven't got as much sense as our horses, isn't that so?"

"Yes, ma'am," I humbly replied, "that's perfectly true. God willed it so."

"The Turcomans loot and rob and carry you off bodily, and sell you to anyone they choose, and you can't find any way to stop them."

"True, ma'am," I replied again. "You see, the Turcomans have their wits about them, and we're a lot of asses."

Then she would burst out laughing again and it never dawned on her that her stock of milk and butter was dwindling to my advantage. I have repeatedly observed that the people of the strongest physique have the least brains. Take the Europeans; you can fool them to your heart's content, yet they go swaggering about as if they had bought the place, just because they happen to have the whip hand. They don't know, and they never will know, that mind is far superior to matter. The Turcomans are exactly the same. They, too, are brutes.

I was employed by my masters in hewing wood, drawing water, and driving the sheep to pasture. When I had no particular job in hand, I would take a walk in the country. I had made some friends, and I used to do a little singing. I knew also how to make traps for mice, and I taught some of the women to cook Persian dishes, and the men liked them tremendously. I got things in return, such as buttered tea and cakes. There were also a good number of weddings, where I gave an exhibition of dancing, to the great amusement of the company. They were in a particularly joyous mood, as well they might be. Our camp, the camps adjoining it, in fact the whole country were in a very festive state on account of the victory. There were crowds of prisoners, and their captors counted on making big money out of them. Then, when the initial fit of temper had passed, the various widows were enchanted with their situation, which is not to be wondered at. You see, a Turcoman spinster fetches only five gold *tomans,* and the circumstances must be not a little abnormal for a man to consider a spinster when he wants to marry. A widow, on the other hand, commands a high price on account of her house-keeping knowledge, her reputation for thrift, and her ability to run a house. Moreover, one knows for certain whether she can, or cannot, bear children. As for love, you will readily conceive that, with the sort of face and figure these ladies are blest with, the question does not arise. No one thinks about it; in fact no one has any idea what it means. Once I tried to tell my mistress about the beautiful and touching passion Mejnun entertained for Leila, and that, by recalling Leila to my mind, sent me off into transports of grief. My mistress gave me an outrageous thrashing for daring to bore her with such a lot of rubbish. She was still quite young, yet she had had two husbands already, before the one she acknowledged at the moment, and three children into the bargain. For this reason her reputation was immense, and it was a feather in my cap, and well I knew it, to belong to such a woman.

I had been living like this for about three months, jogging along pretty peacefully, and I was beginning to get accustomed to my lot (in truth, as I have explained, it was no very hard one) when one morning, as I was strolling about the camp at loose ends, I was accosted by two other slaves, Persians like myself, men belonging to the Kum contingent, who told me they knew for a fact—swearing by their heads—that we were to be set free during the day and sent back to Mashad.

This rumor had been put about so often, and just as often proved baseless, that I began to laugh. I told my comrades not to put too much faith in what they had heard, and not to give up adding to their stock of patience. However, when I had left them, I felt, as I always did, whenever I heard such tidings, very anxious and disturbed. I know that many things are done amiss in Iran and that there is plenty to find fault with there; still, it is Iran, the best and most sacred country in the world. Nowhere else does one experience such pleasure, such joy. Once you've lived there you're always yearning to get back again, and when you're there, that's where you want to lay your bones. I didn't believe a word of what my two comrades had said;

nevertheless my heart was thumping, and I felt wistful, so terribly wistful that, instead of continuing my walk, I went back to my master's abode.

It chanced that he had just alighted from his horse and was engaged in conversation with his wife. Seeing me, he called me over.

"Aga," said he, "thou art my slave no longer, thou art my guest, and thou art about to start for Mashad."

I was so overcome you could have knocked me down with a feather, and the tent seemed to be going round and round.

"Is this true?" I cried.

"What stupids these Persians are," said his wife with a laugh. "What is there wonderful about it? Thy Government has ransomed its men at ten *tomans* a head. We might have sold them for more than that, but, since the folly's been done and we've had our money, be off home and don't be a fool."

I hardly listened to what the creature said. The whole thing passed like a dream before my eyes. I saw, yes I saw, the lovely vale of Khamseh, the place where I was born; I saw, quite plainly, the stream, the willows, the lush grass, the flowers, the tree at whose roots I had buried my money, my beautiful, my darling Leila in my arms, my hunting grounds, my gazelles, my tigers, my dear Kerim, the excellent Sulaiman, the staunch Abdullah, all my cousins, the bazaar at Teheran, the grocer's, the cookshop, the faces of the people I knew; yes, yes, my whole life came up before me at that moment. I was absolutely drunk with joy. I felt like dancing, singing, weeping. I felt as if I could hug everybody who came into my mind at this moment of supreme felicity, and I cried aloud in my agony.

"Idiot!" said the woman. "Thou didst soak raki last night, and, for all I know, this morning, too. If ever I catch thee at it again . . ."

"But that will never happen," said her husband with a laugh. "He's off today, and, I tell thee again, Aga, from this morning onward, thou art a free man."

"I'm a free man!" I shouted. Out of the tent I dashed

and made for the big square in the middle of the camp. From all the habitations came pouring my poor comrades, every whit as excited as I was. We flung our arms around one another, nor did we omit to offer thanks to God and the Imams, crying aloud with heart and voice, "Iran! Dear Iran! Light of my eyes!" And then I learned, little by little, how it was we were issuing all of a sudden out of the shadows into so lovely a light.

It seems that, since the loss of our army and the beginning of our captivity, a number of things had happened. The King of Kings, on hearing what had befallen, flew into a mighty rage with his generals, accusing them of leaving his poor soldiers to go on all alone against the enemy, instead of going with them. He accused them further of selling the foodstuffs, arms, powder, and clothing that should have been assigned to the men, and, finally, he announced his firm resolve to have all the culprits beheaded.

Perhaps he would have been well advised to put this threat into execution. Yet after all what good would it have done? The present generals would have been succeeded by others in all respects their fellows. It is the way of the world, and you cannot change it. In the circumstances His Majesty adopted a far wiser line. He laid aside his choler. All that happened was that the ministers and pillars of the empire received a prodigious number of presents from the accused officers. One or two of these latter were recalled for a few months. The king came in for some magnificent gifts, and it was decided that the commanders should ransom all the men who had been taken prisoner by the Turcomans and that they should do so out of their own pockets, seeing that they were responsible for the misfortunes that had befallen the poor devils.

The matter having been thus settled, the generals had of course taken the colonel and majors aside, the said colonels and majors having done precisely what they themselves had done. They threatened to have them beaten, to reduce them to the ranks and even to cut off their heads, and so well did they work matters, that, at last, they too managed to bring about an agreement. The colonels and majors gave presents to their superiors, and so these latter recouped themselves, in some measure, for the expenses that, to safe-guard their own interests, they had been forced to incur at Teheran.

Meantime they had sent forth envoys among the Turco-man tribes to negotiate for the ransom of the captives. They had had some difficulty in coming to terms, but at length an agreement was arrived at. And this was how, after a period of incredible excitement, a sort of ecstasy of happi-ness, we finally came to take leave of our former masters and our Turcoman friends, and set out on the road to Ma-shad, marching, you can take my word for it, like birds about to spread their wings.

The weather was superb. By night the stars glittered like diamonds in the sky; by day, a glorious sun deluged earth and sky with flakes of gold that poured in torrents from his flaming orb. The whole universe smiled on us, on us poor hapless soldiers, yea the most luckless, the most for-lorn, the most ill-treated of human beings, emerging from the very depths of misfortune to regain the realms at least of hope. We marched blithely, and we sang lustily, and so came at length to within two hours of Mashad. We saw things taking clear and definite shape before us on the sky's deep blue, the cupolas, the minarets and the gleaming walls of the sacred mosque, and the countless rows of houses in the town. And as we fell to thinking on all the good things we should soon be finding in the heart of that celestial scene, we were suddenly brought to an abrupt halt by two regi-ments drawn up across the road with a group of officers in front of them. We stopped short and bowed low.

A mullah advanced toward us from the group of officers. When he had got within earshot, he lifted up his hands on high and harangued us as follows:

"My children," he said, "glory to God the Lord of the Universe, mighty and merciful, who rescued the prophet Yunès from the whale's belly, and you from the hands of the fell Turcomans."

"Amen!" responded all our lads.

"It is meet that ye should thank Him by entering humbly

into Mashad, humbly, I say, as befits a band of miserable prisoners."

"We are ready so to do," we made reply.

"So be it, then, my children; now you will, all of you, like pious men and faithful Mussulmans, put chains upon your wrists, and all the people, moved to tears by this proof of your sufferings, will shower blessings upon you; yea, blessings, and alms to boot."

We thought this a capital idea, and were delighted with it. Thereupon, some soldiers from each of the two regiments left the ranks and approached us. They put iron rings about our necks and shackles on our wrists, and then split us up into groups of eight to ten chained together. This made us laugh heartily and we fancied ourselves very highly in this guise, though the weight of the metal was a little fatiguing. However, it was only a matter of putting up with it for a few hours, and that was a trifle.

When we were all rigged out, the drummers, the band, and the officers of one of the regiments marched on in front, we came next, in our lamentable getup, but very pleased with ourselves. Close behind us followed the other regiment. Before long we beheld a multitude of Mashadis who had turned out to meet us. We saluted and had the joy of hearing ourselves covered with blessings. Meanwhile, the drums rolled, the band played, and several pieces of artillery were fired off in our honor.

Once inside the city, we were split up; some took one street, some another, and soldiers escorted us. As for myself and my seven chained comrades, all of us handcuffed, with iron collars clamped around our necks, we were marched off to a guardhouse where we were allowed to sit on a platform. The sergeant in charge of our escort encouraged us to solicit the charity of the passers-by. This was a first-rate idea, and we put it into immediate execution with amazing success. Men, women, and children brought us rice, meat, and even dainties, without stint. We did not get much in the way of cash. I have a notion that the good folk who contributed to our assistance were not too flush with it themselves.

At night an officer arrived. We asked him to set us free and let us go about our own affairs. As for myself, my one prevailing idea was to go and put in a good night's sleep, and I greatly needed it, at the house of my friend and kinsman, Mullah Sulaiman. This is what the officer replied:

"My lads, you must listen to reason. You see it's like this: you fellows have been redeemed from captivity through the incomparable, the superhuman generosity of my uncle, General Ali Khan. For each of you he gave your masters ten *tomans*. Would it be fair, I ask you, that he should lose such a large sum? Of course it wouldn't; you will agree to that. But then, if he were to let you go, although you are all very honest, and incapable of repudiating your debts, and all that, the fact, the unfortunate fact, is that you have not got any assets. How could a lot of beggarly soldiers be expected to have any money? Realizing this, my uncle, who is the very personification of kindness, will put you in the way of getting some. By leaving you with chains about your necks, until you have each collected fifteen *tomans*, which you will give to him, he will show you how to touch the hearts of the Mussulmans and to stimulate the flow of public charity. Do not take it too much to heart. Tell people the whole story of your sufferings; go on begging from any and everyone who comes your way. Hail them, call out to every one of the good folk who pass by. They will come. You see they are already feeding you very satisfactorily. Keep on, and, by and by, pity will move them more and more, and their purse strings will be loosed. In a few days, when there is no more likelihood of your picking up anything much here, you will be sent away somewhere else. Thus, you will go back to Teheran, from there you will go on to Ispahan, Shiraz, Karmanshah, and all the cities of Iran the Well-Guarded, and so at last you will pay off the debt."

The officer ended. We flew into a fearful rage. Despair took hold of us, and we began calling him son of a dog, and were in a fair way to include his uncle, and his uncle's wives, mother, and daughters if he had any, in the same category, when at a sign from our bully of an officer, our warders fell on us, beat us, flung us to the ground, and kicked us. I nearly had a rib stove in, and my head was swollen with two great bumps. There was nothing for it but to give them best. Everybody caved in. As for me, when I had wept in a corner a good half hour, I resigned myself to my fate and again began in doleful tones to solicit the charity of the passers-by.

There was no lack of charitable folk, and everybody knows, thanks be to God Almighty, that there is in Islam a notable readiness to come to the aid of the unhappy. The women, in particular, gathered in great numbers about us. They gazed upon us and wept. They asked us to tell them about the trials we had endured. Great as they were, we made, as may well be imagined, no attempt to diminish them. On the contrary, we never omitted to add to our tales, that our wives and our little ones—five, six, seven, eight of them—were waiting for us at home and dying of hunger. By this means we collected a lot of small change, and, now and then, a little silver. However, some of us were luckier than the others.

It is well known that our regiments are recruited from the poorer classes, who, having neither friends nor protectors, have no means of evading military service. When soldiers are required, the recruiting gangs pick up in the streets and taverns of the cities, or in country cottages, anyone and everyone who has no one of influence to protect him. So there we were, all on our chain, grown men, youngsters of fifteen, old fellows of seventy, for, when you're a soldier, you're a soldier for life, unless you can manage to get your release, or to run away.

Those who had the most given to them were the youngsters. There was one, a good-looking lad of sixteen, born at Zanjan, who got his freedom at the end of a fortnight, owing to the fuss that was made of him everywhere. It is true that he had the face of an angel. As for me, I succeeded in getting word to Mullah Sulaiman, letting him know my dismal plight. The good fellow came at once, flung his arms around my neck, and in the name of our beloved Leila, gave me a *toman*. It was a lot of money. Possibly I might

have got more out of him, only the next day we were compelled to leave Mashad en route for Teheran.

My comrades and I composed a song about our trials
and tribulations, and we sang it to the country folk along
our way. That always brought us in a bit. Moreover, the
Mussulmans in their charity fed us poor captives with
greater liberality than they had previously regaled the soldiers of the king, and our guards benefited by it no less
than we did. The only thing was, we had to keep a sharp
eye on our little takings, for, naturally, both we and the
soldiers who had charge of us had but one thought, and
that was to get hold of as much as possible of other people's
belongings. For my part I kept my bit of money wrapped
up in a piece of blue cotton stuff. I never showed it to anyone and I had it tied on to me under my clothes with a
piece of string. When we arrived at the capital, I could
state with truth that, including the gold *toman* my cousin
gave me, some silver *sahabgrans,* and a mass of coppers,
I had, all told, about three and a half *tomans.* Some of my
friends were, I am sure, better off than I was, but others
hadn't so much. An old artilleryman named Ibrahim, who
was my nearest chainmate, never had anything at all given
him; he was so ugly.

On arriving at Teheran, we were taken straight to my
old guard post and we were all put up on show on a platform. The people of the neighborhood, recognizing me,
came along in crowds. I told them the whole story of our
misfortunes and they were on the point of handing out a
considerable sum, when a positive miracle happened. God
be praised! Blessed be the sainted Imams! May their holy
names be lifted up on high! Amen! Amen! Glory to God,
the Lord of Creation! Glory to God!

A miracle, I say, happened, and this was the manner of
it. As usual, a great number of women had gathered around
to inspect us. They shoved their way forward, pressing on
one another's heels, doing their utmost to get a good view
of us. So it happened that I, who was telling the story of
our tribulations, found myself face to face with a wall of

blue and white veils. I had got to this passage, which I repeated several times, in tones of despair:

"O Mussulmans! O Mussulmans! Islam is no more! Religion is dead! I hail from the Khamseh! Alas! Alas! I come
from the borderland of Zanjan! I have a poor blind mother,
my father's two sisters are crippled, my wife is paralyzed,
and my eight little ones are dying of hunger, and I shall
die of despair!"

At that moment I heard a piercing shriek quite near me.
I recognized the voice at once. It went through me like a
red-hot arrow.

"In God! By God! For God!" it cried. "It's Aga!"

"Leila!" I shouted without a moment's hesitation.

Despite the thickness of the veil she was wearing, her
face positively glowed as I gazed upon it. I was borne away
with joy to the topmost summit of the seventh sphere.

"Let not thy heart be troubled," said she, "thou shalt be
delivered this very day, or at the latest, on the morrow."

Thereupon she turned away and disappeared, together
with two women who were in her company. That evening,
as I was dying with impatience, an officer arrived with a
vekil. My chain was sundered, and the officer spoke to me,
saying:

"Go thy way, thou art free."

Even as he was saying these words, I found myself
clasped in the arms, in the arms I say of—whom do you
think? Why, of my cousin Abdullah! God! How glad I was
to see him!

"Ah, my friend, my brother, my well beloved," said he.
"What joy! What a meeting! When I learned from our
cousin Kerim that thou hadst been carried off by the militia,
I knew not to what depths of despair I was ready to abandon myself."

"Noble Kerim!" I exclaimed. "We were always very fond
of each other, he and I, though sometimes, I confess, I used
to like Sulaiman better, and by the way, do you know that
Sulaiman . . ." And then I went on to tell him what had
happened to our worthy cousin and how he was about to
become a very learned mullah and a personage of great

importance at Mashad. Abdullah was delighted to hear this.

"I grieve," he said, "that our cousin Kerim has failed to do equally well. It was to some extent his own fault. He had, it will be remembered, a most regrettable habit of indulging to excess in cold tea."

"Cold tea," of course, as is well known in respectable circles, signifies that abominable liquor commonly called raki. I shook my head with a gesture of mingled sorrow and anger.

"Kerim," I replied, "was indeed addicted to cold tea, as I know only too well. For a long time I did my best to wean him from this shameful habit. I never succeeded."

"All the same," Abdullah went on, "he might be worse off. I employ him as a muleteer and he carts goods for me on the Tabriz-Trebizond Road. He makes a decent living by it."

"What is that? What is that thou sayest? Thou has become a trader?"

"Yes, my brother," answered Abdullah modestly, "I have amassed a certain amount of capital, and that is how I was able to come to thy assistance today, when my wife told me of your distressing plight."

"Thy wife?"

I was absolutely dumfounded.

"Yes, my wife. Kerim, you see, not having the wherewithal to support that adorable creature in the comfort she deserved, agreed to a divorce, and then I married her."

I wasn't any too pleased at this, but what could I do? Nothing but bow to my fate. There's no getting away from fate; time and again I've had to recognize that. Now here was another blow, and I confess I felt it. However, I didn't say anything. I went along with Abdullah. When we got near the New Gate, he took me into an exceedingly attractive house, and showed me into the *enderun*.

There I found Leila, seated on a rug. She welcomed me very kindly. Unfortunately for me, I thought her looking prettier and more appealing than ever, and my heart grew big with tears. She noticed this, and when, after tea, Abdullah, who had business to attend to, left us alone, she said:

"My poor Aga, I see thou art a little sad."

"I am, very," I replied, hanging my head.

"Now, let's be sensible," she went on. "I will not hide anything from thee. I confess I was very fond of thee; and so I am now. At the same time, I was not insensible to Sulaiman's good qualities; Kerim's gaiety and high spirits delighted me, and I am full of esteem and regard for the meritorious Abdullah. If anyone asked me to declare which of my four cousins I liked the best, I should request that, of the four, they should make one sole man, and him, I am sure, I should love passionately and for ever. But, I ask you, is that possible? Be assured, thou wilt live for ever in my heart. I could not marry Sulaiman because he had no money. I came to you; you have been a trifle irresponsible, but I forgive that. I know that thou lovest me tenderly. Kerim put me on the high road to starvation. Abdullah has made me rich. I owe it to him to be a good wife in return, and I shall be faithful to him till death, though thinking of you three as of men. . . . But there, I've said enough. Abdullah is your cousin. Love him; serve him. He will do for you all that in him lies. I shall not hinder him, you may be sure of that."

She said a number of other affectionate things that, at the time, only increased my sorrow. However, since there was nothing else for it, as I realized only too well, I resigned myself to being, as far as Leila was concerned, nothing more than the son of her uncle.

Abdullah, in his capacity as trader, frequently had dealings with persons of importance. He did them services, and stood high in their esteem. Thanks to him, I was made sultan in the Khasseh, or Private, Regiment, which always remains at Teheran, in the palace there, mounting guard, drawing water, hewing wood, and doing building work. So then, I was a captain, and I began to feed on my soldiers, even as in the past I had been fed on myself. This soon procured me a very honorable status, and I have nothing to grumble about.

We are in the King's Bodyguard. It has often been proposed that we should be given a magnificent uniform, and the matter is still under discussion. Sometimes it is suggested that we should be arrayed like the men who watch over the life of the emperor of the Russias; they, according to all accounts, wear green, with gold stripes and embroidery. Some, on the other hand, favor red, also with stripes, and embroidery and facings as aforesaid. But if the men were thus attired, of what use could they possibly be? Meanwhile, until the question is decided, they go about in tattered breeches and often with nothing on their heads.

Being now an officer, I made up my mind to live with men of my own standing, and I added considerably to my acquaintance. Among my new friends I found myself chiefly drawn to a certain sultan, a young man of charming disposition. He had lived a long time with the Feringhis, having been sent to their country in order to complete his education. He told me some very curious things. One evening, when we had drunk rather more cold tea than usual, he delivered himself of some opinions I thought were perfectly sound.

"You see, Brother," said he, "all Iranians are brutes, and all Europeans are fools. I know, because I've been brought up among them. To begin with, I was put in college, and then, as I had learned just as well as those swine, what you have to do to get through examinations, I entered their military academy, the place they call St. Cyr. I put in two years there, like the rest of them. Then, having become an officer, I came back home. There they wanted to make use of me, and asked me questions about military practice. I told them, but they didn't like it; they jeered, and took a dislike to me. They said I was disloyal and insolent, and gave me the rod. At first I wished I was dead, for that is the sort of thing Europeans regard as a terrible dishonor."

"The fools!" I cried, emptying my glass.

"Yes, they *are* fools. They don't realize that everything out here—habits, emotions, interests, climate, air, soil, our past, our present—makes what is perfectly natural for them utterly impossible for us. When I realized that I wasn't going to do any good by dying, I began my education all over again. I gave up having opinions, and trying to reform things, blaming here and contradicting there, and I became like all the rest of you. I kissed the hands of the powers that be, and I said, 'Yes, most certainly,' to the most glaring absurdities. After that, they gradually gave up making my life a burden to me, but still, even now, they don't really trust me, and I shall never be more than a captain. We know, both of us, you and I, generals of fifteen and marshals of eighteen. We also know doughty warriors who don't know how to load a rifle. Here am I, a man of fifty and upward, and I shall die in poverty, under a cloud of incurable suspicion, all because I know how to handle troops and to polish off these Turcoman frontiersmen in a matter of three months or so. Confound those European knaves who brought all this misery upon me! Pass the raki."

That night we drank so deeply that it was the evening of the next day before I was able to get up off the carpet on which I had fallen, and I left my comrade still lying on it.

Thanks to Abdullah's good offices, I confidently expect to be promoted major this year, unless, that is, they make a colonel of me. *Inshallah! Inshallah!*

The Mysterious Sketch

BY ÉMILE ERCKMANN AND
ALEXANDRE CHATRIAN

TRANSLATED BY JOHN D. GRAYSON

ÉMILE ERCKMANN
1822–99
and
ALEXANDRE CHATRIAN
1826–90

These two Alsatians (Erckmann was born in Pfalzburg; Chatrian, in nearby Soldatenthal) collaborated for over forty years (1848–89) on some of the best-selling novels of the nineteenth century. Their specialty was historical romances dealing with the French Revolution and the Napoleonic Wars: *The Invasion* (1852), *Madame Thérèse* (1863), *Friend Fritz* (1864), *The History of a Conscript* (1864), *Waterloo* (1865). Although they were accused by recalcitrant patriots of defeatist pacifism and democratic ideology, their novels and plays were enjoyed for their engrossing plots and straightforward style. Of particular interest to contemporary readers are their tales of fantasy, *Histoires et contes fantastiques* (1849), one of which is included here.

ABOUT ERCKMANN-CHATRIAN: Nothing worth while in English; in French, L. Schoumacker's excellent dissertation, University of Strasbourg (Paris, Belles Lettres, 1933), and the biographical study by Émile Hinzelin (Paris, Ferenczi, 1922).

I

At the corner of the Hellebardieren-Strasse in Nuremberg, opposite the chapel of St. Sebalt, there stands a little inn. It is a tall, narrow structure with grimy windowpanes, its Gothic gable surmounted by a plaster Madonna. Here it was that I spent the saddest days I have ever known.

I had come to Nuremberg to study the old German masters, but, lacking money, I was obliged to earn my living by painting portraits. And what portraits they were! Of fat matrons who posed with their pet cats on their knees, of periwigged aldermen and burgomasters in three-cornered hats, all bespattered with the liveliest ochre and vermilion my palette could provide.

From portraits I sank to sketches, and from sketches to silhouettes.

There is nothing more pitiable than to have a landlord forever dogging your footsteps, tight-lipped and scolding, greeting you every morning with: "Well, now, will you pay me soon, sir? Do you know how high you have run up your bill? Ah no—that doesn't distress you! The heavenly Father feedeth the fowls of the air. You can eat, drink, and sleep with perfect tranquillity. Your bill, sir, amounts to two hundred florins and ten kreutzers. Scarcely worth mentioning!"

Those who have never been regaled with such a sermon cannot imagine its terrible effect. Your imagination, your love of art, even your enthusiasm for beauty—all wither and die before the cruel blast. You become awkward and timid, all your energy vanishes, to say nothing of your self-

respect, and you find yourself bowing to Burgomaster
Schneegans across the way with the greatest deference.

One evening, penniless as usual and threatened with
debtors' prison by my landlord, the worthy Mr. Rap, I resolved to bankrupt him by cutting my own throat. Seated
on my cot opposite the window and absorbed in this happy
thought, I entertained myself with a thousand more or less
cheerful reflections.

"What is man," I mused to myself, "but an omnivorous
animal? His jaws, furnished with canine teeth, incisors and
molars, make this quite clear. The canine teeth are for rend-
ing flesh; the incisors, for biting into fruits; and the molars,
for chewing, grinding and crushing animal and vegetable
matter, agreeable to nose and palate. However, when there
is nothing to be chewed, man has no function in nature. He
is meaningless—a superfluity—the fifth wheel to a cart."

Such were my thoughts. I did not venture to open my
razor, for fear that the incontestable force of my logic might
inspire me with the courage to do away with myself then
and there. After debating a while in this fashion I blew
out my candle, resolving to postpone the act until the following morning.

The unspeakable Rap had demoralized me completely.
As far as art was concerned, I thought of nothing but silhouettes, and my greatest wish was to make enough money
to rid myself of his hateful presence. However, that same
night, a curious revolution took place in my mind. About
an hour later I awoke, relit my lamp, and, putting on a
gray smock, I took up a piece of paper and made a rapid
sketch in the Dutch manner. The result was something
strange and fantastic, entirely unlike the rest of my work.

Picture a dark courtyard, bounded by high, crumbling
walls. These walls are provided with hooks, some seven or
eight feet from the ground. Clearly the yard belongs to a
butcher's shop.

On the left there is a kind of trellis, and through it, hanging from an archway by a system of enormous ropes and
pulleys, you see a quartered steer. Great rivers of blood

glide over the flagstones and flow together into a ditch filled with shapeless rubbish.

The lighting emanates from above, from between chimneys with weather vanes that cut into a patch of sky about the size of your hand, and the roofs of the surrounding houses cast somber shadows onto the stories beneath.

There is a shed in the background, and under it a woodbin, some ladders, a few bundles of straw, some coils of rope, a chicken coop, and an old, empty rabbit hutch.

How did all these bizarre details enter my consciousness? I cannot tell. I had never visited such a spot, and yet each stroke of the pencil seemed to be reproducing a scene that was somehow real. My work was effortless, rapid, and sure.

On the right, however, one corner of the sketch remained blank. At first I did not know what belonged there, but I sensed that in that corner something had stirred and was moving about. Suddenly I could visualize—a foot! A foot, not planted firmly on the ground, but in the air, and almost upside down. Despite the improbability of such a position, I followed the inspiration; the foot was extended into a leg, partially covered by a flapping skirt. Soon an old woman appeared, pale, wasted, and disheveled—and she was leaning backward over a pit, fighting frantically against a hand that was cutting her throat.

It was a murder scene I was sketching. The pencil fell from my grasp.

I was frightened by that old woman, precariously perched on the edge of the pit, her face contorted by terror, her shriveled hands clutching the arm of the assassin. I could not bring myself to look at her. But the man himself, except for that one murderous arm, would not appear. I could not complete the picture.

"I'm tired," I told myself, my forehead bathed in sweat. "All that remains is that one figure, and I shall finish it tomorrow. It will be simple."

And I returned to bed, still somewhat shaken by the experience. Five minutes later I was sleeping soundly.

The following morning I was up and about by daybreak.

I had just finished dressing and was preparing to resume my work, when there came two short raps at the door.

"Come in," I called.

The door was opened, and a tall, thin man, already old and dressed in black, appeared on the threshold. The features of the man, his close-set eyes, his great aquiline nose, long, pointed chin, and broad, bony forehead, gave him a dignified but somewhat stern aspect.

"Mr. Christian Venius, the painter?" he enquired, bowing gravely.

"That is my name, sir."

He bowed again and said, "I am Baron Friedrich von Spreckdal."

Amazed that Baron von Spreckdal, the rich art collector and judge of the Criminal Court, should appear in my wretched lodgings, I glanced furtively over the worm-eaten furniture, the moldy hangings, and the dusty floor. I was humiliated by the shabbiness of the room, but Von Spreckdal seemed to be unaware of it. He sat down next to my little table.

"Mr. Venius," he began, "I have come to——"

But at that moment his eyes fell on the unfinished sketch and he said no more. I was sitting on the edge of the cot, and the unexpected attention that this great man was giving to my drawing made my heart pound with anticipation.

After an interval Von Spreckdal raised his head.

"Did you do this?" he asked, looking at me closely.

"Yes, sir."

"What is the price?"

"I do not sell my sketches. It is only the plan for a painting."

"I see," he said, lifting the sheet with his long yellow fingers. Then he took a magnifying glass from his waistcoat pocket and proceeded to study the drawing in silence.

Slanting sunbeams from the dormer window fell upon the baron as he sat scanning the paper, his heavy eyebrows contracted, and his long, lean cheeks crisscrossed by a thousand minute wrinkles. The stillness was so deep that

I distinctly heard the plaintive buzzing of a fly caught in a cobweb.

"Well, Mr. Venius," he said at last, without looking at me, "what will be the dimensions of this painting?"

"Three feet by four."

"And the price?"

"Fifty ducats."

Von Spreckdal replaced the sketch on the table and drew from his pocket a pear-shaped, green silk purse.

"Here are the fifty ducats."

I was too dumfounded to speak.

The baron rose, bade me good morning, and I heard his ponderous ivory-headed cane striking each step until he reached the bottom of the last flight of stairs. Then, recovering from my stupor, I suddenly remembered that I had not even thanked him, and I dashed down the five flights like lightning. However, by the time I reached the front door, the street was deserted.

"How very curious!" I exclaimed.

And, still panting for breath, I climbed back up to my lodgings.

II

The miraculous manner in which Von Spreckdal had appeared threw me into a state of near-ecstasy. "Yesterday," I said to myself, as I contemplated the pile of ducats glistening in the sunlight, "yesterday, I was sinfully planning to cut my throat for a couple of miserable florins, and today, I find that a fortune has fallen into my lap out of thin air. Decidedly, I did well in not opening my razor, and if the temptation to suicide ever seizes me again, I shall take care to put off the business until the next day."

After these judicious observations I sat down to finish the sketch. Half a dozen strokes of the pencil and it would be complete. But in this I was mysteriously deceived. Ponder as I might, I had lost the thread of my inspiration, and the hidden assassin would not be disentangled from the clutches of my brain. Desperately I sought to evoke him, to sketch him, to ensnare him, but he did not match the rest. It was like a figure of Raphael on the cover of a cigar box.

It was at this moment of crisis that Rap, according to his usual praiseworthy custom, opened my door without knocking and walked in. Immediately the pile of ducats caught his greedy eye, and, turning to me, he screeched:

"Aha, I've caught you! Will you still insist, Mr. Painter, that you have no money?" And his hooked fingers reached out with that nervous tremor that the sight of gold always produces in the miser.

At first I could not answer him. Then, suddenly, the recollection of all the insults and indignities I had suffered at his hands overwhelmed me, and his covetous glance and impudent smile were more than I could bear. With a single bound, I caught hold of him and, pushing him out of the room with both hands, slammed the door in his face.

The incident had occurred in a matter of seconds. However, no sooner had I flattened his nose with the door, than the old villain began hammering and pounding from the other side.

"My money! Thief! My money!"

His yelps brought the other lodgers out of their chambers. "What's the matter? What's going on?"

By way of explanation I flung the door open, and, planting a kick on Mr. Rap's backbone that sent him rolling and tumbling down twenty steps or more, I bellowed, "That's what's going on!" Whereupon, I slammed the door shut again and double-locked it, amid bursts of laughter from my neighbors in the passage.

Pleased with what I had done, I rubbed my hands together. The adventure had so revived my spirits that I took up my work again, and was about to finish the sketch, when a new sound reached my ears. It was the thump of rifle butts striking the pavement of the street.

Looking out of my window, I beheld three constables, their cocked hats askew, standing on duty at the downstairs door.

"Could the scoundrel have broken a bone when he fell?" I wondered, dismayed.

How strange and capricious is the mind of man! There I was—I, who had wished to cut my throat the night before—trembling to the very marrow of my bones, because I might be hanged if Rap were dead!

The stair well was filled with a confusion of sounds. It was a mounting flood of footsteps, the clank of arms and short, sharp commands.

Suddenly, someone tried to open my door. But it was locked! Then there followed a general clamor.

"Open in the name of the law!"

I stood up shaking, my legs melting under me.

"Open up!" repeated the same voice.

It occurred to me that I might save myself by fleeing over the roof tops, but scarcely had I passed my head through the little skylight when I recoiled, overcome by giddiness. In a flash I had caught a glimpse of all the windows below, their panes shining like mirrors, and of their flowerpots, bird cages, and gratings. And farther down, the balcony; and still farther, the street lamp; and below that, the hanging sign of the Rote Faesschen, adorned with spikes. Finally, I had spotted three flashing bayonets down below, just waiting to run me through from head to toe, like meat on a spit. On the roof of the next house a huge red cat, lying in wait behind a chimney pot, was preparing to spring upon a flock of sparrows who were quarreling and chirping in the drain.

You cannot imagine what precision, what range of vision, what speed of observation, the human eye can attain when its owner is stimulated by fear!

There came a third summons.

"Open up, or we'll break the door down!"

Seeing that flight was impossible, I tottered to the door and drew back the bolts.

At once two hands seized me by the collar. A squat little man, who reeked of wine, declared, "You are under arrest!"

He was wearing a bottle-green frock coat, buttoned up to his chin, a stovepipe hat, and rings on all his fingers. He had

enormous side whiskers and his name was Passauf. He was
the chief of police.

Five bulldog heads wearing little flat caps, their noses
like pistol barrels, and their lower jaws bristling with teeth
and fangs, were regarding me warily from the passage.

"What is it you want?" I demanded of Passauf.

"Come downstairs!" he shouted roughly, signaling to one
of his men to lay hold of me.

And so I was dragged away, more dead than alive, while
the others ransacked my room from top to bottom. Down
the stairs I was borne, held up like a consumptive in his
final stages, my hair hanging in my eyes, and stumbling
and tripping at every step. I was hustled into a hackney
coach and flung down between two merry brutes who
thoughtfully made sure I saw the clubs they carried, fastened to their wrists by a leather strap. Then the coach
started off, with every urchin in the neighborhood trailing
along behind.

"But what have I done?" I asked one of my guards.

The guard looked at the other with a nasty smile.

"Hans," he said, "he wants to know what he's done." That
smile turned my blood to ice.

Presently the dark shadow of a building loomed up before us, and the horses came to a halt under a stone archway. We were coming into the Raspelhaus, a place about
which one might say:

> *Of those who step inside this den,*
> *A few come out; but how?—and when?*

Life is not all sweetness in this world. Freed from the
clutches of Mr. Rap, I was now about to be shut up in a
dismal dungeon. And I knew that, once imprisoned, many
a poor devil never has the luck to breathe the free air
again.

A series of great dark courtyards; windows in rows, as in
a hospital, but heavily barred; not a patch of greenery, nor
a bit of ivy, nor even a weather vane to be seen—this was
my new home. I could have wept and torn the hair from
my head by the handful.

The constables, accompanied by the jailer, placed me temporarily in a cell. The jailer, if I remember rightly, was called Kaspar Schluessel. With his gray woolen cap, a bunch of keys at his waist, and the stem of a pipe clenched between his teeth he reminded me of the Owl-God of the Caribs. He had big, round yellow eyes that could see in the dark, a nose like a comma, and a neck almost buried in his shoulders.

Schluessel locked me up absent-mindedly, his thoughts elsewhere, as if he were putting away a pair of socks in a dresser drawer. As for me, I must have stood in the same spot for more than ten minutes, my hands clasped behind my back and my head almost resting on my chest. At last I was roused by a hopeful idea.

"When he fell," I thought desperately, "Rap cried out: 'I'm being murdered!' but he didn't say by whom. I shall tell them it was my neighbor, the old man who sells spectacles. Then he'll be hanged instead of me."

This scheme soothed me greatly, and I sighed deeply. I looked around my cell. It had recently been whitewashed, and the walls were still unadorned, except for one corner in which my predecessor had crudely sketched a gibbet. What light there was came in through a little oval window about nine or ten feet from the floor. Except for a pail and a heap of straw there were no furnishings.

I sank down onto the straw, again overcome by dejection, and put my arms about my knees. I could scarcely see clearly, but, remembering suddenly that before dying Rap had indeed named me as his murderer, I felt my legs go numb with terror and I stood up, coughing as if the noose were already biting into my throat.

At almost the same instant I heard Schluessel cross the corridor. He opened the cell and ordered me to follow him. As before, the jailer was escorted by two burly constables, so resignedly I fell into step between my guards.

We marched down long, murky corridors, lighted at intervals by inside windows. In one cell I recognized the notorious Jick-Jack, who was to be executed the following day. He wore a strait jacket and was singing in a raucous voice:

"I am the mon-arch of these moun-tains!"

As he caught sight of me, he called out, "Hey, there, comrade! I'll save a place for you on my right!"

The two guards and the Owl-God looked at one another and grinned, but I could feel my back crawl with goose flesh.

III

Schluessel thrust me forward into a high, dark chamber, furnished with a semicircle of benches. The appearance of that empty room, with its two high, barred windows, its image of Christ of old polished oak, the arms extended and head mournfully resting on one shoulder, filled me with a religious awe as well as terror. All my schemes of false accusation melted away, and my lips moved in silent prayer.

I had not prayed for many years, but misfortune always brings us back to piety. Man is, after all, such a helpless creature!

Two figures were seated before me on a raised bench, but since the light was behind them, their faces were left in shadow. However, I recognized Von Spreckdal by his aquiline profile, outlined by a slanting ray of light from the window. The other man was fat, his cheeks were round and full, and his hands short and pudgy. Like Von Spreckdal, he wore a judge's gown.

Below them, sitting at a low writing table, was the court clerk, Konrad, who from time to time tickled the base of his ear with his pen. When I entered, he stood up and stared at me curiously.

I was directed to sit down, and Von Spreckdal, raising his voice, said to me, "Christian Venius, how did you come by this sketch?"

He held up my sketch of the previous night and had it passed down to me. After examining it I answered, "It was I who drew it."

There followed a rather long silence. The court clerk, Konrad, was writing down my reply. As I listened to his pen scratch across the paper, I pondered, "What on earth has the drawing to do with the kick I gave Rap?"

"It was you who drew it," said Von Spreckdal. "Very well. What, then, is the subject of the sketch?"

"The subject is one of fantasy."

"You did not copy these details from life?"

"No, sir, I imagined them all."

"Prisoner Christian," said the judge severely, "I beg you to reflect. Do not lie to us!"

I colored, and in a passionate voice, I cried out, "I have spoken the truth!"

"Write it down, Clerk," said Von Spreckdal.

The pen dashed on again.

"And that woman," pursued the magistrate, "that woman who is being murdered at the edge of the pit—did you imagine her also?"

"Yes, certainly."

"You have never seen her?"

"Never."

Von Spreckdal rose angrily from his place, but immediately sat down again and leaned over to consult with his colleague. Those two dark profiles, silhouetted against the shining background of the window—the three men stationed behind me—the silence of the room—all made me quake with apprehension.

"What do they want of me? What have I done?" I murmured.

Abruptly Von Spreckdal said to the guards, "Take the prisoner back to the carriage. We are going to the Metzger-Strasse."

Then he addressed me. "Christian Venius," he thundered, "you stand here in a lamentable condition. Compose yourself, and remember that if man's justice is inflexible, you may still enjoy the mercy of God. Perhaps you will be worthy of it if you confess your crime."

His words stunned me like a hammer blow. "Oh, what

a frightful nightmare!" I shrieked. And then I fell back fainting into the arms of my guards.

When I regained consciousness, the coach was rolling slowly down the street, preceded by another. The two constables were still on either side of me. During the ride one of them offered a pinch of snuff to his companion. Mechanically my fingers reached toward the snuffbox, and he snatched it back abruptly. A blush of shame rose to my cheeks, and I turned my face away to hide my emotions.

"If you persist in looking outside," warned the man with the snuffbox, "we shall be obliged to handcuff you."

"The devil take you, you damned scoundrel," I thought to myself. And as the coach had just halted, one of them climbed out while the other held me by the collar. Then, seeing that his companion was ready to take charge of me, he shoved me rudely out.

These endless precautions to prevent my escaping seemed to bode no good, but I was still unable to comprehend the full gravity of the crime with which I stood charged, when a terrible occurrence finally opened my eyes and plunged me into the deepest despair.

I was pushed into a filthy alley, paved with rough and broken stones. A foul-smelling, yellowish moisture oozed from the walls, and as I walked along followed by the guards, my panic increased with every step. Farther on I could discern the outlines of a shadowy courtyard, and, overcome by a piercing anxiety, I recoiled instinctively.

"Go on, go on!" cried one of the constables, clapping a hand on my shoulder. "Keep on walking!"

Imagine my horror when, at the end of the passage, I found the courtyard I had sketched the previous night, its walls provided with hooks, its piles of old iron, its chicken coop and rabbit hutch! Not a garret window, large or small, high or low, not a cracked pane of glass, not a single detail had I omitted!

The two judges, Von Spreckdal and Richter, were standing by the pit. At their feet lay the corpse of the old woman, her long gray hair disheveled, her face bluish, her tongue clenched between her teeth, and her wide-open eyes staring hideously and blankly upward. It was a ghastly spectacle!

"Well," Von Spreckdal said solemnly, "what have you got to say?"

I could not reply.

"Do you admit that you threw this woman, Theresa Becker, into this pit after you strangled her to steal her money?"

"No!" I cried. "No! I do not know the woman. I have never seen her before. Oh, God help me!"

"That will do," he said dryly. And without another word he walked rapidly away with his colleague.

For the return trip the constables thought it wise to handcuff me. I was carried back to the Raspelhaus in a complete stupor, and now I no longer knew what to think. Over and over I kept asking myself if I actually had killed the old woman!

In the eyes of my jailers, I was already condemned.

I shall not tell you of my emotions that night in the Raspelhaus, when, lying on my heap of straw opposite the window and the gibbet, I listened to the watchman call into the silence, "Sleep, citizens of Nuremberg, the Lord watches over you! One o'clock!—Two o'clock!—Three o'clock, and all's well!"

Every reader can imagine for himself what such a night must be. It is all very well to say that it is better to be hanged innocent than guilty. For the soul's sake this is perfectly true, but to the body it makes very little difference. On the contrary, the body resists, and, cursing its fate, it seeks to escape the end that awaits it on the rope. I might add that it repents only of having enjoyed this life too little —of having listened to a conscience that preached moderation and abstinence.

"Ah, if I had only known," it weeps, "you wouldn't have led me about on a leash, with your fancy words, your fine phrases and pretty maxims! You wouldn't have seduced me with promises! Instead, I might have spent some delightful hours that will never come again. You said to me, 'Subdue your passions.' Very well; I did subdue them, and what a

lot of good has come of it! I am going to be hanged, and
afterward they will call *you* a noble soul, a stoical spirit, a
martyr to the errors of justice. But I—*I* shall be left out
altogether!"

At last morning came. First, pale and uncertain, it shone
with a faint glimmer on the bars and back wall of my cell
where it glistened like tinsel. Outside the street was coming
to life again; it was Friday—market day. I listened to the
carts rumble by, loaded with vegetables, and the chatter
of peasants from the Schwarzwald as they bustled along,
basket on arm, to the booths and stalls of the market hall.
I heard the butter maids gossiping under my window, and
the cackle of chickens as they were carried past.

With the light of day my heart also felt somewhat lighter.
Some of my gloomiest fears were dispelled, and I had an
irresistible urge to see what was happening outside.

Other prisoners before me had climbed up to the window. They had hollowed out little footholds in the wall in
order to reach it more easily, and I in turn clambered up
by this means. By bending almost double, and resting my
chin on my chest, I was able to cram my body into the
small aperture, but as I watched the life, the crowds, the
busy confusion of the market, my cheeks were wet with
tears. I no longer thought of suicide. Instead, I hungered
for the open air, for life, as never before.

"Ah," I thought, "to live is to be happy! They can set me
to pushing a wheelbarrow. They can fasten a ball and chain
to my ankle. Nothing matters, if only I can live!"

The old market hall, its roof like a candle snuffer resting on heavy columns, was a striking sight. There were old
women, seated next to their hampers of vegetables, their
poultry coops, their baskets of eggs, and behind them,
swarthy Jewish merchants, dealers in old clothes. There
were the butchers, who, with sleeves rolled up, were cutting
meat in their stalls; and the peasants, calm and impassive,
who pushed back wide-brimmed felt hats and leaned on
their staves, puffing away tranquilly at their pipes. Then
the uproar, the noise of the crowd—shrill words, quarrel-
some words, serious, loud, and short words—the gesticula-

tions—the casual expressions and attitudes that betray even at a distance the tenor of the conversation and reveal so clearly the character of the individual. In short, everything I beheld captivated my soul, and despite my sad state I felt happy at being back in the world again.

However, as I was looking on, I noticed a man pass—a butcher, who carried an enormous side of beef on his bent back. His arms were bare, with the elbows above his bowed head, and his flowing hair hid his face from me. Yet, at first glance, I gave a start.

"That is the man!" I said to myself.

All my blood seemed to choke my heart. Trembling to the tips of my toes, I came down from my perch with chattering teeth. My face grew pale and I stuttered in a strangled voice:

"That is the man! That's he—there! And I am to die for the crime he committed! Oh, God, what am I to do?"

Then a divine inspiration came to me. I thrust my hand into my coat pocket, and there was my box of charcoal pencils!

Dashing to the wall, I began to sketch the murder scene with incredible swiftness. My uncertainty had vanished; I groped no longer. Now I knew the man. I could see him. He was actually posing for me!

At ten o'clock the jailer entered my cell, and his owl-like impassivity gave way to astonishment.

"Is it possible?" he exclaimed.

"Bring my judges," I called over my shoulder as I pursued my work more and more feverishly.

Schluessel replied, "They are waiting for you in the examination room."

"Let them come here," I insisted. "I wish to disclose some information." Another few strokes and my picture would be complete.

The jailer departed.

Some minutes later the two judges appeared.

"There is your murderer!" I exclaimed, pointing to the frightening figure which stood out so boldly against the white background of the wall.

At first Von Spreckdal said nothing. Then he asked me, "What is his name?"

"I do not know it, but at this moment he is in the market hall. Go in by the Hellebardieren-Strasse and you will find him chopping meat at the third stall on the left."

"What do you think?" he asked, turning to his colleague.

"The man must be found," answered Richter gravely.

A couple of guards who were standing in the passage hastened to obey the order. Meanwhile the two judges remained there, still staring in amazement at the sketch. As for myself, I collapsed onto the straw, utterly exhausted, my knees drawn up and my head resting against them.

Soon some steps rang out in the distance, from beneath the arches. Reader, if you have never awaited your hour of deliverance, counting the minutes that pass like centuries —if you have never keenly felt terror, or hope, or doubt— then you cannot imagine my inner trembling at that moment. I could have distinguished the step of the murderer, walking along between the guards, from a thousand others. Now they were approaching the cell. Now even the judges seemed impatient. With pounding heart I raised my head and stared fixedly at the door.

At last it opened, and the man entered, his cheeks flushed and his jaws clenched so tightly that the muscles stood out below his ears. I noticed that under his reddish-blond eyebrows his little eyes were restless and tawny, like a wolf's.

Wordlessly Von Spreckdal pointed to the sketch.

The burly man looked, and in an instant his ruddiness became a deathly pallor. He gave a bellow that froze us all with terror, threw out his arms, and gave a leap backward to knock down the guards. There was a frightening struggle in the passage. I heard the panting of the butcher, muffled curses, short, sharp words, and the footsteps of the guards pounding on the pavement.

It all lasted perhaps a minute.

Finally the murderer was brought in, his head hanging and his hands tied behind his back. Once more he turned his blackened eyes to the sketch, appeared to deliberate, and then spoke softly, as if to himself.

"But who could have seen me at midnight?" he said.

I was saved!

Many years have passed since that terrible adventure. I no longer make silhouettes, thank heaven, nor even portraits of the burgomaster. By dint of work and perseverance I have won a place in the sun, and I earn my living honestly by painting works of art—the only objective, to my mind, that all true artists should strive to attain. But the memory of the sketch I made that night has always remained in my thoughts. Sometimes, in the middle of my work, my mind is carried back to it. Then I lay down my palette and dream for whole hours!

How could a crime, committed by a man I did not know, in a place I had never seen, be reproduced by my pencil to the smallest detail? Was it chance? No, indeed! What is chance, after all, but the effect of a cause that escapes us?

Perhaps Schiller was right when he said, "The immortal self shares in no way the weaknesses of the material. While the body sleeps, the soul unfolds its shining wings and flies away to God knows where! What it does there none can tell, but sometimes our inspiration carries back to us the secret of its nightly wanderings."

Who can say? Nature is more daring in her reality than man's imagination in its fantasy.

Vera

BY VILLIERS DE L'ISLE ADAM

TRANSLATED BY JOHN D. GRAYSON

AUGUSTE VILLIERS DE L'ISLE ADAM
1838–89

Villiers de l'Isle Adam came from a family of the ancient Catholic nobility, impoverished but steeped in grand, if eccentric, chivalric traditions. At nineteen he left his birthplace, the Breton seaport of St. Brieux, to go to Paris, where he cut a picturesque figure in bohemian circles. Baudelaire became his friend and introduced him to the writings of Edgar Allan Poe, which served him as models for most of his *Contes cruels* (1883), from which "Vera" is taken, as well as his *Nouveaux contes cruels* (1888) and *Histories insolites* (1888). All these works were saturated with occultism, terror, and Hoffmannesque fantasy. One of his poetic plays, *Axel* (1890), is of considerable significance in the history of symbolism and has influenced, among others, Maeterlinck and Yeats.

ABOUT VILLIERS DE L'ISLE ADAM: Robert du Pontavice de Heussey, *Villiers de l'Isle Adam*, N.Y., Dodd, Mead & Co., 1894; Peter Quennell, *Baudelaire and the Symbolists*, London, Weidenfeld & Nicolson, 1954 (rev. ed.); Edmund Wilson, *Axel's Castle*, N.Y., Scribner's, 1954 (new ed.); in French, Max Daireaux, *Villiers de l'Isle Adam, l'homme et l'oeuvre* (Paris, 1936), and Pierre Castex, *Contes cruels, étude historique et littéraire*, Paris, Corti, 1956.

"Love is stronger than death," said King Solomon. And indeed its mysterious power is limitless.

Our story begins in Paris, on an evening in autumn, several years ago. Through the twilight some carriages, already lighted, were rolling toward the dark St. Germain quarter from their hour in the Bois. One of them halted before the gate of a vast, regal town house, encircled by venerable gardens. The entrance was surmounted by a stone escutcheon, bearing the arms of the ancient line of the Counts of Athol: a silver star and crown trimmed in ermine on a field of azure, below which appeared the motto "Pallida Victrix." The heavy doors of the house were thrown open and a man of some thirty-five years, deathly pale and dressed in mourning, alighted from the carriage. On the steps a group of silent servants lifted their torches. Without seeing them he mounted the steps and entered. It was Count d'Athol.

Reeling, the count continued up the white staircase to the room where, earlier that day, he had placed his wife in a velvet-lined coffin, wreathed in violets and billows of cambric—Vera, his pale lady of pleasure and his despair. He opened the door noiselessly and pushed aside the hangings.

Everything was as the countess had left it, for death had come upon her unexpectedly. The previous night his beloved wife had become so deeply enraptured, had lost herself in embraces so exquisite, that her heart had failed. Suddenly her lips were stained with a deathly purple.

Scarcely had she had time to smile at her husband and give
him a wordless farewell kiss. Then her long lashes, like
mourning veils, were lowered over the beautiful night of
her eyes.

The nameless day had passed.

Toward noon, after the dreadful obsequies in the family
vault, Count d'Athol had sent away the train of black-clad
mourners from the cemetery. Then, pulling the iron door
of the mausoleum closed after him, he had shut himself up
within the four marble walls, alone with his shrouded wife.
Some incense was burning on a tripod before the coffin and
a shining arc of lamps at the young woman's head studded
her body with twinkling stars.

All day long, half in reverie, the count remained standing there, overcome with mingled emotions of tenderness
and despair. At six o'clock, when it had begun to grow dark,
he came out and secured the door behind him. Then, drawing the silver key out of the lock, he stood on the top step
and threw it gently through the trefoil above the entrance,
onto the flags in the interior of the vault. Why had he done
so? No doubt he had made the strange resolution never to
return there again.

And now the count was examining the bedroom they had
once shared.

Under the heavy mauve hangings of cashmere figured
in gold, the window sash was raised, and through the opening the last rays of the afternoon light shone on a large
portrait of the dead woman, mounted in an antique wooden
frame. The count looked about him—at the gown flung
onto an armchair the night before, at the jewels on the
mantelpiece, the pearl necklace, the half-closed fan, the
heavy flasks of perfume whose scent she would never
breathe again. On the ebony bed, with its twisted posts,
lying near the lacy pillow that still bore the impression of
her head was a crumpled handkerchief reddened with flecks
of blood, where her young soul had fluttered for an instant.
He saw the open piano, holding a melody never to be
played; the Indian flowers she had cut in the conservatory,
wilting in an antique pair of Saxe vases; and at the foot of

the bed, on a black fur rug, the tiny slippers of Oriental velvet on which she had worked a funny little motto in pearls: Qui verra Véra l'aimera—"Who sees Vera will love her." The bare feet of his beloved had played here yesterday morning, caressed at each step by swan's-down! And there, there in the shadows, was the clock whose spring he had smashed so that it would never ring the hours again.

So she had gone away. But where? And was he to continue living? It was pointless, impossible, absurd.

And the count sought refuge in his recollections of former days. Six months had slipped by since his marriage. Wasn't it abroad, at an embassy ball, that he had seen her for the first time? Yes; the moment came to life again, distinctly, before his eyes, and she appeared to him there, radiant as ever. That evening their eyes had met, and both were instantly aware that they shared the same temperament and were destined to love forever.

The idle, deceitful comments, the mocking smiles, the insinuations—all the obstacles the world invents to delay the inevitable happiness of those who belong to each other—had vanished like a flock of night birds re-entering the shadows, the moment they exchanged their first words.

Vera, weary of her insipid companions, had come to him after the first irritating incident, thus simplifying in queenly fashion the banal ceremonies in which so much of life's precious time is lost. No sooner had they spoken than each one felt a calm and tranquil certainty of the other. What smiles passed between them! What indescribable joy they felt at their first embrace!

However, their natures were of a most singular sort. They were two beings gifted with a remarkable, but totally worldly, power of reason. They experienced emotion with a disquieting and lasting intensity in which they forgot their very selves. Yet certain ideas, like those of the soul, the infinite, or of God Himself, seemed to be veiled from their understanding. The faith so many others possessed in the supernatural was nothing more to them than the motive for a vague astonishment—a sealed document that did not concern them, since they lacked the knowledge either to confirm or to deny. They knew also that the world was alien to them, and so upon their marriage they had isolated themselves in that dark old mansion, where the density of the gardens served to muffle the noises of the life outside.

There the lovers were swallowed up in a sea of those languid pleasures that unite the spirit with the mysterious flesh. With shudders and caresses they exhausted the violence of their desire, and each became the heartthrob of the other's being. In them flesh and spirit were so commingled that their bodies seemed to them pure mind, and their embraces the links that bound them together in an ideal fusion. Then, suddenly, the spell was broken. A terrible accident had wrenched her from his arms. What specter had taken his beloved wife from him? No, she was not dead. Is the soul of a violin carried off by the snap of one of its strings?

The hours passed.

The count looked through the window at the advancing night, and night seemed to be a woman, a melancholy queen marching into exile. The evening star, shining above the treetops, was the diamond clasp of her mourning tunic, lost in a background of blue.

"That is Vera," he thought.

At the sound of her name, spoken very softly, he started like a man who is awakened from a deep sleep. Then, straightening up, he looked about him.

The objects in the room stood out against the bluish shadows in the gleam of a vigil lamp that, now that it had grown quite dark, burned brighter and brighter, like another star. It stood before an icon that had been in Vera's family for generations. The triptych, made of an old and precious wood, was hung between the looking-glass and the portrait. A reflection of its gold fell tremulously on the necklace that lay among the jewels on the mantelpiece.

The delicate red lines of a Byzantine cross, dissolved by the light, gave a rosy tinge to the halo of the regally clad Madonna and turned the pearls the color of blood. Since her childhood, Vera, with her great eyes, had pitied the Madonna, with her pure, motherly face, but alas—being by nature unable to feel any love for her except a superstitious one—she sometimes offered her this much, naïvely, when she happened to pass before the vigil lamp.

The count, touched by these painful memories in the most secret part of his soul, stood erect, hastily blew out the sacred light, and, groping in the shadows, seized the fringed bell cord and rang.

A manservant appeared. He was an old man dressed in black, and he carried a lamp that he placed in front of the portrait of the countess. When he turned around, it was with a shudder of superstitious terror that he beheld his master, standing there and smiling as if nothing had happened.

"Raymond," the count said calmly, "this evening the countess and I are worn out with fatigue. You will serve the soup around ten. By the way, we have decided to remain by ourselves as much as possible beginning tomorrow. I do not wish any one of my servants, except yourself, to spend another night in the house. You are to give them three years' wages and see to it that they leave. Then you will close and bar the front door and light the candles downstairs in the dining room. You will be quite enough for us. In future, we shall receive no one."

Trembling, the old man looked intently at him.

The count lit a cigar and went down to the gardens.

At first it seemed to Raymond that the excessive grief and despair had impaired his master's reason. However, he was aware that the shock of a sudden awakening can prove fatal to the sleepwalker. He had known the count from childhood, and his first duty was to respect his secret.

The servant bowed his head. Was he to obey the count and become his accomplice? Was he to continue to serve *them* and overlook death itself? What a strange notion it was! And how long would the dream endure? Until tomorrow? Perhaps; but who could be certain? Well, after all, what right had he to consider or to judge?

He left the room, carried out the count's orders to the letter, and on that same evening their strange life began.

The discomfort of the first few days was soon over. Raymond, at first in a kind of stupor, then out of deference and affection for the count, played his part so skillfully that before three weeks had elapsed he sometimes felt the dupe of his own good intentions. He half forgot the original motive for the terrible illusion he was helping to create and, overcome by giddiness, had constantly to tell himself that the countess was actually dead. So well had he joined in that macabre game that it was becoming increasingly difficult to return to reality. Soon he needed more than a word to convince himself of the true state of affairs, and he perceived that he would end by abandoning himself entirely to the frightening magnetism with which the count was charging the atmosphere about them. He was afraid, with an indecisive, unspoken fear.

D'Athol, in fact, was living as if entirely unaware of his beloved's death. Indeed, how could he help but feel her presence, when the being of the young woman had become so united with his own? On sunny days, seated on a bench in the garden, he would read aloud the poetry she used to love. In the evenings, in front of the fire, while two cups of tea reposed on the drum table, he would chat with the Illusion, who (in his eyes) was smiling across at him from the opposite armchair.

The days, the nights, the weeks flew by. Neither the count nor the manservant knew any longer what they were doing. And, in truth, such odd things were happening now that the real and the imaginary seemed one and the same. A presence floated in the air. A form sought to cross the barrier, to weave itself into the fabric of a space whose outlines had grown dim.

Like a mystic, d'Athol led two lives. A sweet, pallid face, half perceived in the twinkling of an eye, like a flash of lightning; a feeble tune struck suddenly at the piano; a kiss that closed his mouth just as he was about to speak; *feminine* thoughts that stirred in him in response to something he had said—in short, there was such a doubling of himself that he could catch the dizzyingly sweet scent of his beloved's perfume trailing after him like a fluid mist. Between waking and sleeping he would hear words softly murmured. Everything brought her back to him. It was the negation of death, elevated at last to a strange, unknown force.

Once d'Athol heard and saw her so clearly before him that he tried to take her in his arms, but at this the form dissolved.

"Child," he murmured, smiling. And he fell asleep again, like a lover who is sulky with a drowsy mistress.

On her birthday, as a jest, he placed a sprig of live-forever in the bouquet he laid on Vera's pillow.

"It is because she believes herself dead," he said.

Thanks to the all-powerful will of Count d'Athol, who, by dint of love, had re-created the living presence of his wife in the lonely mansion, this existence had at last acquired a somber and persuasive charm. Even Raymond no longer felt any terror, having gradually become accustomed to their way of life.

The glimpse of a black velvet gown at the turning of a passage; a laughing voice that called to him in the drawing room; the tinkle of a bell when he awoke in the morning, just as before—all this had become familiar to him. One might have said that the dead woman was playing at being invisible, like a child. She felt herself so loved; it was all quite innocent!

A year slipped by.

The evening of the anniversary of Vera's death the count, seated before the fire in her room, had just read her a Florentine fabliau, *Callimachus*. He closed the book and took up his tea.

"Dushka," he said, "do you remember the Valley of Roses, on the banks of the Lahn, and the Castle of the Four Towers? This story reminded you of them, did it not?"

He rose, and in the bluish glass he noticed that he was paler than usual. He picked up a pearl bracelet in a casket and looked carefully at the pearls. Had not Vera just removed them from her arm before undressing? The pearls still felt warm and their luster seemed subtler, as if from the warmth of her flesh. And the opal of that Siberian necklace, which so loved to rest on Vera's lovely bosom, that it sickened and grew pale in its gold filigree whenever she forgot to wear it for any space of time. How the countess had loved that trinket for its fidelity! This evening the opal shone as if she had just taken it off, as if it were still permeated by the exquisite fascination of the beautiful dead woman. On replacing the bracelet and the gem the count's hand chanced to brush against the cambric handkerchief, on which the drops of blood shone moist and red, like roses in the snow. There, on the piano—who could have turned the last page of that old song? What! The holy light of the vigil lamp had been kindled before the shrine! Yes, its golden flame strangely illuminated the face of the Madonna, with her closed eyes. And those Oriental flowers, newly cut, which were opening in the old Saxe vases—what hand had just arranged them there? The room seemed joyful and endowed with a life more intense, more meaningful, than usual. But nothing could surprise the count. It all appeared so ordinary to him that he did not even notice that the clock, which had been silent for a year, was now striking the hour.

One might have said that on that evening, from the depths of the shadows, Countess Vera was striving to return to that room, which was so full of her essence, where she had left so much of herself. Everything that had formed a part of her existence drew her there. Surely the fury of her husband's enduring passion had broken the misty bonds of the invisible around her!

Surely she must long to smile again into that mysterious glass where she had so often admired her lily face. His sweet Vera must have stirred among her violets under the burned-out lamps. His beloved must have awakened and, seeing the silver key on the flags of her tomb, wished to come away to him. Death is a final event only to those who hope for heaven—but for her, was not their embrace heaven, and life, and death? A single kiss from her husband was drawing her lips forth from the shadows. The sound of old melodies, the intoxicating words once spoken, the garments that used to cover her body and retained her scent, those magic gems that longed for her with dark affection—and most of all, the powerful and absolute certainty of her presence, a sensation shared by the very objects in the room—all of these had been calling to her, drawing her back during the past year. And gradually she had returned, so that the only thing now lacking was her actual self, cured of the sleep of death.

Ah, ideas are living things! The count had stolen from the air to reshape his beloved, and perhaps it was necessary to fill the void that remained with the only being compatible with it; otherwise the universe might have crumbled. At that moment he had the definite and absolute impression that she must be in the room; he could almost see her! He was as calmly certain of it as of his own existence. All that was missing was Vera herself, and surely she would appear to him, solid and tangible. Surely the great dream of life and death would open its infinite portals ever so slightly! Faith had sent her the way to resurrection.

A youthful peal of laughter seemed to light up the marriage bed with its gay brightness. The count turned around. And there, before his eyes, fashioned of longing and of remembrance, reclining gracefully on the lacy pillow and holding back her heavy, black hair, the Countess Vera was looking at him, a little sleepily still, with her mouth half open in a delightful smile of pleasure.

"Roger," she said in a faraway voice.

He came close to her. Their lips met in a rapture that was divine, intoxicating, immortal! Time soared upward, to that lofty ecstasy where, for the first time, heaven and earth were united.

And then they understood that, in reality, they were only one, single being.

Suddenly the count shivered, as if struck by a fatal memory.

"Ah, now I remember!" he exclaimed. "What is the matter with me? You are dead!"

At that word the mysterious flame of the vigil lamp before the icon flickered out. The pale, feeble light of morning —an ordinary morning, grayish and rainy—filtered into the room through the chinks in the curtains. The candles grew

pale and went out, leaving red wicks smoking acridly; the
fire disappeared under a bed of warm cinders; the flowers
faded and withered in a moment; the pendulum of the
clock gradually came to a standstill. The "certainty" of all
the objects in the room had suddenly vanished. The opal,
dead, shone no longer; the drops of blood on the cambric
near her pillow seemed less distinct; and, slipping from the
despairing arms that still sought in vain to restrain her, the
burning white vision dissolved into air. A faint sigh of farewell, clear but far off, reached Roger's consciousness. He
rose, and at last he realized that he was alone. His dream
had been dispelled by a single word; he had snapped the
magnetic wire of her life at one stroke. Now the atmosphere
of the room was like that of a tomb.

Like those drops of glass, illogically formed, and yet so
solid that the blow of a hammer at their thickest part will
not smash them, but that crumble suddenly to fine powder
if the sharp, fine end is broken—so had everything vanished.

"Oh," he murmured. "Then it is finished! You are lost
and alone. Tell me—how can I reach you? Show me the
way that will lead me to you!"

Suddenly, like a reply, a shining object fell from the marriage bed with a metallic clink onto the black fur rug. It
shone in the light of the wretched morning. The forsaken
lover bent down, his hand closed over it, and when he
recognized what he held, a sublime smile lit his face. It
was the key to the tomb.

Maldoror

BY ISIDORE DUCASSE, COMTE DE LAUTRÉAMONT

TRANSLATED BY ANGEL FLORES

ISIDORE DUCASSE
"Comte de Lautréamont"
1846–70

The excerpt from *Maldoror* (1869) included here is the work of the twenty-three-year-old Isidore Ducasse, who was born in Montevideo and signed himself Count of Lautréamont in admiration of Eugène Sue's blasphemous hero. At fourteen he was sent to France to study, where he showed tremendous promise in mathematics and the sciences. *Maldoror* was written in a frenzy as he was about to enter the École Polytechnique. Only a year later he died of tuberculosis in a Montmartre hospital, aged twenty-four. *Maldoror* illustrates some of the excesses of romanticism, which, paradoxically enough, Lautréamont hated, particularly the puffing of the ego to superhuman dimensions. Its hero, Maldoror, a sort of Zarathustra or Byronic Satan, incarnates the agonies and uncertainties of his creator. Intoxicated with despair "as if it were some powerful wine," he rebels, challenges God himself, and like some apocalyptic beast, changing from cricket to eagle, from swan to octopus, haunts the world with his evil doings.

ABOUT LAUTRÉAMONT: Except for the brief essay by S. A. Rhodes, "Lautréamont Redivivus," in the *Romanic Review* in 1931 (Vol. 22, pp. 285–90) there is very little in English. In German: Hans Rudolf Linder, *Lautréamont, sein Werk und sein Weltbild* (University of Basel dissertation, 1947); and in French: Philippe Soupault, *Lautréamont* (Paris, 1946); Marcel Jean, *Maldoror* (Paris, 1947); and Maurice Blanchot, *Lautréamont et Sade* (Paris, 1949).

I sat down on a rock by the sea. A ship had just spread all its sails to set off, when an imperceptible dot appeared on the horizon and approached closer and closer: a squall was rushing the ship along. The storm was about to begin its attack and already the sky was darkening, turning almost as hideously black as the heart of man. The vessel, a big warship, dropped anchor so as not to be hurled upon the rocks of the coast. The wind blew furiously from the four points of the compass, tearing the sails to shreds. Thunder reverberated amid lightning flashes without muffling the sounds of lamentation that issued from the foundationless house, the floating sepulcher. The masses of water buffeted the anchor chains yet could not break them; nevertheless they ripped open a hole in the side of the vessel for the water to pour in. A gaping hole and the pumps were inadequate to bail out the huge mountains of salt water that rushed foamingly across the deck. The stricken ship fired cannon shots to give the alarm, but she sank slowly . . . majestically. Whoever has not witnessed the sinking of a boat in the midst of a hurricane, with intermittent lightning and deepest darkness, while the passengers are overwhelmed by despair—whoever has not seen this knows nothing of life's contingencies. At last a universal shout of immense anguish escaped from the ship while the sea redoubled its fearful attacks. The shout announces that all human strength has been abandoned. Everyone wraps himself in the mantle of resignation and commits his fate to the hands of God. They crowd together like a flock of sheep. The stricken ship goes on firing cannon shots to give the alarm but she sinks slowly . . . majestically. They have been working the pumps all day long. To no avail. Night comes, implacable and dense, bringing to a close the gracious performance. Each tells himself that once down in the water he will no longer be able to breathe, for, as far as he can remember, he can count no fish among his ancestors. But he exhorts himself to hold his breath as long as possible in order to prolong his life for two or three seconds. This is the avenging irony he wishes to dedicate to death. . . . The stricken ship fires cannon shots to give the alarm, but she sinks slowly . . . majestically. He does not know that, as she sinks, the ship produces a powerful circumvolution of billows that the slimy ooze has mixed with the troubled waters, and that a submarine force, set in motion by the havoc-making storm above, stirs the element into jerky, nervous movements. Thus, despite the calculated cold-bloodedness he musters beforehand, the man about to be drowned, should after further reflection feel happy if he can prolong his life in the vortex of the abyss by half an ordinary breath, for good measure. It will be impossible for him to defy death, his supreme desire. The stricken ship fires cannon shots to give the alarm, but she sinks slowly . . . majestically. It is a mistake. She fires cannon shots no longer—she is sinking.

The nutshell has been swallowed up completely. Oh heavens! How can one live after experiencing such intense pleasure? It so happened that I was offered the opportunity of witnessing the death pangs of my fellow-men. Minute by minute I followed the vicissitudes of their agony. Now the bellowing of some old woman who had gone crazy with fear dominated everything; at others, the wailing of a suckling infant prevented one from hearing the captain's orders. The ship was too far away for me to discern clearly the moans brought to me by the squall, but my will power permitted me, and the optical illusion was perfect. Every fifteen minutes, when a gust raising its lugubrious voice above the squawking of the frightened petrels dislocated the ship in longitudinal cracks and increased the groan of those about to be offered in holocaust to death, I would jab the sharp point of an iron into my cheek and think to myself: "They are suffering more!" I had at least a basis for comparison. From the shore I addressed them, hurling at them curses and threats. I imagined they must hear me! I felt that my hatred and my words, spanning the distance, annulled the laws of acoustics, and their ears, deafened by the bellowing of the raging ocean. I felt that they must be thinking about me, venting their vengeance in impotent wrath! From time to time I cast my glance toward the cities asleep on terra firma, and, seeing that no one suspected that a ship was about to sink a few miles from the shore, with a crown of birds of prey and a pedestal of empty-bellied aquatic giants, I again took heart and began to hope: I was now sure of disaster! None would escape! As an extreme precaution I fetched my double-barreled gun so that if some castaway tried to swim across to the rocks to escape imminent death, a bullet in the shoulder would shatter his arm and prevent him from carrying out his plan. At the height of the storm I saw a robust head with hair standing on end desperately trying to keep above the waves. He was tossing about like a cork, swallowing many quarts of water and sinking. But soon he reappeared with dripping hair and, staring at the shore, seemed to defy death. He was marvelously calm. A wide bleeding wound caused by some hidden reef scarred his noble, intrepid face. He could not have been more than sixteen; one could but faintly perceive the peach bloom on his upper lip in the night lit by flashes of lightning. And now he was only six hundred feet from the cliff and I could see him clearly. What courage! What indomitable spirit! How stalwartly his head seemed to defy fate while he vigorously breasted the waves whose furrows opened with difficulty before him . . . !

I had made up my mind in advance. I owed it to myself to keep my promise: the last hour had sounded once and for all—and none must escape. I had made my resolution and nothing could change it . . . ! A sharp report was

heard and immediately the head sank, never to reappear.
I did not derive as much pleasure from this murder as one
might think, precisely because I was so sated with so much
killing that henceforth I murdered from sheer unalterable
habit, which provides only slight pleasure. Feelings become
blunted, hardened. What delight could I experience in the
death of this one human being when there were more than
a hundred others about to offer to me the spectacle of
their final struggles against the waves as the ship sank?
For me this death did not even have the allure of danger,
for human justice cradled by the hurricane of that horrid
night was dozing in houses only a few steps away from
me. Now that the years weigh down upon my body, I
confess in all sincerity, as a supreme, solemn truth, that I
was not so cruel as men claimed afterward, but there were
times when their own wickedness wrought its persistent
havoc for years on end. Then my fury knew no bounds; I
underwent a paroxysm of cruelty and became terrible to
anyone who drew near my haggard eyes, if he still belonged to the same race as I. As for horses and dogs, I let
them go by untouched, think of it!

Unfortunately on the night of the storm I was under-
going one of those fits; my reason had flown (for ordinarily
I was just as cruel, but more circumspect), and this time
everything that fell into my hands was doomed to perish:
I make no excuses for my misdeeds. My fellow-men are
not entirely to blame. I simply state what it is that makes
me scratch the nape of my neck beforehand while waiting
for Judgment Day . . . What do I care for the Last Judgment? My reason never runs away with me, as I said before, in order to deceive you. And when I commit a crime
I know exactly what I am doing: I do just as I please!

As I stood upon the rock, while the hurricane whipped
my hair and cloak, I watched in ecstasy the power of the
tempest falling upon a ship beneath a starless sky. In an
attitude of triumph I followed all the vicissitudes of the
drama, from the moment when the vessel cast anchor to
the moment she was engulfed, like a fatal garment dragging down into the entrails of the sea all those who wore it.

But the moment was approaching when I was about to participate in those scenes of natural upheaval. When the place where the vessel had waged combat showed clearly that she had gone to spend the rest of her days on the ground floor of the sea, then some who had been swept away by the waves partly reappeared on the surface. In groups of twos and threes they grabbed one another by the waist: a sure way of not saving their lives, for they hindered each other's movements and sank like jars with holes in them. . . . What is this army of sea monsters cleaving the waves so swiftly? There are six of them slicing the billowy surf with their powerful fins. Of all those humans moving their four limbs in this shifting continent the sharks soon make only an eggless omelet and share it according to the law of the mightiest. Blood mingles with the water and the water mingles with blood. Their fierce eyes light up the scene of carnage well enough. . . .

But what is this new disturbance in the water over there on the horizon? One would say a waterspout was approaching. What oar strokes! I see what it is: a huge female shark is coming for her share of liver paste and cold cuts. Upon her arrival she is ravenous with hunger. She fights other sharks over the few palpitating limbs that float here and there, saying nothing, on the surface of the red cream. To right and left she deals mortal wounds. But three living sharks still surround her and she is compelled to turn in all directions to outwit their maneuvers. With mounting emotion, unknown till then, the spectator on the shore follows this new type of naval battle. His eyes are fixed upon that courageous, strong-toothed female shark.

He hesitates no longer but shoulders his gun and, with his usual skill, lodges his second bullet in the gills of one of the sharks at the moment it shows itself above a wave. Now the two remaining sharks manifest even greater fierceness. From the top of the rock the man with the salty saliva plummets into the sea and swims toward the charmingly colored carpet, holding in his hand the steel knife that never leaves him. Now each shark must face the enemy. He advances toward his tired adversary and, biding

his time, plunges his sharp blade into its belly. The mobile
fortress easily eliminates the last enemy. . . . The swimmer finds himself face to face with the female shark he has
saved. They stare at each other for a while, each astonished
to discover so much ferocity in the glances of the other.
They swim in circles, without losing sight of one another,
soliloquizing: "I was mistaken till now: there is someone
wickeder than I."

Then, by common agreement, one glides toward the
other in mutual admiration—the female shark cleaving the
water with her fins, Maldoror beating the waves with his
arms—and held their breath in deep veneration, each anxious to contemplate for the first time his living image.
Arrived at a distance of ten feet, they suddenly fall one
against the other like two magnets and embrace with dignity and gratitude, as tenderly as brother and sister. Carnal
desire immediately follows this display of friendship. Like
two leeches, two sinewy thighs cling closely to the monster's
viscous skin; arms and fins interlace about the body of the
beloved object which they encircle lovingly. Soon throats
and breasts make but one glaucous mass redolent of seaweed. Amid flashes of lightning and with the foaming wave
for marriage bed, swept along by a submarine current as
though in a cradle, and gyrating toward the depths of the
abyss, amid the eternally havoc-wreaking tempest they become united in one long, chaste, hideous copulation. At
last I had found someone who resembled me! Henceforth
I was no longer alone in life! She had the same ideas as
I . . . ! I beheld my first love!

Who Knows?

BY GUY DE MAUPASSANT

TRANSLATED BY CLAIRE NOYES

GUY DE MAUPASSANT
1850–93

Maupassant spent his childhood with his mother in Étretat after his parents were separated. He was educated at Yvetot's seminary and the Lycée Corneille at Rouen, served as a conscript in the Franco-Prussian War, and worked for ten years thereafter in the Ministries of Marine and of Public Education. He was encouraged to write by his godfather, Gustave Flaubert, and became known in 1880 when his story "Boule de suif" was included in the collection, *Les Soirées de Médan,* which contained works by Zola and his naturalist friends. From then until 1890, when his health began to suffer, Maupassant produced over three hundred short stories, six novels, four plays, and three travel books, all of which earned him vast sums of money. Acute observer of life and accomplished craftsman, he has been regarded as a master of the short story. The imaginative "Who Knows?" included here is a felicitous blend of humor and fantasy, not at all typical of his usual slick style. Maupassant died in an insane asylum at the age of forty-three following an attempt at suicide.

ABOUT MAUPASSANT: Ernest Boyd, *Guy de Maupassant,* N.Y., Knopf, 1926; S. Jackson, *Guy de Maupassant,* London, Duckworth, 1938; R. H. Sherard, *The Life, Work, and Evil Fate of Guy de Maupassant,* London, Laurie, 1926; Francis Steegmuller, *Maupassant, a Lion in His Path,* N.Y., Universal (Grosset & Dunlap), 1958; E. D. Sullivan, *Maupassant the Novelist,* Princeton Univ. Press, 1954.

Thank God! At last I shall write what happened! But can I? Do I dare? It is so fantastic, so inexplicable, so incomprehensible, so mad!

If I were not sure of what I saw, sure that there was no flaw in my reasoning, no error in my conclusions, no gap in the inflexible sequence of my observations, I should believe myself simply subject to hallucinations, the victim of a strange vision. After all, who knows?

Today I am in a sanatorium, but I entered voluntarily, out of prudence, or was it fear? One man alone knows my story, the house doctor. Now I shall set it all down, I don't know quite why. Perhaps to unburden myself of the thing inside me that haunts me like some dreadful nightmare. Anyhow, here it is.

I have always been a recluse, a dreamer, a kind of philosopher, detached and kindly, satisfied with little, harboring no bitterness against men and no grudge against heaven. I have always lived alone, because a kind of uneasiness seizes me in the presence of others. How can I explain it? I cannot. It's not that I shun society. I enjoy chatting or dining with my friends but when I feel them near me for any length of time, even the most intimate, I get bored, tired, unnerved, and feel a growing, obsessive desire to have them leave me to myself, to be alone.

This desire is more than a need, it is an irresistible necessity. And if I were to be forced to remain with people, if I had to give lengthy attention to their conversation, some-

thing would happen. What? Ah! Who knows? Possibly only
a fainting spell? Of course, probably only a fainting spell.

I am so fond of being alone that I cannot even endure
the nearness of others sleeping under my roof; I cannot
live in Paris because living there is for me a constant agony.
I die inside, and for me it is both physical and nervous
torture to sense this huge swarming crowd, breathing
around me even in their sleep. Ah! The sleep of others is
even more painful to me than their speech. And I can never
rest, when I know or feel that there are other beings, on
the other side of the wall, who suffer this nightly suspension
of consciousness.

Why am I this way? Who knows? Perhaps the reason is
quite simple: I tire very quickly of anything outside myself.
There are many people like me.

There are **two** kinds of people. Those who need others,
who are distracted, amused, soothed by company, while
loneliness assails, exhausts, and destroys them, as would the
ascent of a terrible glacier or the crossing of the desert. And
those who, on the contrary, are worried, bored, irritated,
and cramped, by contact with others, while solitude gives
them peace and rest in the freedom and fantasy of their
thoughts.

It is, in fact, a recognized psychological phenomenon.
The former are meant to live the life of the extrovert; the
latter, that of the introvert. In my own case, my attention
to outward things is brief and quickly exhausted, and, when
it reaches its limits, I am conscious of an unbearable physical and mental discomfort.

The result has been that I am, or rather was, very much
attached to inanimate objects, which take on for me the
importance of human beings, and that my house has, or
rather had, become a world in which I lived a lonely but
active life, surrounded by things, furniture, and ornaments
that I knew and loved like friends. I had gradually filled my
life with them, and embellished it with them, and felt content and satisfied, happy as in the arms of a loving woman
whose familiar caress has become a calm and gentle need.

I had had this house built in a beautiful garden that

separated it from the roads, not far from a town, where I could enjoy the social amenities, of which I felt the need from time to time. All my servants slept in a building at the far end of a walled kitchen garden. In the silence of my house, hidden as it was and buried under the foliage of tall trees, the enveloping darkness of the nights was so restful and welcome that I always put off going to bed for several hours, so that I might enjoy it longer.

That evening *Sigurd* had been given at the local theater. It was the first time I had heard this beautiful fairy play with music and I had thoroughly enjoyed it.

I was returning home on foot, at a lively pace, with scraps of melody running in my head, and entrancing scenes still vivid in my mind. It was dark, pitch black; I could hardly see the road, and several times I nearly fell headlong into the ditch. From the tollhouse to my place is a little more than half a mile or about twenty minutes' slow walking. It was one o'clock in the morning, one or one-thirty; the sky suddenly cleared a little before me and the crescent moon appeared, the melancholy crescent of the waning moon. The moon in its first quarter, when it rises at four or five in the evening, is bright, with cheerful, silvery light, but in the last quarter, when it rises after midnight, it is a dull copper color, and ominous—a real witches' Sabbath moon. All night walkers must have noted this. The first quarter's crescent, even when slender as a thread, sheds a faint but cheerful gleam, which lifts the heart, and throws clearly defined shadows on the ground; the last quarter's crescent sheds a feeble, fitful light that casts almost no shadow.

The dark silhouette of my garden loomed ahead and for some reason I felt rather hesitant at the idea of going in. I slackened my pace. The night was very mild. The great mass of trees looked like a tomb, in which my house lay buried.

I opened my garden gate and went down the long driveway leading to the house. The rows of sycamores, arched overhead, made a lofty tunnel that flowed by dense clusters of green and wound around the lawn on which flower beds in the lightening darkness formed oval patches of no particular color.

Nearing the house, I felt curiously uneasy. I paused. There was not a sound, not a breath of air stirring in the leaves. "What's wrong with me?" I thought. For ten years I had been coming home like this without ever feeling nervous. I was not afraid. I have never been afraid of the dark. The sight of a man, a burglar or a thief, would merely have thrown me into a rage, and I would have jumped on him without a moment's hesitation. Besides, I was armed. I had my revolver. But I did not put my hand on it, because I wanted to resist the fear stirring within me.

What was it? A foreboding? The mysterious premonition that grips a man's mind at the approach of the supernatural? Perhaps. Who knows?

As I went on, I felt shivers running down my spine, and when I was close to the wall of my great shuttered house, I felt that I must wait a few minutes before opening the door and entering. So I sat down on a garden seat under the drawing-room windows. I stayed there, trembling, leaning my head against the wall, staring into the blackness of the foliage. During those first moments I noticed nothing unusual around me. I was aware of a buzzing in my ears, but I often hear that. I sometimes think I can hear trains passing, bells ringing, or crowds tramping.

But soon the humming became more distinct, more definite, more recognizable. I had been wrong. It was not the usual throbbing of my arteries that caused these noises in my ears, but a definite, though confused, noise that was coming, no doubt about it, from inside my house.

I could hear it through the wall, a continuous noise, no, more a rustling than a noise, a faint stirring of things, as of many objects being moved about, as if someone were shifting all my furniture and dragging it about.

Naturally, for some time I thought I must be mistaken. But, having put my ear against a shutter to hear the strange noises in my house more clearly, I was quite firmly convinced that something abnormal and inexplicable was going on inside. I was not afraid, but, I was—how shall I say?

—bewildered and astonished. I did not cock my revolver, suspecting—and how right I was!—that it would be of no use. I waited.

I waited a long while, unable to come to a decision, with my mind perfectly clear but deeply disturbed. I waited motionless, listening to the growing noise, which kept gaining in intensity until it finally rose to an impatient, angry rumble.

Then, suddenly, ashamed of my cowardice, I seized my bunch of keys, chose the one I needed, thrust it into the lock, turned it twice, and, pushing in the door with all my strength, I sent it crashing against the wall inside.

The bang echoed like a gunshot, and the crash was answered by a fearful uproar from cellar to attic. It was so sudden, so terrifying, so deafening that I stepped back several paces, and, although I realized it was useless, I drew my revolver from its holster.

I still waited, but not for long. I could now distinguish an extraordinary sound of tramping, not of human feet or shoes, but of crutches, wooden stumps, iron stumps that rang out like cymbals.

Suddenly, on the threshold of the front door I saw an armchair, my big reading chair, come strutting out. It moved off into the garden. It was followed by others from the drawing room; next came the low sofas crawling along like crocodiles on their stumpy legs, then all the rest of my chairs, leaping like goats, and the little footstools hopping along like rabbits.

Imagine my feelings! I slipped into a flower bed where I crouched, my eyes glued on this exodus of my furniture. It all came out, one piece after another, quickly or slowly, according to shape and weight. My piano, a concert grand, galloped past like a runaway horse, with a faint jangle of music still inside it; the smaller objects, brushes, cut glass, goblets, slid over the gravel like ants, gleaming like glow-worms in the moonlight. The carpets and hangings crawled away, with all the oozing elasticity of devil fish. Then I saw my desk appear, a rare eighteenth-century collector's item, containing all my letters and the whole painful record of my heart's spent passion. And in it were also my photographs.

Suddenly I was no longer afraid, I threw myself upon it, I grappled it as one grapples with a thief a woman in flight, but it pursued its irresistible course, and in spite of my utmost efforts, I could not even slow it up. As I wrestled like a madman with this terrible force, I fell to the ground in the struggle. Then it rolled me over and over, dragging me through the gravel, and the other furniture close on its heels had already begun to tread on me, trampling and bruising my legs, then, when I let go, the others swept over my body like a cavalry charge over an unhorsed soldier.

At last, mad with terror, I managed to drag myself out of the main path and I hid again in the trees, watching the disappearance of the smallest, tiniest, humblest pieces I had ever owned.

Presently I heard, in the distance, inside my house, now as sonorous as it was empty, a terrific din of doors being shut. They banged from attic to basement, until at last the hall door, which I myself had left open in my mad flight, slammed shut with a final bang.

I fled at a run toward the town and did not recover my composure until I got to the streets and met some people coming home late. I rang the bell of a hotel where I was known. I had dusted off my clothes, and I explained that I had lost my keys, including the key of the kitchen garden where my servants slept in a separate house, behind the garden wall that protected my fruit and vegetables from thieves.

I buried myself in the bed they gave me, but I couldn't sleep, so I waited for daylight, listening to the violent beating of my heart. I had given orders for my servants to be informed at dawn, and my valet knocked at my door at seven in the morning.

He looked upset.

"A terrible thing happened last night, sir," he said.

"What?"

"All your furniture has been stolen, sir, everything, down to the smallest things."

This news cheered me. Why? Who knows? I was calm, sure that I could conceal my feelings and never tell anyone what I had seen. I would hide it, bury it in my mind like some ghastly secret. I answered:

"Then they are the same people who stole my keys. The police must be informed immediately. I'm getting up and will be with you in a few moments."

The inquiry lasted five months. Not even the smallest of my ornaments or the slightest trace of the thieves was ever found. Good God! If I had told what I knew—if I had told —they would have put away, not the thieves, but me, the man who could have seen such a thing!

Of course, I knew how to keep my mouth shut. But I did not furnish my house again. It was no good. It would only have happened again. I never wanted to go back to it again. I never did. In fact, I never saw it again.

I went to a hotel in Paris and consulted doctors about my state of nerves, which had been worrying me since that dreadful night.

They prescribed travel and I took their advice. I began with a trip to Italy. The sun did me good. For six months I wandered from Genoa to Venice, from Venice to Florence, from Florence to Rome, from Rome to Naples. Next I toured Sicily, that land of such wonderful scenery and monuments, relics left by the Greeks and Normans. I crossed to Africa and traveled at my leisure through the great desert, so yellow and calm, where still camels, gazelles, and nomadic Arabs roam, where, in the clear, dry air no obsession can persist by night or day.

I returned to France via Marseilles, and in spite of the gaiety of Provence the diminished intensity of the sunlight depressed me. On my return to the continent, I had the odd feeling of a patient who thinks he is cured but who is warned by a dull pain that the source of illness has not been eradicated.

I went back to Paris, but after a month I was bored. It was autumn, and I wanted to tour Normandy, which was new ground to me, before winter set in.

I began with Rouen, of course, and for a week I wan-

dered about, intrigued, delighted, and thrilled in this medieval town, the amazing museum of rare Gothic monuments.

Then, one afternoon, about four o'clock, as I was walking down an extraordinary street, along which flowed an
inky black stream, called Eau de Robec, my attention, previously centered on the strange and ancient appearance of
the houses, was caught suddenly by a row of secondhand
furniture shops.

They had, indeed, chosen the right spot, these seedy
junk dealers in this fantastic alley of houses overlooking
this sinister stream, under pointed roofs of tile or slate on
which the weather vanes of a vanished age still creaked.

Stacked in the rear of the dark shops could be seen
carved chests, china from Rouen, Nevers, and Moustiers,
statues, some painted, others carved in wood, crucifixes,
Madonnas, saints, church ornaments, vestments, copes,
even chalices and an old gilded wooden tabernacle now
vacated by God. What extraordinary storerooms in these
great, lofty houses, packed from cellar to attic with all sorts
of objects whose usefulness was really at an end, and that
had outlived their natural owners, their century, their period, their fashion, to be bought as curios by later generations.

My passion for antiques revived in this collector's paradise. I went from shop to shop, crossing in two strides the
bridge made of four rotten planks thrown over the stinking
flow of the Eau de Robec. Then—God have mercy!—I felt
my heart in my throat! I saw one of my finest wardrobes
at the edge of a vault crammed with junk and that looked
like the entrance to the catacombs of some cemetery of
old furniture. I drew near, trembling all over, trembling to
such an extent that I did not dare touch it. I put out my
hand, then I hesitated. But it *was* mine—a unique Louis
XIII, unmistakable to anyone who had ever seen it. Suddenly, peering farther along toward the darker interior of
this gallery, I noticed three of my petit-point chairs, and,
farther off, my two Henry II tables, which were so rare
that people came from Paris to see them.

Imagine, just imagine my state of mind!

Then I went forward, dazed and gripped by emotion, but I persisted, for I am no coward. I went on as a knight of the Dark Ages would have penetrated a magic circle. As I advanced, I found all my belongings, my tapestries, my weapons, everything, except the desk containing my letters, which I could not discover anywhere.

And so I continued, descending to dark corridors to climb up again to the upper stories. I was alone. I called but there was no answer. I was alone; there was no one in this huge, winding labyrinth of a building.

Night came on and I had to sit down in the dark on one of my own chairs, for I wouldn't go away. From time to time I called out, "Hello! Anybody there?"

I must have been there for more than an hour when I heard footsteps, light, slow steps; I could not tell where they were coming from. I nearly ran away, but, pulling myself together, I called out again and saw a light in the next room.

"Who's there?" said a voice.

I answered, "A customer."

The answer came: "It's rather late; we're closed."

I retorted, "I've been waiting for more than an hour."

"You could have come back tomorrow."

"No. Tomorrow, I am leaving Rouen."

I did not dare go to him and he did not come to me. All this time I saw the reflection of his candle shining on a tapestry, in which two angels were hovering over the dead on a battlefield. That, too, belonged to me. I said:

"Well! Are you coming?"

He replied, "I'm waiting for you."

I got up and went toward him.

In the center of a large room stood a very short man, very short and very fat, phenomenally, hideously fat.

He had a sparse beard, straggling, ill-kept, dirty yellow beard, and not a hair on his head, not one! As he held his candle raised at arm's length in order to see me, the dome of his bald head looked like a miniature moon shining in this huge room stacked with old furniture. His face was wrinkled and bloated, his eyes mere slits.

I bargained for three of my chairs, paid a large sum for them, then and there, giving him merely the number of my suite at the hotel. They were to be delivered the next day before 9 A.M.

Then I left. He saw me to the door quite politely.

I went straight to the police station, where I told the inspector of the theft of my furniture and the discovery I had just made.

He got in touch immediately by telegraph with the magistrate who had first investigated the theft at my home, and asked me to wait for the answer. An hour later it was received and completely confirmed my story.

"I'll have him arrested and questioned at once," he said, "for he might become suspicious and move your belongings. You had best have your dinner and come back in two hours. I'll have him here and interrogate him in your presence."

"Fine! And thank you very much."

I had dinner at my hotel, and my appetite was better than I should have thought possible. I was rather pleased. My man was caught.

Two hours later I was back at the police station, where the officer was waiting for me.

"Well, sir," he said, seeing me approach. "We didn't find your man. My men couldn't lay their hands on him."

I felt faint.

"But—you have found the house?" I asked.

"Of course. It will be watched until he comes back. But he has disappeared."

"Disappeared?"

"Yes. He usually spends the evening with his neighbor, a queer old hag, a widow called Madame Bidoin, a second-hand dealer like himself. She hasn't seen him this evening and couldn't help us. We shall have to wait until tomorrow."

I left. The streets of Rouen now seemed sinister and threatening, with the disturbing effect of a haunted house.

I slept badly, plagued by nightmares whenever I dozed.

Since I did not want to seem too worried or impatient, I waited until ten o'clock the next morning before going back to the police.

The dealer had not returned. His shop was still closed.

The inspector said, "I have taken the necessary steps. The prosecutor has been informed. We'll go together to the shop, have it opened, and you can show me what belongs to you."

We took a cab. Officers were stationed, along with a locksmith, in front of the shop door, which had been opened.

When I entered, I saw that my wardrobe, my chairs, my tables, and all my household effects were gone. And the night before I had not been able to take a single step without bumping into one of my possessions! The superintendent, surprised, looked at me, with suspicion at first.

"Well, sir," I said, "the disappearance of my furniture coincides strangely with the disappearance of the dealer."

He smiled.

"That's true. You were wrong to buy and pay for your own belongings, yesterday. It tipped him off."

I replied, "What I can't understand is that all the space occupied by my things is now filled with other pieces."

"Oh," said the superintendent, "he had all night, and accomplices, no doubt. This building must communicate with the neighboring houses. Don't fear, sir, I'll see to this business myself. The thief will not escape us for long, we've got his hideout."

My heart was pounding so violently I thought it would burst.

I stayed on for two weeks in Rouen. The man never came back. Unbelievable! God knows nobody could outwit or trap a man like that!

Then on the following morning I received this strange letter from my gardener, who had been acting as caretaker for my house, which had remained unoccupied since the robbery.

Dear Sir:

*I beg to inform you that last night something hap-
pened, which we can't explain, nor the police either.
All the furniture has come back; all of it, even the
smallest bits. The house is now just as it was the night
of the robbery. It's enough to make you doubt your
sanity! It all happened the night of Friday and in the
early hours of Saturday. The paths are cut up as if
everything had been dragged from the garden gate to
the door. It was just the same the day it all disappeared.*

I await your return and remain,

Your respectful servant,
Philippe Raudin

No, no, never! I will not return there!

I took the letter to the chief inspector in Rouen.

"Now that's a very clever way of making restitution. Let's
play possum. We'll catch our man one of these days."

But they didn't catch him. No! They never caught him,
and now I am as terrified of him as if a wild animal were
loose on my track.

Disappeared, escaped, this monster with the bald head
like a full moon! They'll never catch him. He'll never go
back to his shop. Why should he? I am the only one who
can find him and I refuse to.

I won't, I won't!

And if he does go back, if he returns to his shop, who
can prove that my furniture was ever there? There is only
my word against his, and I have a feeling it is becoming
suspect.

No! My life was getting impossible. And I couldn't keep
the secret of what I had seen. I could not go on living
normally with the fear that this horror might begin again.

I went and consulted the doctor who is director of this
sanatorium and told him the whole story.

After questioning me thoroughly, he said:

"My dear sir, would you be willing to stay here a while?"

"Of course, Doctor."

"You have means?"

"Yes, Doctor."

"Would you like a private apartment?"

"Yes, Doctor."

"Would you like your friends to come and see you?"

"No, no. No one. The man from Rouen might venture to pursue me here to get even with me."

And I have been alone, completely alone here for three months now. My mind is almost at ease. I am afraid of only one thing—supposing the antiquary went mad—and was sent to this asylum— Even prisons aren't safe!——

The Party Favor

BY LÉON BLOY

TRANSLATED BY MARTIN NOZICK

LÉON BLOY
1846–1917

Bloy was born in Périgueux of a lower-middle-class family. He was educated in the local schools and also at home by his mother, who was an intensely religious Spanish Catholic. At the age of eighteen he went to Paris in search of fame and adventure. There he earned a precarious living, spending all his leisure time in art studios and in the company of such influential contemporaries as Barbey d'Aurevilly (to whom he became private secretary and who stimulated his interest in becoming a writer), Balzac, Baudelaire, and the philosopher Blanc de Saint-Bonnet. After his experiences in the Franco-Prussian War, Bloy, "the pauper prophet," became a mouthpiece of spiritual values. Like Blanc de Saint-Bonnet, he waged war against rationalism and naturalism, against the rich and the powerful, and the corruption of his epoch. In addition to his disquisitions and polemical essays, Bloy wrote short stories, novels, and an illuminating autobiography, all of which were imbued with his religious spirit.

ABOUT BLOY: Albert Béguin, *Léon Bloy, A Study in Impatience*, London, Sheed & Ward, 1947; Sister Mary Rosalie Brady, *Thought and Style in the Works of Léon Bloy*, Washington, D.C., The Catholic University of America, 1945; Rayner Heppenstal, *Léon Bloy*, Cambridge, Bowes & Bowes, and Yale University Press, 1954; Raissa Maritain (ed.), *Pilgrim of the Absolute*, N.Y., Pantheon, 1947; Raissa Maritain, *We Have Been Friends Together*, N.Y., Longmans, Green, 1942; and *Adventures in Grace*, N.Y., Longmans, Green, 1945; Karl Pfleger, *Wrestlers with Christ*, N.Y., Sheed & Ward, 1936; Emmanuela Polimeni, *Léon Bloy, The Pauper Prophet*, London, D. Dobson, 1947.

A fine young man and a lovely young lady were so passionately in love that they were married. After the ceremony, when they were finally alone, and comfortably seated facing each other, their eyes met; they said nothing but were overcome by horror.—CONTEMPORARY HISTORY IN A NUTSHELL

Monsieur Tertullien had just turned fifty, his hair was still glossy black, his business was booming, and his credit growing daily, when his poor wife died.

It was a terrible blow, for not by the wildest stretch of the imagination could you think of a more satisfactory helpmate.

She was twenty years younger than her husband, with the most tempting little face in the world and such a charming disposition that she never once failed to delight all and sundry.

The magnanimous Tertullien had accepted her without a penny, thus following the example of most businessmen who are inconvenienced by celibacy and yet do not have the time to devote themselves to the seduction of difficult virgins.

He had married her, he would say playfully, "between two cheeses." For he was a wholesale cheese merchant and had gone through the serious process of taking a wife in the interval between delivering quite an order of Chester and getting in a fine lot of Parmesan.

The union, I regret to say, was childless: the only shadow cast upon an otherwise perfect arrangement.

Whose fault was it? That was a very serious question debated by the grocers and fruit dealers of the Gros Caillou. One rather hirsute butcher woman, whom the handsome Tertullien had jilted, accused him openly of impotence but was roundly refuted by a pimply mattress maker who claimed she spoke from personal experience.

However, the pharmacist asserted that they should wait
before jumping to any conclusions, and the kindly conci-
erges, with nothing to lose, approved of such philosophical
circumspection.

With great authority they argued that Rome was not
built in a day, that all's well that ends well, that he who
wishes to live long, avoids excess, etc., and therefore there
was every reason to believe that any day now the happy
event would occur to crown the cheese merchant's dazzling
fortunes.

You would have thought that an heir to the crown of
France was involved.

There was great consternation when it was learned that
sudden death had put an end to such reasonable hopes.

Unless Tertullien married again promptly, a hypothesis
that, in the light of his grief, could not for a single moment
be entertained, the business he had nurtured like a child
and had built up from nothing would eventually find its
way into the hands of a stranger.

Such an unhappy prospect was enough to make the sorrow of the mourning husband particularly bitter.

In fact, he seemed on the verge of succumbing to complete despair.

I do not know to what extent the dream of an heir for
his cheeses had gnawed at him, but my ears did bear witness to his grievous bellowing and the extralegal sum-
monses he served upon himself to follow his Clémentine to
the grave without delay, although he was less than specific
about the date.

For ten years I had done business with this fine gentleman; I therefore had had plenty of time to study him
closely and was aware of an admirable, although not well-
known, quality of his character.

He was horribly afraid of being cuckolded. All his ancestors, for two or three hundred years, had grown horns,
and his tender feelings for his wife stemmed mainly from

an unshakable certainty that she kept his forehead completely unencumbered.

There had been something touching and droll about his *gratitude*. Come to think of it, it almost ended up by being tragic, and sometimes I used to wonder, with some shock, whether Clémentine's unbelievable sterility could be attributed to certain strange doubts Tertullien might have had about his *own* identity, or to the sublime fear he had of cuckolding himself—by making her fruitful.

But all this was far too beautiful, far too incomprehensible for the Marolles, the Bondons, or the Livarots, and the banal thing that was meant to happen did happen.

When Clémentine surrendered her soul to her Maker, the unfortunate widower's immediate reaction was a series of unpremeditated and very natural groans and sobs.

When he had paid his initial respects—to use an expression he adopted—he resolved to put the effects of his late, adored wife in order before facing the ordeal of the last rites.

He was rushing head-on to meet his unhappy fate. The sad history of the Tertulliens was about to repeat itself.

In a mysterious drawer of a commode so innocent-looking that even the most distrustful of husbands would never have suspected it, he discovered a packet of letters of such volume and variety that he was overwhelmed.

All his friends and acquaintances were represented. Except for me, they had all been his wife's lovers.

Even his employees—they had written her on pink paper —had enjoyed her favors.

There was not a particle of doubt that the deceased had deceived him day and night, in all kinds of weather, and in all sorts of places. In his bed, in the cellar, in the attic, in his shop, undaunted by the steady gaze of the Gruyère and the emanations of the Roquefort and Camembert.

We need scarcely add that they did not give a hang about him in those shocking letters. From the first line to the last he was taken over the coals.

A telegraph operator, widely known for the sharpness of

his wit, made the most cutting remarks about Tertullien's business and dropped allusions and advice we would not dare to print.

But there was one thing so unheard of, so outrageous, so fantastic that it could conceivably throw the constellation of Capricorn into confusion.

Attached to this humiliating dossier was an endless series of small sticks that amazed and mystified him. But as he summoned up the cunning of a crafty Apache warrior following the scent of a trail, a blinding light flooded his brain and he perceived that the number of these objects was exactly that of the admirers his wife had encouraged, and each one bore a number of notches like those to be seen on butchers' blocks.

Evidently Clémentine had been a very systematic woman, fond of keeping score.

The widower, crushed by humiliation, begged to be left alone with the deceased and locked himself up for two or three hours like a man wishing to give himself up to his grief without restraint.

Several weeks later Tertullien threw a sumptuous dinner party to celebrate the Epiphany.

Twenty male guests, carefully selected, were seated around the table. Before them was displayed unparalleled magnificence. Rare, abundant dishes were served. It looked like the farewell dinner proffered by some opulent ruler about to abdicate.

Yet a few guests experienced a moment of embarrassment as they surveyed the funereal décor, which the memory of some melodrama had inspired the now lugubrious imagination of the cheese merchant to copy.

The walls, even the ceiling, were covered in black, the tablecloth was black, and light came from black candles burning in black candlesticks. Everything was black.

The telegraph operator was completely baffled and wanted to leave. A jovial pork dealer held him back and declared that "he should enter into the spirit of the occasion" because he thought it all "very funny."

The others, who had wavered for a brief moment, decided to snap their fingers at death. Soon the bottles were making the rounds and dinner reached a pitch of hilarity. With the champagne, the puns began to fly and it was time for dirty jokes. Then a gigantic cake was brought in.

"Gentlemen," said Tertullien, rising from his seat, "let us lift our glasses to the memory of our beloved deceased. Each one of you knew and appreciated the goodness of her heart. You certainly cannot have forgotten her charming, tender heart. I beg you then to make a *very special* effort to evoke her memory before we cut the cake of the Magi, which she would so much have loved to share with you."

Since I had never been the lover of the cheese merchant's wife—probably because I never met her—I had not been invited to the dinner and could not find out to whose lot the party favor fell.

But I do know that the diabolical Tertullien got into some trouble with the law for having put into the enormous flanks of the almond cake, the *heart* of his wife, the little decomposing heart of the delightful Clémentine.

Nausicaa

BY JULES LEMAÎTRE

TRANSLATED BY ANGEL FLORES

JULES LEMAÎTRE
1853–1914

Lemaître, born in Vennecy, was educated at Catholic schools in Orléans and Paris and at the École Normale Supérieure. He taught in Havre and Algiers and, after receiving his doctorate, became a professor at the universities of Besançon and Grenoble. An impassioned attack against Ernest Renan, paradoxically the writer who had influenced him most deeply, made Lemaître famous overnight; he then became the dramatic critic for the *Journal des Debats*. Later his criticism was collected in *Les Contemporains* (7 vols., 1885–99) and *Impressions de théâtre* (7 vols., 1888–98), which were largely responsible for his election to the French Academy in 1895. Although his novel, *Les Rois* (1893), was a fiasco, and his plays, *Revoltée* (1889)—the French *Doll's House—Le Deputé Leveau* (1891), *Mariage blanc* (1891), etc., only moderately successful, Lemaître demonstrated his gifts as a storyteller in his charmingly ironical versions of old myths, like "Nausicaa," which appeared in his collection *Myrrha, vierge et martyre* (1894).

ABOUT LEMAÎTRE: Nothing worth while in English; in French, Myriam Harry, *La vie de Jules Lemaître* (Paris, 1946); E. Seillière, *Jules Lemaître, historien de l'évolution naturiste* (Paris, 1935); his work as playwright and critic is analyzed by Alfred Knopf in *Jules Lemaître als Dramatiker*.

After having slain the suitors with his arrows, the ingenious Ulysses, wise and full of memories, spent his days placidly in his palace at Ithaca. Every evening, seated between his wife Penelope and his son Telemachus, he told them over and over again about his many travels.

One of the adventures he used to retell most willingly had to do with his meeting with Nausicaa, the daughter of Alcinous, the king of the Phaeacians.

"I shall never forget," he would say, "how beautiful, charming, and helpful she was to me. For three days and three nights I had been floating on the vast sea, clinging to a beam of my broken raft. Finally a huge wave lifted me up in the air and hurled me toward the mouth of a river. I succeeded in getting to the bank; a forest was near; I piled up leaves, and since I was naked, I buried myself in them and fell asleep. . . . All of a sudden a sound of splashing water and shouts woke me up. I opened my eyes and I beheld some young women who were playing ball on the riverbank. The ball had just fallen into the rapid current. I stood up, taking good care to hide my naked body with a leafy branch. I drew near the most beautiful of the young girls——"

"You have told us that a thousand times before, my dear," interrupted Penelope.

"Quite likely," said Ulysses.

"What's the difference?" said Telemachus.

Ulysses resumed:

"I can still see her on her cart driving the mules with their sweet tinkling bells. The cart was full of fine white linen and gowns made from dyed wool that the young princess had just washed in the river with the help of her companions. She stood, slightly arched, pulling the reins as the evening breeze ruffled her golden hair (ill-held by her headbands) and pressed her supple robe against her well-formed limbs."

"And what then?" asked Telemachus.

"She was perfectly brought up," Ulysses went on. "When we came close to the city she asked me to leave her so that nobody could gossip about her on seeing her with a man. But from the way I was received in Alcinous's palace I gathered that she had said nice things about me to her noble parents. I did not see her again until my departure. She said to me, 'I salute you, my dear guest, so that when in your fatherland you will forget me not for it is to me that you owe your life.' And I replied, 'Nausicaa, daughter of the magnanimous Alcinous, if Hera's powerful husband wishes me to enjoy my return and that I should enter my dwelling, I will address to you, as to a goddess, my daily prayers, for you were the one who saved me.' No prettier or wiser young woman have I ever met, and since I will never travel again, I am positive I will meet none like her, ever."

"Do you think she's married now?" asked Telemachus.

"She was then only fifteen and not yet engaged."

"Did you tell her that you had a son?"

"I did. And I also told her that I was dying to see him again."

"And did you speak well of me to her?"

"I did, though I hardly knew you, for I left Ithaca when you were only a baby in your mother's arms."

Meanwhile, anxious to marry off her son, Penelope introduced Telemachus to the fairest maidens of the land: to the daughters of the princes of Dulichios, of Samos, of Zacynthos. Each time Telemachus said to her:

"I don't want to marry any of these for I know a fairer and wiser maid."

"Who then?"

"Nausicaa, the daughter of the king of the Phaeacians."

"How can you claim to know her when you have never laid eyes on her?"

"Well, I shall see her," replied Telemachus.

One day he said to his father:

"My heart wishes, O illustrious Father, that, cleaving the fish-abounding sea in a vessel, I sail toward the island of the Phaeacians, and that I go and ask King Alcinous for beautiful Nausicaa's hand. For I die of love for that maid upon whom I have not laid my eyes; and if you present any objection to my plan I will age in your palace and give you no grandchildren."

The ingenious Ulysses replied:

"A god has probably infused this desire into you. Since my description of the princess, who was washing her clothes in the river, you look down upon the succulent viands served at our table and dark circles appear under your eyes. Take thirty men with you in a fast-sailing vessel and seek her whom you know not but without whom you are not able to exist any longer. But I must first warn you of the dangers of the trip. If the wind drives you toward Polyphemus's island, take care not to land there; however, if a storm casts you on the shore, hide yourself and as soon as your ship is ready to sail, flee and keep away from the Cyclops. Some time ago I put out his eye and, though blind, remember, he's still formidable. Also keep away from the island of the Lotus-Eaters, but if you are forced to land among them, eat not the flower that will be offered to you, for it will cause you to lose your memory. Fear also the island of Ææa, the kingdom of the blond Circe, whose magic wand changes men into swine. If perchance your ill-fortune wills that you meet her during your voyage, here is a plant whose root is black and its flower white as milk. The gods call it *moly* and it was given to me by Mercury. Through it you will render powerless the evil spell of the famous sorceress."

Ulysses added other advice anent the dangers of the island of the Sirens, of the island of the Sun, and of the island
of the Laestrygonians. He said, to conclude:

"Remember my words, Son, for I would not want you
to repeat my ill-fated adventures."

"I will remember," said Telemachus. "And as far as that
goes, hostile to me will be any obstacle and even any pleasure that could delay my arrival in the island of the wise
Alcinous."

And so Telemachus departed, his heart full of Nausicaa.

A gale threw him off course and as his vessel skirted
Polyphemus's island, he felt like seeing the giant whom his
father had formerly fooled. He said to himself:

"The danger can't be too great, considering that Polyphemus is blind!"

He disembarked alone, leaving his vessel anchored in the
far end of a bay, and went exploring the fertile, undulating
fields sprinkled with flocks and clumps of trees. On the horizon, from behind a hillock, there emerged an enormous
head, then shoulders similar to those polished rocks that jut
out in the sea, then a chest as bushy as a ravine.

Shortly thereafter a huge hand caught hold of Telemachus who saw, looking down on him, an eye as large as a
shield.

"You are not blind then?" he asked the giant.

"My father Neptune cured me," replied Polyphemus. "A
little man of your own species took away from me the light
of day—and that's why I'm going to eat you up!"

"You would commit a bad mistake," said Telemachus,
"because if you let me live I would entertain you by spinning beautiful yarns for you."

"I'm listening," said Polyphemus.

Telemachus began the story of the Trojan War. At nightfall the Cyclops said:

"It is time to sleep; I will not eat you up tonight because
I want to know how the story ends."

Each night the Cyclops repeated the same thing, and
this lasted for three years.

The first year Telemachus told about the siege of Priam's city.

The second year about the return of Menelaus and Agamemnon.

The third year about Ulysses's home-coming, and his adventures and bewildering ruses.

"You are quite bold, I declare," said Polyphemus, "to be praising right under my nose the little man who did me so great harm!"

"But," Telemachus replied, "the more I show you the sharpness of that little man, the less shameful your defeat appears."

"Quite plausible," said the giant, "and I pardon you for it. It would be a different matter, of course, had not a god restored my sight—but past evils are only dreams!"

By the end of the third year Telemachus had a hard time searching his memory: he no longer found anything to tell the giant. So he began over again the same stories. Nonetheless Polyphemus enjoyed them equally well, and this lasted another three years.

But Telemachus did not find courage to repeat a third time the story of the siege of Ilium and of the return of the heroes. He confessed it to Polyphemus, adding:

"I prefer you to eat me. I will only regret to have died without seeing beautiful Nausicaa."

He raved for a long while about his love and his grief, and suddenly he saw in the Cyclops's eye a tear as big as a pumpkin.

"Go," said the Cyclops, "go and find your beloved! Why didn't you speak sooner?"

"I see that I should have begun there," thought Telemachus. "I have lost six years—all my fault! Shyness kept me from revealing my secret. If I revealed it, it was only because I believed I was going to perish for sure."

He built a boat (for the vessel he had left in the bay had long since disappeared) and set off once more over the deep sea.

Another storm hurled him over to Circe's island.

He saw at the entrance to a dense forest, on a swing made of lianas interlaced with garlands of flowers, a woman who was gently swinging.

She wore a headdress covered with rubies; her long eyebrows joined together over her eyes; her mouth was redder than a newly inflicted wound; her breasts and arms were yellow as saffron; flowers formed of precious stones were strewn over her transparent hyacinth-hued gown; and she smiled through her tawny hair, which completely enveloped her.

Her magic wand, like a sword, hung from her girdle.

Circe watched Telemachus.

The young hero looked under his tunic for the *moly*, the white and black flower handed to him by his father at his departure. He became aware of the fact that he no longer had it.

"I am lost," he thought. "She will strike me with her wand and I shall be just like the acorn-eating swine."

But Circe said to him gently:

"Follow me, young stranger, and come to sleep with me."

He followed her. Soon they reached her palace, which was a hundred times more beautiful than that of Ulysses.

All along the way, from the depths of the forest and ravines, swine and wolves that had once been men shipwrecked on the island rushed after the footsteps of the sorceress and although she pricked them cruelly with a long iron rod, they tried to lick her bare feet.

For three years Telemachus slept with the sorceress.

Then, one day, he grew ashamed; he felt extremely tired, and he discovered that he had not ceased to love Alcinous's daughter, the innocent blue-eyed virgin he had never seen.

But he was thinking:

"Were I to express a desire for departing, the sorceress, angered, will change me into an animal and thus I shall never see Nausicaa."

Circe, on her part, was getting fed up with her companion. She began to hate him for her having fallen in love with him. So one night she rose from her purple bed, picked up her wand and struck him over his heart.

But Telemachus kept his form and his face. This was because at that instant he was thinking of Nausicaa and his heart was full of his love.

"Go away! Go away!" shrieked the sorceress.

Telemachus found again his boat, set forth once more on the sea, and a third storm hurled him onto the island of the Lotus-Eaters.

These were polite men, full of intelligence, even-tempered, charming.

Their king offered Telemachus a lotus flower.

"I will not eat anything," said the young hero, "for this is the flower of forgetfulness and I want to remember."

"Nevertheless forgetfulness is a great privilege," said the king. "Thanks to this flower, which is our only nourishment, we are able to overlook sorrow, regrets, desire, and all the passions that trouble unfortunate mankind. But, at any rate, we do not force anyone to eat the divine flower."

Telemachus lived for some weeks on provisions he had saved from his shipwreck but, later on, since there were no fruits or animals fit to eat in the island, he fed, as best he could, on clams and fish.

One day he asked the king:

"Does the lotus flower make men forget even what they most desire or what causes them greatest pain?"

"Of course," the king answered.

"Oh," said Telemachus, "it will never make me forget beautiful Nausicaa."

"Try and see!"

"If I try it, it is because I am quite sure that the lotus flower could not do what the artifices of a magician failed to do."

He ate the flower and fell asleep.

Another way of saying that he went on living as the gentle Lotus-Eaters, enjoying the present hour and worrying about nothing. Only at times he felt deep in his heart some-

thing like a twinge of his old wound without being able to
ascertain exactly what it was.

When he awoke he could not forget Alcinous's daughter;
but twenty years had elapsed without his realizing it: all
that time was required by his love to overcome the influence
of the flower of forgetfulness.

"Those were the best twenty years of your existence," the
king told him.

But Telemachus did not believe it.

Politely he took leave of his hosts.

I shall pass over other adventures in which he was engaged, now due to necessity, now due to his curiosity of
seeing new things, be it at the island of the Sirens, be it at
the island of the Sun, be it at the island of the Laestrygonians—nor will I repeat how love was strong enough to
extricate him from all these dangers and to tear him away
from the various stopping places.

A final storm drove him toward the mouth of a river, in
the desired island, in the land of the Phaeacians. He reached
the shore; a forest was near. He piled up leaves and, as he
was naked, he covered himself with them. He fell asleep.
. . . All of a sudden the sound of splashing water woke
him up.

Telemachus opened his eyes and saw servant maids
washing clothes under the supervision of a richly clad old
woman.

He stood up, taking care of covering his naked body with
a leafy branch, and drew near the old lady. She was rather
stout and locks of gray hair escaped from her headbands.

One could readily see that she had once been beautiful,
but was so no longer.

Telemachus asked her for hospitality. She replied kindly
and had her servants give him clothes.

"And now, my guest, I am going to take you to the king's
palace."

"Are you perhaps the queen?" asked Telemachus.

"You have said it, stranger."

And so Telemachus, rejoicing in his heart, exclaimed:

"May the gods grant long life to the mother of the beautiful Nausicaa!"

"Nausicaa? That's me!" the queen replied. "But what's wrong with you, venerable old man . . . ?"

In his boat, hastily repaired, the old Telemachus gained the open sea, without turning once to look back.

Salomé

BY JULES LAFORGUE

TRANSLATED BY WILLIAM E. SMITH

JULES LAFORGUE
1860–87

Laforgue was born in Montevideo of French parents and educated in France. He worked for a while as secretary to the editor of the *Gazette de Beaux-Arts* and then went to Berlin as reader to the Empress Augusta. It was there that he wrote *Complaintes* (1885), *Imitation de Notre-Dame la Lune* (1886) and *Dernier vers*, which was published posthumously. These, together with his prose tales, *Moralités Légendaires*, which were satirical versions of the old legends (Hamlet, Salomé, Pan, Lohengrin), make up his entire work. The charmingly baroque "Salomé" included here was one of these tales and is an ornate parody of Flaubert's "Hérodias." After five years in Germany Laforgue married an English girl and returned to Paris, where he died of consumption within the year. Melancholy and frustrated in his life, Laforgue tried in his work to be lighthearted, to make fun of his own bitterness. His verse and tales capture this mixture of exasperation and humor and show the virtuosity that has had so great an influence on the early work of T. S. Eliot, Ezra Pound, and Hart Crane.

ABOUT LAFORGUE: Warren Ramsey, *Jules Laforgue and the Ironic Inheritance*, N.Y., Oxford, 1953; see also Angel Flores, *An Anthology of French Poetry from Nerval to Valéry*, N.Y., Doubleday Anchor Books, 1958.

To be born is to depart; to die is to return.
PROVERBS FROM THE KINGDOM OF ANNAM,
COLLECTED BY FATHER JOURDAIN OF FOREIGN
MISSIONS.

I

The dog days had come and gone two thousand times since
an elementary rhythmic revolution of the Palace Mandarins
had elevated the first Tetrarch, a minor Roman proconsul,
to this throne (hereditary, henceforth, but through careful
selection) of the Esoteric White Islands (henceforth, lost to
history), but that unusual title of Tetrarch was retained
because it had as sacred a ring to it as Monarch, and im-
plied in addition the seven symbols of statehood clinging
to the prefix "tetra" but not to "monos."

With pylons, three blocks of them, squat and stark, inner
courtyards, galleries, vaults, and the famous Hanging
Park, its jungles undulating in the Atlantic breezes, and the
Observatory's one eye on the lookout six hundred feet up,
near the sky, and a hundred flights of sphinxes and cyno-
cephali: the tetrarchic palace was no more than a monolith,
carved, excavated, hollowed, compartmented, and finally
burnished into a mountain of black basalt streaked with
white, extended by a pier of sonorous pavement, with a
double row of poplars, funereal violet, in tubs, projecting
far out into the shifting solitude of the sea, until it reached
an eternal rock, very much like an ossified sponge, holding
out a pretty comic-opera beacon toward the night-prowling
junks.

Titanic hulk of gloom, streaked with pallor! Those ivory-
black façades give so mysterious a reflection of today's July
sun, that sun above the sea, darkly reflected, which the owls

of the Hanging Park can contemplate without eyestrain
from the tops of their dusty fir trees.

At the pier's edge the galley that had come, the day
before, carrying those two unwelcome princes who claimed
to be the son and nephew of a certain northern satrap,
swayed in its moorings, discussed by a few languid silhouettes.

Now, while high noon stagnated on (the festival would
not begin officially until three o'clock), the palace slept
away the afternoon, postponed the stretch that would end
its siesta.

The followers of those northern princes and the Tetrarch's
men could be heard laughing loudly, in the court where the
conduits met, laughing without understanding one another,
playing quoits, exchanging tobacco. A lesson was offered to
these foreign colleagues on the proper grooming of white
elephants. . . .

"But there are no white elephants in our country," they
tried to say.

And they saw how the grooms blessed themselves, as if
warding off blasphemous ideas. And then they gaped at the
peacocks strutting above the fountain, moving in circles,
their tails iridescent in the sunlight; and then they entertained themselves—they really went too far!—with the gut-
tural echoes of their barbaric shouts.

The Tetrarch, Emerald-Archetypas, appeared on the
central terrace, taking off his gloves in honor of the sun,
universal Artist of the Zenith, Firefly of the Higher Sky,
etc.; and that rabble rushed back inside to attend to their
business.

Oh, see the Tetrarch on the terrace, see the dynastic
caryatid!

Behind him the city, already humming festively (drying
out its copious irrigation); and farther on, beyond those
ridiculous ramparts and their enamelwork of tiny yellow
flowers, how contentedly the fields were sprawling—the fine
roads covered with small fragments of crushed flint, the
checkered complexity of crops! Before him the sea, the sea,

eternally novel and respectable, called the sea because
there is no other name to give it.

And to punctuate this silence, nothing now but the joyous, clear barking of dogs down below, as the street Arabs,
their bodies gleaming naked amid the mica of the scorching
sand, whistled exotically and launched the animals against
the foaming scrollwork at the rim of the sea, the sea on the
surface of which these children had been converting their
worn arrowheads into stones for skipping. And so, through
the clematis of the terrace, through the cool hush of invisible streams, disjointed spirals of smoke arose, sadly and
artlessly, as the Tetrarch, propped on his elbows, puffed
sulkily on his midday hookah. There had been a moment,
yesterday, after a messenger had put in a shady appearance
and announced those northern princes, when his pregnant
destiny on these pregnant islands had wavered between
his immediate domestic terrors and an absolute dilettantism
that could go for the highest stakes even at the moment of
ruin.

For *he* was one of those sons of the North, those eaters
of meat—he, that wretched Iokanaan, who had turned up
here one fine morning, with his spectacles and his uncut red
beard, hawking (in that country's own language) some
pamphlets that he was distributing gratis, but delivering
his sales talk in such an inflammatory style that the people
had nearly stoned him—so that now he was thinking things
over in the depths of the tetrarchic palace's only dungeon.

Would the twentieth centenary of the Emerald-Archetypas dynasty be celebrated by a war with the outside
world, after so many centuries of esotericism, lost to history?
Iokanaan had described his fatherland as a country stunted
by want, famished for the property of others, fostering warfare as a national industry. And those two princes might
very possibly have come to claim this fellow, who was a
talented sort after all, and a subject of theirs—and they
might build on this pretext, extend their rights of jurisdiction
over the occidentals. . . .

But fortunately!—and thanks to the inexplicable interces-
sion of his daughter Salomé—he had not yet interfered with

the executioner's traditional, honorary sinecure, nor sent
him after Iokanaan armed with the sacred Kris!

However, false alarm! The two princes were merely on a
voyage of circumnavigation, looking in on dubiously occupied colonies, and they had only approached the White
Islands because they were passing nearby, out of curiosity.
But what a surprise! Could it be in this corner of the world
that their notorious Iokanaan was going to end up on the
gallows? The idea had made them eager for details of the
tribulations of this poor soul, who was already so little of a
prophet in his own country.

And so the Tetrarch sucked on his midday hookah, with
a vacant look, his mood impaired, as it always was at this
climactic hour of the day—even more impaired than usual
today, with those mounting noises of the national festival,
firecrackers and choristers, bunting and lemonade. . . .

The next morning, over the horizon, which was so infinite
in spite of everything, but beyond which—so they said—
many other races existed under the same sun, those two
gentlemen and their galley would vanish.

Now, leaning across the syrupy clematis on his earthen-
ware balustrade, throwing cake crumbs down to the fish in
the ponds below, Emerald-Archetypas reminded himself
that now he could no longer count on even the small income that his hidden talents might bring in, since his venerable carcass definitely resisted all impulses toward art,
toward meditation, toward congenial spirits, or toward industry.

To think that, on the day of his birth, a remarkable tempest had burst over the black dynastic palace, and many
trustworthy persons had seen a lightning-flash calligraph
"alpha" and "omega"! How many noonday hours had he
killed in sighing over that mystical folderol? And nothing
out of the ordinary had come to pass. Besides, a message
like "alpha," "omega"—that leaves a lot of leeway.

And so, for nearly two months now, relinquishing the interests of youth and pummeling his thighs to regain some
of that old enthusiasm about resigning himself to the nothingness that had asceticized his twentieth year, he had se-

riously gone about taking up a course of daily visits to the necropolis (so cool in the summer, besides) of his ancestors. Winter was on its way; the ceremonies of the Snow Cult, his grandson's investiture. And besides, Salomé would stay at his side—she wouldn't hear a word about the joys of hymeneal bliss, the dear child!

Emerald-Archetypas was about to reach for a hand bell and request some more consecrated cake for those resplendent July fish, when he heard on the flagstones, behind him, the sound of the cane belonging to the Commander-of-a-Thousand-Trifles. The northern princes had returned from a visit to the city; they awaited the Tetrarch in the hall of the Palace Mandarins.

II

The aforementioned northern princes, belted, pomaded, braided, gloved, beards combed out, hair parted along the occiput (with bangs smoothed down on the temples to suggest the medallion-profile look), were waiting, one hand of each pressing his helmet against his right thigh, the other hand caressing the hilt of his saber, with the waddling gait of a stallion that smells powder everywhere, in spite of himself. They were making conversation with the aristocrats: the high Mandarin, the Lord High Supervisor of Libraries, the Arbiter of Elegance, the Preserver of Symbols, the Tutor and Selector of the Gynecium, the Pope of Snow, and the Administrator of Death, surrounded by two rows of scrawny, nervous scribes, armed with quills at their sides and inkstands tucked in their sleeves.

Their Highnesses congratulated the Tetrarch and themselves on the "fortunate wind which . . ." "on such a glorious day . . ." "upon these islands . . ." and concluded with a eulogy of the capital, especially of the White Basilica, where they had heard a "Tedium Laudamus" played on the Hand Organ of the Seven Sorrows, and of

the Cemetery of Beasts and Objects—nor were these the
only curiosities of such magnitude.

A snack was served. And because the princes swore that
they felt compelled not to touch meat in the company of
their hosts, so orthodox in their devotion to vegetarianism
and ichthyophagy, the table was a picture, with its delicate arrangement, among fine crystals, of a smattering of
artichokes in the shell, swimming in iron husks that stood
erect and worked on hinges, asparagus served on mats of
pink rushes, pearly-gray eels, date cakes, assorted fruit
compotes, and several sweet wines.

Afterward, preceded by the Commander-of-a-Thousand-
Trifles, the Tetrarch and his entourage did what they could
to show their guests the honors of the palace, of the titanic,
gloomy palace streaked with pallor.

Their first stop would be at the panorama of the Islands,
as seen from the Observatory; afterward they would descend from one story to the next, through the Park, the
Menagerie, and the Aquarium, all the way down to the
vaults.

Hoisted to the heights (and pneumatically at that), the
procession hastily crossed, on tiptoe, the apartments that
Salomé occupied, to an accompaniment of countless slam-
ming doors into which disappeared two or three Negresses'
backs, with vertebrae of oiled bronze. What was more,
in the exact center of a room tapestried with majolicas (so
very yellow!) they found an abandoned and enormous
ivory basin, a good-sized white sponge, some moist satins,
a pair of pink sandals (so very pink!). Then, a room filled
with books; next, another crammed with metallotherapeu-
tic equipment; a spiral staircase; and finally they breathed
the upper air of the platform—ah! just in time to see the
disappearance of a young girl, harmoniously bemuslined
in spidery jonquil with black dots, who was manipulating
the pulleys so as to let herself glide into space, down toward the lower stories . . . !

The princes were already falling all over themselves with
gallant salaams about their intruding, but they quieted
down altogether when they saw a ring of astonished eyes,

full of the apparent confession: "Well, well, after all, nothing up here is any of our business."

And then a promenade in the open air, with terse expressions of stifled appreciation, around the Observatory Dome, which contained a huge equatorial telescope fifty-four feet long, a movable dome, decorated with waterproof frescoes, whose bulk of one hundred tons was balanced on fourteen steel bars in a vat of magnesium chloride and could rotate in two minutes, the story ran, under a single pressure from Salomé's hand.

Come to think of it, suppose these exotic freaks should dream up the idea of pitching us over the edge, these two princes thought, with a simultaneous shudder. . . . But they were ten times more vigorous, the two of them in their skin-tight uniforms, than this whole dozen of nobles, all pale, hairless, their fingers laden with rings, wrapped up like priests in their shining gilt brocades. And they diverted themselves by singling out their galley, down below in the harbor, like a coleopteron with a thorax of rubbed sheet-iron.

And they listened to an enumeration of the islands, an archipelago of natural cloisters, each one with its own caste, etc.

They descended through a chamber of Perfumes where the Arbiter of Elegance made a note of the gifts which Their Highnesses would like to take along, all of them secretly sabotaged by Salomé: make-up without carbonate of lead, powder without white lead or bismuth, rejuvenators without cantharis, lustral waters without mercurial protochloride, depilatories without arsenic sulphide, milk without corrosive sublimate or hydrated lead oxide, genuinely vegetable dyes without silver nitrate, hyposulphide of soda, copper sulphate, sodium sulphide, potassium cyanide, acetate of lead (can such things be!) and two demijohns containing perfume bouquets for spring and for autumn.

At the end of a dank, interminable corridor with a smell of ambush about it, the Commander opened a door that was green with moss, covered with fungi as sumptuous as jewels, and they were surprised to find themselves in the midst of the vast silence of that famous Hanging Park—ah, just in time to see, around the bend of a path, the disappearance of a svelte young form, hermetically bemuslined in spidery jonquil with black dots, escorted by molossine bats and greyhounds, whose playful barking, almost sobbing for sheer loyalty, gradually faded away into distant echoes.

Oh, everywhere, echoes from unknown passages, filling that austere green solitude, kilometrically deep, sprinkled with patches of light, furnished exclusively with an army of rigid pines, whose bare trunks of a salmon-flesh tint spread, far above, far above, their dusty horizontal parasols. The bars of sunlight lay down between these tree trunks with the same gentle calm they might have between the pillars of some claustral chapel with grillwork vents. A sea breeze tried to penetrate this lofty timber, with a strange distant murmur, like an express train in the night. Then the high-altitude silence took shape again and made itself at home. Nearby, oh, somewhere, a bulbul discharged some rewarding remarks; from a great distance another answered; just as if this were their home, their century-old dynastic aviary. And the group moved on, hazarding guesses as to the thickness of this artificial soil, with its thick felt of dead leaves and pine-needle cushions left by a thousand yesteryears, forming a comfortable lodging for the roots of those pines, so patriarchal! Next were vast gulfs of lawn, grassy slopes like dreams about a faun's kermis; and stagnant sheets of water where swans that wore earrings far too heavy for their spindle necks were immersed in ennui and old age; and endless decamerons of polychromatic statues with fractured pedestals, but posing with surprising—nobility.

Finally, the gazelle enclosure acted as a transition—it didn't pretend to be anything else—between the orchards on one extreme, the Menagerie and the Aquarium on the other.

The deer hardly condescended to raise their eyelids; the elephants shifted their weight to the tune of a harsh crack-crack of plaster, but their thoughts were elsewhere; the giraffes were dressed modestly in soft coffee-and-cream, but they had exaggerated mannerisms and stubbornly

stared over the heads of this brilliant court; the monkeys
never for a moment interrupted the domestic scenes of their
phalanstery; the aviaries' glitter was deafening; the reptiles,
for nearly a week, had been endlessly shedding skin; and
the stables just happened to be deprived of their finest animals, stallions, mares, and zebras, which had been lent to
the municipality for a special cavalcade in honor of the day.

The Aquarium! Ah! This is it, the Aquarium! We'll stop
here. How silently it gyrates . . . !

Labyrinth of grottoes, corridors to the right, to the left,
each compartment revealing through glass luminous vistas
of undersea nations.

Their moors, everywhere dolmens studded with viscous
gems, arenas with graded basalt seats, where crabs wallow
together in couples, stubborn and fumbling in their after-
dinner good spirits, their small eyes roguish and hard-bitten.

Their plains, plains of fine sand, so fine that it sometimes
lifts in the breeze after the waving tail of some flat fish
just arrived from far away, fluttering like a liberty banner,
scrutinized, as he passes and leaves us behind and goes his
way, by large eyes that dot the sand in spots and have no
other interest in life.

And the desolation of their steppes, housing only one
blasted and petrified tree, colonized by trembling clusters
of sea horses . . .

And, crossed by natural bridges, their mossy hollows,
where the slated carapaces of king crabs with rattails rumi-
nate, wallowing, some capsized and flailing, but no doubt
intentionally, so as to exercise . . .

And, below the chaotic ruins of their arches of triumph,
the sea needles moving along like frivolous ribbons; and the
haphazard navigations of hairy nuclei, a tuft of bristles
around the matrix, which can fan itself thus when traveling
becomes tedious . . .

And their fields of sponges, sponges like lung remains;
thickets of truffles, all in orange velvet; and a great cemetery for pearly molluscs; and those plantations of asparagus,
tumefied and pickled in the alcohol of Silence . . .

And, as far as the eye can see, their prairies, prairies

dotted with white anemones, fat and healthy onions, bulbs
of violet mucus, bits of intestine that got lost and, indeed,
began existing again, stumps with antennae that blink at
a coral reef nearby, a thousand aimless warts; an entire
flora, fetal, claustral, vibratile, fermenting that eternal
dream, of someday achieving a mutual whisper of congratulations among themselves about their condition . . .

Oh, just look, that high plateau: hanging on like a leech,
a polyp keeps its vigil, the area's gross and glabrous mino-
taur . . . !

Before departing the Pope of Snow turns to the halted
procession and speaks, as if reciting an ancient lesson:

"No day, no night, my friends, no winter, nor spring,
nor summer, nor autumn, nor any other weathercocks. Loving, dreaming, without a change of position, in the cool
repose of the imperturbably blind. O world of contentment,
yours is a sightless, supreme beatitude, while we, we are
being dehydrated by other-worldly hunger pangs. And
why are our antennae, our own senses, not bounded by the
Blind, the Opaque, the Silent, why do they follow a scent
that leads outside of our realm? And why are we so incapable of curling up in our own little corner and sleeping
off the drunken stupor of our sad little Self?

"But, O submarine villegiatures, we do have two feasts to
glut our other-worldly hunger pangs that are worthy of
you: the face of the too-beloved, shut up tight on the pillow, a flattened headband glued down by the final sweat,
an agonized mouth opening on pallid teeth in an aquarium
ray of the Moon (oh, pluck not, pluck not!)—and the Moon
herself, a sunflower, yellow, crushed, desiccated by agnosti-
cism. (Oh! Try, try to pluck her!)"

And this was the Aquarium: but could those foreign
princes have understood?

And, in single file, speedily and cautiously, they moved
down the main corridor of the Gynecium, with its paintings
of callipedic scenes and the rotten melancholy of its feminine odors: all they heard was the trickle of a waterspout
—to the left? to the right?—whose freshness moistened the

thin thread of a cantilena, unforgettably oppressed, miserable and sterile.

And lest their ignorance of the fertility rites might lead them to commit some fatal error, the princes continued at the same discreet pace across the tetrarchic necropolis: two rows of cupboards, masked by life-size portraits, containing urns and thousands of realistic relics, but only affecting to the family, you know what I mean.

But, look here, what they absolutely insisted upon, was seeing their old friend Iokanaan again!

So they followed an official with a key embroidered at right angles to his spine, who stopped at the end of an old sewer that smelled of niter, and, pointing out a grating, lowered it to waist height with a mechanism; and they could approach and perceive, inside a small cell, that unfortunate European, who was getting to his feet, having been interrupted as he lay flat on his stomach, his nose in a mess of ragged papers.

Hearing two voices wish him a polite good-morning in his native tongue, Iokanaan stood erect and straightened his thick spectacles, which had been patched up with wire.

Oh, good Lord, his princes had come! How many dirty winter nights, with his clogs soaking up the muddy snow, he had been at the head of all the paupers going home after a day of wage-earning, and, pausing for a moment there, while tyrannical policemen on horseback restrained the crowd, he had watched these two dismount, covered with plumes, from their heavy, pompous coaches, and climb between two banks of drawn sabers up the great staircase of their palace, that palace with *a giorno* windows at which, as he moved on, he shook his fist, muttering every time that an "era" had to come! And now, it had come, that era! In his own country, the long-promised revolution was a fact! And its poor old prophet, Iokanaan, was a belated god! And this personalized royal measure, this far-flung heroic expedition his princes had undertaken to deliver him, was certainly the moving ceremony the people had demanded in confirmation of the advent of this Universal Easter Day!

At first he automatically doubled up in a bow, in the
manner of his own country, trying to think of a speech that
would be memorable, historic, fraternal of course, but dignified as well. . . .

Illico, his words were cut off short by the northern
satrap's nephew, an apoplectically bald army veteran, who
insisted on mumbling irrelevantly to everyone that, following the example of Napoleon I, he detested "ideologists":
"Ah, ha! Look at you, an ideologist, a scribbler, a dishonor-
able discharge, a bastard of Jean Jacques Rousseau. So
this is where you finally decided to be hanged, you classless
pamphleteer! Good riddance! I hope your grimy pate is
quick about finding your colleagues from the Bas-Bois at
the bottom of a guillotine basket! Yes, I mean the Bas-Bois
conspiracy, yesterday's fresh heads."

Oh, the brutes, the indestructible brutes! And the Bas-
Bois plotting had failed! His brothers, assassinated! And
there was no one to give him the affecting details of the
affair. Finished, finished; nothing left but to be ground, like
his brothers, under the Constitutional Heel. The wretched
publicist resolved to stick to a rigid silence, waiting for the
upper classes to leave so that he could accept death in his
corner; two long white tears flowed out under his spectacles
along his emaciated cheeks toward the meager beard. And
suddenly they saw him raise himself to his bare feet,
stretching his hands after an apparition, to which he gur-
gled some of the softest diminutives of his mother tongue.
They turned around—ah!—just in time to see the disappearance, in a tinkling of keys, through the lambency of that
in pace, a young form unmistakably bemuslined in spidery
jonquil with black dots. . . .

And Iokanaan once again fell flat on his stomach among
his litter, and, noticing that he had upset the inkwell into
his stack of papers, he began blotting the ink, tenderly, like
a child.

The procession climbed away, without comment; the
northern satrap's nephew fingered the stickpin of his military collar and chewed over his principles.

III

In a mode uniting joy and fatalism an orchestra of ivory instruments was improvising a unanimous miniature overture.

The court came in and was hailed by a lush hullabaloo from two hundred luxurious guests who raised themselves on their fine couches. A brief halt was made before a pyramid of shelves containing presents offered to the Tetrarch on this occasion. The two northern princes nudged each other with their elbows and excitedly took from around their necks the Necklace of the Iron Fleece, which they bestowed on their host. But neither one dared to put it around his neck. The aesthetic mediocrity of that necklace was glaring enough, especially here. And as for its honorific value, they felt, not having observed anything similar around them, that the explanations required to make it clear definitely risked falling flat, or at best merely achieving a polite success.

Everyone took his place; Emerald-Archetypas introduced his son and his grandson, two magnificent specimens (magnificent, that is, of course, from the esoteric, white point of view), emblematically attired.

And then, in that windy hall strewn with rushes as yellow as jonquils, those deafening aviaries intoning on all sides, while in the center a fountain sprang up and at its height pierced a gaudy velarium of India rubber, on which the water could be heard falling back in a fine rain, icy and pelting; there were all told, paralleling the semicircular tables, ten rows of couches, each decorated with an eye to the guests' specialities—and, facing them, an Alcazar stage, amazingly deep, where the cream of the mountebanks, jugglers, beauties, and virtuosi of the Islands would come to be tasted.

A wily breeze scuttled along the velarium, but weighted

down in spite of itself by that incessant downpour from the fountain.

And the aviaries, overjoyed by the clashing colors, regretfully stopped their noise when the music began to accompany everyone's supper.

The poor Tetrarch! This assortment of music, this audience of sumptuous effusion on this pompous occasion grieved him in his heart. He barely nibbled at that ingenious sequence of sweetmeats, pecking at them with spatulas of hardened snow, his attention wandering like a child's, gaping at the bizarre circus frieze that was evolving on the Alcazar stage.

On the Alcazar stage there appeared:

The serpent girl, thin, in viscous scales of blue, green, and yellow, her bosom and belly soft pink: she undulated and twisted, never tiring of her own touch, and lisped that hymn that begins, "Biblis, Sister Biblis, you, yes, you have changed into a wellspring!"

Next a parade of costumes, all sacramentally curtailed, each one symbolizing a separate human desire. The refinement of all this!

Next the entr'actes, presenting horizontal cyclones of electrified flowers, and a horizontal waterspout of berserk bouquets . . . !

Next came musical clowns, wearing over their hearts their insignia, the crank of a genuine hand organ, which they turned with the look of Messiahs who refuse to be influenced and will go to any lengths to follow their apostleship.

And other clowns took the roles of the Idea, the Will, and the Unconscious. The Idea rattled on about everything, the Will beat his head against the scenery, and the Unconscious made big, mysterious gestures, like a person who is sure of being far better informed than he can express in words as yet. Moreover, this trinity had one single, unchanging refrain:

> *Our Canaan, I guess,*
> *Is nothing less*
> *Than good old Nothingness.*

> *Non-being, I mean,*
> *The Meca far-seen*
> *Toward which libraries lean.*

It obtained a howling success.

Next virtuosi of the flying trapeze, describing nearly sidereal ellipses . . . !

Next, a rink of natural ice was brought in, and there emerged an adolescent skater, his arms crossed over those Brandenburg trimmings in white Astrakhan fur on his chest, only stopping after he had described every combination of all the known curves; then he waltzed on his points, like a ballerina; then he etched on the ice a flamboyant Gothic cathedral, not omitting one rose window or grill! Then he designed a three-part fugue, and ended with a labyrinthine twirl, like that of a fakir possessed *del diavolo,* finally leaving the stage, his feet in the air, skating on his steel fingernails . . . !

And it was all concluded by a batch of living pictures, nudities as chaste as vegetables, symbols becoming ever more eurhythmic, by means of a Crucifixion of the Aesthetic.

The calumets had been carted in; the conversation moved into the general; Iokanaan, who could hardly have been amused at hearing this festival going on over his head, was the chief staple of news. The northern princes spoke in favor of armed authority, the supreme religion, that guardian of repose, of bread, and of international competition, but they lost the thread and tried to make an end by quoting this distich, as a kind of epiphonema:

> *Besides, every decent person preaches*
> *The perfectibility of the Species.*

The Mandarins were of the opinion that the sources of social competition should be atrophied, neutralized, that society should be organized into cliques of exclusive initiates, scraping along in peace, with great walls of China between them, etc., etc.

And the music, playing on alone, seemed to complete the

sense of what the speakers were too ephemeral to formulate.

In the end, you could hear the silence growing larger, like the pale mesh of a fish net cast out on an evening of fishing; the company arose; apparently it was Salomé.

She entered, descended the spiral staircase, tense in her muslin sheath; with one hand she signed to them to recline again; a small, black lyre dangled from her wrist; with the tips of her fingers she flicked a kiss toward her father.

And she came and took her place, facing them, on the platform, behind her the drawn curtain of the Alcazar stage; she waited for them to exhaust the possibilities of observing her, but saved appearances by pretending to sway on her pallid feet, spreading their toes wide apart.

She took no notice of anyone. Powdered with exotic pollens, her hair fell loosely onto her shoulders in flat locks, while on her forehead it was entangled with yellow flowers and bits of straw; supported over her bare shoulders by two armlets of pearl was a dwarf peacock's spread tail, with an ever-changing background, silken, azure, golden, emerald, a halo against which her pure face was etched, that superior face, but politely indifferent to the knowledge that it was unique, that pinched neck, those eyes exhausted by their iridescent expiations, those lips, a circumflex accent of pale pink setting off those teeth, and those gums, of an even paler pink, in that too crucified smile.

Oh! The celestial, sweet creature, so understandably aesthetic, the delicate recluse of the White Esoteric Islands . . . !

Hermetically bemuslined in a spidery jonquil with black dots, which several fibulae pinned together here and there, exposing the arms in their angelic nudity and forming, between those soupçons of breasts, whose nipples were dotted with tiny pinks, a sash embroidered on her eighteenth birthday; then, a little above that adorable umbilical dimple, joining a jeweled girdle of an intense, jealous yellow, casting an inviolable shadow into the hollow between those meager thighs, and halting at her ankles only to reascend her back as two sashes, fluttering apart, finally joining again at the pearl armlets below the dwarf peacock's tail and its changing background, azure, silken, emerald, gold, a halo for that pure superior face; she swayed on her feet, her pallid feet, spreading their toes wide apart, bare except for anklets from which rained a dazzling fringe of yellow silk.

Oh! The little Messiah, complete with womb! How burdensome her head was for her! She didn't know what to do with her hands, even her shoulders seemed ill at ease. Who was it that crucified her smile, that poor little Immaculate Conception? And who exhausted those blue eyes? —Oh! Their hearts exulted, how simple her skirt must feel! Art is so long and life so short! Oh, just to chat with her in a corner, near a fountain, to find out not her Why, but her How, and then to die . . . ! To die, unless . . .

Do you think she may make a speech, after all . . . ?

Craning forward out of his heap of silken cushions, his wrinkles dilating, his pupils jutting out from the battlements of his tarnished lids, pretending to be interested in fingering the Seal, which hung around his neck, the Tetrarch had just handed a page the pineapple he had been nibbling and his towered tiara.

"Look inward! Look inward, before you do anything, O Idea and Contour, Caryatid of these islands without history!" he pleaded.

Then he smiled at everyone, like a contented father, as if to say: "You will see what you will see," giving the necessary information to his guests, the princes, in highly disorganized form, so that the two of them gathered that the Moon had been bled white in order to cast the horoscope of the little creature before them, and that she was generally admitted (a council had been devoted to the question) to be the foster sister of the Milky Way (she has everything!).

Now, delicately planted on her right foot, her thigh raised, her other leg bent behind her in the manner of Niobe, Salomé, permitting herself a small coughing laugh, perhaps with an idea of suggesting that the last thing to do was to imagine that she took herself seriously, plucked on her lyre until she drew blood, and, in a voice without timbre or sex, like that of an invalid calling for his dose,

which neither he (nor you, nor I) ever actually needed,
she improvised as follows:

"O Non-being, by which I mean the latent Life to come
day-after-tomorrow, but no sooner, how worthy you are,
how forgiving, coexisting with the Infinite, the ultimate in
clarity!"

Was she mocking? She went on:

"Love! That compulsive mania that refuses to accept an
absolute death (feeble subterfuge!). O traitorous Brother,
I cannot honestly say that we have reached a time for
mutual explanations. For all eternity, things are as they
are. But how real it would be to make each other some
concessions in the realm of the five existent senses, in the
name of the Unconscious!

"O latitudes, altitudes of those Nebulae of good intentions, filled with little fresh-water jellyfish, please do me one
good turn—come and graze in empirical meadows. O tran-
sients on this earth, so eminently *idem* as incalculable
others, all equally alone in a life indefinably infinite in its
strivings! The active Essence loves itself (listen carefully,
now), loves itself dynamically, more or less freely: it is like
a profound soul forever playing solitaire with itself, exactly
as it pleases. I command you, be the passives of nature;
enter the Discipline of the Benevolent Harmony, but automatically as Everything! And let me know how it feels.

"Yes, you hydrocephalic theosophists, you are like the
tame fowls of the people, nothing but arbitrary groups of
phenomena without any guarantee of being governed from
beyond: go back to existences tainted by negligence, and
in my name browse, for your daily meal, for your seasonal
sustenance, on those deltas without sphinxes, whose angles
equal two rights in spite of all. O you generations of incurable pubescence, behold the true decorum; and whatever else you do, pretend to be utterly enmeshed in the
irresponsible limbo of the potentialities of which I speak.
The Unconscious *farà da se*.

"And you, O fatal Jordans, O baptismal Ganges, insub-
mergible sidereal currents, cosmogonies like Mamas! When
entering, wash yourselves clean of the more or less original

stain of the Systematic; first of all, let us be minced into
lint to help out the Great Curative Power (or should we
call it Palliative?), which sews up all holes, in the prairie,
in the epidermis, etc.—*Quia est in ea virtus dormitiva.*
Go . . ."

Salomé stopped short, brushing back her hair (powdered
with exotic pollens), and her soupçons of breasts churned
so that the pinks fell away from them (widowing their
nipples). Trying to recover herself, she took her black lyre
and plucked out an irrelevant fugue. . . .

"Oh! Go on, go on, tell all you know!" Emerald-
Archetypas moaned, clapping his hands like a child. "I give
you my tetrarchic word! You will be given anything you
desire: the University? my Seal? the Snow Cult? Inoculate
us with your Immaculate Conception charm . . . I am so
bored, we are so bored! Am I wrong, gentlemen?"

Actually the company was breathing a murmur of unspoken discomfort; some of the tiaras tottered. Each one
felt ashamed of the others, but the weakness of the human
heart, even among so correct a race . . . (neighbor, you
get my drift).

Having summarily slaughtered a number of theogonies,
theodicies, and formulas of national wisdom (all in the
offhand tone of a chorus master who says: "All right, now,
one measure to get our breath?"), Salomé, a little delirious,
returned to her mystical gabble, her head quickly thrown
back, her Adam's apple leaping frightfully—her whole being soon becoming little more than a spidery fabric, her
soul like a transitory meteor drop.

O tides, lunar oboes, promenades, twilight gardens, ob-
solete breezes of November, hay-gathering, missed callings,
animal gazes, vicissitudes!—Jonquil muslins with funereal
dots, exhausted eyes, crucified smiles, adorable navels, peacock halos, dropped pinks, irrelevant fugues! There was a
rebirth of non-culture granted to all, and their youth was
restored besides, the systematic spirit died in spirals amid
showers with a turmoil that was doubtlessly definitive, for
the earth's own good, thoroughly understood everywhere,

touched by Varuna, the Omniversal Atmosphere, who gave each one the test of readiness.

And Salomé insanely insisted:

"It is pure being, I tell you! O sectarians of the consciousness, why label yourselves as individuals and therefore indivisible? Why not breathe on the embers of some other sciences, in the Sunrise of my Septentrions?

"Do you call it life to inquire stubbornly after the details of self and whatever else there is, with the inevitable question after each step: Ah! well, whom am I deceiving now?

"Get rid of contexts, species, realms! Nothing is lost, nothing is gained, everything belongs to everyone; and everything is already full of submission, no need for confessionals, ready for the Prodigal Son (he won't be allowed to explain, only to relax).

"And these are not just devices for expiations followed by relapses; they are the trampled vintage of the Infinite; not experimental, but inevitable; because . . .

"You are the other sex, and we are the little darlings of childhood (always as unattainable Psyches, at that). So, before the evening is over, let us immerse ourselves in the harmonious mildness of pre-established moralities; let us drift along, exposing our flourishing abdomen to the air; surrounded by prodigality's perfumes and some appropriate hecatombs; toward the beyond where no one will hear his heart's beating or the pulse of his consciousness.

"It all advances as in stanzas, my pulse rate swells like cannon shells, in our lust's furor no caesura, our priestly dress a flattened mess, leave it behind and let us wind along the shore of Nevermore; I must vault up out of me! —(You can see it's not my fault.)"

The little yellow oratress in black dots broke her lyre over her knee and reclaimed her dignity.

The company, intoxicated, kept up appearances by mopping their brows. There passed a silence of ineffable confusion.

The northern princes were afraid to look at their watches,

and even more so to ask, "And when is her bedtime?" It couldn't possibly be later than six o'clock.

The Tetrarch examined the embroidery of his cushions; it was all over; Salomé's hard voice suddenly made him look up.

"And now, Father, I want you to tell them to bring up to my room, in a plate or something, the head of Iokanaan. That's that. I'll go upstairs and wait for it."

"But, my child, you can't mean it! That foreigner . . ."

But all those present in the hall fervently urged the tiara to fulfill Salomé's will on that occasion; and the aviaries ended the discussion by resuming their deafening glitter.

Emerald-Archetypas sneaked a side glance at the northern princes; not the slightest sign of approval or of disapproval. Doubtless it was none of their concern.

Decreed!

The Tetrarch threw his Seal to the Administrator of Death.

The guests were already dispersing, changing the subject, in the direction of the evening bath.

IV

Leaning her elbows on the Observatory parapet, Salomé, fugitive from festivals of state, listened to the familiar sea sound of beautiful nights.

A full outfit of stars on one of those nights! Eternities of braziers in the zenith! Oh, for the means of making an escape, so to speak, on an Exile Express, etc.!

Salomé, the foster sister of the Milky Way, never really gave of herself except to the stars.

According to a color photograph (ectoplasmic) of the stars called yellow, red, white, of sixteenth magnitude, she had had diamonds cut in precise imitation and sprinkled them into her hair and her other charms, even her evening dress (funereal violet muslin with gold dots), in order to

commune *tête-à-tête* on terraces with her twenty-four million stars, just as a sovereign about to receive his peers or
satellites will wear the insignia of their territories.

Salomé had nothing but contempt for vulgar trinkets of
first, second magnitude, etc. Up to the fifteenth magnitude,
no star was her social equal. Besides, her special passion
was nebulae matrices, not fully formed nebulae with already planetiform disks, but the amorphous, the perforated,
the tentacled. And the Orion nebula, that gaseous pasty of
sickly rays, had always remained the favorite son of all the
jewels in her flickering crown.

Ah, dear companions of the astral prairies, Salomé had
ceased to be our little Salomé! And that night was to inau-
gurate a new era of relating and etiquette!

In the beginning, after being exorcised from her dress's
virginity, she felt a new connection with those nebulae
matrices: that she, like them, had been impregnated with
an orbital path.

Later, this drastic sacrifice to the cult (although she was
really lucky to have extricated herself so discreetly) had
made it necessary, if she wanted to dispose of the originator,
that she perform the act (a serious one, in spite of what
they say) called homicide.

Finally, in order to bring about the silence of the tomb
for the Originator, she had had to present a diluted specimen to all those present of the elixir she had been distilling
in the anguish of a hundred nights formed like this one.

Well, after all, that was her life; she was a speciality, a
minor speciality.

Now in her presence, on a cushion, among the fragments
of her ebony lyre, the head of John (in the tradition of the
head of Orpheus) glowed, dipped in phosphorus, rouged,
curled, grimacing at those twenty-four million stars.

When the object was handed over, Salomé had cleared
her scientific conscience by trying out those notorious experiments after decapitation that have caused so much
talk, but as she had anticipated, all the electric shocks produced only a facial rictus of minor consequence.

Now she would try her own theory.

But, think of it, she had stopped lowering her eyes before Orion! She steeled herself and stared at that mystical nebula that had presided over her puberty, for ten full minutes. How many nights, how many future nights, to the winner of the last word . . . !

And those choristers, those firecrackers, below her, in the city!

Finally Salomé consulted her reason, shook herself, and pulled up her shawl, then she unclasped the opal of Orion from her person, a mottled jewel, sprinkled with gray-gold, put it in John's mouth like a Host, kissed the mouth mercifully and hermetically, and sealed the mouth with her own corrosive seal (an instantaneous process).

She waited, a minute passed . . . ! Nothing signaled to her out of the night . . . ! With a "Well?" that sounded rebellious and irritable she picked up that jovial object in her little feminine hands . . .

She wanted the head to fall intact into the sea, without first smashing against the cliff rocks, and so she exerted all her strength. The missile described a convincing phosphorescent parabola. Oh, such a noble parabola! But that unfortunate little astronomer had failed abominably in calculating her distance, and, flying over the parapet, she gave her first human cry, and she fell, winding down from rock to rock, to rattle her last in a picturesque channel bathed by the tides, far from the sound of that festival of state, lacerated to the bone, her sidereal diamonds tearing into her flesh, her skull shattered, paralyzed by vertigo, in short sick unto death, in agony for more than an hour.

Nor did she finally attain the viaticum of seeing the head of John, a phosphorescent star, upon the sea . . .

As for the endless distances of heaven, they remained distant . . .

Thus ended the existence of Salomé, I mean the one from the Esoteric White Islands; she was less a victim of illiterate destiny than she was one who wanted to live in the world of artifice, instead of simply from day to day, as all of us do.

The Dark Lantern

BY JULES RENARD

TRANSLATED BY WILLIAM E. SMITH

JULES RENARD
1864–1910

Jules Renard, born of a middle-class family at Châlons, completed his elementary studies in Nevers and later attended the Lycée Charlemagne in Paris. While holding a modest job he began contributing to various periodicals. In 1888 he married and, two years later, joined the original staff of the *Mercure de France*, in which his criticism and stories occasionally appeared. Although his work never gained a wide audience, it was noticed with favor by the novelist Alphonse Daudet, the poet Jean Richepin, and many of the symbolist writers. Renard's stories of rural life in his native Nivernais region, written in a witty and pungent style, show his remarkable gift for depicting the country and countrymen. His major successes were the novels *L'Écornifleur* [The Sponger] (1892), *Poil de Carotte* (1894), which he adapted for the stage and which was later made into a successful motion picture, and his *Histoires naturelles* (1896), which inspired Maurice Ravel. Three years before his death Renard was elected to the Goncourt Academy.

ABOUT RENARD: Helen Brewster Coulter, *The Prose Work and Technique of Jules Renard*, Washington, D.C., Gibian Bros., 1935 [Columbia University Ph.D. dissertation]; Arthur Knodel, *Jules Renard as Critic*, University of California Press, 1951; in French, Marcel Pollitzer, *Jules Renard*, Paris, La Colombe, 1956.

I. CRAZY TIENNETTE

Christ Punished

As she passes the foot of the cross set outside the village, apparently to protect it from surprises, crazy Tiennette notices that the Christ has fallen down.

No doubt, that night, a heavy wind has weakened the nails and thrown him to the ground.

Tiennette blesses herself and rights the Christ with many precautions, as she would a person still alive. She cannot set him back upon the tall cross; she cannot leave him all alone, at the side of the path.

What is more, he has hurt himself in the fall and some of his fingers are off.

"I must bring the Christ to the carpenter," she says, "and he will mend him."

She hugs him reverently around the middle and bears him off, not running. But he is so heavy he slips through her arms, and she must often hoist him up again with a rough jolt.

And when she does, the nails that pierce the Christ's feet hook to Tiennette's skirt and raise it a little and uncover her legs.

"Will you stop that now, Lord!" she says to him.

And Tiennette, simple, gives the Christ's cheeks a few light slaps, but delicately, with all respect.

The Snowchild

Snow is falling, and through the streets, bareheaded, crazy Tiennette is running like a crazy woman. She plays all alone, catches the white flies as they fall in her violet hands, sticks out her tongue to dissolve the light candy she can just taste, and, with the tip of her finger, draws sticks and rings on the bright sheet.

Farther on she guesses that this little star print has fallen from a bird, this big one from a goose, and this other strange one from the sky maybe.

Then the shoes that made her as tall as the roof thatch and dizzied her so come loose. She topples and stays on the ground a long while, making a cross, being good, until her portrait sinks in.

Then she makes herself a snowchild.

His limbs are twisted and shrunken from the cold. His eyes have been gouged out, his nose has one hole to take the place of two, his mouth has no teeth, and his skull has no hair, because hair and teeth are too hard.

"The poor little thing!" says Tiennette.

She clasps him to her heart and whistles a lullaby, then, once he starts to melt, she changes him quickly and gives him a maternal roll in the fresh snow so the bed that envelops him will be clean.

Tiennette Lost

Tiennette goes out at her pleasure, walks where she will; and her innocence protects her. She walks hurriedly, never strolls, always seems in flight.

This morning, having left home one hour ago by the clock, she stops and says:

"Oh God! I've lost myself!"

She searches, reflects, worried, hunting for herself.

The countryside has vanished under snow. It fills the tree branches; this one seems to have dressed as a traveler waiting for the coach.

But Tiennette spies her own tracks, still fresh, in the snow, and the idea comes to her: she will follow and find herself again.

Sometimes she softly sets her feet inside the deep prints, and if other tracks cross hers she stoops and sets them right. Sometimes she runs, losing her breath, as if there were wolves at her back.

When she reaches the village and recognizes her house among the crouching shapes:

"I probably went back home," she thinks.

She stops hurrying. She takes a breath, drops her anxiety from her shoulders like a shawl grown too heavy, pushes open the door, and says calmly:

"I knew it; there I am!"

The Stick

Tiennette rolls a stick between her fingers, scratches it with her nails, bites it with the tips of her teeth, strips its bark off. She moves on down the road and says to the trees:

"You must have heard that this is my wedding day. I'm serious, I mean it. He loves me, I expect him soon."

She gives them smiles left and right, already rehearsing the ceremony.

But a voice from among the trees gives her an order:

"Take off your cap, Tiennette."

She pauses, looks at the trees, hears breathing among them, and asks, trembling:

"Is it really you this time?"

"Yes, Tiennette; take off your cap."

Reassured, she throws away her cap, just as she threw away the leaves she pulled from her stick.

"Take off your jacket, Tiennette."

She obeys, throws away her jacket just as she threw away the thin branches she pulled from her stick.

"Take off your skirt, Tiennette."

She reaches a hand around to undo the knotted strings, but she sees the stick in her other hand, naked, its bark pulled off, and, abruptly waking up, Tiennette shame-

facedly picks up her cap and jacket and runs away, far
from the libertine who wanted to trap her again and who
stays there, behind the trees, laughing.

II. TIENNOT

The Cherry Man

Tiennot, walking through the market place, sees baskets
filled with cherries so fat and red they cannot be real. He
says to the owner:

"Let me eat as many cherries as I want, and we'll settle
for ten pennies."

The owner agrees, sure of a profit, because cherries aren't
scarce this year and he could afford to give away a bar-
rowful for ten pennies, at the price they bring in.

Tiennot lies down on his right side among the baskets.

Not hurrying, he chooses the finest cherries and eats them
one by one.

Slowly he empties the first basket, then the second.

The owner smiles. Now and then some market people
come to watch. The druggist shows up, then the café
owner. Everyone gives Tiennot encouragement.

He carefully keeps from answering. Without moving he
methodically opens and closes his mouth. At times, when
a passing cherry is more juicy than the others, he seems
to be asleep.

The owner, already uneasy, thinks:

"I may not lose anything on this, but I won't gain much
by it."

And the ten-cent piece clenched between his teeth
shrinks in value.

Suddenly reviving, he says:

"Well?"

Tiennot stirs, tries to lift himself, but the effort seems
painful. In the end he only changes position, rolls over on
his left side, gropes for another basket.

But he has worked up an appetite, and now he begins to devour the cherry stones as well.

The Spring and the Sugar

Tiennot is quenching his thirst with spring water. His hand serves as a cup at first; later he prefers a straight drink and he lies down over the spring, wetting his chin and nose. When he stops to breathe, he looks around at the animals and the water's white plume as it rises.

"It tastes good," he says, "but I know it would taste better with sugar."

He runs to the village, buys a piece of sugar, and steals back at nightfall to drop it into the spring.

"Tomorrow morning," he says just for himself, "I will have a feast."

All the people are still asleep when Tiennot leaves his bed and hurries to the spring.

Before he tastes the water, he says, sucking with his lips: "Oh! What a fine taste!"

He bends down, tastes, and says, letting his lips relax: "Yes. No. There's no more sugar in it than there was yesterday."

He is baffled, he fixes his eyes on his crestfallen reflection.

"My God! What a fool I am!" he shouts. "A child would know: water runs, and my melted sugar ran along with it. It left the spring behind and ran away across the field; it can't be going fast, I can catch it."

And Tiennot departs, walking beside the brook. He carefully counts out twenty paces and then stops. He takes a mouthful of water and savors it. But then he tosses his head, suddenly, and departs again in pursuit of his sugar.

The Fist of God

In a short smock and a shaggy top hat Tiennot is coming home from the fair. All he had to sell is sold, his pig, his cheese, and his two old hens, but the hens were sold for pullets, after he gave them wine and made them drunk.

They were full of life, their eyes glittered, they had fever in their wings and claws, they deceived a trusting woman who may be weighing them again, surprised and angry to see them dangling, cold, broken. Tiennot smiles; he feels no remorse; he has put it over many times. He zigzags, his legs give, he wanders all over the road, for while the hens were pecking up drops of wine out of a bowl, he was drinking the rest of the bottle.

Then a cyclist shouts, a bell sounds, a horn trumpets right behind him. He hears nothing. He goes back and forth across the road, waving his arms, gesticulating, feeling compassion, as if he were selling his hens a second time.

And suddenly a fist blow crushes down his shaggy top hat.

Tiennot stops, bends double, his head a prisoner, surrounded by night down to the ears. He tries to lift his hat off; he tries for some time; but his head is caught, the circle around his skull hurts him. Tiennot struggles, heaves, bellows, finally frees himself.

He looks around: nobody on the road, nobody ahead, nobody behind. He looks over the hedge, first left, then right.

He sees nothing.

And Tiennot, who got his hens drunk and sold them, mechanically makes the sign of the cross.

The Fine Corn

On the dry road, under the burning sun, Tiennot and Baptiste are driving back home in their donkey cart. They pass near a field of ripe corn, and Baptiste, who knows all about corn, says:

"What fine corn!"

Tiennot is driving and says nothing; he bows his back. Baptiste bows his own in imitation, and their necks, exposed, tough, slowly broil, shine like copper pans.

Like a machine, Tiennot pulls or shakes the reins. Sometimes he raises a stick and aims a lively blow at the donkey's buttocks, as if they were a bespattered pair of breeches.

The donkey never changes pace; he bends his head, probably to watch the play of his hoofs as they move in and out, one after another, never mistaking. The cart follows along after him as best it can; a roundish shadow drags after; Tiennot and Baptiste bend down still farther.

They pass through villages that look deserted because of the heat. They meet a few scarce people who give only a single sign. They close their eyes against the road's white glare.

And yet they arrive that night, very late. In the end one always arrives. The donkey halts before the door, perks its ears. Baptiste and Tiennot, sluggish, stir themselves, and Tiennot answers Baptiste:

"Yes, it is fine corn."

A CATALOG OF SELECTED
DOVER BOOKS
IN ALL FIELDS OF INTEREST

A CATALOG OF SELECTED DOVER
BOOKS IN ALL FIELDS OF INTEREST

DRAWINGS OF REMBRANDT, edited by Seymour Slive. Updated Lippmann, Hofstede de Groot edition, with definitive scholarly apparatus. All portraits, biblical sketches, landscapes, nudes. Oriental figures, classical studies, together with selection of work by followers. 550 illustrations. Total of 630pp. 9⅛ × 12¼.
21485-0, 21486-9 Pa., Two-vol. set $25.00

GHOST AND HORROR STORIES OF AMBROSE BIERCE, Ambrose Bierce. 24 tales vividly imagined, strangely prophetic, and decades ahead of their time in technical skill: "The Damned Thing," "An Inhabitant of Carcosa," "The Eyes of the Panther," "Moxon's Master," and 20 more. 199pp. 5⅜ × 8½. 20767-6 Pa. $3.95

ETHICAL WRITINGS OF MAIMONIDES, Maimonides. Most significant ethical works of great medieval sage, newly translated for utmost precision, readability. Laws Concerning Character Traits, Eight Chapters, more. 192pp. 5⅜ × 8½.
24522-5 Pa. $4.50

THE EXPLORATION OF THE COLORADO RIVER AND ITS CANYONS, J. W. Powell. Full text of Powell's 1,000-mile expedition down the fabled Colorado in 1869. Superb account of terrain, geology, vegetation, Indians, famine, mutiny, treacherous rapids, mighty canyons, during exploration of last unknown part of continental U.S. 400pp. 5⅜ × 8½. 20094-9 Pa. $6.95

HISTORY OF PHILOSOPHY, Julián Marías. Clearest one-volume history on the market. Every major philosopher and dozens of others, to Existentialism and later. 505pp. 5⅜ × 8½. 21739-6 Pa. $8.50

ALL ABOUT LIGHTNING, Martin A. Uman. Highly readable non-technical survey of nature and causes of lightning, thunderstorms, ball lightning, St. Elmo's Fire, much more. Illustrated. 192pp. 5⅜ × 8½. 25237-X Pa. $5.95

SAILING ALONE AROUND THE WORLD, Captain Joshua Slocum. First man to sail around the world, alone, in small boat. One of great feats of seamanship told in delightful manner. 67 illustrations. 294pp. 5⅜ × 8½. 20326-3 Pa. $4.95

LETTERS AND NOTES ON THE MANNERS, CUSTOMS AND CONDI-TIONS OF THE NORTH AMERICAN INDIANS, George Catlin. Classic account of life among Plains Indians: ceremonies, hunt, warfare, etc. 312 plates. 572pp. of text. 6⅛ × 9¼. 22118-0, 22119-9 Pa. Two-vol. set $15.90

ALASKA: The Harriman Expedition, 1899, John Burroughs, John Muir, et al. Informative, engrossing accounts of two-month, 9,000-mile expedition. Native peoples, wildlife, forests, geography, salmon industry, glaciers, more. Profusely illustrated. 240 black-and-white line drawings. 124 black-and-white photographs. 3 maps. Index. 576pp. 5⅜ × 8½. 25109-8 Pa. $11.95

THE BOOK OF BEASTS: Being a Translation from a Latin Bestiary of the Twelfth Century, T. H. White. Wonderful catalog real and fanciful beasts: manticore, griffin, phoenix, amphivius, jaculus, many more. White's witty erudite commentary on scientific, historical aspects. Fascinating glimpse of medieval mind. Illustrated. 296pp. 5⅜ × 8¼. (Available in U.S. only) 24609-4 Pa. $5.95

FRANK LLOYD WRIGHT: ARCHITECTURE AND NATURE With 160 Illustrations, Donald Hoffmann. Profusely illustrated study of influence of nature—especially prairie—on Wright's designs for Fallingwater, Robie House, Guggenheim Museum, other masterpieces. 96pp. 9¼ × 10¾. 25098-9 Pa. $7.95

FRANK LLOYD WRIGHT'S FALLINGWATER, Donald Hoffmann. Wright's famous waterfall house: planning and construction of organic idea. History of site, owners, Wright's personal involvement. Photographs of various stages of building. Preface by Edgar Kaufmann, Jr. 100 illustrations. 112pp. 9¼ × 10. 23671-4 Pa. $7.95

YEARS WITH FRANK LLOYD WRIGHT: Apprentice to Genius, Edgar Tafel. Insightful memoir by a former apprentice presents a revealing portrait of Wright the man, the inspired teacher, the greatest American architect. 372 black-and-white illustrations. Preface. Index. vi + 228pp. 8¼ × 11. 24801-1 Pa. $9.95

THE STORY OF KING ARTHUR AND HIS KNIGHTS, Howard Pyle. Enchanting version of King Arthur fable has delighted generations with imaginative narratives of exciting adventures and unforgettable illustrations by the author. 41 illustrations. xviii + 313pp. 6⅛ × 9¼. 21445-1 Pa. $5.95

THE GODS OF THE EGYPTIANS, E. A. Wallis Budge. Thorough coverage of numerous gods of ancient Egypt by foremost Egyptologist. Information on evolution of cults, rites and gods; the cult of Osiris; the Book of the Dead and its rites; the sacred animals and birds; Heaven and Hell; and more. 956pp. 6⅛ × 9¼. 22055-9, 22056-7 Pa., Two-vol. set $21.90

A THEOLOGICO-POLITICAL TREATISE, Benedict Spinoza. Also contains unfinished *Political Treatise*. Great classic on religious liberty, theory of government on common consent. R. Elwes translation. Total of 421pp. 5⅜ × 8½. 20249-6 Pa. $6.95

INCIDENTS OF TRAVEL IN CENTRAL AMERICA, CHIAPAS, AND YUCATAN, John L. Stephens. Almost single-handed discovery of Maya culture; exploration of ruined cities, monuments, temples; customs of Indians. 115 drawings. 892pp. 5⅜ × 8½. 22404-X, 22405-8 Pa., Two-vol. set $15.90

LOS CAPRICHOS, Francisco Goya. 80 plates of wild, grotesque monsters and caricatures. Prado manuscript included. 183pp. 6⅝ × 9⅝. 22384-1 Pa. $4.95

AUTOBIOGRAPHY: The Story of My Experiments with Truth, Mohandas K. Gandhi. Not hagiography, but Gandhi in his own words. Boyhood, legal studies, purification, the growth of the Satyagraha (nonviolent protest) movement. Critical, inspiring work of the man who freed India. 480pp. 5⅜ × 8½. (Available in U.S. only) 24593-4 Pa. $6.95

ILLUSTRATED DICTIONARY OF HISTORIC ARCHITECTURE, edited by Cyril M. Harris. Extraordinary compendium of clear, concise definitions for over 5,000 important architectural terms complemented by over 2,000 line drawings. Covers full spectrum of architecture from ancient ruins to 20th-century Modernism. Preface. 592pp. 7½ × 9⅜. 24444-X Pa. $14.95

THE NIGHT BEFORE CHRISTMAS, Clement Moore. Full text, and woodcuts from original 1848 book. Also critical, historical material. 19 illustrations. 40pp. 4⅝ × 6. 22797-9 Pa. $2.50

THE LESSON OF JAPANESE ARCHITECTURE: 165 Photographs, Jiro Harada. Memorable gallery of 165 photographs taken in the 1930's of exquisite Japanese homes of the well-to-do and historic buildings. 13 line diagrams. 192pp. 8⅜ × 11¼. 24778-3 Pa. $8.95

THE AUTOBIOGRAPHY OF CHARLES DARWIN AND SELECTED LETTERS, edited by Francis Darwin. The fascinating life of eccentric genius composed of an intimate memoir by Darwin (intended for his children); commentary by his son, Francis; hundreds of fragments from notebooks, journals, papers; and letters to and from Lyell, Hooker, Huxley, Wallace and Henslow. xi + 365pp. 5⅜ × 8. 20479-0 Pa. $5.95

WONDERS OF THE SKY: Observing Rainbows, Comets, Eclipses, the Stars and Other Phenomena, Fred Schaaf. Charming, easy-to-read poetic guide to all manner of celestial events visible to the naked eye. Mock suns, glories, Belt of Venus, more. Illustrated. 299pp. 5¼ × 8¼. 24402-4 Pa. $7.95

BURNHAM'S CELESTIAL HANDBOOK, Robert Burnham, Jr. Thorough guide to the stars beyond our solar system. Exhaustive treatment. Alphabetical by constellation: Andromeda to Cetus in Vol. 1; Chamaeleon to Orion in Vol. 2; and Pavo to Vulpecula in Vol. 3. Hundreds of illustrations. Index in Vol. 3. 2,000pp. 6⅛ × 9¼. 23567-X, 23568-8, 23673-0 Pa., Three-vol. set $37.85

STAR NAMES: Their Lore and Meaning, Richard Hinckley Allen. Fascinating history of names various cultures have given to constellations and literary and folkloristic uses that have been made of stars. Indexes to subjects. Arabic and Greek names. Biblical references. Bibliography. 563pp. 5⅜ × 8½. 21079-0 Pa. $7.95

THIRTY YEARS THAT SHOOK PHYSICS: The Story of Quantum Theory, George Gamow. Lucid, accessible introduction to influential theory of energy and matter. Careful explanations of Dirac's anti-particles, Bohr's model of the atom, much more. 12 plates. Numerous drawings. 240pp. 5⅜ × 8½. 24895-X Pa. $4.95

CHINESE DOMESTIC FURNITURE IN PHOTOGRAPHS AND MEASURED DRAWINGS, Gustav Ecke. A rare volume, now affordably priced for antique collectors, furniture buffs and art historians. Detailed review of styles ranging from early Shang to late Ming. Unabridged republication. 161 black-and-white drawings, photos. Total of 224pp. 8⅜ × 11¼. (Available in U.S. only) 25171-3 Pa. $12.95

VINCENT VAN GOGH: A Biography, Julius Meier-Graefe. Dynamic, penetrating study of artist's life, relationship with brother, Theo, painting techniques, travels, more. Readable, engrossing. 160pp. 5⅜ × 8½. (Available in U.S. only) 25253-1 Pa. $3.95

HOW TO WRITE, Gertrude Stein. Gertrude Stein claimed anyone could understand her unconventional writing—here are clues to help. Fascinating improvisations, language experiments, explanations illuminate Stein's craft and the art of writing. Total of 414pp. 4⅝ × 6⅜.   23144-5 Pa. $5.95

ADVENTURES AT SEA IN THE GREAT AGE OF SAIL: Five Firsthand Narratives, edited by Elliot Snow. Rare true accounts of exploration, whaling, shipwreck, fierce natives, trade, shipboard life, more. 33 illustrations. Introduction. 353pp. 5⅜ × 8½.   25177-2 Pa. $7.95

THE HERBAL OR GENERAL HISTORY OF PLANTS, John Gerard. Classic descriptions of about 2,850 plants—with over 2,700 illustrations—includes Latin and English names, physical descriptions, varieties, time and place of growth, more. 2,706 illustrations. xlv + 1,678pp. 8½ × 12¼.   23147-X Cloth. $75.00

DOROTHY AND THE WIZARD IN OZ, L. Frank Baum. Dorothy and the Wizard visit the center of the Earth, where people are vegetables, glass houses grow and Oz characters reappear. Classic sequel to *Wizard of Oz*. 256pp. 5⅜ × 8.
24714-7 Pa. $4.95

SONGS OF EXPERIENCE: Facsimile Reproduction with 26 Plates in Full Color, William Blake. This facsimile of Blake's original "Illuminated Book" reproduces 26 full-color plates from a rare 1826 edition. Includes "The Tyger," "London," "Holy Thursday," and other immortal poems. 26 color plates. Printed text of poems. 48pp. 5¼ × 7.   24636-1 Pa. $3.50

SONGS OF INNOCENCE, William Blake. The first and most popular of Blake's famous "Illuminated Books," in a facsimile edition reproducing all 31 brightly colored plates. Additional printed text of each poem. 64pp. 5¼ × 7.
22764-2 Pa. $3.50

PRECIOUS STONES, Max Bauer. Classic, thorough study of diamonds, rubies, emeralds, garnets, etc.: physical character, occurrence, properties, use, similar topics. 20 plates, 8 in color. 94 figures. 659pp. 6⅛ × 9¼.
21910-0, 21911-9 Pa., Two-vol. set $15.90

ENCYCLOPEDIA OF VICTORIAN NEEDLEWORK, S. F. A. Caulfeild and Blanche Saward. Full, precise descriptions of stitches, techniques for dozens of needlecrafts—most exhaustive reference of its kind. Over 800 figures. Total of 679pp. 8⅛ × 11. Two volumes.   Vol. 1 22800-2 Pa. $11.95
Vol. 2 22801-0 Pa. $11.95

THE MARVELOUS LAND OF OZ, L. Frank Baum. Second Oz book, the Scarecrow and Tin Woodman are back with hero named Tip, Oz magic. 136 illustrations. 287pp. 5⅜ × 8½.   20692-0 Pa. $5.95

WILD FOWL DECOYS, Joel Barber. Basic book on the subject, by foremost authority and collector. Reveals history of decoy making and rigging, place in American culture, different kinds of decoys, how to make them, and how to use them. 140 plates. 156pp. 7⅞ × 10¾.   20011-6 Pa. $8.95

HISTORY OF LACE, Mrs. Bury Palliser. Definitive, profusely illustrated chronicle of lace from earliest times to late 19th century. Laces of Italy, Greece, England, France, Belgium, etc. Landmark of needlework scholarship. 266 illustrations. 672pp. 6⅛ × 9¼.   24742-2 Pa. $14.95

ILLUSTRATED GUIDE TO SHAKER FURNITURE, Robert Meader. All furniture and appurtenances, with much on unknown local styles. 235 photos. 146pp. 9 × 12. 22819-3 Pa. $7.95

WHALE SHIPS AND WHALING: A Pictorial Survey, George Francis Dow. Over 200 vintage engravings, drawings, photographs of barks, brigs, cutters, other vessels. Also harpoons, lances, whaling guns, many other artifacts. Comprehensive text by foremost authority. 207 black-and-white illustrations. 288pp. 6 × 9. 24808-9 Pa. $8.95

THE BERTRAMS, Anthony Trollope. Powerful portrayal of blind self-will and thwarted ambition includes one of Trollope's most heartrending love stories. 497pp. 5⅜ × 8½. 25119-5 Pa. $8.95

ADVENTURES WITH A HAND LENS, Richard Headstrom. Clearly written guide to observing and studying flowers and grasses, fish scales, moth and insect wings, egg cases, buds, feathers, seeds, leaf scars, moss, molds, ferns, common crystals, etc.—all with an ordinary, inexpensive magnifying glass. 209 exact line drawings aid in your discoveries. 220pp. 5⅜ × 8½. 23330-8 Pa. $4.50

RODIN ON ART AND ARTISTS, Auguste Rodin. Great sculptor's candid, wide-ranging comments on meaning of art; great artists; relation of sculpture to poetry, painting, music; philosophy of life, more. 76 superb black-and-white illustrations of Rodin's sculpture, drawings and prints. 119pp. 8⅜ × 11¼. 24487-3 Pa. $6.95

FIFTY CLASSIC FRENCH FILMS, 1912–1982: A Pictorial Record, Anthony Slide. Memorable stills from Grand Illusion, Beauty and the Beast, Hiroshima, Mon Amour, many more. Credits, plot synopses, reviews, etc. 160pp. 8¼ × 11. 25256-6 Pa. $11.95

THE PRINCIPLES OF PSYCHOLOGY, William James. Famous long course complete, unabridged. Stream of thought, time perception, memory, experimental methods; great work decades ahead of its time. 94 figures. 1,391pp. 5⅜ × 8½. 20381-6, 20382-4 Pa., Two-vol. set $19.90

BODIES IN A BOOKSHOP, R. T. Campbell. Challenging mystery of blackmail and murder with ingenious plot and superbly drawn characters. In the best tradition of British suspense fiction. 192pp. 5⅜ × 8½. 24720-1 Pa. $3.95

CALLAS: PORTRAIT OF A PRIMA DONNA, George Jellinek. Renowned commentator on the musical scene chronicles incredible career and life of the most controversial, fascinating, influential operatic personality of our time. 64 black-and-white photographs. 416pp. 5⅜ × 8¼. 25047-4 Pa. $7.95

GEOMETRY, RELATIVITY AND THE FOURTH DIMENSION, Rudolph Rucker. Exposition of fourth dimension, concepts of relativity as Flatland characters continue adventures. Popular, easily followed yet accurate, profound. 141 illustrations. 133pp. 5⅜ × 8½. 23400-2 Pa. $3.50

HOUSEHOLD STORIES BY THE BROTHERS GRIMM, with pictures by Walter Crane. 53 classic stories—Rumpelstiltskin, Rapunzel, Hansel and Gretel, the Fisherman and his Wife, Snow White, Tom Thumb, Sleeping Beauty, Cinderella, and so much more—lavishly illustrated with original 19th century drawings. 114 illustrations. x + 269pp. 5⅜ × 8½. 21080-4 Pa. $4.50

SUNDIALS, Albert Waugh. Far and away the best, most thorough coverage of ideas, mathematics concerned, types, construction, adjusting anywhere. Over 100 illustrations. 230pp. 5⅜ × 8½. 22947-5 Pa. $4.50

PICTURE HISTORY OF THE NORMANDIE: With 190 Illustrations, Frank O. Braynard. Full story of legendary French ocean liner: Art Deco interiors, design innovations, furnishings, celebrities, maiden voyage, tragic fire, much more. Extensive text. 144pp. 8⅜ × 11¾. 25257-4 Pa. $9.95

THE FIRST AMERICAN COOKBOOK: A Facsimile of "American Cookery," 1796, Amelia Simmons. Facsimile of the first American-written cookbook published in the United States contains authentic recipes for colonial favorites—pumpkin pudding, winter squash pudding, spruce beer, Indian slapjacks, and more. Introductory Essay and Glossary of colonial cooking terms. 80pp. 5⅜ × 8½. 24710-4 Pa. $3.50

101 PUZZLES IN THOUGHT AND LOGIC, C. R. Wylie, Jr. Solve murders and robberies, find out which fishermen are liars, how a blind man could possibly identify a color—purely by your own reasoning! 107pp. 5⅜ × 8½. 20367-0 Pa. $2.50

THE BOOK OF WORLD-FAMOUS MUSIC—CLASSICAL, POPULAR AND FOLK, James J. Fuld. Revised and enlarged republication of landmark work in musico-bibliography. Full information about nearly 1,000 songs and compositions including first lines of music and lyrics. New supplement. Index. 800pp. 5⅜ × 8¼. 24857-7 Pa. $14.95

ANTHROPOLOGY AND MODERN LIFE, Franz Boas. Great anthropologist's classic treatise on race and culture. Introduction by Ruth Bunzel. Only inexpensive paperback edition. 255pp. 5⅜ × 8½. 25245-0 Pa. $5.95

THE TALE OF PETER RABBIT, Beatrix Potter. The inimitable Peter's terrifying adventure in Mr. McGregor's garden, with all 27 wonderful, full-color Potter illustrations. 55pp. 4¼ × 5½. (Available in U.S. only) 22827-4 Pa. $1.75

THREE PROPHETIC SCIENCE FICTION NOVELS, H. G. Wells. *When the Sleeper Wakes, A Story of the Days to Come* and *The Time Machine* (full version). 335pp. 5⅜ × 8½. (Available in U.S. only) 20605-X Pa. $5.95

APICIUS COOKERY AND DINING IN IMPERIAL ROME, edited and translated by Joseph Dommers Vehling. Oldest known cookbook in existence offers readers a clear picture of what foods Romans ate, how they prepared them, etc. 49 illustrations. 301pp. 6⅛ × 9¼. 23563-7 Pa. $6.50

SHAKESPEARE LEXICON AND QUOTATION DICTIONARY, Alexander Schmidt. Full definitions, locations, shades of meaning of every word in plays and poems. More than 50,000 exact quotations. 1,485pp. 6½ × 9¼. 22726-X, 22727-8 Pa., Two-vol. set $27.90

THE WORLD'S GREAT SPEECHES, edited by Lewis Copeland and Lawrence W. Lamm. Vast collection of 278 speeches from Greeks to 1970. Powerful and effective models; unique look at history. 842pp. 5⅜ × 8½. 20468-5 Pa. $11.95

THE BLUE FAIRY BOOK, Andrew Lang. The first, most famous collection, with many familiar tales: Little Red Riding Hood, Aladdin and the Wonderful Lamp, Puss in Boots, Sleeping Beauty, Hansel and Gretel, Rumpelstiltskin; 37 in all. 138 illustrations. 390pp. 5⅜ × 8½. 21437-0 Pa. $5.95

THE STORY OF THE CHAMPIONS OF THE ROUND TABLE, Howard Pyle. Sir Launcelot, Sir Tristram and Sir Percival in spirited adventures of love and triumph retold in Pyle's inimitable style. 50 drawings, 31 full-page. xviii + 329pp. 6½ × 9¼. 21883-X Pa. $6.95

AUDUBON AND HIS JOURNALS, Maria Audubon. Unmatched two-volume portrait of the great artist, naturalist and author contains his journals, an excellent biography by his granddaughter, expert annotations by the noted ornithologist, Dr. Elliott Coues, and 37 superb illustrations. Total of 1,200pp. 5⅜ × 8.

Vol. I 25143-8 Pa. $8.95
Vol. II 25144-6 Pa. $8.95

GREAT DINOSAUR HUNTERS AND THEIR DISCOVERIES, Edwin H. Colbert. Fascinating, lavishly illustrated chronicle of dinosaur research, 1820's to 1960. Achievements of Cope, Marsh, Brown, Buckland, Mantell, Huxley, many others. 384pp. 5¼ × 8¼. 24701-5 Pa. $6.95

THE TASTEMAKERS, Russell Lynes. Informal, illustrated social history of American taste 1850's-1950's. First popularized categories Highbrow, Lowbrow, Middlebrow. 129 illustrations. New (1979) afterword. 384pp. 6 × 9.

23993-4 Pa. $6.95

DOUBLE CROSS PURPOSES, Ronald A. Knox. A treasure hunt in the Scottish Highlands, an old map, unidentified corpse, surprise discoveries keep reader guessing in this cleverly intricate tale of financial skullduggery. 2 black-and-white maps. 320pp. 5⅜ × 8½. (Available in U.S. only) 25032-6 Pa. $5.95

AUTHENTIC VICTORIAN DECORATION AND ORNAMENTATION IN FULL COLOR: 46 Plates from "Studies in Design," Christopher Dresser. Superb full-color lithographs reproduced from rare original portfolio of a major Victorian designer. 48pp. 9¼ × 12¼. 25083-0 Pa. $7.95

PRIMITIVE ART, Franz Boas. Remains the best text ever prepared on subject, thoroughly discussing Indian, African, Asian, Australian, and, especially, Northern American primitive art. Over 950 illustrations show ceramics, masks, totem poles, weapons, textiles, paintings, much more. 376pp. 5⅜ × 8. 20025-6 Pa. $6.95

SIDELIGHTS ON RELATIVITY, Albert Einstein. Unabridged republication of two lectures delivered by the great physicist in 1920-21. *Ether and Relativity* and *Geometry and Experience*. Elegant ideas in non-mathematical form, accessible to intelligent layman. vi + 56pp. 5⅜ × 8½. 24511-X Pa. $2.95

THE WIT AND HUMOR OF OSCAR WILDE, edited by Alvin Redman. More than 1,000 ripostes, paradoxes, wisecracks: Work is the curse of the drinking classes, I can resist everything except temptation, etc. 258pp. 5⅜ × 8½. 20602-5 Pa. $4.50

ADVENTURES WITH A MICROSCOPE, Richard Headstrom. 59 adventures with clothing fibers, protozoa, ferns and lichens, roots and leaves, much more. 142 illustrations. 232pp. 5⅜ × 8½. 23471-1 Pa. $3.95

PLANTS OF THE BIBLE, Harold N. Moldenke and Alma L. Moldenke. Standard reference to all 230 plants mentioned in Scriptures. Latin name, biblical reference, uses, modern identity, much more. Unsurpassed encyclopedic resource for scholars, botanists, nature lovers, students of Bible. Bibliography. Indexes. 123 black-and-white illustrations. 384pp. 6 × 9. 25069-5 Pa. $8.95

FAMOUS AMERICAN WOMEN: A Biographical Dictionary from Colonial Times to the Present, Robert McHenry, ed. From Pocahontas to Rosa Parks, 1,035 distinguished American women documented in separate biographical entries. Accurate, up-to-date data, numerous categories, spans 400 years. Indices. 493pp. 6½ × 9¼. 24523-3 Pa. $9.95

THE FABULOUS INTERIORS OF THE GREAT OCEAN LINERS IN HISTORIC PHOTOGRAPHS, William H. Miller, Jr. Some 200 superb photographs capture exquisite interiors of world's great "floating palaces"—1890's to 1980's: *Titanic, Ile de France, Queen Elizabeth, United States, Europa,* more. Approx. 200 black-and-white photographs. Captions. Text. Introduction. 160pp. 8⅜ × 11¼. 24756-2 Pa. $9.95

THE GREAT LUXURY LINERS, 1927–1954: A Photographic Record, William H. Miller, Jr. Nostalgic tribute to heyday of ocean liners. 186 photos of Ile de France, Normandie, Leviathan, Queen Elizabeth, United States, many others. Interior and exterior views. Introduction. Captions. 160pp. 9 × 12. 24056-8 Pa. $9.95

A NATURAL HISTORY OF THE DUCKS, John Charles Phillips. Great landmark of ornithology offers complete detailed coverage of nearly 200 species and subspecies of ducks: gadwall, sheldrake, merganser, pintail, many more. 74 full-color plates, 102 black-and-white. Bibliography. Total of 1,920pp. 8⅜ × 11¼. 25141-1, 25142-X Cloth. Two-vol. set $100.00

THE SEAWEED HANDBOOK: An Illustrated Guide to Seaweeds from North Carolina to Canada, Thomas F. Lee. Concise reference covers 78 species. Scientific and common names, habitat, distribution, more. Finding keys for easy identification. 224pp. 5⅜ × 8½. 25215-9 Pa. $5.95

THE TEN BOOKS OF ARCHITECTURE: The 1755 Leoni Edition, Leon Battista Alberti. Rare classic helped introduce the glories of ancient architecture to the Renaissance. 68 black-and-white plates. 336pp. 8⅜ × 11¼. 25239-6 Pa $14.95

MISS MACKENZIE, Anthony Trollope. Minor masterpieces by Victorian master unmasks many truths about life in 19th-century England. First inexpensive edition in years. 392pp. 5⅜ × 8½. 25201-9 Pa. $7.95

THE RIME OF THE ANCIENT MARINER, Gustave Doré, Samuel Taylor Coleridge. Dramatic engravings considered by many to be his greatest work. The terrifying space of the open sea, the storms and whirlpools of an unknown ocean, the ice of Antarctica, more—all rendered in a powerful, chilling manner. Full text. 38 plates. 77pp. 9¼ × 12. 22305-1 Pa. $4.95

THE EXPEDITIONS OF ZEBULON MONTGOMERY PIKE, Zebulon Montgomery Pike. Fascinating first-hand accounts (1805-6) of exploration of Mississippi River, Indian wars, capture by Spanish dragoons, much more. 1,088pp. 5⅜ × 8½. 25254-X, 25255-8 Pa. Two-vol. set $23.90

A CONCISE HISTORY OF PHOTOGRAPHY: Third Revised Edition, Helmut Gernsheim. Best one-volume history—camera obscura, photochemistry, daguerreotypes, evolution of cameras, film, more. Also artistic aspects—landscape, portraits, fine art, etc. 281 black-and-white photographs. 26 in color. 176pp. 8⅜ × 11¼. 25128-4 Pa. $12.95

THE DORÉ BIBLE ILLUSTRATIONS, Gustave Doré. 241 detailed plates from the Bible: the Creation scenes, Adam and Eve, Flood, Babylon, battle sequences, life of Jesus, etc. Each plate is accompanied by the verses from the King James version of the Bible. 241pp. 9 × 12. 23004-X Pa. $8.95

HUGGER-MUGGER IN THE LOUVRE, Elliot Paul. Second Homer Evans mystery-comedy. Theft at the Louvre involves sleuth in hilarious, madcap caper. "A knockout."—Books. 336pp. 5⅜ × 8½. 25185-3 Pa. $5.95

FLATLAND, E. A. Abbott. Intriguing and enormously popular science-fiction classic explores the complexities of trying to survive as a two-dimensional being in a three-dimensional world. Amusingly illustrated by the author. 16 illustrations. 103pp. 5⅜ × 8½. 20001-9 Pa. $2.25

THE HISTORY OF THE LEWIS AND CLARK EXPEDITION, Meriwether Lewis and William Clark, edited by Elliott Coues. Classic edition of Lewis and Clark's day-by-day journals that later became the basis for U.S. claims to Oregon and the West. Accurate and invaluable geographical, botanical, biological, meteorological and anthropological material. Total of 1,508pp. 5⅜ × 8½.
21268-8, 21269-6, 21270-X Pa. Three-vol. set $25.50

LANGUAGE, TRUTH AND LOGIC, Alfred J. Ayer. Famous, clear introduction to Vienna, Cambridge schools of Logical Positivism. Role of philosophy, elimination of metaphysics, nature of analysis, etc. 160pp. 5⅜ × 8½. (Available in U.S. and Canada only) 20010-8 Pa. $2.95

MATHEMATICS FOR THE NONMATHEMATICIAN, Morris Kline. Detailed, college-level treatment of mathematics in cultural and historical context, with numerous exercises. For liberal arts students. Preface. Recommended Reading Lists. Tables. Index. Numerous black-and-white figures. xvi + 641pp. 5⅜ × 8½.
24823-2 Pa. $11.95

28 SCIENCE FICTION STORIES, H. G. Wells. Novels, *Star Begotten* and *Men Like Gods,* plus 26 short stories: "Empire of the Ants," "A Story of the Stone Age," "The Stolen Bacillus," "In the Abyss," etc. 915pp. 5⅜ × 8½. (Available in U.S. only)
20265-8 Cloth. $10.95

HANDBOOK OF PICTORIAL SYMBOLS, Rudolph Modley. 3,250 signs and symbols, many systems in full; official or heavy commercial use. Arranged by subject. Most in Pictorial Archive series. 143pp. 8⅛ × 11. 23357-X Pa. $5.95

INCIDENTS OF TRAVEL IN YUCATAN, John L. Stephens. Classic (1843) exploration of jungles of Yucatan, looking for evidences of Maya civilization. Travel adventures, Mexican and Indian culture, etc. Total of 669pp. 5⅜ × 8½.
20926-1, 20927-X Pa., Two-vol. set $9.90

DEGAS: An Intimate Portrait, Ambroise Vollard. Charming, anecdotal memoir by famous art dealer of one of the greatest 19th-century French painters. 14 black-and-white illustrations. Introduction by Harold L. Van Doren. 96pp. 5⅜ × 8½.
25131-4 Pa. $3.95

PERSONAL NARRATIVE OF A PILGRIMAGE TO ALMANDINAH AND MECCAH, Richard Burton. Great travel classic by remarkably colorful personality. Burton, disguised as a Moroccan, visited sacred shrines of Islam, narrowly escaping death. 47 illustrations. 959pp. 5⅜ × 8½.   21217-3, 21218-1 Pa., Two-vol. set $17.90

PHRASE AND WORD ORIGINS, A. H. Holt. Entertaining, reliable, modern study of more than 1,200 colorful words, phrases, origins and histories. Much unexpected information. 254pp. 5⅜ × 8½.   20758-7 Pa. $5.95

THE RED THUMB MARK, R. Austin Freeman. In this first Dr. Thorndyke case, the great scientific detective draws fascinating conclusions from the nature of a single fingerprint. Exciting story, authentic science. 320pp. 5⅜ × 8½. (Available in U.S. only)   25210-8 Pa. $5.95

AN EGYPTIAN HIEROGLYPHIC DICTIONARY, E. A. Wallis Budge. Monumental work containing about 25,000 words or terms that occur in texts ranging from 3000 B.C. to 600 A.D. Each entry consists of a transliteration of the word, the word in hieroglyphs, and the meaning in English. 1,314pp. 6⅜ × 10.
23615-3, 23616-1 Pa., Two-vol. set $27.90

THE COMPLEAT STRATEGYST: Being a Primer on the Theory of Games of Strategy, J. D. Williams. Highly entertaining classic describes, with many illustrated examples, how to select best strategies in conflict situations. Prefaces. Appendices. xvi + 268pp. 5⅜ × 8½.   25101-2 Pa. $5.95

THE ROAD TO OZ, L. Frank Baum. Dorothy meets the Shaggy Man, little Button-Bright and the Rainbow's beautiful daughter in this delightful trip to the magical Land of Oz. 272pp. 5⅜ × 8.   25208-6 Pa. $4.95

POINT AND LINE TO PLANE, Wassily Kandinsky. Seminal exposition of role of point, line, other elements in non-objective painting. Essential to understanding 20th-century art. 127 illustrations. 192pp. 6½ × 9¼.   23808-3 Pa. $4.50

LADY ANNA, Anthony Trollope. Moving chronicle of Countess Lovel's bitter struggle to win for herself and daughter Anna their rightful rank and fortune—perhaps at cost of sanity itself. 384pp. 5⅜ × 8½.   24669-8 Pa. $6.95

EGYPTIAN MAGIC, E. A. Wallis Budge. Sums up all that is known about magic in Ancient Egypt: the role of magic in controlling the gods, powerful amulets that warded off evil spirits, scarabs of immortality, use of wax images, formulas and spells, the secret name, much more. 253pp. 5⅜ × 8½.   22681-6 Pa. $4.50

THE DANCE OF SIVA, Ananda Coomaraswamy. Preeminent authority unfolds the vast metaphysic of India: the revelation of her art, conception of the universe, social organization, etc. 27 reproductions of art masterpieces. 192pp. 5⅜ × 8½.
24817-8 Pa. $5.95

CHRISTMAS CUSTOMS AND TRADITIONS, Clement A. Miles. Origin, evolution, significance of religious, secular practices. Caroling, gifts, yule logs, much more. Full, scholarly yet fascinating; non-sectarian. 400pp. 5⅜ × 8½.
23354-5 Pa. $6.50

THE HUMAN FIGURE IN MOTION, Eadweard Muybridge. More than 4,500 stopped-action photos, in action series, showing undraped men, women, children jumping, lying down, throwing, sitting, wrestling, carrying, etc. 390pp. 7⅞ × 10⅝.
20204-6 Cloth. $19.95

THE MAN WHO WAS THURSDAY, Gilbert Keith Chesterton. Witty, fast-paced novel about a club of anarchists in turn-of-the-century London. Brilliant social, religious, philosophical speculations. 128pp. 5⅜ × 8½.   25121-7 Pa. $3.95

A CEZANNE SKETCHBOOK: Figures, Portraits, Landscapes and Still Lifes, Paul Cezanne. Great artist experiments with tonal effects, light, mass, other qualities in over 100 drawings. A revealing view of developing master painter, precursor of Cubism. 102 black-and-white illustrations. 144pp. 8¾ × 6⅜.   24790-2 Pa. $5.95

AN ENCYCLOPEDIA OF BATTLES: Accounts of Over 1,560 Battles from 1479 B.C. to the Present, David Eggenberger. Presents essential details of every major battle in recorded history, from the first battle of Megiddo in 1479 B.C. to Grenada in 1984. List of Battle Maps. New Appendix covering the years 1967–1984. Index. 99 illustrations. 544pp. 6½ × 9¼.   24913-1 Pa. $14.95

AN ETYMOLOGICAL DICTIONARY OF MODERN ENGLISH, Ernest Weekley. Richest, fullest work, by foremost British lexicographer. Detailed word histories. Inexhaustible. Total of 856pp. 6½ × 9¼.
21873-2, 21874-0 Pa., Two-vol. set $17.00

WEBSTER'S AMERICAN MILITARY BIOGRAPHIES, edited by Robert McHenry. Over 1,000 figures who shaped 3 centuries of American military history. Detailed biographies of Nathan Hale, Douglas MacArthur, Mary Hallaren, others. Chronologies of engagements, more. Introduction. Addenda. 1,033 entries in alphabetical order. xi + 548pp. 6½ × 9¼. (Available in U.S. only)
24758-9 Pa. $11.95

LIFE IN ANCIENT EGYPT, Adolf Erman. Detailed older account, with much not in more recent books: domestic life, religion, magic, medicine, commerce, and whatever else needed for complete picture. Many illustrations. 597pp. 5⅜ × 8½.
22632-8 Pa. $8.95

HISTORIC COSTUME IN PICTURES, Braun & Schneider. Over 1,450 costumed figures shown, covering a wide variety of peoples: kings, emperors, nobles, priests, servants, soldiers, scholars, townsfolk, peasants, merchants, courtiers, cavaliers, and more. 256pp. 8⅜ × 11¼.   23150-X Pa. $7.95

THE NOTEBOOKS OF LEONARDO DA VINCI, edited by J. P. Richter. Extracts from manuscripts reveal great genius; on painting, sculpture, anatomy, sciences, geography, etc. Both Italian and English. 186 ms. pages reproduced, plus 500 additional drawings, including studies for *Last Supper*, *Sforza* monument, etc. 860pp. 7⅞ × 10¾. (Available in U.S. only) 22572-0, 22573-9 Pa., Two-vol. set $25.90

THE ART NOUVEAU STYLE BOOK OF ALPHONSE MUCHA: All 72 Plates from "Documents Decoratifs" in Original Color, Alphonse Mucha. Rare copyright-free design portfolio by high priest of Art Nouveau. Jewelry, wallpaper, stained glass, furniture, figure studies, plant and animal motifs, etc. Only complete one-volume edition. 80pp. 9⅜ × 12¼. 24044-4 Pa. $8.95

ANIMALS: 1,419 COPYRIGHT-FREE ILLUSTRATIONS OF MAMMALS, BIRDS, FISH, INSECTS, ETC., edited by Jim Harter. Clear wood engravings present, in extremely lifelike poses, over 1,000 species of animals. One of the most extensive pictorial sourcebooks of its kind. Captions. Index. 284pp. 9 × 12. 23766-4 Pa. $9.95

OBELISTS FLY HIGH, C. Daly King. Masterpiece of American detective fiction, long out of print, involves murder on a 1935 transcontinental flight—"a very thrilling story"—NY Times. Unabridged and unaltered republication of the edition published by William Collins Sons & Co. Ltd., London, 1935. 288pp. 5⅜ × 8½. (Available in U.S. only) 25036-9 Pa. $4.95

VICTORIAN AND EDWARDIAN FASHION: A Photographic Survey, Alison Gernsheim. First fashion history completely illustrated by contemporary photographs. Full text plus 235 photos, 1840–1914, in which many celebrities appear. 240pp. 6½ × 9¼. 24205-6 Pa. $6.00

THE ART OF THE FRENCH ILLUSTRATED BOOK, 1700–1914, Gordon N. Ray. Over 630 superb book illustrations by Fragonard, Delacroix, Daumier, Doré, Grandville, Manet, Mucha, Steinlen, Toulouse-Lautrec and many others. Preface. Introduction. 633 halftones. Indices of artists, authors & titles, binders and provenances. Appendices. Bibliography. 608pp. 8⅜ × 11¼. 25086-5 Pa. $24.95

THE WONDERFUL WIZARD OF OZ, L. Frank Baum. Facsimile in full color of America's finest children's classic. 143 illustrations by W. W. Denslow. 267pp. 5⅜ × 8½. 20691-2 Pa. $5.95

FRONTIERS OF MODERN PHYSICS: New Perspectives on Cosmology, Relativity, Black Holes and Extraterrestrial Intelligence, Tony Rothman, et al. For the intelligent layman. Subjects include: cosmological models of the universe; black holes; the neutrino; the search for extraterrestrial intelligence. Introduction. 46 black-and-white illustrations. 192pp. 5⅜ × 8½. 24587-X Pa. $6.95

THE FRIENDLY STARS, Martha Evans Martin & Donald Howard Menzel. Classic text marshalls the stars together in an engaging, non-technical survey, presenting them as sources of beauty in night sky. 23 illustrations. Foreword. 2 star charts. Index. 147pp. 5⅜ × 8½. 21099-5 Pa. $3.50

FADS AND FALLACIES IN THE NAME OF SCIENCE, Martin Gardner. Fair, witty appraisal of cranks, quacks, and quackeries of science and pseudoscience: hollow earth, Velikovsky, orgone energy, Dianetics, flying saucers, Bridey Murphy, food and medical fads, etc. Revised, expanded In the Name of Science. "A very able and even-tempered presentation."—The New Yorker. 363pp. 5⅜ × 8. 20394-8 Pa. $6.50

ANCIENT EGYPT: ITS CULTURE AND HISTORY, J. E Manchip White. From pre-dynastics through Ptolemies: society, history, political structure, religion, daily life, literature, cultural heritage. 48 plates. 217pp. 5⅜ × 8½. 22548-8 Pa. $4.95

CATALOG OF DOVER BOOKS

SIR HARRY HOTSPUR OF HUMBLETHWAITE, Anthony Trollope. Incisive, unconventional psychological study of a conflict between a wealthy baronet, his idealistic daughter, and their scapegrace cousin. The 1870 novel in its first inexpensive edition in years. 250pp. 5⅜ × 8½.   24953-0 Pa. $5.95

LASERS AND HOLOGRAPHY, Winston E. Kock. Sound introduction to burgeoning field, expanded (1981) for second edition. Wave patterns, coherence, lasers, diffraction, zone plates, properties of holograms, recent advances. 84 illustrations. 160pp. 5⅜ × 8¼. (Except in United Kingdom)   24041-X Pa. $3.50

INTRODUCTION TO ARTIFICIAL INTELLIGENCE: SECOND, EN-LARGED EDITION, Philip C. Jackson, Jr. Comprehensive survey of artificial intelligence—the study of how machines (computers) can be made to act intelli-gently. Includes introductory and advanced material. Extensive notes updating the main text. 132 black-and-white illustrations. 512pp. 5⅜ × 8½.   24864-X Pa. $8.95

HISTORY OF INDIAN AND INDONESIAN ART, Ananda K. Coomaraswamy. Over 400 illustrations illuminate classic study of Indian art from earliest Harappa finds to early 20th century. Provides philosophical, religious and social insights. 304pp. 6⅜ × 9⅜.   25005-9 Pa. $8.95

THE GOLEM, Gustav Meyrink. Most famous supernatural novel in modern European literature, set in Ghetto of Old Prague around 1890. Compelling story of mystical experiences, strange transformations, profound terror. 13 black-and-white illustrations. 224pp. 5⅜ × 8½. (Available in U.S. only)   25025-3 Pa. $5.95

ARMADALE, Wilkie Collins. Third great mystery novel by the author of *The Woman in White* and *The Moonstone*. Original magazine version with 40 illustrations. 597pp. 5⅜ × 8½.   23429-0 Pa. $9.95

PICTORIAL ENCYCLOPEDIA OF HISTORIC ARCHITECTURAL PLANS, DETAILS AND ELEMENTS: With 1,880 Line Drawings of Arches, Domes, Doorways, Facades, Gables, Windows, etc., John Theodore Haneman. Sourcebook of inspiration for architects, designers, others. Bibliography. Captions. 141pp. 9 × 12.   24605-1 Pa. $6.95

BENCHLEY LOST AND FOUND, Robert Benchley. Finest humor from early 30's, about pet peeves, child psychologists, post office and others. Mostly unavailable elsewhere. 73 illustrations by Peter Arno and others. 183pp. 5⅜ × 8½.
                     22410-4 Pa. $3.95

ERTÉ GRAPHICS, Erté. Collection of striking color graphics: *Seasons, Alphabet, Numerals, Aces* and *Precious Stones*. 50 plates, including 4 on covers. 48pp. 9⅜ × 12¼.   23580-7 Pa. $6.95

THE JOURNAL OF HENRY D. THOREAU, edited by Bradford Torrey, F. H. Allen. Complete reprinting of 14 volumes, 1837–61, over two million words; the sourcebooks for *Walden*, etc. Definitive. All original sketches, plus 75 photographs. 1,804pp. 8½ × 12¼.   20312-3, 20313-1 Cloth., Two-vol. set $80.00

CASTLES: THEIR CONSTRUCTION AND HISTORY, Sidney Toy. Traces castle development from ancient roots. Nearly 200 photographs and drawings illustrate moats, keeps, baileys, many other features. Caernarvon, Dover Castles, Hadrian's Wall, Tower of London, dozens more. 256pp. 5⅜ × 8¼.
                     24898-4 Pa. $5.95

CATALOG OF DOVER BOOKS

AMERICAN CLIPPER SHIPS: 1833–1858, Octavius T. Howe & Frederick C. Matthews. Fully-illustrated, encyclopedic review of 352 clipper ships from the period of America's greatest maritime supremacy. Introduction. 109 halftones. 5 black-and-white line illustrations. Index. Total of 928pp. 5⅜ × 8½.
25115-2, 25116-0 Pa., Two-vol. set $17.90

TOWARDS A NEW ARCHITECTURE, Le Corbusier. Pioneering manifesto by great architect, near legendary founder of "International School." Technical and aesthetic theories, views on industry, economics, relation of form to function, "mass-production spirit," much more. Profusely illustrated. Unabridged translation of 13th French edition. Introduction by Frederick Etchells. 320pp. 6⅛ × 9¼.
(Available in U.S. only) 25023-7 Pa. $8.95

THE BOOK OF KELLS, edited by Blanche Cirker. Inexpensive collection of 32 full-color, full-page plates from the greatest illuminated manuscript of the Middle Ages, painstakingly reproduced from rare facsimile edition. Publisher's Note. Captions. 32pp. 9⅜ × 12¼. 24345-1 Pa. $4.95

BEST SCIENCE FICTION STORIES OF H. G. WELLS, H. G. Wells. Full novel *The Invisible Man*, plus 17 short stories: "The Crystal Egg," "Aepyornis Island," "The Strange Orchid," etc. 303pp. 5⅜ × 8½. (Available in U.S. only)
21531-8 Pa. $4.95

AMERICAN SAILING SHIPS: Their Plans and History, Charles G. Davis. Photos, construction details of schooners, frigates, clippers, other sailcraft of 18th to early 20th centuries—plus entertaining discourse on design, rigging, nautical lore, much more. 137 black-and-white illustrations. 240pp. 6⅛ × 9¼.
24658-2 Pa. $5.95

ENTERTAINING MATHEMATICAL PUZZLES, Martin Gardner. Selection of author's favorite conundrums involving arithmetic, money, speed, etc., with lively commentary. Complete solutions. 112pp. 5⅜ × 8½. 25211-6 Pa. $2.95

THE WILL TO BELIEVE, HUMAN IMMORTALITY, William James. Two books bound together. Effect of irrational on logical, and arguments for human immortality. 402pp. 5⅜ × 8½. 20291-7 Pa. $7.50

THE HAUNTED MONASTERY and THE CHINESE MAZE MURDERS, Robert Van Gulik. 2 full novels by Van Gulik continue adventures of Judge Dee and his companions. An evil Taoist monastery, seemingly supernatural events; overgrown topiary maze that hides strange crimes. Set in 7th-century China. 27 illustrations. 328pp. 5⅜ × 8½. 23502-5 Pa. $5.95

CELEBRATED CASES OF JUDGE DEE (DEE GOONG AN), translated by Robert Van Gulik. Authentic 18th-century Chinese detective novel; Dee and associates solve three interlocked cases. Led to Van Gulik's own stories with same characters. Extensive introduction. 9 illustrations. 237pp. 5⅜ × 8½.
23337-5 Pa. $4.95

Prices subject to change without notice.
Available at your book dealer or write for free catalog to Dept. GI, Dover Publications, Inc., 31 East 2nd St., Mineola, N.Y. 11501. Dover publishes more than 175 books each year on science, elementary and advanced mathematics, biology, music, art, literary history, social sciences and other areas.